DISCOVERING THE WESTERN PAST

A LOOK AT THE EVIDENCE

VOLUME II: SINCE 1500

SIXTH EDITION

Merry E. Wiesner
University of Wisconsin—Milwaukee

Julius R. Ruff
Marquette University

William Bruce Wheeler
University of Tennessee

HOUGHTON MIFFLIN COMPANY   Boston   New York

Publisher: Patricia Coryell
Sponsoring Editor: Nancy Blaine
Senior Marketing Manager: Katherine Bates
Senior Development Editor: Jeffrey Greene
Project Editor: Aimee E. Chevrette
Art and Design Manager: Jill Haber Atkins
Cover Design Manager: Anne S. Katzeff
Photo Editor: Jennifer Meyer Dare
Composition Buyer: Chuck Dutton
New Title Project Manager: Susan Brooks-Peltier
Editorial Assistant: Adrienne Zicht
Marketing Assistant: Lauren Bussard
Editorial Assistant: Andrew Laskey

Cover Image: Sharon Beavan (born 1956), *Angel*, 1989. Oil on canvas. Courtesy of the artist.

Printed in the U.S.A.

Library of Congress Control Number: 2007926453

Instructor's exam copy:
ISBN-13: 978-0-618-83419-8
ISBN-10: 0-618-83419-2

For orders, use student text ISBNs:
ISBN-13: 978-0-618-76611-6
ISBN-10: 0-618-76611-1

6789-EB-00 09 08 07 06

CONTENTS

PREFACE   IX

CHAPTER ONE
The Spread of the Reformation   1

  THE PROBLEM   1
  SOURCES AND METHOD   3
  THE EVIDENCE   6
          Martin Luther's sermon in Erfurt, Germany, 1521. Three 16th-century hymns.
          Illustrations by Matthias Gerung, 1546. Woodcuts by Lucas Cranach and an
          unknown artist of religious pamphlets. Anonymous German pamphlet, 1523.
  QUESTIONS TO CONSIDER   20
  EPILOGUE   22

CHAPTER TWO
Staging Absolutism   24

  THE PROBLEM   24
  SOURCES AND METHOD   27
  THE EVIDENCE   32
          Jean Bodin, *The Six Books of the Republic*, 1576. Jacques Bénigne Bossuet,
          Politics Drawn from the Very Words of the Holy Scriptures, 1678. The Duke
          of Saint-Simon on the Reign of Louis XIV. Royal portraits. The Mask of
          Apollo. Engravings of Louis XIV as Roman Emperor in Carousel of 1662.
          Illustrations of Versailles and Marly.
  QUESTIONS TO CONSIDER   48
  EPILOGUE   49

CHAPTER THREE
The Mind of an Age: Science and Religion Confront
Eighteenth-Century Natural Disaster   51

  THE PROBLEM   51
  SOURCES AND METHOD   53
  THE EVIDENCE   58

Gabriel Malagrida and John Wesley on the cause of the Lisbon earthquake. Voltaire on Newtonian physics, 1733. Alexander Pope's *An Essay on Man*, 1734. Observation, from Denis Diderot's *Encyclopedia*, ca 1765. *Natural History, General and Specific*, by George-Louis Leclerc. Poem on the Lisbon Disaster, by Voltaire and a letter to Voltaire from Jean-Jacques Rousseau regarding the poem. David Hume's "The Essay on Miracles," 1748. *The System of Nature* by Paul-Henry Thiry, Baron d'Holbach, 1770.
QUESTIONS TO CONSIDER   77
EPILOGUE   78

CHAPTER FOUR
European Material Life, 1600–1800   81

THE PROBLEM   81
SOURCES AND METHOD   82
THE EVIDENCE   94
Spring Agricultural Labor from a fifteenth-century French book of hours, Jean, Duc de Berry. Table of agricultural yields, 1600–1820. The Effects of Harvest Failure. A Meal of Gruel in a Dutch Peasant Family, 1653. A Peasant Kitchen with an Open Fire in the South Tyrol. Baltic grain exports, 1562–1650. Exports of slaves from Africa. Sugar imports in France, England, and Wales. Imports of groceries into England and Wales, 1559–1800. Illustration, "The Coffee House Patriots; or News from St. Eusatia," 1781. Value of wardrobes and linen, Paris, 1700–1789. "The Grumbling Hive: or, Knaves Turn'd Honest," Bernard Mandeville. Tables of ownership of consumer goods.
QUESTIONS TO CONSIDER   107
EPILOGUE   108

CHAPTER FIVE
A Day in the French Revolution: July 14, 1789   110

THE PROBLEM   110
SOURCES AND METHOD   113
THE EVIDENCE   120
The Bastille as a Symbol: The *Mémoires* of Simon-Nicolas-Henri Linguet. Photograph of the rue du Fer-à-Moulin, 1870. Floor plan of a typical residential building in Faubourg St.-Antoine. Graphs depicting wheat prices in Paris and France in the eighteenth century. Table of bread and wage earner's budget. Map of Paris by economic circumstances of residents, 1790. Table of the trades of the Bastille insurgents, 1789. Marguerite Painaigre's petition to the French National Assembly. Travel account, Arthur Young, 1789. Duke of Dorset's report on Paris to the Foreign Office in London.
QUESTIONS TO CONSIDER   134
EPILOGUE   135

CHAPTER SIX
Labor Old and New: The Impact of the Industrial Revolution 138

THE PROBLEM   138
SOURCES AND METHOD   142
THE EVIDENCE   147

Sabastien Le Prestre de Vaubans description of agricultural labor in France, about 1700. Testimony of an agricultural worker's wife and former factory worker, 1842. List of holidays during the work year in 17th-century Lille, France. Guild regulations in the Prussian woolen industry, 1797. La Rochefoucauld describes the putting-out system in Rouen, France, 1781–1783. Scenes of weaving in Germany and England. Luddite labor protest in Yorkshire, 1812. Rules for workers in the foundry and engineering works of the Royal Overseas Trading Company, Berlin, 1844. Apprenticeship contract for young women employed in the silk mills of Tarare, France, 1850s. Report of the Sadler Committee, 1832. Working conditions of a female textile worker in Germany, 1880s and 1890s. Report on the employment of children in three British mines, 1841–1842.

QUESTIONS TO CONSIDER   170
EPILOGUE   172

CHAPTER SEVEN
Two Programs for Social and Political Change: Liberalism and Socialism   174

THE PROBLEM   174
SOURCES AND METHOD   176
THE EVIDENCE   180

Alexis de Tocqueville's views on history, the problems of democracy, revolution, ideals of government. Karl Marx's writings on history from *The Communist Manifesto*, the Revolution of 1848 in Paris, ideals of government and economy.

QUESTIONS TO CONSIDER   201
EPILOGUE   203

CHAPTER EIGHT
Vienna and Paris, 1850–1930: The Development of the Modern City   206

THE PROBLEM   206
SOURCES AND METHOD   209

THE EVIDENCE   218

   Illustrations of Vienna and Paris in the 1850s, leather workers on the
   Bièvre River, Paris. Drawing and photograph of the Viennese Ringstrasse.
   Maps of Paris and photographs of the construction of and the completed
   Avenue de l'Opera. Illustrations of Ringstrasse apartment building, Paris
   apartment building. Floor plan of Paris apartment building. Illustrations
   of the Prater, Vienna; the Buttes-Chaumont Park, Paris; 19th-century
   working-class Paris suburb; the Lemoine Forges in 1881; Vienna workers
   tenement, early 20th century; Viennese S-Bahn and station; Parisian bus
   and tramway stop in 1936. Photographs of Karl Marx Hof in Vienna, floor
   plan of Parisian low-cost housing, and photograph of Viennese
   Kongressbad.

QUESTIONS TO CONSIDER   240
EPILOGUE   241

CHAPTER NINE
Expansion and Public Opinion: Advocates of the "New Imperialism"   243

THE PROBLEM   243
SOURCES AND METHOD   247
THE EVIDENCE   250

   Friedrich Farbi's *Bedarf Deutschland der Kolonien?*, 1879. John G. Paton's
   letter urging British possession of the New Hebrides, 1883. Jules Ferry's
   appeal to the French to build the second colonial empire, 1890. Joseph
   Chamberlain's speech to the West Birmingham Relief Association, 1894.
   Ferdinando Martini, from *Cose affricane*, 1897. G.W. Steevens on the
   Sudan, 1898.

QUESTIONS TO CONSIDER   261
EPILOGUE   262

CHAPTER TEN
Women in Russian Revolutionary Movements   266

THE PROBLEM   266
SOURCES AND METHOD   270
THE EVIDENCE   275

   From the *Memoirs* of Elizabeta Kovalskaia, Moscow, 1926; Olga
   Liubatovich, Moscow, 1906; Praskovia Ivanoskaia, Moscow, 1926; and Eva
   Broido, Berlin, 1926. Alexandra Kollontai, *Towards a History of the Working
   Women's Movement in Russia,* 1920. Petition to the Duma, 1906. Petition to
   the Provisional Government, 1917. Alexandra Kollontai, "In the Front
   Line of Fire," *Pravda,* 1917; and from the pamphlet "Working Woman and
   Mother," 1914.

QUESTIONS TO CONSIDER   293
EPILOGUE   294

CHAPTER ELEVEN
World War I: Total War   298

THE PROBLEM   298
SOURCES AND METHOD   300
THE EVIDENCE   307
    World War I verse by Rupert Brooke, Charles Péguy, and Ernst Lissauer. *The Front Lines,* German infantry attack, 1912. British infantry going "Over the Top" in an attack on Kemmel Hill, April, 1918. *Under Fire,* by Henri Barbusse, 1916. Erich Remarque's *All Quiet on the Western Front,* 1928. Verse by Siegfried Sassoon and Wilfred Owen. Letter from a former German student serving in France, 1914. Vera Brittain's account of a London air raid, 1917. German wartime civilian rations, 1918. Report on French public opinion in the Department of the Isère. Tables depicting the employment of women in wartime British industry and estimated military casualties by nation.
QUESTIONS TO CONSIDER   331
EPILOGUE   332

CHAPTER TWELVE
Selling a Totalitarian System   335

THE PROBLEM   335
SOURCES AND METHOD   340
THE EVIDENCE   344
    Excerpts from Hitler's *Mein Kampf.* Joseph Goebbel's directives for the presidential campaign of 1932. Adolf Hitler's S.A. Order 111, 1926. Photographs of Regensburg S.A. banners and S.A. propaganda rally in Spandau, 1932. Report of a Nazi meeting held in a heavily communist quarter of Berlin, February 1927. Political posters from 1924 and 1932. Photograph of a National Socialist rally in the Berlin Sports Palace, 1930. Verses from The Horst Wessel Song. Otto Dietrich's description of Hitler's campaign by airplane, 1932. Text from a Nazi pamphlet, ca 1932. Graph depicting types and amounts of political violence in Northeim, Germany, 1930–1932. *My Part in Germany's Fight,* by Joseph Goebbels, 1934. Report on the problem of stemming the spread of Nazi ideas in the Protestant youth movement, 1931. William L. Shirer's reactions to the Nazi party rally at Nuremberg, 1934.
QUESTIONS TO CONSIDER   361
EPILOGUE   363

CHAPTER THIRTEEN
The Perils of Prosperity: The Unrest of Youth in the 1960s   365

THE PROBLEM   365
SOURCES AND METHOD   372
THE EVIDENCE   376
Pamphlet of the March 22 Movement. Leaflet issued by student and worker groups in France in 1968. Slogans of the Sorbonne Occupation Committee, May 16, 1968. French political posters and cartoons. "Ten Commandments for a Young Czechoslovak Intellectual," March 1968. Ivan Sviták, "Wherefrom, with Whom, and Whither?." The action program of the Communist Party of Czechoslovakia. Czechoslovakian political cartoons.
QUESTIONS TO CONSIDER   395
EPILOGUE   396

CHAPTER FOURTEEN
The European Nation State and Regional Ethnic Nationalism   399

THE PROBLEM   399
SOURCES AND METHOD   400
THE EVIDENCE   409
Douglas Hyde on the revival of Gaelic, 1892. Significant European Regional Ethnic Minorities, ca 1989. Jacque Atatli, "The End of One France." Excerpts from the Finnish Constitution. Luis Núñez Astrain, "The KAS Alternative," 1978. Map of the USSR, 1989. Ethnic composition of the Soviet Union's successor states. Anna Politkovskaya, "Monsters and Human Beings," 1999. Map of national and ethnic minorities in the former Yugoslavia. Emir Suljagic, "Ethnic Cleansing" in Bosnia, 1992.
QUESTIONS TO CONSIDER   425
EPILOGUE   426

PREFACE

The title of this book begins with a verb, a choice that reflects our basic philosophy about history. History is not simply something one learns about; it is something one does. One discovers the past, and what makes this pursuit exciting is not only the past that is discovered but also the process of discovery itself. This process can be simultaneously exhilarating and frustrating, enlightening and confusing, but it is always challenging enough to convince those of us who are professional historians to spend our lives at it. And our own students, as well as many other students, have caught this infectious excitement.

The recognition that history involves discovery as much as physics or astronomy does is often not shared by students, whose classroom experience of history frequently does not extend beyond listening to lectures and reading textbooks. The primary goal of *Discovering the Western Past: A Look at the Evidence* is to allow students enrolled in Western Civilization courses to *do* history in the same way we as historians do—to examine a group of original sources in order to answer questions about the past.

The unique structure of this book clusters primary sources around a set of historical questions that students are asked to "solve." Unlike a source reader, this book prompts students to actually *analyze* a wide variety of authentic primary source material, to make inferences, and to draw conclusions in much the same way that historians do.

The evidence in this book is more varied than that in most source collections. We have included such visual evidence as coins, paintings, statues, literary illustrations, historical photographs, maps, cartoons, advertisements, and political posters. In choosing written evidence we again have tried to offer a broad sample—eulogies, wills, court records, oral testimonies, and statistical data all supplement letters, newspaper articles, speeches, memoirs, and other more traditional sources.

In order for students to learn history the way we as historians do, they must not only be confronted with the evidence but must also learn how to use that evidence to arrive at a conclusion. In other words, they must learn historical methodology. Too often methodology (or even the notion that historians *have* a methodology) is reserved for upper-level majors or graduate students; beginning students are simply presented with historical facts and interpretations without being shown how these were unearthed or formulated.

Students may learn that historians hold different interpretations of the significance of an event or individual or different ideas about causation, but they are not informed of how historians come to such conclusions.

Thus, along with evidence, we have provided explicit suggestions about how one might analyze that evidence, guiding students as they reach their own conclusions. As they work through the various chapters, students will discover both that the sources of historical information are wide-ranging and that the methodologies appropriate to understanding and using them are equally diverse. By doing history themselves, students will learn how intellectual historians handle philosophical treatises, economic historians quantitative data, social historians court records, and political and diplomatic historians theoretical treatises and memoirs. They will also be asked to consider the limitations of their evidence, to explore what historical questions it cannot answer as well as those it can. Instead of remaining passive observers, students become active participants.

Following an approach that we have found successful in many different classroom situations, we have divided each chapter into five parts: The Problem, Sources and Method, The Evidence, Questions to Consider, and Epilogue. The section called "The Problem" presents the general historical background and context for the evidence offered and concludes with the central question or questions explored in the chapter. Your students should refer to the central questions frequently as they analyze the evidence in the chapter. These serve as guideposts for their analysis, and can always be found right at the end of "The Problem" section.

The section titled "Sources and Method" provides specific information about the sources and suggests ways in which students might best study and analyze this primary evidence. It also discusses how previous historians have evaluated such sources and mentions any major disputes about methodology or interpretation. In keeping with the active learning that this book encourages, "Sources and Methods" often guides students by posing specific questions about the evidence. These are meant to encourage careful reading, and certainly do not all need to be answered.

"The Evidence" forms the core of each chapter, presenting a variety of original sources for students to use in completing the central task. In "Questions to Consider," suggestions are offered about connections among the sources, and students are guided to draw deductions from the evidence. Again, possible connections among pieces of evidence are often proposed in the form of questions rather than statements, for we believe this technique helps reinforce the process of discovering. "Questions to Consider" is just that—additional issues for students to think about as they develop answers to the chapter's central questions.

The final section, "Epilogue," traces both the immediate effects of the issue under discussion and its impact on later developments.

Within this framework, we have tried to present a series of historical issues and events of significance to the instructor as well as of interest to the student. We have also aimed to provide a balance among political, social, diplomatic, intellectual, and cultural history. In other words, we have attempted to create a kind of historical sampler that we believe will help students learn the methods and skills used by historians. These skills—analyzing arguments, developing hypotheses, comparing evidence, testing conclusions, and reevaluating material—will not only enable students to master historical content; they will also provide the necessary foundation for critical thinking in other college courses and after college as well.

Discovering the Western Past is designed to accommodate any format of the Western Civilization course, from the small lecture/discussion class of a liberal arts or community college to the large lecture with discussions led by teaching assistants at a sizable university. The chapters may be used for individual assignments, team projects, class discussions, papers, and exams. Each is self-contained, so that any combination may be assigned. The book is not intended to replace a standard textbook, and it was written to accompany any Western Civilization text the instructor chooses. The *Instructor's Resource Manual*, written by the authors of the text, offers suggestions for class discussions, suggestions for ways in which students' learning may be evaluated, and annotated lists of suggestions for further reading.

New to the Sixth Edition

The first five editions of *Discovering the Western Past: A Look at the Evidence* elicited a very positive response from instructors and students alike, and that response encouraged us to proceed with this Sixth Edition. As authors, we were particularly gratified by the widespread acceptance of the central goal of *Discovering the Western Past*, that of making students active analysts of the past and not merely passive recipients of its factual record.

The Sixth Edition of *Discovering the Western Past* incorporates the responses to the book that we have received from our own students, as well as from student and faculty users of the book around the country. Many of the chapters in the two volumes have received some reworking, and new chapters are included in each volume.

Volume I includes new chapters on barbarian invaders and medieval village life, and the return of a chapter on the Reformation brought back by request from users of the book. Volume II offers a new chapter on European material life (1600–1800), a chapter on women in Russian revolutionary movements, and a new final chapter on the European nation-state and regional ethnic nationalism.

Acknowledgments

In the completion of this book, the authors received assistance from a number of people. Our colleagues and students at the University of Wisconsin—Milwaukee, Marquette University, and the University of Tennessee, Knoxville, have been generous with their ideas and time. Merry E. Wiesner (-Hanks) wishes especially to thank Judith Bennett, Judith Beall, Martha Carlin, Abbas Hamdani, and Marci Sortor for their critiques and suggestions, and Neil Wiesner-Hanks and Kai and Tyr Wiesner-Hanks for their help in maintaining the author's perspective. Julius Ruff acknowledges the assistance of two valued colleagues who aided in preparing all six editions of this work: the Reverend John Patrick Donnelly, S.J., of Marquette University and Michael D. Sibalis of Wilfrid Laurier University. He also wishes to thank Laura, Julia, and Charles Ruff for their continued support. William Bruce Wheeler wishes to thank Owen Bradley and John Bohstedt for their valuable assistance.

We wish to acknowledge particularly the following historians who read and commented on the manuscript of this Sixth Edition as it developed:

Steve Alvin, *Illinois Valley Community College*

William S. Arnett, *West Virginia University*

Anne M. Breedlove, *Las Positas College*

Christopher Carlsmith, *University of Massachusetts-Lowell*

Marie Seong-Hak Kim, *St. Cloud State University*

Lynn Lubamersky, *Boise State University*

Matthew R. Lungerhausen, *Winona State University*

Sherri Olson, *University of Connecticut*

Jeremy D. Popkin, *University of Kentucky*

Paul Townend, *University of North Carolina-Wilmington*

Finally, the authors extend their thanks to the staff of Houghton Mifflin Company for their enthusiastic support.

M.E.W.

J.R.R.

W.B.W.

CHAPTER ONE

THE SPREAD

OF THE REFORMATION

THE PROBLEM

In 1517, an Augustinian monk in the German province of Saxony named Martin Luther (1483–1546) began preaching and writing against papal *indulgences*, those letters from the pope that substituted for earthly penance or time in Purgatory for Christians who earned or purchased them. Luther called for an end to the sale of indulgences because this practice encouraged people to believe that sins did not have to be taken seriously but could be atoned for simply by buying a piece of paper. In taking this position, he was repeating the ideas expressed more than one hundred years earlier by John Hus (1369?–1415), a Czech theologian and preacher. Many of Luther's other ideas had also been previously expressed by Hus, and even earlier by John Wyclif (1328–1384), an English philosopher and theologian. All three objected to the wealth of the Church and to the pope's claims to earthly power; called for an end to pilgrimages and the veneration of saints;

said that priests were no better than other people, and that in fact all believers were priests; and believed that the Bible should be available for all people to read for themselves in their own language.

Though Luther's beliefs were quite similar to those of Wyclif and Hus, their impact was not. Wyclif had gained a large following and died peacefully in his bed; less than twenty years after his death, however, English rulers ordered anyone espousing his beliefs to be burned at the stake as a heretic, and so the movement he started was more or less wiped out. Hus himself was burned at the stake in 1415 at the Council of Constance, which ordered the bones of Wyclif to be dug up and burned as well. Hus's followers were not as easily steered back to the fold or stamped out as Wyclif's had been, but his ideas never spread beyond Bohemia (modern-day Czech Republic). Martin Luther's actions, on the other hand, led to a permanent split in Western Christianity, dividing an institution that had existed as a unified body for almost 1,500 years. Within only a few years, Luther gained a huge number of followers in Germany and other countries, inspiring other religious reformers to break with the Catholic church in developing their own ideas. This movement has come to be known collectively as the "Protestant Reformation," though perhaps *Revolution* might be a more accurate term.

To understand why Luther's impact was so much greater than that of his predecessors, we need to examine a number of factors besides his basic set of beliefs. As with any revolution, social and economic grievances also played a role. Many different groups in early-sixteenth-century German society were disturbed by the changes they saw around them. Peasants wanted the right to hunt and fish as they had in earlier times and objected to new taxes that their landlords imposed on them. Bitter at the wealth of the Church, they believed that the clergy were more interested in collecting money from them than in providing spiritual leadership. Landlords, watching the price of manufactured goods rise even faster than they could raise taxes or rents, blamed urban merchants and bankers, calling them greedy and avaricious. Those with only small landholdings were especially caught in an inflationary squeeze and often had to sell off their lands. This was particularly the case for the free imperial knights, a group of about 3,000 individuals in Germany who owed allegiance directly to the emperor but whose landholdings were often less than one square mile. The knights were also losing their reason for existence because military

campaigns increasingly relied on infantry and artillery forces rather than mounted cavalry. All these groups were becoming nationalistic and objected to their church taxes and tithes going to the pope, whom they regarded as primarily an Italian prince rather than an international religious leader.

Political factors were also important in the Protestant Revolution. Germany was not a centralized monarchy like France, Spain, and England, but a collection of hundreds of semi-independent territories loosely combined into a political unit called the Holy Roman Empire, under the leadership of an elected emperor. Some of these territories were ruled by nobles such as princes, dukes, or counts; some were independent cities; some were ecclesiastical principalities ruled by archbishops or bishops; and some were ruled by free imperial knights. Each territory was jealous of the power of its neighbors and was equally unwilling to allow the emperor any strong centralized authority. This effect usually worked to the benefit of the individual territories, but it could also work to their detriment. For example, the emperor's weakness prevented him from enforcing such laws against alleged heretics as the one the English king had used against Wyclif's followers, with the result that each territory was relatively independent in matters of religion. On the other hand, he was unable to place limits on papal legal authority or tax collection in the way the stronger kings of western Europe could, with the result that Germany supported many more indulgence peddlers than England or Spain.

The decentralization of the Holy Roman Empire also left each territory more vulnerable than before to external military threats, the most significant of which in the early sixteenth century was the Ottoman Turks. Originating in central Asia, the Turks had adopted the Muslim religion and begun a campaign of conquest westward. In 1453 they took Constantinople, and by 1500 they were nearing Vienna, arousing fear in many German rulers. The Turkish threat combined with social and economic grievances among many sectors of society to make western Europeans feel that the end of the world was near or look for a charismatic leader who would solve their problems.

Technological factors also played a role in the Protestant Revolution. The printing press was developed in Germany around 1450, and by Luther's time there were printers in most of the major cities in Europe. The spread of printing was accompanied by a rise in literacy, so that many more people were able to read than in the time of Wyclif or Hus. They were also more able to buy books and pamphlets, for the rag paper used by printers was much cheaper than the parchment or vellum used by copyists in earlier centuries. Owning a Bible or part of a Bible to read in one's own language was now a realistic possibility.

In many ways, then, the early sixteenth century was a favorable time for a major religious change in western Europe. Your task in this chapter will be to assess how that change occurred. How were the ideas of Luther disseminated so widely and so quickly? How were they made attractive to various groups within German society?

SOURCES AND METHOD

Before you look at the evidence in this chapter, think about how ideas are spread in modern American society. What would be the best ways to reach the greatest number of people if you wanted to discuss a new issue or present a new concept? You might want to use health issues as an example, for these often involve totally new ideas and information on one hand and are regarded as vitally important on the other. Think, for example, about the means by which the dangers of cigarette smoking or information about the spread of AIDS is communicated. To answer the first question, we will need to examine the sixteenth-century equivalents of these forms of communication. Health is an appropriate parallel because the most important such issue for many people in the sixteenth century was the health of their souls, a problem directly addressed by Luther and the other reformers.

The spread of the Reformation was perhaps the first example of a successful multimedia campaign; in consequence, as you might imagine, we will be using a wide variety of sources. As you read the written sources and look at the visual evidence, keep in mind that people were seeing, hearing, and reading all these materials at once. As in any successful advertising or propaganda campaign, certain ideas were reinforced over and over again to make sure the message was thoroughly communicated. You will need to pay particular attention, then, to those points that come up in more than one type of source.

Though they were seeing, hearing, or reading the same message, different groups within German society interpreted Protestant ideas differently. They latched on to certain concepts that had relevance for their own situations and often attached Protestant ideas to existing social, political, or economic grievances. Artists and authors spreading the Protestant message often conveyed their ideas in ways they knew would be attractive to various social groups. In answering the second question, it is important to note the portrayal of various social groups and pay attention to the frequency with which these portrayals appear. Thus, as you look at the visual sources and read the written ones, jot down one list of the ideas expressed and another of the ways in which various types of people are depicted. In this way, you will begin to see which ideas are central and perceived as popular, and which might be interpreted differently by different people.

Source 1 is a sermon delivered in 1521 by Martin Luther in Erfurt on his way to the Diet of Worms, a meeting of the leaders of the territories in the Holy Roman Empire. It is not based on Luther's own notes but was written down by a person in the audience, who then gave the transcript to a local printer. This sermon is thus a record of both how the Reformation message was spread orally—so many people wanted to hear him that the church where Luther preached could not hold them all—and how it was spread in written form, for seven editions of the sermon appeared in 1521 alone. What teachings of the Catholic church did Luther criticize, and what ideas of his own did he emphasize? In assessing how ideas are spread, we have to pay attention not only to the content of the message but also to the form. In what sorts of words and images did Luther convey his ideas to his large audience?

The next sources—three hymns—also serve as both oral and written evidence. Martin Luther believed that congregational hymn singing was an important part of a church service and an effective way to teach people about theology. In this tactic he anticipated modern advertisers, who recognize the power of a song or jingle in influencing people's choices. The first two hymns were written by Luther and the third by Paul Speratus, an early follower. As you read them, pay attention to both their content and their images. What ideas from Luther's sermon are reinforced in the hymns? What sorts of mental pictures do the words produce? (Keep in mind that you are reading these simply as poetry, whereas sixteenth-century people sang them. You may know the tune of "A Mighty Fortress," which is still sung in many Protestant congregations today; if so, you can use your knowledge of its musical setting to help you assess the impact of the hymn and its message.)

The Lutheran message would certainly not have spread as widely as it did if church services were its only forum. The remaining sources are those that people might have encountered anywhere. The woodcuts all come from Protestant pamphlets—small, inexpensive paperbound booklets written in German that were readily available in any city with a printer—or *broadsheets*—single-sheet posters that were often sold alone or as a series. These documents are extremely complex visually and need to be examined with great care. Most of the images used would have been familiar to any sixteenth-century person, but they may not be to you. Here, then, are some clues to help guide your analysis.

In Source 5, the person on the right wearing the triple crown with money on the table in front of him is the pope. The devils in front of the table are wearing the flat hats worn by cardinals; the pieces of paper with seals attached that they are handing out are indulgences. At the bottom are the flames of hell; at the top, heaven with a preacher and people participating in the two Church sacraments that the Protestants retained, baptism and communion.

Source 6, another heaven and hell image, shows Christ at the top deciding who will stay in heaven and two linked devils at the bottom dragging various people to hell. The right-hand devil wears the triple-crowned papal tiara, the left-hand one, the rolled turban worn by Turks. Included in the hell-bound group on the right are men wearing the flat cardinal's hat, the pointed hat of bishops, and the distinctive haircut of monks.

Source 7 comes from a series of woodcut contrasts. The left pictures show biblical scenes and the right the contemporary Church. The top left picture shows Christ with his disciples; the top right, the pope. From their hats and haircuts you can recognize some of the people gathered in front of the pope; those kneeling are wearing crowns, which in the sixteenth century were worn only by rulers. The bottom left picture shows Christ and the moneychangers at the temple at Jerusalem; the bottom right, the pope and indulgences.

Source 8 is the cover of a pamphlet called "The Wolf's Song." By now you recognize the hats and haircuts of the wolves at the top and sides; some of the geese wear crowns, and many carry jeweled necklaces. The choice of animals is intentional. Wolves were still a threat to livestock in sixteenth-century Europe, and geese were regarded as foolish, silly creatures willing to follow their leader blindly into dangerous situations.

Source 9 is a woodcut by the well-known German artist Lucas Cranach, whom Luther commissioned to illustrate his pamphlet "Against the Papacy at Rome, Founded by the Devil" (1545). It shows two men defecating into the papal triple crown.

Taking all of the images into account, what message do the woodcuts convey about the pope and other Catholic clergy? About the Protestant clergy? Which images and ideas are frequently repeated? How do these fit in with what was preached or sung in church?

The last source is a pamphlet by an unknown author printed in 1523. It is written in the form of a dialogue, a very common form for these Reformation printed materials. Read it, as you did the sermon and the hymns, for both content and tone. Why do you think the author chose these two characters to convey his message? What do they criticize about Catholic practices? How do the ideas expressed here compare with those in Luther's sermon? Which of the woodcuts might have served as an illustration for this pamphlet?

THE EVIDENCE

Source 1 from John W. Doberstein, editor, Luther's Works, *vol. 51 (Philadelphia: Fortress, 1959), pp. 61–66. Reprinted by permission.*

1. Sermon Preached by Martin Luther in Erfurt (Germany), 1521

Dear friends, I shall pass over the story of St. Thomas this time and leave it for another occasion, and instead consider the brief words uttered by Christ: "Peace be with you" [John 20:19] and "Behold my hands and my side" [John 20:27], and "as the Father has sent me, even so I send you" [John 20:21]. Now, it is clear and manifest that every person likes to think that he will be saved and attain to eternal salvation. This is what I propose to discuss now.

You also know that all philosophers, doctors and writers have studiously endeavored to teach and write what attitude man should take to piety. They have gone to great trouble, but, as is evident, to little avail. Now genuine and true piety consists of two kinds of works: those done for others, which are the right kind, and those done for ourselves, which are unimportant. In order to find a foundation, one man builds churches; another goes on a pilgrimage to St. James'[1] or St. Peter's[2]; a third fasts or prays, wears a cowl, goes barefoot, or does something else of the kind. Such works are nothing whatever and must be completely destroyed. Mark these words: none of our works have any power whatsoever. For God has chosen a man, the Lord Christ Jesus, to crush death, destroy sin, and shatter hell, since there was no one before he came who did not inevitably belong to the devil. The devil therefore thought he would get a hold upon the Lord when he hung between the two thieves

---

1. St. James of Compostella, a cathedral in northern Spain.
2. A cathedral in Rome.

and was suffering the most contemptible and disgraceful of deaths, which was cursed both by God and by men [cf. Deut. 21:23; Gal. 3:13]. But the Godhead was so strong that death, sin, and even hell were destroyed.

Therefore you should note well the words which Paul writes to the Romans [Rom. 5:12–21]. Our sins have their source in Adam, and because Adam ate the apple, we have inherited sin from him. But Christ has shattered death for our sake, in order that we might be saved by his works, which are alien to us, and not by our works.

But the papal dominion treats us altogether differently. It makes rules about fasting, praying, and butter-eating, so that whoever keeps the commandments of the pope will be saved and whoever does not keep them belongs to the devil. It thus seduces the people with the delusion that goodness and salvation lies in their own works. But I say that none of the saints, no matter how holy they were, attained salvation by their works. Even the holy mother of God did not become good, was not saved, by her virginity or her motherhood, but rather by the will of faith and the works of God, and not by her purity, or her own works. Therefore, mark me well: this is the reason why salvation does not lie in our own works, no matter what they are; it cannot and will not be effected without faith.

Now, someone may say: Look, my friend, you are saying a lot about faith, and claiming that our salvation depends solely upon it; now, I ask you, how does one come to faith? I will tell you. Our Lord Christ said, "Peace be with you. Behold my hands, etc." [John 20:26–27]. [In other words, he is saying:] Look, man, I am the only one who has taken away your sins and redeemed you, etc.; now be at peace. Just as you inherited sin from Adam—not that you committed it, for I did not eat the apple, any more than you did, and yet this is how we came to be in sin—so we have not suffered [as Christ did], and therefore we were made free from death and sin by God's work, not by our works. Therefore God says: Behold, man, I am your redemption [cf. Isa. 43:3], just as Paul said to the Corinthians: Christ is our justification and redemption, etc. [I Cor 1:30]. Christ is our justification and redemption, as Paul says in this passage. And here our [Roman] masters say: Yes, *Redemptor*, Redeemer; this is true, but it is not enough.

Therefore, I say again: Alien works, these make us good! Our Lord Christ says: I am your justification. I have destroyed the sins you have upon you. Therefore only believe in me; believe that I am he who has done this; then you will be justified. For it is written, *Justicia est fides*, righteousness is identical with faith and comes through faith. Therefore, if we want to have faith, we should believe the gospel, Paul, etc, and not the papal breves,[3] or the decretals,[4] but rather guard ourselves against them as against fire. For everything that comes from the pope cries out: Give, give; and if you refuse, you are of

3. **breve:** letter of authority.
4. **decretal:** decree on matters of doctrine.

the devil. It would be a small matter if they were only exploiting the people. But, unfortunately, it is the greatest evil in the world to lead the people to believe that outward works can save or make a man good.

At this time the world is so full of wickedness that it is overflowing, and is therefore now under a terrible judgment and punishment, which God has inflicted, so that the people are perverting and deceiving themselves in their own minds. For to build churches, and to fast and pray and so on has the appearance of good works, but in our heads we are deluding ourselves. We should not give way to greed, desire for temporal honor, and other vices and rather be helpful to our poor neighbor. Then God will arise in us and we in him, and this means a new birth. What does it matter if we commit a fresh sin? If we do not immediately despair, but rather say within ourselves, "O God, thou livest still! Christ my Lord is the destroyer of sin," then at once the sin is gone. And also the wise man says: *Septies in die cadit iustus et resurgit.*" "A righteous man falls seven times, and rises again" [Prov. 24:16].

The reason why the world is so utterly perverted and in error is that for a long time there have been no genuine preachers. There are perhaps three thousand priests, among whom one cannot find four good ones— God have mercy on us in this crying shame! And when you do get a good preacher, he runs through the gospel superficially and then follows it up with a fable . . . or he mixes in something of the pagan teachers, Aristotle, Plato, Socrates, and others, who are all quite contrary to the gospel, and also contrary to God, for they did not have the knowledge of the light which we possess. Aye, if you come to me and say: The Philosopher says: Do many good works, then you will acquire the habit, and finally you will become godly; then I say to you: Do not perform good works in order to become godly; but if you are already godly, then do good works, though without affectation and with faith. There you see how contrary these two points of view are.

In former times the devil made great attacks upon the people and from these attacks they took refuge in faith and clung to the Head, which is Christ; and so he was unable to accomplish anything. So now he has invented another device; he whispers into the ears of our Junkers[5] that they should make exactions from people and give them laws. This way it looks well on the outside; but inside it is full of poison. So the young children grow up in a delusion; they go to church thinking that salvation consists in praying, fasting, and attending mass. Thus it is the preacher's fault. But still there would be no need, if only we had right preachers.

The Lord said three times to St. Peter: "*Petre, amas me? etc.; pasce oves meas*" [John 21:15–17]. "Peter, feed, feed, feed my sheep." What is the meaning of *pascere*? It means to feed. How should one feed the sheep? Only by preaching the Word of God, only by preaching faith. Then our Junkers come along

5. **junker:** member of the landowning nobility.

and say: *Pascere* means *leges dare*, to enact laws, but with deception. Yes, they are well fed! They feed the sheep as the butchers do on Easter eve. Whereas one should speak the Word of God plainly to guide the poor and weak in faith, they mix in their beloved Aristotle, who is contrary to God, despite the fact that Paul says in Col. [2:8]: Beware of laws and philosophy. What does "philosophy" mean? If we knew Greek, Latin, and German, we would see clearly what the Apostle is saying.

Is not this the truth? I know very well that you don't like to hear this and that I am annoying many of you; nevertheless, I shall say it. I will also advise you, no matter who you are: If you have preaching in mind or are able to help it along, then do not become a priest or a monk, for there is a passage in the thirty-third and thirty-fourth chapters of the prophet Ezekiel, unfortunately a terrifying passage, which reads: If you forsake your neighbor, see him going astray, and do not help him, do not preach to him, I will call you to account for his soul [Ezek. 33:8; 34:10]. This is a passage which is not often read. But I say, you become a priest or a monk in order to pray your seven canonical hours and say mass, and you think you want to be godly. Alas, you're a fine fellow! It [i.e., being a priest or monk] will fail you. You say the Psalter, you pray the rosary, you pray all kinds of other prayers, and say a lot of words; you say mass, you kneel before the altar, you read confession, you go on mumbling and maundering; and all the while you think you are free from sin. And yet in your heart you have such great envy that, if you could choke your neighbor and get away with it creditably, you would do it; and that's the way you say mass. It would be no wonder if a thunderbolt struck you to the ground. But if you have eaten three grains of sugar or some other seasoning, no one could drag you to the altar with red-hot tongs.[6] You have scruples! And that means to go to heaven with the devil. I know very well that you don't like to hear this. Nevertheless, I will tell the truth, I must tell the truth, even though it cost me my neck twenty times over, that the verdict may not be pronounced against me [i.e., at the last judgment].

Yes, you say, there were learned people a hundred or fifty years ago too. That is true; but I am not concerned with the length of time or the number of persons. For even though they knew something of it then, the devil has always been a mixer, who preferred the pagan writers to the holy gospel. I will tell the truth and must tell the truth; that's why I'm standing here, and not taking any money for it either. Therefore, we should not build upon human law or works, but rather have true faith in the One who is the destroyer of sin; then we shall find ourselves growing in Him. Then everything that was bitter before is sweet. Then our hearts will recognize God. And when that happens we shall be despised, and we shall pay no regard to human law, and then the pope will come and excommunicate us. But then we shall be so

---

6. Because of the rule that the priest must say mass fasting.

united with God that we shall pay no heed whatsoever to any hardship, ban, or law.

Then someone may go on and ask: Should we not keep the man-made laws at all? Or, can we not continue to pray, fast, and so on, as long as the right way is present? My answer is that if there is present a right Christian love and faith, then everything a man does is meritorious; and each may do what he wills [cf. Rom. 14:22], so long as he has no regard for works, since they cannot save him.

In conclusion, then, every single person should reflect and remember that we cannot help ourselves, but only God, and also that our works are utterly worthless. So shall we have the peace of God. And every person should so perform his work that it benefits not only himself alone, but also another, his neighbor. If he is rich, his wealth should benefit the poor. If he is poor, his service should benefit the rich. When persons are servants or maidservants, their work should benefit their master. Thus no one's work should benefit him alone; for when you note that you are serving only your own advantage, then your service is false. I am not troubled; I know very well what man-made laws are. Let the pope issue as many laws as he likes, I will keep them all so far as I please.

Therefore, dear friends, remember that God has risen up for our sakes. Therefore let us also arise to be helpful to the weak in faith, and so direct our work that God may be pleased with it. So shall we receive the peace he has given to us today. May God grant us this every day. Amen.

Source 2 from Ulrich Leupold, editor, Luther's Works, *vol. 53 (Philadelphia: Fortress, 1965), p. 305. Copyright © 1965 Fortress Press. Used by permission of Augsburg Fortress.*

2. Luther, *Lord, Keep Us Steadfast in Thy Word*, hymn, 1541–1542

1. Lord, keep us steadfast in thy Word,
And curb the pope's and Turk's vile sword,
Who seek to topple from the throne
Jesus Christ, thine only Son.

2. Proof of thy might, Lord Christ, afford,
For thou of all the lords art Lord;
Thine own poor Christendom defend,
That it may praise thee without end.

3. God Holy Ghost, who comfort art,
Give to thy folk on earth one heart;
Stand by us breathing our last breath,
Lead us to life straight out of death.

Sources 3 and 4 from Lutheran Book of Worship *(Minneapolis: Augsburg, 1978), hymn 229; hymn 297. Source 3: Copyright © 1978. Used by permission of Augsburg Publishing House. Source 4: Copyright © 1941 Concordia Publishing House. Used by permission.*

3. Luther, *A Mighty Fortress Is Our God*, hymn, 1527–1528

1.   A mighty fortress is our God,
A sword and shield victorious;
He breaks the cruel oppressor's rod
And wins salvation glorious.
The old satanic foe
Has sworn to work us woe!
With craft and dreadful might
He arms himself to fight.
On earth he has no equal.

2.   No strength of ours can match his might!
We would be lost, rejected.
But now a champion comes to fight,
Whom God himself elected.
You ask who this may be?
The Lord of hosts is he!
Christ Jesus, mighty Lord,
God's only Son, adored.
He holds the field victorious.

3.   Though hordes of devils fill the land
All threat'ning to devour us,
We tremble not, unmoved we stand;
They cannot overpow'r us,
Let this world's tyrant rage;
In battle we'll engage!
His might is doomed to fail;
God's judgment must prevail!
One little word subdues him.

4.   God's Word forever shall abide,
No thanks to foes, who fear it;
For God himself fights by our side
With weapons of the Spirit.
Were they to take our house,
Goods, honor, child, or spouse,
Though life be wrenched away,

They cannot win the day.
The Kingdom's ours forever!

4. Paul Speratus, *Salvation unto Us Has Come*, hymn, 1524

1.   Salvation unto us has come
By God's free grace and favor;
Good works cannot avert our doom,
They help and save us never.
Faith looks to Jesus Christ alone,
Who did for all the world atone;
He is our mediator.

2.   Theirs was a false, misleading dream
Who thought God's law was given
That sinners might themselves redeem
And by their works gain heaven.
The Law is but a mirror bright
To bring the inbred sin to light
That lurks within our nature.

3.   And yet the Law fulfilled must be,
Or we were lost forever;
Therefore God sent his Son that he
Might us from death deliver.
He all the Law for us fulfilled,
And thus his Father's anger stilled
Which over us impended.

4.   Faith clings to Jesus' cross alone
And rests in him unceasing;
And by its fruits true faith is known,
With love and hope unceasing.
For faith alone can justify;
Works serve our neighbor and supply
The proof that faith is living.

5.   All blessing, honor, thanks, and praise
To Father, Son, and Spirit,
The God who saved us by his grace;
All glory to his merit
O triune God in heav'n above,
You have revealed your saving love;
Your blessed name we hallow.

Source 5 from Kupferstichkabinett Staatliche Museen zu Berlin, Preussischer Kulturbesitz, Berlin. Photograph by Jorg P. Anders.

5. Matthias Gerung, Broadsheet, Lauingen (Germany), 1546

Source 6 from the Mitchell Collection, London.

6. Matthias Gerung, Broadsheet, Lauingen, 1546

7. Lucas Cranach, Pamphlet, Wittenberg (Germany), 1521

9. Lucas Cranach, Pamphlet, Wittenberg, 1545[7]

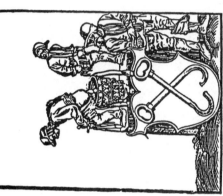

Bapst hat dem reich Christi gethon
Wie man hie handelt seine Cron.
Was ir zweifeltig: spricht der geist
Sy werdt getroffen ein: Gott ists der heist.
Mart. Luth.

7. The lines below the woodcut read, "The pope has done to the kingdom of Christ / What is here being done to his own crown."

8. Unknown Artist, Pamphlet, Augsburg (Germany), 1522

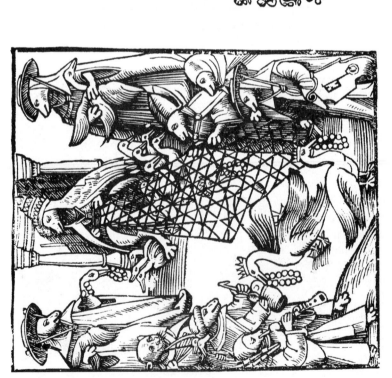

Source 10 from Oskar Schade, Satiren und Pasquille aus der Reformationszeit, *vol. 2, no. 15 (Hannover: 1863). Selection translated by Merry E. Wiesner.*

10. Anonymous German Pamphlet, 1523

A dialogue between two good friends named Hans Tholl and Claus Lamp, talking about the Antichrist[8] and his followers.

They are in a good mood while drinking wine and sit and discuss some ideas from the letters of Paul.

PREFACE

Dear Christians and brothers, if we want to recognize and know the Antichrist, we have to go to the brothers who can read, so that they will read us the second chapter of the second letter of Paul to the Thessalonians. There we will clearly find him, with his gestures and manners, how he acted and still acts, how he is now revealed so that we do not have to wait any longer but can know him despite his masks. How the devil sends his followers to knock us down, and how the old women and bath maids see him. We have long been blind to the lies and deceits of Satan, the devil. Because we have not paid attention to the divine warnings from Daniel, Paul, Christ, Peter, and the apocalypse of John, God has tormented us with ghosts and apparitions who will take us all with them to hell. Why should this cause God to suffer when He has offered you His holy word? If you don't want it, then go to the devil, for he is here now. He sees, finds, and possesses.

It happened that Hans Tholl and Claus Lamp were looking for each other and finally found each other in the evening.

CLAUS: My friend Hans, where have you been all day? I've been looking for you. The innkeeper has a good wine for two cents, and I wanted to drink a glass of wine with you.

HANS: Dear friend, I've been in a place that I wouldn't take six glasses of wine for.

CLAUS: So tell me where you have been.

HANS: I've got exciting news.

CLAUS: Well, what is it then? Tell me!

HANS: I was in a place where a friend read to four of us from the Bible. He read in the second chapter of the second letter of Paul to the Thessalonians about the Antichrist and how one is to recognize him.

8. **Antichrist:** the devil.

CLAUS: Oh I would have given a penny to have been there.

HANS: I want you to believe that I haven't heard anything like this in my whole life; I wouldn't have given three pennies to miss it.

CLAUS: Can't you remember anything, Hans? Can you tell me something about it?

HANS: I think I can tell you about almost the whole chapter, and only leave a little out.

CLAUS: So tell me! But let's get some wine first. I'll pay for yours.

HANS: Here's to your money!

CLAUS: Innkeeper, bring some wine.

HANS: What does he get for it?

CLAUS: He gets two cents. Now, tell me! I really want to hear what you will say about the Antichrist.

HANS: I'll tell you, but it will seem strange to you.

CLAUS: Why?

HANS: It seemed strange and odd to me, too, that people or states are the Antichrist.

CLAUS: Go ahead, then, you're boring me.

HANS: Stop that. All right, here's what the chapter says: "Dear brothers," Paul writes to the Thessalonians, "We ask you in the name of the coming of Christ and our coming together for the same, that you not be moved in your senses (or from your senses), or frightened by the spirit or the word or by letters supposedly coming from us, saying that the day of the Lord has come or will be coming soon. Let no one deceive you in any way, it will come only when there is disagreement and disunity (even though they all say they are preaching and believing nothing but the Gospel and Christianity) and the man of lawlessness will be disclosed, the son of damnation, who is against the gospel. Then he will be raised up (here Claus Lamp began to understand) above everything that is called a god (or is worshipped as a god) until he sits in the temple of God and lets himself be prayed to as if he were God." Claus, what are you thinking about? Do you know this man of lawlessness?

CLAUS: Now all the devils will come for you! He is no other beast than the Pope and his realm. I would never in my whole life have realized that if you hadn't been there [to hear it]. I'll buy you a second glass of wine!

HANS: Be quiet! I want to tell you more.

CLAUS: My dear friend, still more?

HANS: Of course. First I'll tell you the reason why I was talked to for so long.

CLAUS: My friend, for God's sake keep talking!

HANS: So listen! Here is the text: Paul says: "Don't you remember the things that I told you when I was with you? And now you know what is holding him (or what you should pay attention to), and that he will be revealed in his time. I tell you, that now he is doing so many evil and underhanded things, that only those who stop it now will stop it when his time comes fully. And then he will be revealed, the lawless one"—listen here, Claus—" who the lord Jesus Christ will slay with the breath of His mouth and will totally destroy with the light of His coming. But the coming of the Antichrist is through the activity of Satan, the devil, with great power and supposed signs and wonders, and with mis-guided celebration of the evil of those who will be destroyed. Because they would not accept the love of truth" (this clearly refers to the Gospel)" and be saved, God sends them the results of their errors, a great delusion, so that they believe the lies and are all condemned who did not believe the truth but agreed to the evil (and took it on themselves)." See that, Claus! Now you have heard why God has allowed error. Even though we have long wanted not to do wrong, we still hard-headedly keep doing it.

CLAUS: That says a lot. I would set my life on it, if it were only half as important. Now I hear and see that God allows very little understanding.

HANS: Yes, and why? People don't want to know very much and don't go to the Bible. God has hardened them and we are so godless. God will make us suffer because we don't ask about the truth. If we only had half as much con-cern about the health of our souls as we have about material goods, we wouldn't have come so far from the right path. As you have just heard, it isn't God who sent the so-called preachers [to lead us astray]. Here, I'll say it to you straight: Paul goes on to say: "Dear brothers, we should give thanks to God at all times because he chose you from the beginning, and he called you through the Gospel" (and not through other fairy-stories, as people are now saying).

CLAUS: Unfortunately you are right. Right now I hear strange things about the beast of the Antichrist from priests and monks. God help us!

HANS: Yes, we need to pray earnestly to God to send us good preachers, that preach the pure Gospel and leave the fairy stories at home.

CLAUS: My friend, I am still thinking about the Antichrist, that he has begun so many devilish things and made the whole world to be his fool.

HANS: That astonishers me, too. But you have now heard from Paul, when he says: "God has allowed them to be deluded because they have not accepted the truth." We haven't noticed this, and the priests have hidden it from us.

CLAUS: I believe that the devil has possessed them all so that they haven't preached to us about these things.

HANS: They are afraid that people would recognize that their God, the Pope, is the Antichrist. People are supposed to honor and pray to him, just like Paul says about the Antichrist. So they are afraid.

CLAUS: That's really true. They've thought: If we tell the lay people this, they will notice and think about how they have to kiss the Pope's foot and call him "most holy." And some know-it-alls even say: The Pope can't do any wrong; he can't sin.

HANS: It's amazing that God has allowed this to happen for so long, that it hasn't been made clear that we have been so blind. What really matters is that we have deserted the truth, my dear Claus. Let's ask God for the true faith!

I see clearly that everything will soon be over, that the Last judgment stands right before the door!

CLAUS: My dear brother Hans, I've thought that for a long time. Shall we go home?

HANS: Yes, let's drink up and go.

CLAUS: I don't want to drink any more, because I have been so seized by pity and compassion. I see that things will end soon. My dear Hans, I want to take this thing to its end with you, so I have to ask: what do you think about the fact that there is such a commotion now about Luther and his writings?

HANS: I think it's because he has discovered the Antichrist. He can't stand it, and I believe he will make many martyrs. I've heard that it has already started in some places; in Antwerp three people have been burnt because of his teachings. And I've heard that in some places they are imprisoning people and hunting them down.

CLAUS: If that's true, that's what's supposed to happen. I have always heard that the Antichrist will make martyrs and will pay money so that people will kill those who do not believe in him but instead preach the word of God.

HANS: I've heard that, too. Now to the next thing: when I want to hear more things read, I'll tell you.

CLAUS: My dear friend, I'll let everything be open to you, because I see clearly what will come out of it. I see clearly, if I want to be saved, I have to come back to the true faith, from which without a doubt the Antichrist and his horde have led us. God give you a good night!

HANS: Same to you! See that you don't forget what I've said.

CLAUS: I won't for the rest of my life. God be praised.

QUESTIONS TO CONSIDER

In exploring how the Reformation movement grew and took root throughout Europe, many scholars point to the printing press as the key factor in explaining why Luther's reforms had a much greater impact than those of Wyclif and Hus. After examining the sources, would you agree? What difference did it make that Luther's sermons were not only delivered but also printed? That hymns were taught not simply to choirs of monks or clergymen but to congregations of laypeople, out of hymnals that were printed and might be purchased by any fairly well-to-do member? That small pamphlets such as the one reproduced here were written in German and appeared in paperback?

Several historians have also pointed to the opposite effect, that the Protestant emphasis on individual reading of the Bible dramatically increased the demand for books. Judging by the language, what sort of person might have bought Luther's sermon or the pamphlet? What effects would you expect the Protestant Reformation to have had on literacy? The religious conflict itself was also a spur to book production and book buying, and religious works were the best sellers of the sixteenth century. What techniques did the pamphlet writer use to make his work more appealing to a buyer? How might including some of the woodcuts have affected sales?

Of course, the great majority of people in the sixteenth century could not read, so it may be wrong to overemphasize written sources of communication. As you noticed in the dialogue, however, people who could not read often turned to their neighbors who could, and so printed pamphlets were often heard by many who could not read them themselves. This dialogue itself was probably read out loud and may even have been acted out, which we know was the case with more elaborate dialogues containing stage directions and a whole cast of characters. Do you think this dialogue would have been effective read aloud rather than silently? The printing press also increased the circulation of visual images; woodcuts such as those reproduced here often became best sellers. Why did so many people purchase these woodcuts? If a person's only contact with Protestant thinking were images such as these, how would his or her beliefs have differed from those of a person who could read Luther's words as well?

To answer the second question—how the Protestant message was made attractive to people—look at your list of frequently repeated ideas and images. Which seem directed to all Christians? For example, what do the sources say about the role of good works in helping a person achieve salvation? The role of faith? Why might these ideas have been appealing? What was wrong with the Catholic clergy? In contrast, what did "good preachers" do and emphasize? Why might the contrast have made Luther's ideas attractive?

Though ideas and images were often repeated, not everyone understood them in the same way or was attracted to them for the same reasons. Different groups within German society responded to different parts of the Protestant message and must be examined separately. Begin with the peasants. How are they depicted in the various sources? Why did the pamphlet writer and the artist of Source 9 choose to make their characters peasants? In the heaven and hell woodcuts, where are peasants and poor people? Why would peasants have been particularly attracted to the criticism of indulgences? Why would Luther's ideas about the value of good works have appealed to them? Source 5 shows nobles in fancy feathered hats near hell, and Source 8 depicts rulers as geese; how would peasants have responded to these images? In the dialogue, Claus and Hans both agree that the Last Judgment is near. Why might sixteenth-century peasants have accepted this idea of the imminence of the end of the world?

Now consider the nobles and rulers. We have already noted that several of the woodcuts portray them negatively. How did Luther portray them in his sermon? Though hostility to nobles and rulers is evident in the Protestant message, many of the movement's ideas and images appealed to this class. Look, for example, at the upper-right picture in Source 7. How does this scene reflect the hostility of rulers to the papacy? The noble class was primarily responsible for military actions in sixteenth-century Germany. How would they have responded to the language of the hymns? What effect might linking the Turks and the pope in the hymn in Source 2 and the woodcut of Source 6 have had? Sources 1, 3, 6, and 10 all include devils attacking people or dragging them to hell at the Last Judgment. Why might nobles have been attracted to such imagery? What message would they have gotten from imagery linking such devils with the pope? In what ways did the reasons why Luther's ideas appealed to nobles contradict the reasons they appealed to peasants?

Other groups in German society appear only rarely in the sources given here, so you will not be able to discover as much about the ways in which the Protestant message attracted them as you can in the case of peasants and nobles. You may, however, want to review the sources for evidence relating to the middle class, which you can find most easily in the woodcuts. Which of your answers about the reasons certain ideas were appealing to peasants or nobles would also apply to middle-class people?

You are now ready to answer both questions posed in this chapter. How were the basic concepts of the Reformation communicated to a wide range of the population? How were these concepts made attractive to different groups?

EPILOGUE

Though Luther's initial message was one of religious reform, people quickly saw its social, economic, and political implications. The free imperial knights used Luther's attack on the wealth of the Church and his ideas about the spiritual equality of all Christians to justify their rebellion in 1521. Quickly suppressed, this uprising was followed by a more serious rebellion by peasants in 1525. Peasants in south Germany added religious demands, such as a call for taxes, to their long-standing economic grievances and took up arms. The Peasants' War spread eastward and northward but was never unified militarily, and it was brutally put down by imperial and noble armies later in the same year.

Given some of Luther's remarks about rulers and human laws (as you read in the sermon), the peasants expected him to support them. He did not, but urged them instead to obey their rulers, for in his opinion religion was not a valid justification for political revolution or social upheaval. When the peasants did not listen and continued their rebellion, Luther turned against them, calling them "murdering and thieving hordes." He supported the rulers in their slaughter of peasant armies, and his later writings became much more conservative than the sermon you read here.

The nobles and rulers who accepted Luther's message continued to receive his support, however. Many of the German states abolished the Catholic Church and established their own Protestant churches under their individual ruler's control. This expulsion led to a series of religious wars between Protestants and Catholics that were finally ended by the Peace of Augsburg in 1555. The terms of the peace treaty allowed rulers to choose between Catholicism and Lutheran Protestantism; they were further given the right to enforce religious uniformity within their territories. By the middle of the sixteenth century, then, the only people who could respond as they chose to the Protestant message were rulers.

Achieving religious uniformity was not as simple a task as it had been earlier, however. Though rulers attempted to ban materials they did not agree with and prevent their subjects from reading or printing forbidden materials, religious literature was regularly smuggled from city to city. Because printing presses could produce thousands of copies of anything fairly quickly, ideas of all types spread much more quickly than they had earlier. Once people can read, it is much more difficult to control the information they take in; though rulers could control their subjects' outward religious activities, they could not control their thoughts.

Rulers were not the only ones who could not control thinking and the exchange of ideas during the sixteenth century. As Luther discovered to his dismay, once ideas are printed and widely disseminated, they take on a life of their own; no matter how much one might wish, they cannot be called back or be made to conform to their original meaning. Not only did German knights and peasants interpret Luther's message in their own way, but other religious reformers, building on what he had written, developed their own interpretations of the Christian message. They used the same variety of methods that had been so successful in spreading Luther's ideas to communicate their own, and the Protestant Reformation became a multifaceted movement with many different leaders and numerous plans for action.

The Catholic Church, learning from Protestant successes, began to publish its own illustrated pamphlets with negative images of Luther and other Protestant leaders along with explanations of its theology in easy-to-understand language. In this chapter we have looked exclusively at Lutheran propaganda, but the oral, written, and visual techniques of communication presented here were employed by all sides in the sixteenth-century religious conflict. Later they would be adapted for other political and intellectual debates.

CHAPTER TWO

STAGING ABSOLUTISM

The "Age of Absolutism" is the label historians often apply to the history of Europe in the seventeenth and eighteenth centuries. In many ways it is an appropriate description because, with the exception of the Dutch Republic and England (where the Civil War of 1642–1648 and the Glorious Revolution of 1688 severely limited royal power), most major European states in this era had monarchs who aspired to absolute authority in their realms.

The royal absolutism that evolved in seventeenth-century Europe represents an important step in governmental development. In constructing absolutist states, monarchs and their ministers both created new organs of administration and built on existing institutions of government to supplant the regional authorities of the medieval state with more centralized state power. In principle, this centralized authority was subject to the absolute authority of the monarch; in practice, royal authority was nowhere as encompassing as that of a modern dictator. Poor communication systems, the persistence of traditional privileges that exempted whole regions or social groups from full royal authority, and other factors all set limits on royal power. Nevertheless, monarchs of the era strove for the ideal of absolute royal power, and France was the model in their work of state building.

French monarchs of the seventeenth and early eighteenth centuries more fully developed the system of absolute monarchy. In these rulers' efforts to overcome impediments to royal authority, we can learn much about the creation of absolutism in Europe. Rulers in Prussia, Austria, Russia, and many smaller states sought not only the real power of the French kings, but also the elaborate court ceremony and dazzling palaces that symbolized that power.

Absolutism in France was the work of Henry IV (r. 1589–1610), Louis XIII (r. 1610–1643) and his minister Cardinal Richelieu, and Louis XIV (r. 1643–1715). These rulers established a system of centralized royal political authority that destroyed many remnants of the feudal monarchy. The reward for their endeavors was great: With Europe's largest population and immense wealth, France was potentially the mightiest country on the Continent in 1600 and its natural leader, if only these national strengths could be unified and directed by a strong government. Just as importantly, these monarchs endeavored to create strong central governments as proof against internal disorders, like rebellion and civil warfare, that plagued the medieval state. But French rulers confronted formidable problems, common to many early modern states, in achieving their goals. Nobles everywhere still held considerable power, in part a legacy of the system of feudal monarchy. In France they possessed military power, which they used in the religious civil wars of the sixteenth century and in their Fronde revolt against growing royal power in the mid-seventeenth century. Nobles also exercised considerable political power through such representative bodies as the Estates General and provincial assemblies, which gave form to their claims for a voice in government. Moreover, nobles served as the judges of the great law courts, the *parlements,* which had to register all royal edicts before they could take effect.

A second obstacle to national unity and royal authority in many states, in an age that equated national unity with religious uniformity, was the presence of a large and influential religious minority. In France the Protestant minority was known as the Huguenots. Not only did they forswear the Catholic religion of the king and the majority of his subjects, but they possessed military power through their rights, under the Edict of Nantes,[1] to fortify their cities.

A third and major impediment to unifying a country under absolute royal authority was regional differences. The medieval monarchy of France had been built province by province over several centuries, and the kingdom was not well integrated. Some provinces, like Brittany in the north, retained local estates or assemblies with which the monarch actually had to bargain for taxes. Many provinces had their own cultural heritage that separated them from the king's government centered in Paris. These differences might be as simple as matters of local custom, but they might also be as complex as unique systems of civil law. A particular problem was the persistence of local dialects, which made the French of royal officials a foreign and incomprehensible tongue in large portions of the kingdom.

The only unifying principle that could overcome all these centrifugal forces was royal authority. The task in the seventeenth century was to build a theoretical basis for a truly powerful monarch, to endow the king with tangible power that gave substance to theory, and to place the sovereign in a setting that would never permit the country to forget his new power.

To establish an abstract basis for absolutism, royal authority had to be strengthened and reinforced by a

1. **Edict of Nantes:** In this 1598 decree, King Henry IV sought to end the civil warfare between French Catholics and Huguenots. He granted the Protestants basic protection, in the event of renewed fighting, by allowing them to fortify some 200 of their cities. The edict also accorded the Protestants freedom of belief with some restrictions, and civil rights equal to those of Catholic Frenchmen.

veritable cult of kingship. Seventeenth-century French statesmen built on medieval foundations in this task. Medieval kings had possessed limited tangible authority but substantial religious prestige; their vassals had rendered them religious oaths of loyalty. French monarchs since Pepin the Short had been anointed in a biblically inspired coronation ceremony in which they received not only the communion bread that the Catholic Church administered to all believers, but also the wine, which was normally reserved for clerics; once crowned, they claimed to possess mystical religious powers to heal with the royal touch. All these trappings served to endow the monarch with almost divine powers, separating him from and raising him above his subjects. Many seventeenth-century thinkers emphasized this traditional divine dimension of royal power. Others, as you will see, found more practical grounds for great royal power.

To achieve greater royal power, Henry IV reestablished peace after the religious civil warfare of the late sixteenth century, and Cardinal Richelieu curbed the military power of the nobility. With the creation of loyal provincial administrators, the *intendants,* and a system of political patronage that he directed, the cardinal also established firmer central control in the name of Louis XIII. Richelieu, moreover, ended Huguenot political power by crushing their revolt in 1628, and he intervened in the Thirty Years' War to establish France as a chief European power.

The reign of Louis XIV completed the process of consolidating royal authority in France. Louis XIV created much of the administrative apparatus necessary to centralize the state. The king brought the nobility under even greater control, building in Europe's largest army a force that could defeat any aristocratic revolt and creating in Versailles a court life that drew nobles away from provincial plotting and near to the king, where their actions could be observed. The king also sought to extend royal authority by expanding France's borders through a series of wars and to eliminate the Huguenot minority completely by revoking the religious freedoms embodied in the Edict of Nantes.

The king supplemented his military and political work of state building with other projects to integrate France more completely as one nation. With royal patronage, authors and scholars flourished and, by the example of their often excellent works, extended the French dialect in the country at the expense of provincial tongues. In the king's name, his finance minister, Jean-Baptiste Colbert (1619–1683), sought to realize a vision of a unified French economy. He designed mercantilist policies to favor French trade and build French industry, and he improved transportation to bind the country together as one unit. The result of Louis's policies, therefore, was not only a stronger king and a more powerful France but a more unified country as well.

Far more than previous French monarchs, Louis XIV addressed the third task in establishing absolutism. In modern terms, it consisted of effective public relations, which required visible evidence of the new royal authority. The stage setting for the royal display of the symbols of absolute authority was Versailles, the site of a new royal palace. Built between 1661 and 1682, the palace itself was massive, with a façade one-quarter mile long pierced by 2,143 windows. It was set in a park of 37,000 acres, of which 6,000 acres were embellished with formal gardens. These gardens contained 1,400 fountains that required massive hydraulic works to supply them with water, an artificial lake one mile long for royal boating parties, and 200 statues. The palace grounds contained various smaller palaces as well, including Marly, where the king could entertain small, select groups away from the main palace, which was the center of a court life embracing almost 20,000 persons (9,000 soldiers billeted in the town; and 5,000 royal servants, 1,000 nobles and their 4,000 servants, plus the royal family, all housed in the main palace). Because the royal ministers and their secretaries also were in residence, Versailles was much more than a palace: It was the capital of France.

Royal architects deliberately designed the palace to impart a message to all who entered. As a guidebook of 1681 by Laurent Morellet noted regarding the palace's art:

The subjects of painting which complete the decorations of the ceilings are of heroes and illustrious men, taken from history and fable, who have deserved the titles of Magnanimous, of Great, of Fathers of the People, of Liberal, of Just, of August and Victorious, and who have possessed all the Virtues which we have seen appear in the Person of our Great Monarch during the fortunate course of his reign; so that everything remarkable which one sees in the Château and in the garden always has some relationship with the great actions of His Majesty.[2]

The court ritual and etiquette enacted in this setting departed markedly from the simpler court life of Louis XIII and were designed to complement the physical presence of the palace itself in teaching the lesson of a new royal power.

In this chapter we will analyze royal absolutism in France. What was the theoretical basis for absolute royal authority? What was traditional and what was new in the justification of royal power as expressed in late-sixteenth- and seventeenth-century France? How did such early modern kings as Louis XIV communicate their absolute power in the various ceremonies and symbols of royal authority presented in the evidence that follows?

SOURCES AND METHOD

This chapter assembles several kinds of sources, each demanding a different kind of historical analysis. Two works of political theory that were influential

2. Laurent Morellet, *Explication historique de ce qu'il y a de plus remarquable dans la maison royale de Versailles et en celle de Monsieur à Saint-Cloud* (Paris, 1681), quoted in Robert W. Hartle, "Louis XIV and the Mirror of Antiquity" in Steven G. Reinhardt and Vaughn L. Glasgow, eds., *The Sun King: Louis XIV and the New World* (New Orleans: Louisiana State Museum Foundation, 1984), p. 111.

in the formation of absolutism open the evidence. To analyze these works effectively, you will need some brief background information on their authors and on the problems these thinkers discussed.

Jean Bodin (1530–1596) was a law professor, an attorney, and a legal official. His interests transcended his legal education, however. He brought a wide reading in Hebrew, Greek, Italian, and German to the central problem addressed in his major work, *The Six Books of the Republic* (1576), that of establishing the well-ordered state. Writing during the religious wars of the sixteenth century, when government in France all but broke down, Bodin offered answers to this crisis. Especially novel for the sixteenth century was his call for religious toleration. Although he was at least formally a Catholic[3] and recognized unity in religion as a strong unifying factor for a country, Bodin was unwilling to advocate the use of force in eliminating Protestantism from France. He believed that acceptance was by far the better policy.

Bodin's political thought was also significant, and his *Republic* immediately was recognized as an important work. Published in several editions and translated into Latin, Italian, Spanish, and German, the *Republic* influenced

a circle of men, the *Politiques*, who advised Henry IV. Through the process of seeking to explain how to establish the well-ordered state, Bodin contributed much to Western political theory. Perhaps his most important idea was that there was nothing divine about governing power. Men created governments solely to ensure their physical and material security; to meet those needs, the ruling power had to exercise a sovereignty on which Bodin placed few limits.[4] Indeed, Bodin's concept of the ruler's power is his most important contribution to political thought. What is the essence of royal sovereignty for Bodin? What other governing power did the monarch possess? How did Bodin's vision point to the end of the feudal state that still partially existed in his time?

The second work of political theory was written by Jacques Bénigne Bossuet (1627–1704), Bishop of Meaux. A great orator who preached at the court of Louis XIV, Bossuet was entrusted with the education of the king's son and heir, the Dauphin. He wrote three works for that prince's instruction, including the one excerpted in this chapter, *Politics Drawn from the Very Words of the Holy Scripture* (1678).

As tutor to the Dauphin and royal preacher, Bossuet expressed what has been called the *divine right* theory of kingship: that is, the king was God's deputy on earth, and to oppose him was to oppose divine law. Here, of course, the bishop was drawing on

---

3. Bodin's religious thought evolved in the course of his life. Although he was brought up a Catholic and was briefly a Carmelite friar, his knowledge of Hebrew and early regard for the Old Testament led some to suspect that he was a Jew. The writings of his middle years indicate some Calvinist leanings. Later in life, his thought seems to have moved beyond traditional Catholic and Protestant Christianity. He was nevertheless deeply religious.

4. Bodin saw the sovereign power as limited by natural law and the need to respect property (which meant that the ruler could not tax without his subjects' consent) and the family.

those medieval beliefs and practices imputing certain divine powers to the king. Because Bossuet was an influential member of the court of Louis XIV, his ideas on royal authority carried considerable weight. Trained as a theologian, he buttressed his political theories with scriptural authority. In this selection, determine the extent of the royal link to God. Why might such a theory be particularly useful to Louis XIV?

Source 3 is a selection from the *Memoirs* of Louis de Rouvroy, duke of Saint-Simon (1675–1755). Saint-Simon's memoirs of court life are extensive, comprising forty-one volumes in the main French edition. They constitute both a remarkable record of life at Versailles and, because of their style, an important example of French literature. As useful and important as the *Memoirs* are, however, they must be read with care. All of us, consciously or unconsciously, have biases and opinions, and memoirists are no exception. In fact, memoir literature illustrates problems of which students of history should be aware in everything they read. The way in which authors present events, even what they choose to include or omit from their accounts, reflects their opinions. Because memoir writers often recount events in which they participated, they may have especially strong views about what they relate. Thus, to use Saint-Simon's work profitably, it is essential to understand his point of view. We must also ask if the memoir writer was in a position to know firsthand what he or she is relating or is simply recounting less reliable rumors.

Saint-Simon came from an old noble family that had recently risen to prominence when his father became a royal favorite. Ironically, no one was more deeply opposed to the policies of Louis XIV, which aimed to destroy the traditional feudal power of the nobility in the name of royal authority, than this man whose position rested on that very authority. Saint-Simon was, quite simply, a defender of the older style of kingship, in which sovereignty was limited by the monarch's need to consult with his vassals. His memoirs reflect this view and are often critical of the king. But even with his critical view of the king and his court, Saint-Simon was an important figure there, an individual privy to state business and court gossip, who gives us a remarkable picture of life at Versailles. Analyze the court etiquette and ritual that Saint-Simon describes as a nonverbal message from the king to his most powerful subjects. For example, what message did the royal waking and dressing ceremony convey to the most powerful and privileged persons in France, who crowded the royal bedroom and vied for the privilege of helping the king dress? What message did their very presence convey in turn to Louis XIV? Recall Bossuet's ideas of kingship. Why might public religious rituals such as that attending the royal rising be part of the agenda of a king who was not particularly noted for his piety during the first half of his life?

Studied closely, the three different kinds of written evidence presented— the work of a sixteenth-century political theorist, the writings of a contemporary supporter, and the memoirs of one of the king's opponents—reveal much about the growing power of the French monarchy. What common themes do you find in these works? What were the sources of the king's political authority?

From these written sources, we move on to pictorial evidence of the symbols of royal authority. Symbols are concrete objects possessing a meaning beyond what is immediately apparent. We are all aware of the power of symbols, particularly in our age of electronic media, and we all, perhaps unconsciously, analyze them to some extent. Take a simple example drawn from modern advertising: The lion appears frequently as an image in advertisements for banks and other financial institutions. The lion's presence is intended to convey to us the strength of the financial institution, to inspire our faith in the latter's ability to protect our funds. Using this kind of analysis, you can determine the total meaning of the symbols associated with Louis XIV.

Consider the painting presented as the fourth piece of evidence, *Louis XIV Taking Up Personal Government* in 1661. Louis XIV had been king in name since the age of five after his father's death in 1643, but only in 1661, as an adult, did he assume full power. Remember that such art was generally commissioned by the king and often had an instructional purpose. What do the following elements symbolize: the portrayal of Louis XIV as a Roman emperor; the positioning of a figure representing France on his right; the crowning of the king with a wreath of flowers; the figure of Time (note the hourglass

and scythe) holding a tapestry over the royal head; and the presence of herald angels hovering above?

Now go on to the other pictures and perform the same kind of analysis, always trying to identify the symbolic message that the painter or architect wished to convey. For Source 5, study the royal pose and such seemingly superficial elements in the picture as the king's dress and the background details. Ask yourself what ideas these were intended to convey. Source 6 presents the insignia Louis XIV chose as his personal symbol, which decorated much of Versailles. Reflect on Louis's reasons for this choice in reading his explanation:

The symbol that I have adopted and that you see all around you represents the duties of a Prince and inspires me always to fulfill them. I chose for an emblem the Sun which, according to the rules of this art [heraldry], is the noblest of all, and which, by the brightness that surrounds it, by the light it lends to the other stars that constitute, after a fashion, its court, by the universal good it does, endlessly promoting life, joy, and growth, by its perpetual and regular movement, by its constant and invariable course, is assuredly the most dazzling and most beautiful image of the monarch.[5]

Finally, Source 7 portrays Louis XIV costumed for one of the many pageants enjoyed by the king in his younger years. He wears the garb of a Roman emperor, an official who ruled much of the ancient world. What does the king's choice

5. Quoted in Reinhardt and Glasgow, *The Sun King*, p. 181.

of costume suggest about his vision of his own role in the world?

With Sources 8 through 13, we turn to analysis of architecture, which of course also served to symbolize royal power. You must ask yourself how great that concept of royal power was as you look at the pictures of Versailles. The palace, after all, was not only the royal residence but also the setting for the conduct of government, including the king's reception of foreign ambassadors. At the most basic level, notice the scale of the palace. What impression might its size have been intended to convey? At a second level, examine decorative details of the palace. Why might the balustrade at the palace entry have been decorated with statuary symbolizing Magnificence, Justice, Wisdom, Prudence, Diligence, Peace, Europe, Asia, Renown, Abundance, Force, Generosity, Wealth, Authority, Fame, America, Africa, and Victory?

Observe the views of the palace's interior, considering the functions of the rooms and their details. Source 10 offers a view of the royal chapel at Versailles. Richly decorated in marble and complemented with ceiling paintings such as that depicting the Trinity, the chapel was the site of daily masses as well as of royal marriages and celebrations of victories. Note that the king attended mass in the royal gallery, joining the rest of the court on the main floor only when the mass celebrant was a bishop. Why might such a magnificent setting be part of the palace? More important, what significance do you place on the position the king chose for himself in this grand setting?

Sources 11 and 12 present the sites of the royal rising ceremony described by Saint-Simon. The royal bedroom, Source 11, was richly decorated in gilt, red, and white, and was complemented by paintings of biblical scenes. Notice the rich decoration of the Bull's Eye Window Antechamber (Source 12), just outside the bedroom, where the courtiers daily awaited the king's arising. Why were the rooms decorated in such a fashion?

Source 13 offers an artist's view of Marly. Again, notice the scale of this palace, reflecting that it was, according to Saint-Simon, a weekend getaway spot for Louis XIV and selected favorites. How might the king have used invitations to this château, with the closeness to the royal person they entailed? Examine details of the palace. The central château had twelve apartments, four of which were reserved for the royal family, the others for its guests. The twelve pavilions around the lake in the center of the château's grounds each housed two guest apartments and represented the twelve signs of the zodiac. What symbolic importance might you attach to this?

Finally, return to Source 7, which recreates the pageant known as the Carousel of 1662, one of many such entertainments at court. The scale of such festivals could be huge. In 1662, 12,197 costumed people took part in a celebration that included a parade through the streets of Paris and games. Costumed as ancient Romans, Persians, and others, the participants must have made quite an impression on their audience. What kind of impression do you think it was?

What common message runs through the art and architecture you have analyzed? As you unravel the message woven into this visual evidence, combine it with the evidence you derived from Saint-Simon's portrayal of court life and the political theory of absolutism. Remember, too, the unstated message: that the monarchy of Louis XIV possessed in Europe's largest army the ultimate means for persuading its subjects to accept the divine powers of the king. You should be able to determine from all this material what was new in this conception of royal authority and the ways in which the new authority was expressed.

THE EVIDENCE

Source 1 from Francis William Coker, editor, Readings in Political Philosophy *(New York: Macmillan, 1926), pp. 235–236.*

1. From Jean Bodin, *The Six Books of the Republic*, **Book I,** **1576**

The first and principal function of sovereignty is to give laws to the citizens generally and individually, and, it must be added, not necessarily with the consent of superiors, equals, or inferiors. If the consent of superiors is required, then the prince is clearly a subject; if he must have the consent of equals, then others share his authority; if the consent of inferiors—the people or the senate—is necessary, then he lacks supreme authority. . . .

It may be objected that custom does not get its power from the judgment or command of the prince, and yet has almost the force of law, so that it would seem that the prince is master of law, the people of custom. Custom, insensibly, yet with the full compliance of all, passes gradually into the character of men, and acquires force with the lapse of time. Law, on the other hand, comes forth in one moment at the order of him who has the power to command, and often in opposition to the desire and approval of those whom it governs. Wherefore, Chrysostom[6] likens law to a tyrant and custom to a king. Moreover, the power of law is far greater than that of custom, for customs may be superseded by laws, but laws are not supplanted by customs; it is within the power and function of magistrates to restore the operation of laws which by custom are obsolescent. Custom proposes neither rewards nor penalties; laws carry one or the other, unless it be a permissive law which nullifies the penalty of some other law. In short, a custom has compelling force only as long as the prince, by adding his endorsement and sanction to the custom, makes it a law.

6. **Chrysostom:** Saint John Chrysostom (ca 347–407), an early Father of the Greek church and a brilliant preacher whose religion led him to condemn the vices of the court of the Eastern Roman emperor.

It is thus clear that laws and customs depend for their force upon the will of those who hold supreme power in the state. This first and chief mark of sovereignty is, therefore, of such sort that it cannot be transferred to subjects, though the prince or people sometimes confer upon one of the citizens the power to frame laws (*legum condendarum*), which then have the same force as if they had been framed by the prince himself. The Lacedæmonians bestowed such power upon Lycurgus, the Athenians upon Solon;[7] each stood as deputy for his state, and the fulfillment of his function depended upon the pleasure not of himself but of the people; his legislation had no force save as the people confirmed it by their assent. The former composed and wrote the laws, the people enacted and commanded them.

Under this supreme power of ordaining and abrogating laws, it is clear that all other functions of sovereignty are included; that it may be truly said that supreme authority in the state is comprised in this one thing—namely, to give laws to all and each of the citizens, and to receive none from them. For to declare war or make peace, though seeming to involve what is alien to the term law, is yet accomplished by law, that is by decree of the supreme power. It is also the prerogative of sovereignty to receive appeals from the highest magistrates, to confer authority upon the greater magistrates and to withdraw it from them, to allow exemption from taxes, to bestow other immunities, to grant dispensations from the laws, to exercise power of life and death, to fix the value, name and form of money, to compel all citizens to observe their oaths: all of these attributes are derived from the supreme power of commanding and forbidding—that is, from the authority to give law to the citizens collectively and individually, and to receive law from no one save immortal God. A duke, therefore, who gives laws to all his subjects, but receives law from the emperor, Pope, or king, or has a co-partner in authority, lacks sovereignty.

Source 2 from Richard H. Powers, editor and translator, Readings in European Civilization Since 1500, *1961, pp. 129–130. Reprinted by permission of the Estate of Richard H. Powers.*

2. From Jacques Bénigne Bossuet, *Politics Drawn from the Very Words of the Holy Scripture*, 1678

TO MONSEIGNEUR LE DAUPHIN

God is the King of kings. It is for Him to instruct and direct kings as His ministers. Heed then, Monseigneur, the lessons which He gives them in His Scriptures, and learn . . . the rules and examples on which they ought to base their conduct. . . .

7. **Lacedæmonians:** the Spartans of ancient Greece. **Lycurgus:** traditional author of the Spartan constitution. **Solon:** sixth-century B.C. Athenian lawgiver.

BOOK II: OR AUTHORITY . . .

CONCLUSION: Accordingly we have established by means of Scriptures that monarchical government comes from God. . . . That when government was established among men He chose hereditary monarchy as the most natural and most durable form. That excluding the sex born to obey[8] from the sovereign power was only natural. . . .

BOOK III: THE NATURE OF ROYAL AUTHORITY . . .

FIRST ARTICLE: Its essential characteristics. . . . First, royal authority is sacred; Second, it is paternal; Third, it is absolute; Fourth, it is subject to reason. . . .

SECOND ARTICLE: Royal authority is sacred.

FIRST PROPOSITION: God establishes kings as his ministers and reigns over people through them.—We have already seen that all power comes from God. . . .

Therefore princes act as ministers of God and as His lieutenants on earth. It is through them that he exercises His empire. . . .

Thus we have seen that the royal throne is not the throne of a man, but the throne of God himself. So in Scriptures we find "God has chosen my son Solomon to sit upon the throne of the kingdom of Jehovah over Israel." And further, "Solomon sat on the throne of Jehovah as king."

And in order that we should not think that to have kings established by God is peculiar to the Israelites, here is what Ecclesiastes says: "God gives each people its governor; and Israel is manifestly reserved to Him.". . .

SECOND PROPOSITION: The person of the king is sacred.—It follows from all the above that the person of kings is sacred. . . . God has had them anointed by His prophets with a sacred ointment, as He has had His pontiffs and His altars anointed.

But even before actually being anointed, they are sacred by virtue of their charge, as representatives of His divine majesty, delegated by His providence to execute His design. . . .

The title of *christ* is given to kings, one sees them called *christs* or the Lord's *anointed* everywhere.

Bearing this venerable name, even the prophets revered them, and looked upon them as associated with the sovereign empire of God, whose authority they exercise on earth. . . .

THIRD PROPOSITION: Religion and conscience demand that we obey the prince.—After having said that the prince is the minister of God Saint Paul concluded: "Accordingly it is necessary that you subject yourself to him out of fear of his anger, but also because of the obligation of your conscience. . . ."

And furthermore: "Servants, obey your temporal masters in all things. . . ." Saint Peter said: "Therefore submit yourselves to the order established among

---

8. **sex born to obey:** women. The Salic Law, mistakenly attributed to the medieval Salian Franks, precluded women from inheriting the crown of France.

men for the love of God; be subjected to the king as to God . . . be subjected to those to whom He gives His authority and who are sent by Him to reward good deeds and to punish evil ones."

Even if kings fail in this duty, their charge and their ministry must be respected. For Scriptures tell us: "Obey your masters, not only those who are mild and good, but also those who are peevish and unjust."

Thus there is something religious in the respect which one renders the prince. Service to God and respect for kings are one thing. . . .

Thus it is in the spirit of Christianity for kings to be paid a kind of religious respect. . . .

BOOK IV: CONTINUATION OF THE CHARACTERISTICS OF ROYALTY

FIRST ARTICLE: Royal authority is absolute.

FIRST PROPOSITION: The prince need render account to no one for what he orders. . . .

SECOND PROPOSITION: When the prince has judged there is no other judgment. . . . Princes are gods.

Source 3 from Bayle St. John, translator, The Memoirs of the Duke of Saint-Simon on the Reign of Louis XIV and the Regency, *eighth edition (London: George Allen, 1913), vol. 2, pp. 363–365, vol. 3, pp. 221–227.*

3. The Duke of Saint-Simon on the Reign of Louis XIV

[*On the creation of Versailles and the
            nature of its court life*]

He [Louis XIV] early showed a disinclination for Paris. The troubles that had taken place there during the minority made him regard the place as dangerous;[9] he wished, too, to render himself venerable by hiding himself from the eyes of the multitude; all these considerations fixed him at St. Germains [sic][10] soon after the death of the Queen, his mother. It was to that place he began to attract the world by fêtes and gallantries, and by making it felt that he wished to be often seen.

---

9. During the Fronde revolt of 1648–1653, the royal government lost control of Paris to the crowds and the royal family was forced to flee the city. Because Louis XIV was a minor (only ten years of age) when the revolt erupted, the government was administered by his mother, Anne of Austria, and her chief minister, Cardinal Mazarin.

10. **St. Germains:** St. Germain-en-Layer, site of a royal château overlooking the Seine and dating from the twelfth century, where Louis XIV was born. The court fled there in 1649 during the Fronde.

His love for Madame de la Vallière,[11] which was at first kept secret, occasioned frequent excursions to Versailles, then a little card castle, which had been built by Louis XIII—annoyed, and his suite still more so, at being frequently obliged to sleep in a wretched inn there, after he had been out hunting in the forest of Saint Leger. That monarch rarely slept at Versailles more than one night, and then from necessity; the King, his son, slept there, so that he might be more in private with his mistress; pleasures unknown to the hero and just man, worthy son of Saint Louis, who built the little château.[12]

These excursions of Louis XIV by degrees gave birth to those immense buildings he erected at Versailles; and their convenience for a numerous court, so different from the apartments at St. Germains, led him to take up his abode there entirely shortly after the death of the Queen.[13] He built an infinite number of apartments, which were asked for by those who wished to pay their court to him; whereas at St. Germains nearly everybody was obliged to lodge in the town, and the few who found accommodation at the château were strangely inconvenienced.

The frequent fêtes, the private promenades at Versailles, the journeys, were means on which the King seized in order to distinguish or mortify the courtiers, and thus render them more assiduous in pleasing him. He felt that of real favours he had not enough to bestow; in order to keep up the spirit of devotion, he therefore unceasingly invented all sorts of ideal ones, little preferences and petty distinctions, which answered his purpose as well.

He was exceedingly jealous of the attention paid him. Not only did he notice the presence of the most distinguished courtiers, but those of inferior degree also. He looked to the right and to the left, not only upon rising but upon going to bed, at his meals, in passing through his apartments, or his gardens of Versailles, where alone the courtiers were allowed to follow him; he saw and noticed everybody; not one escaped him, not even those who hoped to remain unnoticed. He marked well all absentees from the court, found out the reason of their absence, and never lost an opportunity of acting towards them as the occasion might seem to justify. With some of the courtiers (the most distinguished), it was a demerit not to make the court their ordinary abode; with others 'twas a fault to come but rarely; for those who never or scarcely ever came it was certain disgrace. When their names were in any way mentioned, "I do not know them," the King would reply haughtily. Those who presented themselves but seldom were thus characterized: "They are people I never see;" these decrees were irrevocable. . . .

---

11. **Madame de la Vallière:** Louise de la Baume le Blanc, Duchesse de la Vallière (1644–1710), the king's first mistress.

12. Saint-Simon greatly admired Louis XIII, who he had never met, and for over half a century attended annual memorial services for the king at the royal tombs in the basilica of St. Denis.

13. Anne of Austria (1601–1666), the mother of Louis XIV.

Louis XIV took great pains to be well informed of all that passed everywhere; in the public places, in the private houses, in society and familiar intercourse. His spies and tell-tales were infinite. He had them of all species; many who were ignorant that their information reached him; others who knew it; others who wrote to him direct, sending their letters through channels he indicated; and all these letters were seen by him alone, and always before everything else; others who sometimes spoke to him secretly in his cabinet, entering by the back stairs. These unknown means ruined an infinite number of people of all classes, who never could discover the cause; often ruined them very unjustly; for the King, once prejudiced, never altered his opinion or so rarely, that nothing was more rare.

[On the royal day and court etiquette]

[The royal day begins.]

At eight o'clock the chief valet de chambre on duty, who alone had slept in the royal chamber, and who had dressed himself, awoke the King. The chief physician, the chief surgeon, and the nurse (as long as she lived), entered at the same time. The latter kissed the King; the others rubbed and often changed his shirt, because he was in the habit of sweating a great deal. At the quarter, the grand chamberlain was called (or, in his absence, the first gentleman of the chamber), and those who had, what was called the *grandes entrées.* The chamberlain (or chief gentleman) drew back the curtains which had been closed again, and presented the holy water from the vase, at the head of the bed. These gentlemen stayed but a moment, and that was the time to speak to the King, if any one had anything to ask of him; in which case the rest stood aside. When, contrary to custom, nobody had aught to say, they were there but for a few moments. He who had opened the curtains and presented the holy water, presented also a prayer-book. Then all passed into the cabinet of the council. A very short religious service being over, the King called, they re-entered. The same officer gave him his dressing-gown; immediately after, other privileged courtiers entered, and then everybody, in time to find the King putting on his shoes and stockings, for he did almost everything himself and with address and grace. Every other day we saw him shave himself; and he had a little short wig in which he always appeared, even in bed, and on medicine days. He often spoke of the chase, and sometimes said a word to somebody. No toilette table was near him; he had simply a mirror held before him.

As soon as he was dressed, he prayed to God, at the side of his bed, where all the clergy present knelt, the cardinals without cushions, all the laity remaining standing; and the captain of the guards came to the balustrade during the prayer, after which the King passed into his cabinet.

He found there, or was followed by all who had the entrée, a very numerous company, for it included everybody in any office. He gave orders to each for the day; thus within a half a quarter of an hour it was known what he meant to do; and then all this crowd left directly. The bastards, a few favourites, and the valets alone were left. It was then a good opportunity for talking with the King; for example, about plans of gardens and buildings; and conversation lasted more or less according to the person engaged in it.

All the Court meantime waited for the King in the gallery, the captain of the guard being alone in the chamber seated at the door of the cabinet.

[The business of government]

On Sunday, and often on Monday, there was a council of state; on Tuesday a finance council; on Wednesday council of state; on Saturday finance council. Rarely were two held in one day or any on Thursday or Friday. Once or twice a month there was a council of despatches[14] on Monday morning; but the order that the Secretaries of State took every morning between the King's rising and his mass, much abridged this kind of business. All the ministers were seated according to rank, except at the council of despatches, where all stood except the sons of France, the Chancellor, and the Duc de Beauvilliers.[15]

[The royal luncheon]

The dinner was always *au petit couvert*,[16] that is, the King ate by himself in his chamber upon a square table in front of the middle window. It was more or less abundant, for he ordered in the morning whether it was to be "a little," or "very little" service. But even at this last, there were always many dishes, and three courses without counting the fruit. The dinner being ready, the principal courtiers entered; then all who were known; and the first gentlemen of the chamber on duty, informed the King.

I have seen, but very rarely, Monseigneur[17] and his sons standing at their dinners, the King not offering them a seat. I have continually seen there the Princes of the blood and the cardinals. I have often seen there also Monsieur,[18] either on arriving from St. Cloud to see the King, or arriving from the council of despatches (the only one he entered), give the King his napkin and remain

---

14. **council of despatches:** the royal council in which ministers discussed the letters from the provincial administrators of France, the *intendants*.

15. **sons of France:** The royal family was distinguished from the rest of the nobility as "children of France." The "sons of France" in the last decade of the seventeenth century thus were the king's son, his grandsons, and his brother. **Duc de Beauvilliers:** Paul de Beauvilliers, Duc de St. Aignan (1648–1714), was a friend of Saint-Simon and tutor of Louis XIV's grandsons, the dukes of Burgundy, Anjou, and Berry.

16. *au petit couvert:* a simple table setting with a light meal.

17. **Monseigneur:** Louis, Dauphin de France (1661–1711), son of Louis XIV and heir to the throne.

18. **Monsieur:** Philippe, Duc d'Orléans (1640–1701), Louis XIV's only sibling. His permanent residence was at the Château of St. Cloud near Paris.

standing. A little while afterwards, the King, seeing that he did not go away, asked him if he would not sit down; he bowed, and the King ordered a seat to be brought for him. A stool was put behind him. Some moments after the King said, "Nay then, sit down, my brother." Monsieur bowed and seated himself until the end of the dinner, when he presented the napkin.

[The day ends.]

At ten o'clock his supper was served. The captain of the guard announced this to him. A quarter of an hour after the King came to supper, and from the ante-chamber of Madame de Maintenon[19] to the table again, any one spoke to him who wished. This supper was always on a grand scale, the royal household (that is, the sons and daughters of France) at table, and a large number of courtiers and ladies present, sitting or standing, and on the evening before the journey to Marly all those ladies who wished to take part in it. That was called presenting yourself for Marly. Men asked in the morning, simply saying to the King, "Sire, Marly." In later years the King grew tired of this, and a valet wrote up in the gallery the names of those who asked. The ladies continued to present themselves.

After supper the King stood some moments, his back to the balustrade of the foot of his bed, encircled by all his Court; then, with bows to the ladies, passed into his cabinet, where on arriving, he gave his orders. He passed a little less than an hour there, seated in an arm-chair, with his legitimate children and bastards, his grandchildren, legitimate and otherwise, and their husbands or wives. Monsieur in another arm-chair; the princesses upon stools, Monseigneur and all the other princes standing.

The King, wishing to retire, went and fed his dogs; then said good night, passed into his chamber to the *ruelle*[20] of his bed, where he said his prayers, as in the morning, then undressed. He said good night with an inclination of the head, and whilst everybody was leaving the room stood at the corner of the mantelpiece, where he gave the order to the colonel of the guards alone. Then commenced what was called the *petit coucher,* at which only the specially privileged remained. That was short. They did not leave until he got into bed. It was a moment to speak to him. Then all left if they saw any one buckle to the King. For ten or twelve years before he died the *petit coucher* ceased, in consequence of a long attack of gout he had had; so that the Court was finished at the rising from supper.

19. **Madame de Maintenon:** Françoise d'Aubigné, Marquise de Maintenon (1635–1719), married Louis XIV after the death of his first wife, Marie Thérèse of Spain.
20. *ruelle:* the area in the bedchamber in which the bed was located and in which the king received persons of high rank.

Sources 4 and 5 from Château de Versailles/Cliché des Musées Nationaux–Paris.

4. Charles Le Brun, *Louis XIV Taking Up Personal Government*, ca 1680, from the Ceiling of the Hall of Mirrors at Versailles

5. Hyacinthe-François-Honoré-Pierre-André Rigaud, *Louis XIV, King of France and Navarre,* **1701**

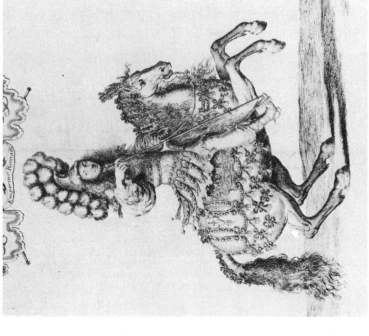

Source 7 from Charles Perrault, Festiva ad captia, 1670. British Library, London.

7. Rousselet, Louis XIV as "Roman Emperor" in an Engraving from the Carousel of 1662

Source 6 from Musée de la Marine, Photographic Service.

6. Mask of Apollo, God of Light, seventeenth century

Sources 8 and 9 from French Government Tourist Office.

8. Garden Façade of Versailles

9. Aerial View of Versailles

Sources 10 through 13 from Château de Versailles/Cliché des Musées Nationaux–Paris.

10. The Royal Chapel at Versailles

11. **Reconstruction of the King's Chamber at Versailles, after 1701**

12. **Antechamber of the Bull's Eye Window at Versailles**

13. Pierre Denis Martin, *Château of Marly, 1724*

QUESTIONS TO CONSIDER

Louis XIV is reputed to have said, "I am the state." Whether the king actually uttered those words is immaterial for our purpose; they neatly summarize the unifying theme in all this chapter's evidence, which demonstrates how royal power was defined as absolute and how that authority was expressed in deeds, art, and architecture.

Consider first the theories of royal authority, comparing the political ideas of Bodin and Bossuet. What are the origins of sovereignty for Bodin and Bossuet? How do they differ? Why can Bodin be said to have justified absolutism on the basis of expediency, that is, that absolute royal power was the only way to ensure order? Do the two thinkers ultimately arrive at the same conclusions? What is the difference between Bodin's conclusion that the royal power permitted the king to hand down laws to his subjects and receive them from no one and Bossuet's definition of the king as virtually a god on earth?

Royal ceremony and etiquette enforced this view of the king. Consider Saint-Simon's *Memoirs* again. The selection describes only limited aspects of court etiquette, but it conveys to us a vivid image of court life. Who was the center of this court made up of the country's most prominent nobles? Analyze individual elements of court ceremony. How does each contribute to a consistent message? Consider the royal dining ritual. To reinforce the lesson of royal power, who was kept standing during the king's luncheon? Who had the task, for most commoners performed by an ordinary waiter, of handing the king his napkin? A message of royal power is being expressed here in a way that is almost theatrical.

Indeed, the image of theater can be useful in further structuring your analysis. The stage setting for this royal display, the palace of Versailles, shows the work of a skilled director in creating a remarkably uniform message in landscape and architecture alike. Who do you suppose that director was? Examine his statement at Versailles. Look first at the exterior views of both Versailles (Sources 8 and 9) and Marly (Source 13). How do the grounds add to the expression of royal power? What view of nature might they suggest to a visitor? How did the stage set enhance the play described by Saint-Simon? How did it encourage the French to accept the authority of Louis XIV?

Look next at the interior of the palace. It was, of course, a royal residence. But do you find much evidence of its function as a place to live in? Examine the royal bedroom and its outer room (Sources 11 and 12). Modern bedrooms are generally intimate in size and decoration; how does the king's differ? Why? Notice, too, the art and use of symbols in the palace. Why might the king's artists and architects have decorated the palace so richly with biblical and classical heroes and themes (Sources 8 through 12)?

Finally, consider the principal actor, Louis XIV. Notice how his self-presentation is consistent with the trappings of the stage set. We find him consciously acting a role in Source 7, portraying an emperor in the Carousel of 1662. That engraving embodies a great deal of indirect information. What details reinforce the aura of royal power? Why should the king be mounted and in Roman costume? What strikes you about the king's attitude atop the prancing horse? Compare this picture with the Le Brun (Source 4) and Rigaud (Source 5) paintings. What elements do you find these pictures to have in common? How does the royal emblem of the sun (Source 6) contribute to the common message?

With these considerations in mind, return now to the central questions of this chapter. What was the theoretical basis for absolute royal authority? What was traditional and what was new in the justification of royal power expressed in late-sixteenth- and seventeenth-century France? How did such early modern kings as Louis XIV communicate their absolute power in the various ceremonies, displays, and symbols of royal authority presented in the evidence?

EPILOGUE

We all know that any successful act produces imitators. In the seventeenth century, the monarchy of Louis XIV looked for a long time like the most successful regime in Europe. Royal absolutism had seemingly unified France. Out of that unity came a military power that threatened to overwhelm Europe; an economic strength, based on mercantilism, that increased French wealth; and an intellectual life that gave the culture of seventeenth- and eighteenth-century Europe a distinctly French accent. Imitators of Louis XIV's work were therefore numerous. At the very least, kings sought physically to express the unifying and centralizing monarchical principle of government in palaces recreating Versailles.[21]

But the work of such monarchs as Louis XIV involved far more than the construction of elaborate palaces in which to stage the theater of their court lives. The act of focusing the state on the figure of the monarch began the transition to the centralized modern style of government and marked the beginning of the end of the decentralized medieval state that bound subjects in an almost contractual relationship to their ruler. The king now emerged as theoretically all-powerful and also as a symbol of national unity.

The monarchs of the age did their work of state building so effectively that the unity and centralization they created often survived the monarchy itself. The French monarchy, for example, succumbed to a revolution in

21. Palaces consciously modeled on Versailles multiplied in the late seventeenth and early eighteenth centuries. They included the Schönbrunn Palace in Vienna (1694); the Royal Palace in Berlin (begun in 1698); Ludwigsburg Palace in Württemberg, Germany (1704–1733); the Würzburg Residenz in Franconia, Germany (1719–1744); and the Stupinigi Palace (1729–1733) near Turin, Italy.

[49]

1789 that in large part stemmed from the bankruptcy of the royal government after too many years of overspending on wars and court life in the name of royal glory. But the unified state endured, strong enough to retain its sense of unity despite challenges in war and changes of government that introduced a new politics of mass participation.

The methods employed by Louis XIV and other monarchs also transcended their age. Modern governments understand the importance of ritual, symbolism, and display in creating the sense of national unity that was part of the absolute monarch's goal. Ritual may now be centered on important national observances. The parades on such days as July 4 in the United States, July 14 in France (commemorating one of the earliest victories of the Revolution of 1789), and the anniversary of the October 1917 Revolution as it was celebrated until 1990 in the former Soviet Union all differ in form from the rituals of Louis XIV. They are designed for a new political age, one of mass participation in politics, in which the loyalty of the whole people, not just that of an elite group, must be won. But their purpose remains the same: to win loyalty to the existing political order.

Modern states also use symbolism to build political loyalty. Artwork on public buildings in Washington, D.C., and the capital cities of other republics, for example, often employs classical themes. The purpose of such artwork is to suggest to citizens that their government perpetuates the republican rectitude of Athens and Rome. Display also is part of the political agenda of modern governments, even governments of new arrivals in the community of nations. This is why newly independent, developing nations of the twentieth and twenty-first centuries expend large portions of their meager resources on such things as grand new capital cities, the most sophisticated military weaponry, and the latest aircraft for the national airline. These are symbols of their governments' successes and thus the basis for these regimes' claims on their peoples' loyalty. These modern rituals, symbols, and displays perform the same function for modern rulers as Versailles did for the Sun King.

CHAPTER THREE

THE MIND OF AN AGE:

SCIENCE AND RELIGION

CONFRONT EIGHTEENTH-CENTURY

NATURAL DISASTER

Because of the tremendous loss of life and damage to property that great natural disasters, such as earthquakes and floods, inflict on their victims, survivors of such events require some explanation of them. What was the reason for the disaster? Why did it occur where it did? In the answers that the thinkers of an age propose for such questions, we may find indications of the general thought patterns that characterize that particular era in history.

In the early twenty-first century, for example, most of us would understand earthquakes scientifically, as the result of pressures along geological faults that occasionally produce cataclysmic movements of the earth's surface. Earlier ages often understood earthquakes in terms of supernatural action. The eighteenth century, the focus of this chapter, is an age whose intellectual life we may investigate with particularly rewarding results. We will find that the intellectual life of this century illustrates the persistence of traditional thought patterns, increasingly challenged by a new, scientific vision of the physical world.

By the middle of the eighteenth century, Europe was approaching the culmination of an intellectual revolution that had been under way since the sixteenth century. Scientific discoveries of the sixteenth and seventeenth centuries, which your textbook describes as the Scientific Revolution, had produced a wholly new outlook on the physical world that was gaining increasing acceptance among educated Europeans. The result of the sixteenth- and seventeenth-century work of Nicholas Copernicus, Johannes Kepler, Galileo Galilei, René Descartes, Sir Isaac Newton, and others was a growing certainty that the physical world could be understood through the

Chapter 3

The Mind of an

Age: Science

and Religion

Confront

Eighteenth-

Century

Natural Disaster

ability of human reason to discern immutable mathematical laws that governed it. No longer did intellectuals explain the world in terms of supernatural action. The physical world increasingly appeared to be a great machine, and many eighteenth-century thinkers, called Deists in their religious outlook, posited a novel relationship between God and the physical world. The movements of the world-machine might have been created by God, but Deists believed that they could not be interrupted by him. Some thinkers also had faith that a divine plan governed the world, affirming that all would be well. But all agreed that nothing happened in such a world without sufficient cause or reason. This was a true revolution in thought, espoused by intellectuals called *philosophes,* who sought to apply their faith in the existence of reasonable and comprehensible natural laws to all aspects of the human experience. Their efforts in this regard constitute the intellectual milieu that historians call the Enlightenment of the eighteenth century.

The Enlightenment's concept of a machine-like universe contradicted much in the traditional Judeo-Christian concept of God. Most important, perhaps, Enlightenment thought precluded any belief in divine intervention in the physical world. Miracles or divinely ordained disasters, for example, simply were impossible for the *philosophes* because they violated natural laws of cause and effect. Traditional religious beliefs, however, were not without their defenders. Often these defenders were clergymen who, using the same tools of

reason employed by the Enlightenment's exponents, strongly disagreed with the *philosophes.* In Catholic Europe, members of the Society of Jesus, or Jesuits, were important defenders of traditional beliefs; in France they even published an influential monthly journal for their cause, the *Journal de Trevoux.* Clergymen in Protestant countries also espoused traditional beliefs concerning a divine presence in the world.

Debate between the proponents of these differing visions of the world's relationship to God had been under way for years before a major earthquake in Lisbon, Portugal, in 1755 forced Western thinkers to focus closely on the problem of explaining the causes of natural disasters. The Lisbon earthquake particularly captured the attention of Western thinkers because it struck a major political capital and international trading center close to Europe's heart.[1] Moreover, it was quite destructive.[2] The earthquake struck the Portuguese capital on November 1, 1755, All Saints' Day. At 9:30 A.M. on that holy day, on which Roman Catholics like the inhabitants of Lisbon are obligated to attend mass in commemoration of all of the church's saints, a loud

1. Other earthquakes of the period struck either on the fringes of the West, as in Jamaica in 1692 and Peru in 1746, or in isolated parts of Europe, as in Sicily in 1693. The few that had occurred in major cities—like London's quakes of 1750—had been slight in comparison to Lisbon's.

2. Modern scientists estimate the Lisbon earthquake's intensity at 8.5 to 8.8 on the Richter scale. By contrast, the San Francisco earthquake of 1906 measured 7.8, while the one that unleashed the tsunami in South Asia on December 26, 2004, which took perhaps 300,000 lives, measured 9.3.

rumbling disturbed a peaceful morning marked by religious observance or preparation for church attendance. Then three great seismic shocks rocked the city and ended its citizens' religious devotions. Churches and homes alike tumbled during this earthquake, whose shocks were felt as far away as Switzerland and northern France, and many persons perished. Other disasters resulting from the earthquake soon increased the loss of life. Fires spread from the hearths of the damaged city and burned for almost a week before they could be extinguished. The trembling of the earth created a tsunami, ocean waves fifteen to twenty feet high that swept up the Tagus River, on which Lisbon is situated, and broke over the city's waterfront. The combined destruction of earthquake, fires, and tidal waves left about 10,000 to 15,000 dead on that holy day of November 1.[3]

3. Estimates on the earthquake toll vary greatly, ranging as high as 60,000 persons. T. D. Kendrick, the author of a modern study, *The Lisbon Earthquake* (Philadelphia: J. B. Lippincott, 1957), accepts 10,000 to 15,000 as the probable number of dead, and, indeed, as the city's population was only about 275,000, the figure of 60,000 dead is difficult to accept.

Natural disasters like that at Lisbon elicited explanations from theologians who sought the work of God's hand in the Portuguese capital. The *philosophes,* however, differed markedly among themselves on the earthquake's significance. By reading selections on the exchange of ideas quickened by the Lisbon earthquake, the background on how some of these ideas developed, and the later implications of these thoughts, you will gain a deeper understanding of eighteenth-century thought about God and his relationship to the world. This was a key issue for the age, and one that was widely debated. Examining it allows us to learn a great deal about the Enlightenment by posing basic questions to the sources presented in this chapter: Why did the Lisbon earthquake present such an intellectual crisis for eighteenth-century thinkers? How did theologians explain the disaster within the framework of their beliefs? How did Enlightenment thinkers explain it? In what direction was their thought on the physical world and its relationship to divine forces leading them?

SOURCES AND METHOD

The problem at hand presents you with questions in the history of ideas, or what historians call "intellectual history." For generations, intellectual historians wrote about the ideas of the past without asking a question that seems central to historians today: "Who, in a certain period, held a particular set of ideas?" or, more precisely, "How representative were these ideas of the society as a whole?" In other words, "How broad was the impact of these ideas in their own time?"

As your text probably notes, literacy was not widespread in eighteenth-century Europe, and so the majority of

Chapter 3

The Mind of an

Age: Science

and Religion

Confront

Eighteenth-

Century

Natural Disaster

the Continent's population never had access to the ideas of the Scientific Revolution or the Enlightenment. Indeed, historians in recent years have come to recognize the persistence of a culture of the people, a popular culture, sometimes pre-Christian in its roots, that coexisted with the ideas of the *philosophes*. The intellectual world of the unlettered was one inhabited by witches and warlocks, in which people readily accepted supernatural explanations for physical phenomena. Such people might be frightened almost to death by an earthquake, but they took little part in the discussion of its philosophical ramifications presented here.

If the majority of the population of eighteenth-century Europe had little or no access to the ideas we will examine, are those ideas still relevant to our study of the past? The answer is certainly yes, although we must take care not to attribute the ideas to all persons. We are discussing ideas that were current among the small, educated elite of the eighteenth century. We must recognize, however, that this privileged group had tremendous influence in a societal and governmental system that accorded little role to anyone born outside that class. Moreover, such persons were the opinion makers of their age. Their ideas would have had considerable influence among those of the middle classes with some education. Thus the thought of this minority of Europe's total population had an impact well outside the boundaries of the social group from which it arose and so is quite worthy of study.

The evidence that follows has been chosen to present you with a broad sample of the thought of Europe's eighteenth-century intellectual elite and the background of its development. The Lisbon earthquake raised the immediate problem of explaining the disaster. This question involved large issues, chief among them the relationship of the physical world to God. Did God intervene in the world's daily operation, as theologians argued? Was he, as Deists said, like a watchmaker, creating a world-machine and then standing back and letting it operate on its own? Or was no divine hand at work in the world at all? In reading these selections, you should gain an understanding of why the Lisbon disaster preoccupied so many eighteenth-century thinkers.

Sources 1 and 2 represent a tendency perhaps as old as humankind, that is, the attempt to explain natural phenomena in terms of supernatural or divine forces. Source 1, "An Opinion on the True Cause of the Earthquake," was a pamphlet written by a Roman Catholic priest, the Jesuit Gabriel Malagrida (1689–1761). Born in Italy, Malagrida spent much of his life in missionary work in Portugal's Brazilian colony and lived in Lisbon after 1754. It is not insignificant that he was a Jesuit; the Society of Jesus was one of the most influential orders in the early modern Roman Catholic Church. The absolute loyalty of the Jesuits to the papacy, combined with their energy and preaching ability, had done much to stem the spread of sixteenth-century European Protestantism. In subsequent centuries, the order's excellent schools had strengthened Catholicism, as had the influence its members wielded as spiritual advisers to monarchs. Malagrida in every way typified his order. He was an excellent preacher and well connected at court, and consequently his attempt to justify the earthquake in theological terms had an impact in Catholic Portugal. How did he account for the earthquake?

Source 2 is a sermon by John Wesley (1703–1791), one of the most influential English Protestant leaders of the eighteenth century. Ordained a priest of the Church of England, Wesley experienced a religious conversion in 1738 that led him to found a new Protestant faith, Methodism. In the eighteenth century, Methodism represented a dynamic new faith, espousing an emotional and personal kind of religion that contrasted with the practices of both Catholics and traditional Protestant groups.

Wesley preached widely in the cause of his faith; he is estimated to have journeyed 250,000 miles in the course of delivering 40,000 sermons, often to large audiences. Because many of his sermons were published in pamphlet form, he reached an even larger public than only those able to attend his sermons. According to this influential Protestant clergyman, what was the cause of the Lisbon earthquake? How might future earthquakes be avoided?

With Source 3 we encounter the thought of the Enlightenment. Voltaire was the pen name of François-Marie Arouet (1694–1778), one of the greatest of the *philosophes* and the author of Source 3. Born the son of a Parisian notary, Voltaire received a traditional

education from French Jesuits but early developed an independence of thought and an irreverence toward established creeds and institutions that plunged him into difficulties. In 1717 the royal government imprisoned him for eleven months for alleged insults to the regent of France. In 1726 his writings provoked the authorities once again, and he avoided a second, lengthy imprisonment by agreeing to leave France for an extended stay in England. Voltaire remained in England for more than two years.

The lack of official tolerance for Voltaire's early writings defined the theme that became a constant in his writings: the cause of toleration. In England, he believed he had found a much freer and more tolerant society than that in France, and his *Letters Concerning the English Nation* (published 1733) contrasted France very unfavorably with England. The book also reflected the deep impact of the ideas of the English thinkers Newton and Locke on Voltaire. He would go on to write an extensive popular version of Newtonian physics, *Elements of the Philosophy of Newton* (1736), but in the earlier work on England, excerpted in Source 3, we find a brief summary of Newton's thought. What sort of world did Newton describe? What was the relationship of God to this world? In what ways does Voltaire express a Deistic interpretation of God's relationship to the physical world?

Source 4 is a passage from the poem "An Essay on Man" by Alexander Pope (1688–1744), an English poet whose acquaintance Voltaire made

[55]

Chapter 3

The Mind of an

Age: Science

and Religion

Confront

Eighteenth-

Century

Natural Disaster

during his English sojourn. As a member of England's Roman Catholic minority, Pope was excluded from educational opportunities open to Protestants, and he was largely self-taught. "An Essay on Man," published in 1734, is therefore remarkable as a summary of the philosophical speculation of the day on God's relationship to the world described by Newton. What is that relationship, according to Pope? Why does Pope tell his readers to accept the world as they find it?

Source 5 is an excerpt from the *Encyclopedia: The Rational Dictionary of the Sciences, the Arts, and the Crafts,* edited by Denis Diderot. Conceived as an attempt to summarize the knowledge of the eighteenth century and especially the results of the Scientific Revolution, the *Encyclopedia* also served to recapitulate Enlightenment thought. Many of the chief *philosophes,* including Voltaire, wrote its articles and brought to the work their criticism of the institutions of their age. Controversy was the immediate result. Church authorities sought to stop publication of the *Encyclopedia,* but slowly, over the years 1751 to 1772, the work appeared in seventeen volumes of text and eleven volumes of illustrations. The entry reproduced here as Source 5 is on the subject "Observation." What methods of research did its anonymous author urge scientific researchers to adopt? How does this article reflect the Scientific Revolution? Is there any role for the intervention of God in this method of amassing knowledge?

In Source 6 we have evidence of the effort to apply these methods of research. This selection is the work of Georges Louis Leclerc, Comte de Buffon (1707–1788), a nobleman and scientist who served as director of the French royal botanical gardens in Paris. In addition, he devoted himself for forty years to writing a forty-four-volume *Natural History,* his attempt to summarize and popularize the results of the Scientific Revolution. Although Buffon may not have been a particularly original thinker and his observation of earthquakes clearly was confined to their above-ground effects, his work was a great success, becoming something of a best seller that greatly influenced his age. Certainly we cannot scientifically accept Buffon's explanation of earthquakes today. But what approach to the physical world does his work represent? Would he in any way be able to accept the ideas of Malagrida or Wesley? Does Buffon see any evidence of divine design? How does his concept of the world grow out of Newton's science?

In Source 7 we encounter a rather different Voltaire from the man who discussed Newton. In his "Poem on the Lisbon Disaster, or An Examination of That Axiom 'All Is Well,'" published twenty years after *Letters,* we have the work of an older Voltaire, whose words reflect a growing doubt about the ideas of the early Enlightenment on the relationship of the physical world to God. What is Voltaire's view of God's role in the physical world in this poem he wrote on receiving the news of the Lisbon disaster? Why can Voltaire accept neither a theological explanation of the event nor the faith of some Deists that a divine plan dictated that all would work out for the best? What possible implications for the later Enlightenment's views on God do you find in this work of the influential Voltaire?

Voltaire's Lisbon poem elicited a forceful response in the form of a letter from Jean-Jacques Rousseau (1712–1778), given here as Source 8. Rousseau was born in Geneva, Switzerland, and his mother died shortly after his birth; his subsequent haphazard upbringing was followed by a wandering life that permitted few lasting relationships. His works, including *The Social Contract*, a work of political theory, and *Emile*, a work of educational philosophy, rank Rousseau among the eighteenth century's greatest thinkers. But he was not part of the company of the *philosophes* and ultimately disassociated himself from them. Rousseau's works glorify the simplicity to be found in nature, and in many ways he was a precursor of the Romantic movement in early-nineteenth-century literature, which consciously sought to negate the Enlightenment.

It was only natural, therefore, for Rousseau to have intellectual differences with Voltaire. When he wrote his letter in 1755, however, Rousseau's great work was still in the future and he was as yet relatively unknown. His letter to Voltaire, who was already an internationally known thinker, was thus rather audacious. What does Rousseau find wrong in Voltaire's

view of the Lisbon earthquake? What relationship between God and humans does Rousseau express?

The author of Source 9, "The Essay on Miracles," was David Hume (1711–1776), a Scottish philosopher who lived for a time in France and who briefly befriended Rousseau. (Hume offered Rousseau a home when the latter was expelled from Bern, Switzerland, for his ideas. Rousseau soon quarreled with Hume, however, as he did with many persons.) Hume's thought reflects the Enlightenment search for hard, observable facts to justify conclusions, whether historical, philosophical, or theological. Could Hume find evidence of the God of Malagrida and Wesley on the one hand or of the God of Newton and the early Voltaire on the other? According to Hume, is any divine scheme at work in the world?

If Hume represents the skepticism of the Enlightenment, the work of Baron d'Holbach, a German-born nobleman who passed much of his life in France, perhaps reflects a logical culmination of Enlightenment thought about the physical world. Source 10 presents an expression of Holbach's views in a selection from his most important work, *The System of Nature*. What room is there for a divinity in Holbach's view, which sees the world as an "uninterrupted succession of causes and effects" in which "matter always existed"? Why do you think Holbach's contemporaries, including Voltaire, criticized his position as atheistic?

As you read these selections, you should be able to answer the central

Chapter 3

The Mind of an

Age: Science

and Religion

Confront

Eighteenth-

Century

Natural Disaster

questions of this chapter: Why did the Lisbon earthquake pose an intellectual crisis for eighteenth-century thinkers? How did theologians explain the disaster? How did Enlightenment thinkers explain it? In what direction was their thought on the physical world and its relationship to divine forces leading them?

Source 1 from T. D. Kendrick, The Lisbon Earthquake *(Philadelphia: Lippincott, 1957), pp. 137–138. Translated by T. D. Kendrick.*

1. Gabriel Malagrida, "An Opinion on the True Cause of the Earthquake," 1756

Learn, O Lisbon, that the destroyers of our houses, palaces, churches, and convents, the cause of the death of so many people and of the flames that devoured such vast treasures, are your abominable sins, and not comets, stars, vapours and exhalations, and similar natural phenomena. Tragic Lisbon is now a mound of ruins. Would that it were less difficult to think of some method of restoring the place; but it has been abandoned, and the refugees from the city live in despair. As for the dead, what a great harvest of sinful souls such disasters send to Hell! It is scandalous to pretend the earthquake was just a natural event, for if that be true, there is no need to repent and to try to avert the wrath of God, and not even the Devil himself could invent a false idea more likely to lead us all to irreparable ruin. Holy people had prophesied the earthquake was coming, yet the city continued in its sinful ways without a care for the future. Now, indeed, the case of Lisbon is desperate. It is necessary to devote all our strength and purpose to the task of repentance. Would to God we could see as much determination and fervour for this necessary exercise as are devoted to the erection of huts and new buildings! Does being billeted in the country outside the city areas put us outside the jurisdiction of God?[4] God undoubtedly desires to exercise His love and mercy, but be sure that wherever we are, He is watching us, scourge in hand.

---

4. Many of Lisbon's citizens fled the danger of the city for the countryside and remained there in shacks and tents until the earthquake danger passed.

Source 2 from The Works of John Wesley, *vol. 11 (Grand Rapids, Mich.: Zondervan, 1958),*
pp. 1–2, 6–7, 8, 11.

2. John Wesley, "Some Serious Thoughts Occasioned by the Late Earthquake at Lisbon," 1755

Tua res agitur, paries quum proximus ardet.[5]

Thinking men generally allow that the greater part of modern Christians are not more virtuous than the ancient Heathens; perhaps less so; since public spirit, love of our country, generous honesty, and simple truth, are scarce anywhere to be found. On the contrary, covetousness, ambition, various injustice, luxury, and falsehood in every kind, have infected every rank and denomination of people, the Clergy themselves not excepted. Now, they who believe there is a God are apt to believe he is not well pleased with this. Nay, they think, he has intimated it very plainly, in many parts of the Christian world. How many hundred thousand men have been swept away by war, in Europe only, within half a century![6] How many thousands, within little more than this, hath the earth opened her mouth and swallowed up! Numbers sunk at Port-Royal, and rose no more! Many thousands went quick into the pit at Lima! The whole city of Catanea, in Sicily, and every inhabitant of it, perished together.[7] Nothing but heaps of ashes and cinders show where it stood. Not so much as one Lot escaped out of Sodom![8]

And what shall we say of the late accounts from Portugal? That some thousand houses, and many thousand persons, are no more! that a fair city is now

5. From the Roman poet Horace: "'Tis your own interest that calls, when flames invade your neighbor's walls."

6. Intense warfare did mark the half-century preceding the earthquake. The great Northern War (1700–1716) pitted Sweden against Russia. In the War of the Spanish Succession (1702–1714), France and Spain fought against England, Holland, the armies of the Holy Roman Emperor, and most of the German states. In the War of the Polish Succession (1733–1735), Spain and France confronted Russia and the forces of the Holy Roman Emperor. Almost all of Europe was involved in the War of the Austrian Succession (1740–1748), in which France, Spain, Prussia, and a number of the German states fought England and Austria. At the time Wesley wrote, fighting between English and French forces had already broken out in North America and would lead to the Seven Years War of 1756–1763. And these were only the major wars! Minor conflicts also raged. One historian reckoned that all of Europe was at peace for only two years in the century spanning 1700–1800.

7. Wesley refers here to the earthquakes of 1692, 1693, and 1746 mentioned in note 1.

8. In the Bible's book of Genesis, chapters 11–14 and 19, God destroyed Sodom and Gomorrah with fire because of their wickedness. Abraham's nephew, Lot, a resident of Sodom, was warned of the destruction and escaped.

Chapter 3

The Mind of an

Age: Science

and Religion

Confront

Eighteenth-

Century

Natural Disaster

in ruinous heaps! Is there indeed a God that judges the world? And is he now making inquisition for blood? If so, it is not surprising, he should begin there, where so much blood has been poured on the ground like water! where so many brave men have been murdered, in the most base and cowardly as well as barbarous manner, almost every day, as well as every night, while none regarded or laid it to heart.[9] "Let them hunt and destroy the precious life, so we may secure our stores of gold and precious stones."[10] How long has their blood been crying from the earth! Yea, how long has that bloody *House of Mercy*,[11] the scandal not only of all religion, but even of human nature, stood to insult both heaven and earth! "And shall I not visit for these things, saith the Lord? Shall not my soul be avenged on such a city as this?". . .

But alas! why should we not be convinced sooner, while that conviction may avail, that it is not chance which governs the world? Why should we not now, before London is as Lisbon, Lima, or Catanea, acknowledge the hand of the Almighty, arising to maintain his own cause? Why, we have a general answer always ready, to screen us from any such conviction: "All these things are purely natural and accidental; the result of natural causes." But there are two objections to this answer: First, it is untrue: Secondly, it is uncomfortable.

First. If by affirming, "All this is purely natural," you mean, it is not providential, or that God has nothing to do with it, this is not true, that is, supposing the Bible to be true. For supposing this, you may descant ever so long on the natural causes of murrain, winds, thunder, lightning, and yet you are altogether wide of the mark, you prove nothing at all, unless you can prove that God never works in or by natural causes. But this you cannot prove; nay, none can doubt of his so working, who allows the Scripture to be of God. For this asserts, in the clearest and strongest terms, that "all things" (in nature) "serve him;" that (by or without a train of natural causes) He "sendeth his rain on the earth;" that He "bringeth the winds out of his treasures," and "maketh a way for the lightning and the thunder;" in general, that "fire and hail, snow and vapour, wind and storm, fulfil his word." Therefore, allowing there are natural causes of all these, they are still under the direction of the Lord of nature: Nay, what is nature itself, but the art of God, or God's method of acting in the material world? . . .

9. In this sentence, Wesley is referring to the executions resulting from trials by the Portuguese Inquisition. The Inquisition was a system of Roman Catholic courts created to identify and judge heretics. Like all continental European courts of the day, these courts could torture the defendant to gather evidence against him or her. Civil, not church, authorities, however, executed sentences.

10. **precious stones:** "Merchants who have lived in Portugal inform us that the King has a large building filled with diamonds; and more gold stored up, coined and uncoined, than all the other monarchs of Europe." [Wesley's note] This may or may not have been true, but Lisbon certainly received gold from New World mines and diamonds from mines discovered in the Portuguese colony of Brazil in the 1730s.

11. **House of Mercy:** "The title which the Inquisition of Portugal (if not in other countries also) takes to itself." [Wesley's note]

A Second objection to your answer is, It is extremely uncomfortable. For if things really be as you affirm; if all these afflictive incidents entirely depend on the fortuitous concourse and agency of blind, material causes; what hope, what help, what resource is left for the poor sufferers by them? . . .

What defence do you find from thousands of gold and silver? You cannot fly; for you cannot quit the earth, unless you will leave your dear body behind you. And while you are on the earth, you know not where to flee to, neither where to flee from. You may buy intelligence, where the shock was yesterday, but not where it will be to-morrow,—to-day. It comes! The roof trembles! The beams crack! The ground rocks to and fro! Hoarse thunder resounds from the bowels of the earth! And all these are but the beginning of sorrows. Now, what help? What wisdom can prevent, what strength resist, the blow? What money can purchase, I will not say deliverance, but an hour's reprieve? Poor honourable fool, where are now thy titles? Wealthy fool, where is now thy golden god? If any thing can help, it must be prayer. But what wilt thou pray to? Not to the God of heaven; you suppose him to have nothing to do with earthquakes. . . .

But how shall we secure the favour of this great God? How, but by worshipping him in spirit and in truth; by uniformly imitating Him we worship, in all his imitable perfections? without which the most accurate systems of opinions, all external modes of religion, are idle cobwebs of the brain, dull farce and empty show. Now, God is love: Love God then, and you are a true worshipper. Love mankind, and God is your God, your Father, and your Friend. But see that you deceive not your own soul; for this is not a point of small importance. And by this you may know: If you love God, then you are happy in God; if you love God, riches, honours, and the pleasures of sense are no more to you than bubbles on the water: You look on dress and equipage, as the tassels of a fool's cap; diversions, as the bells on a fool's coat. If you love God, God is in all your thoughts, and your whole life is a sacrifice to him. And if you love mankind, it is your own design, desire, and endeavour, to spread virtue and happiness all around you; to lessen the present sorrows, and increase the joys, of every child of man; and, if it be possible, to bring them with you to the rivers of pleasure that are at God's right hand for evermore.

Chapter 3

The Mind of an

Age: Science

and Religion

Confront

Eighteenth-

Century

Natural Disaster

Source 3 from Voltaire, Letters Concerning the English Nation *(New York: Burt Franklin Reprints, 1974), pp. 65–66, 96–97, 100, 103, 105–106.*

3. Voltaire on Newtonian Physics, 1733

Not long since, the trite and frivolous Question following was debated in a very polite and learned Company, *viz.* (namely) who was the greatest Man, *Cæsar, Alexander, Tamerlane, Cromwell,* & c.[12]

Some Body answer'd, that Sir *Isaac Newton* excell'd them all. The Gentleman's Assertion was very just; for if true Greatness consists in having receiv'd from Heaven a mighty Genius, and in having employ'd it to enlighten our own Minds and that of others; a Man like Sir *Isaac Newton,* whose equal is hardly found in a thousand Years, is the truly great Man. And those Politicians and Conquerors, (and all ages produce some) were generally so many illustrious wicked Men. That Man claims our Respect, who commands over the Minds of the rest of the World by the Force of Truth, not those who enslave their Fellow Creatures; He who is acquainted with the Universe, not They who deface it. . . .

The Discoveries which gain'd Sir *Isaac Newton* so universal a Reputation, relate to the System of the World, to Light, to Geometrical Infinites; and lastly to Chronology, with which he us'd to amuse himself after the Fatigue of his severer Studies.

I will now acquaint you (without Prolixity if possible) with the few Things I have been able to comprehend of all these sublime Ideas. With Regard to the System of our World, Disputes were a long Time maintain'd, on the Cause that turns the Planets, and keeps them in their Orbits; and on those Causes which make all Bodies here below descend towards the Surface of the Earth.

Having . . . destroy'd the *Cartesian* Vortices,[13] he despair'd of ever being able to discover, whether there is a secret Principle in Nature which, at the same Time, is the Cause of the Motion of all celestial Bodies, and that of Gravity on the Earth. But being retir'd in 1666, upon Account of the Plague, to a Solitude near *Cambridge*; as he was walking one Day in his Garden, and saw some Fruits fall from a Tree, he fell into a profound Meditation on that

12. **Julius Caesar** (102–44 B.C.) dominated Rome during the last years of the republic. **Alexander the Great** (356–323 B.C.) was the king of Macedonia who led the Greeks on wars of conquest to create an empire that included modern Greece, Turkey, Egypt, and much of the Middle East to the borders of India. **Tamerlane** (ca 1336–1405) was a Turkish chieftain who created an empire embracing parts of southern Russia, Turkey, the Middle East, Afghanistan, Pakistan, and northern India. **Oliver Cromwell** (1599–1658) led Parliament's armies against the king in the English Civil War. After the king's defeat and execution, he ruled England as virtual dictator.

13. **Cartesian vortices:** René Descartes (1546–1650), a French philosopher and mathematician, accounted for planetary motion in terms of vortices, that is, a rapid movement of cosmic bodies in a fluid or ether around an axis. Newtonian physics, with its law of gravity, dispensed with such theories.

Gravity, the Cause of which had so long been sought, but in vain, by all the Philosophers, whilst the Vulgar think there is nothing mysterious in it. He said to himself, that from what height soever, in our Hemisphere, those Bodies might descend, their Fall wou'd certainly be in the Progression discover'd by *Galileo*;[14] and the Spaces they run thro' would be as the Square of the Times. Why may not this Power which causes heavy Bodies to descend, and is the same without any sensible Diminution at the remotest Distance from the Center of the Earth, or on the Summits of the highest Mountains; Why, said Sir *Isaac*, may not this Power extend as high as the Moon? And in Case, its Influence reaches so far, is it not very probable that this Power retains it in its Orbit, and determines its Motion? But in case the Moon obeys this Principle (whatever it be) may we not conclude very naturally, that the rest of the Planets are equally subject to it? In case this Power exists (which besides is prov'd) it must increase in an inverse *Ratio* of the Squares of the Distances. All therefore that remains is, to examine how far a heavy Body, which should fall upon the Earth from a moderate height, would go; and how far in the same time, a Body which should fall from the Orbit of the Moon, would descend. To find this, nothing is wanted but the Measure of the Earth, and the Distance of the Moon from it.

This is Attraction, the great Spring by which all Nature is mov'd. Sir *Isaac Newton* after having demonstrated the Existence of this Principle, plainly foresaw that its very Name wou'd offend; and therefore this Philosopher in more Places than one of his Books, gives the Reader some Caution about it. He bids him beware of confounding this Name with what the Ancients call'd occult Qualities; but to be satisfied with knowing that there is in all Bodies a central Force which acts to the utmost Limits of the Universe, according to the invariable Laws of Mechanicks.

Give me Leave once more to introduce Sir *Isaac* speaking: . . . "The Spring that I discover'd was more hidden and more universal, and for that very Reason Mankind ought to thank me the more. I have discover'd a new Property of Matter, one of the Secrets of the Creator; and have calculated and discover'd the Effects of it. After this shall People quarrel with me about the Name I give it."

Vortices may be call'd an occult Quality because their Existence was never prov'd; Attraction on the contrary is a real Thing, because its Effects are demonstrated, and the Proportions of it are calculated. The Cause of this Cause is among the *Arcana*[15] of the Almighty.

Procedes huc, & non amplius.
Hither thou shalt go, and no farther.

14. **Galileo Galilei:** Italian astronomer, mathematician, and physicist (1564–1642) whose work was an important contribution to the Scientific Revolution. He developed the mathematical explanation of the rates at which bodies fall to earth in his law of falling bodies.
15. **Arcana:** secrets or mysteries.

Chapter 3

The Mind of an

Age: Science

and Religion

Confront

Eighteenth-

Century

Natural Disaster

Source 4 from A. W. Ward, editor, The Poetical Works of Alexander Pope *(London: Macmillan, 1879), pp. 199–200.*

4. From Alexander Pope, "An Essay on Man," 1734

All are but parts of one stupendous whole,
Whose body Nature is, and God the soul;
That, chang'd thro' all, and yet in all the same;
Great in the earth, as in th' ethereal[16] frame;
Warms in the sun, refreshes in the breeze,
Glows in the stars, and blossoms in the trees,
Lives thro' all life, extends thro' all extent,
Spreads undivided, operates unspent;
Breathes in our soul, informs our mortal part,
As full, as perfect, in a hair as heart:
As full, as perfect, in vile Man that mourns,
As the rapt Seraph[17] that adores and burns:
To him no high, no low, no great, no small;
He fills, he bounds, connects, and equals all.

Cease then, nor Order Imperfection name:
Our proper bliss depends on what we blame.
Know thy own point: This kind, this due degree
Of blindness, weakness, Heav'n bestows on thee;
Submit.—In this, or any other sphere,
Secure to be as blest as thou canst bear:
Safe in the hand of one disposing Pow'r,
Or in the natal, or the mortal hour.
All Nature is but Art, unknown to thee;
All Chance, Direction, which thou canst not see;
All Discord, Harmony not understood;
All partial Evil, universal Good:
And, spite of Pride, in erring Reason's spite,
One truth is clear, WHATEVER IS, IS RIGHT.

16. **ethereal:** heavenly.
17. **Seraph:** one of the heavenly creatures hovering around the throne of God described in Isaiah 6.

Source 5 from Denis Diderot, The Encyclopedia: Selections, *edited and translated by Stephen J. Gendzier (New York: Harper & Row, 1967), pp. 175–177. Used by permission of Stephen J. Gendzier.*

5. From the *Encyclopedia,* Anonymous Entry on "Observation," ca 1765

OBSERVATION (*Gram. Physic. Med.*) is the attention of the soul focused on objects offered by nature. An experiment is the result of this same attention directed toward phenomena produced by the labors of man. We must, therefore, include within the meaning of the generic noun *observation* the examination of all natural effects, not only of those that present themselves at once and without intermediary to our sight but also those we would not be able to discover without the hand of a worker, provided that this hand has not changed, altered, or disfigured them. The work necessary to reach a mine does not prevent the examination that is made of the metal's distribution, position, quantity, and color from being a simple *observation.* It is also by *observation* that we know the interior geography, that we estimate the number, position, and nature of the layers of earth, although we are obliged to resort to instruments for the excavation that allows us to see the mine. We must not consider as an *experiment* the opening of cadavers, the dissection of plants or animals, and certain analyses or mechanical sorting of mineral matter that scientists are obliged to do in order to be able to *observe* the parts that enter into their composition. The telescope of astronomers, the magnifying glass of the naturalist, and the microscope of the physicist do not prevent the knowledge acquired by these means from being the exact product of *observation.* All these preparations, these instruments only serve to render the different objects of *observation* more concrete, to remove the obstacles that prevent us from perceiving them, or to pierce the veil that hides them. But no change results from this, and there is not the slightest alteration in the nature of the *observed* object. It appears, nevertheless, such as it is; and this is the main difference between an *observation* and an *experiment* which decomposes, combines, and thereby gives use to rather different phenomena from those which nature presents. . . .

Observation is the primary foundation of all the sciences, the most reliable way to arrive at one's goal, the principal means of extending the periphery of scientific knowledge and of illuminating all its points. The facts, whatever they are, constitute the true wealth of the philosopher and the subject of *observation:* the historian collects them, the theoretical physicist combines them, and the experimenter verifies the results of their synthesis. Several facts taken separately appear dry, sterile, and unfruitful. The moment we compare them, they acquire a certain power, assume a vitality that everywhere results from the mutual harmony, from the reciprocal support, and from a chain that binds them together. The connection of these facts and the general cause

[65]

Chapter 3

The Mind of an

Age: Science

and Religion

Confront

Eighteenth-

Century

Natural Disaster

that links them together are some of the objects of reasoning, theories, and systems, while the facts are the materials. The moment a certain number of them have been gathered, some people hasten to construct; and the building is the more solid as the materials are more numerous and each one of them finds a more appropriate place.

Source 6 from Georges Louis Leclerc, Comte de Buffon, Histoire naturelle, générale et particulière, avec description du cabinet du roi, *vol. 1 (Paris: De l'Imprimerie Royale, 1749), pp. 526–529. Translated by Julius R. Ruff.*

6. From Georges Louis Leclerc, Comte de Buffon, *Natural History, General and Specific,* ca 1750

There are two kinds of earthquakes. One type is caused by the action of subterranean fires and by the explosion of volcanoes and is only felt over small distances when volcanoes are active or when they erupt. When the materials which make up subterranean fires begin to ferment, to heat up, and to ignite, the fire expands on all sides and, if it does not naturally find outlets, it heaves up the ground and makes a passage by throwing out the earth in its way. This produces a volcano, the effects of which repeat themselves and endure in proportion to the inflammable materials.

But there is another kind of earthquake, very different as regards its effects and perhaps as regards its causes. These are the earthquakes which are felt over long distances and which shake a large area of terrain without the appearance of a new volcano or an eruption. We have examples of earthquakes which are felt at the same time in England, France, Germany, and as far away as Hungary. These earthquakes always extend over an area much longer than it is wide. They shake a band or zone of the earth with varying force in different locations. They are almost always accompanied by a muffled sound, similar to that of a large, quickly rolling coach.

To understand more fully the causes of this kind of earthquake, it is necessary to remember that all inflammable and explosive materials produce . . . a great deal of air in igniting.[18] This air produced by the fire is in a very highly rarefied state and, because of its state of compression in the depths of the earth, it must produce very violent effects. Let us therefore suppose that at a very great depth, say 600 to 1200 feet, there are found pyrites and other sulphurous materials and that by the fermentation produced by the filtration

18. Buffon advanced this description of combustion a quarter of a century before the great French chemist Antoine Laurent Lavoisier (1743–1794) accurately described combustion and the role of oxygen in this process.

of water or by other causes, these materials ignite. Let us see what must happen. These materials are not regularly arranged in horizontal strata . . . they are, on the contrary, in perpendicular clefts in the caverns . . . where water can penetrate and have an effect. These materials ignite, producing a large quantity of air, the force of which, compressed in a small space like a cavern, not only will shake the terrain above but will look for routes of escape. . . . The routes which are available are caverns and cuts by water and subterranean streams. The rarefied air will rush violently through all of these passages which are open to it. It will form a raging wind in its subterranean paths, the noise of which will be heard on the earth's surface, and it will be accompanied by shock and concussions. This subterranean wind produced by the fire will extend as far as the subterranean cavities and cuts, and will cause a tremor the violence of which will depend on the distance from the source and the narrowness of the passages through which the wind passes. . . . This air will produce no eruption or volcano because it will have found enough space in which to expand or indeed because it will have found escapes and will have left the earth in the form of wind or vapor.[19]

Source 7 from Oeuvres complètes de Voltaire, *nouvelle edition, vol. 9 (Paris: Garnier frères, 1877), p. 470. Translated by Julius R. Ruff.*

7. From Voltaire, "Poem on the Lisbon Disaster, or An Examination of That Axiom 'All Is Well,'" 1755

Oh, miserable mortals! Oh wretched earth!
Oh, dreadful assembly of all mankind!
Eternal sermon of useless sufferings!
Deluded philosophers who cry, "All is well,"
Hasten, contemplate these frightful ruins,
This wreck, these shreds, these wretched ashes of the dead;
These women and children heaped on one another,
These scattered members under broken marble;
One-hundred thousand unfortunates devoured by the earth,[20]

---

19. The article on "Earthquakes" in the *Encyclopedia* edited by Diderot also explains this phenomenon with a theory of subterranean fire. Modern geologists have shown earthquakes to be the result of stresses in the earth's crust. Interestingly, however, modern research also has shown that the eighteenth-century theories of subterranean fire were not entirely incorrect: The earth does have a liquid core of practically molten rock.

20. Voltaire wrote this poem on hearing the first news of the disaster. Those first reports grossly exaggerated the number of deaths, as does the poem.

Chapter 3

The Mind of an

Age: Science

and Religion

Confront

Eighteenth-

Century

Natural Disaster

Who, bleeding, lacerated, and still alive,
Buried under their roofs without aid in their anguish,
End their sad days!
In answer to the half-formed cries of their dying voices,
At the frightful sight of their smoking ashes,
Will you say: "This is the result of eternal laws
Directing the acts of a free and good God!"
Will you say, in seeing this mass of victims:
"God is revenged, their death is the price for their crimes?"
What crime, what error did these children,
Crushed and bloody on their mothers' breasts, commit?
Did Lisbon, which is no more, have more vices
Than London and Paris immersed in their pleasures?
Lisbon is destroyed, and they dance in Paris!

Source 8 from Theodore Bestermann, editor, Voltaire's Correspondence, *vol. 30 (Geneva: In-stitut et Musée Voltaire, 1958), pp. 102–115. Translated by Julius R. Ruff.*

8. From Jean-Jacques Rousseau's Letter to Voltaire Regarding the Poem on the Lisbon Earthquake, August 18, 1756

All my complaints are . . . against your poem on the Lisbon disaster, because I expected from it evidence more worthy of the humanity which apparently inspired you to write it. You reproach Pope[21] and Leibnitz[22] with belittling our misfortunes by affirming that all is well, but you so burden the list of our miseries that you further disparage our condition. Instead of the consolations that I expected, you only vex me. It might be said that you fear that I don't feel my unhappiness enough, and that you are trying to soothe me by proving that all is bad.

Do not be mistaken, Monsieur, it happens that everything is contrary to what you propose. This optimism which you find so cruel consoles me still in

---

21. Alexander Pope, whose "An Essay on Man" is Source 4 in this chapter.

22. **Gottfried Wilhelm von Leibnitz:** a German mathematician and philosopher (1646–1716), the author of *Essays on Theodicy,* in which he examined the origins of evil in the world. Leibnitz saw the universe operating according to a divine plan, and therefore this was the best of all possible worlds. He was not a total optimist, however, because he recognized the existence of evil. Incompletely understanding the thought of Leibnitz, Voltaire satirized him as a blind optimist in his novel *Candide* (1759).

the same woes that you force on me as unbearable. Pope's poem[23] alleviates my difficulties and inclines me to patience; yours makes my afflictions worse, prompts me to grumble, and, leading me beyond a shattered hope, reduces me to despair. . . .

"Have patience, man," Pope and Leibnitz tell me, "your woes are a necessary effect of your nature and of the constitution of the universe. The eternal and beneficent Being who governs the universe wished to protect you. Of all the possible plans, he chose that combining the minimum evil and the maximum good. If it is necessary to say the same thing more bluntly, God has done no better for mankind because (He) can do no better."

Now what does your poem tell me? "Suffer forever unfortunate one. If a God created you, He is doubtlessly all powerful and could have prevented all your woes. Don't ever hope that your woes will end, because you would never know why you exist, if it is not to suffer and die. . . ."

I do not see how one can search for the source of moral evil anywhere but in man. . . . Moreover . . . the majority of our physical misfortunes are also our work. Without leaving your Lisbon subject, concede, for example, that it was hardly nature that there brought together twenty-thousand houses of six or seven stories. If the residents of this large city had been more evenly dispersed and less densely housed, the losses would have been fewer or perhaps none at all. Everyone would have fled at the first shock. But many obstinately remained . . . to expose themselves to additional earth tremors because what they would have had to leave behind was worth more than what they could carry away. How many unfortunates perished in this disaster through the desire to fetch their clothing, papers, or money? . . .

There are often events that afflict us . . . that lose a lot of their horror when we examine them closely. I learned in *Zadig*,[24] and nature daily confirms my lesson, that a rapid death is not always a true misfortune, and that it can sometimes be considered a relative blessing. Of the many persons crushed under Lisbon's ruins, some without doubt escaped greater misfortunes, and . . . it is not certain that a single one of these unfortunates suffered more than if, in the normal course of events, he had awaited [a more normal] death to overtake him after long agonies. Was death [in the ruins] a sadder end than that of a dying person overburdened with useless treatments, whose notary[25] and heirs do not allow him a respite, whom the doctors kill in his own bed at

---

23. **Pope's poem:** "An Essay on Man."

24. *Zadig:* a story published by Voltaire in 1747 that still reflected some faith on his part that a divine order for the world assured that all would work out for the best. In the story, Zadig, the main character, endures a lengthy series of misfortunes.

25. **notary:** in France and other Continental countries, a professional person specializing in drafting wills and inventorying the property involved in them as well as drawing up other property arrangements.

Chapter 3

The Mind of an

Age: Science

and Religion

Confront

Eighteenth-

Century

Natural Disaster

their leisure, and whom the barbarous priests artfully try to make relish death? For me, I see everywhere that the misfortunes nature imposes upon us are less cruel than those which we add to them. . . .

I cannot prevent myself, Monsieur, from noting . . . a strange contrast between you and me as regards the subject of this letter. Satiated with glory . . . you live free in the midst of affluence.[26] Certain of your immortality, you peacefully philosophize on the nature of the soul, and, if your body or heart suffer, you have Tronchin[27] as doctor and friend. You however find only evil on earth. And I, an obscure and poor man tormented with an incurable illness, meditate with pleasure in my seclusion and find that all is well. What is the source of this apparent contradiction? You explained it yourself: you revel but I hope, and hope beautifies everything.

. . . I have suffered too much in this life not to look forward to another. No metaphysical subtleties cause me to doubt a time of immortality for the soul and a beneficent providence. I sense it, I believe it, I wish it, I hope for it, I will uphold it until my last gasp. . . .

I am, with respect, Monsieur,

Jean-Jacques Rousseau

Source 9 from David Hume, Essays: Moral, Political and Literary *(Oxford: Oxford University Press, 1963), pp. 519–521, 524–526, 540–541.*

9. David Hume, "The Essay on Miracles," 1748

There is, in Dr. Tillotson's[28] writings, an argument against the *real presence,*[29] which is as concise, and elegant, and strong, as any argument can possibly be supposed against a doctrine so little worthy of a serious refutation. It is acknowledged on all hands, says that learned prelate, that the authority, either of the Scripture or of tradition, is founded merely on the testimony of the Apostles, who were eye-witnesses to those miracles of our Saviour, by which he proved his divine mission. Our evidence, then, for the truth of the *Christian* religion, is less than the evidence for the truth of our senses; because, even in

26. Voltaire had prospered from his publishings and also had invested well. He owned property in Geneva, Switzerland, and a large estate at Ferney, France, on the Swiss border.

27. **Theodore Tronchin:** a physician (1709–1781) of Geneva, Switzerland. A pioneer in smallpox inoculation in Switzerland, he was a member of Voltaire's circle.

28. **Dr. John Tillotson:** Archbishop of Canterbury (1630–1694), that is, spiritual leader of the Church of England.

29. **real presence:** the presence of Jesus Christ in the sacramental bread and wine of Christian Communion.

the first authors of our religion, it was no greater; and it is evident it must diminish in passing from them to their disciples; nor can any one rest such confidence in their testimony as in the immediate object of his senses. But a weaker evidence can never destroy a stronger; and therefore, were the doctrine of the real presence ever so clearly revealed in Scripture, it were directly contrary to the rules of just reasoning to give our assent to it. It contradicts sense, though both the Scripture and tradition, on which it is supposed to be built, carry not such evidence with them as sense, when they are considered merely as external evidences, and are not brought home to every one's breast by the immediate operation of the Holy Spirit.

Nothing is so convenient as a decisive argument of this kind, which must at least *silence* the most arrogant bigotry and superstition, and free us from their impertinent solicitations. I flatter myself that I have discovered an argument of a like nature, which, if just, will, with the wise and learned, be an everlasting check to all kinds of superstitious delusion, and consequently will be useful as long as the world endures; for so long, I presume, will the accounts of miracles and prodigies be found in all history, sacred and profane.

Though experience be our only guide in reasoning concerning matters of fact, it must be acknowledged, that this guide is not altogether infallible, but in some cases is apt to lead us into errors. One who in our climate should expect better weather in any week of June than in one of December, would reason justly and conformably to experience; but it is certain that he may happen, in the event, to find himself mistaken. However, we may observe that, in such a case, he would have no cause to complain of experience, because it commonly informs us beforehand of the uncertainty, by that contrariety of events which we may learn from a diligent observation. All effects follow not with like certainty from their supposed causes. Some events are found, in all countries and all ages, to have been constantly conjoined together: others are found to have been more variable, and sometimes to disappoint our expectations; so that in our reasonings concerning matter of fact, there are all imaginable degrees of assurance, from the highest certainty to the lowest species of moral evidence.

A wise man, therefore, proportions his belief to the evidence. In such conclusions as are founded on an infallible experience, he expects the event with the last degree of assurance, and regards his past experience as a full *proof* of the future existence of that event. In other cases he proceeds with more caution: he weighs the opposite experiments: he considers which side is supported by the greater number of experiments: to that side he inclines with doubt and hesitation; and when at last he fixes his judgment, the evidence exceeds not what we properly call *probability*. All probability, then, supposes an opposition of experiments and observations, where the one side is found to overbalance the other, and to produce a degree of evidence proportioned to the superiority. A hundred instances or experiments on one side, and fifty on another, afford a doubtful expectation of any event; though a hundred

Chapter 3

The Mind of an

Age: Science

and Religion

Confront

Eighteenth-

Century

Natural Disaster

uniform experiments, with only one that is contradictory, reasonably beget a pretty strong degree of assurance. In all cases, we must balance the opposite experiments, where they are opposite, and deduct the smaller number from the greater, in order to know the exact force of the superior evidence. . . .

A miracle is a violation of the laws of nature; and as a firm and unalterable experience has established these laws, the proof against a miracle, from the very nature of the fact, is as entire as any argument from experience can possibly be imagined. Why is it more than probable that all men must die; that lead cannot, of itself, remain suspended in the air; that fire consumes wood, and is extinguished by water; unless it be that these events are found agreeable to the laws of nature, and there is required a violation of these laws, or, in other words, a miracle to prevent them? Nothing is esteemed a miracle, if it ever happen in the common course of nature. It is no miracle that a man, seemingly in good health, should die on a sudden; because such a kind of death, though more unusual than any other, has yet been frequently observed to happen. But it is a miracle that a dead man should come to life; because that has never been observed in any age or country. There must, therefore, be an uniform experience against every miraculous event, otherwise the event would not merit that appellation. And as an uniform experience amounts to a proof, there is here a direct and full *proof*, from the nature of the fact, against the existence of any miracle. . . .

The plain consequence is (and it is a general maxim worthy of our attention), "That no testimony is sufficient to establish a miracle, unless the testimony be of such a kind, that its falsehood would be more miraculous than the fact which it endeavours to establish: and even in that case there is a mutual destruction of arguments, and the superior only gives us an assurance suitable to that degree of force which remains after deducting the inferior." When any one tells me that he saw a dead man restored to life, I immediately consider with myself whether it be more probable that this person should either deceive or be deceived, or that the fact which he relates should really have happened. I weigh the one miracle against the other; and according to the superiority which I discover, I pronounce my decision, and always reject the greater miracle. If the falsehood of his testimony would be more miraculous than the event which he relates, then, and not till then, can he pretend to command my belief or opinion.

Upon the whole, then, it appears, that no testimony for any kind of miracle has ever amounted to a probability, much less to a proof; and that, even supposing it amounted to a proof, it would be opposed by another proof, derived from the very nature of the fact which it would endeavour to establish. It is experience only which gives authority to human testimony; and it is the same experience which assures us of the laws of nature. When, therefore, these two kinds of experience are contrary, we have nothing to do but to subtract the one from the other, and embrace an opinion either on one side or the other, with that assurance which arises from the remainder. But according to the principle here explained, this subtraction with regard to all popular religions amounts to an entire annihilation; and therefore we may establish it as a maxim, that no human testimony can have such force as to prove a miracle, and make it a just foundation for any such system of religion. . . .

What we have said of miracles, may be applied without any variation to prophecies; and, indeed, all prophecies are real miracles, and as such, only can be admitted as proofs of any revelation. If it did not exceed the capacity of human nature to foretell future events, it would be absurd to employ any prophecy as an argument for a divine mission or authority from heaven. So that, upon the whole, we may conclude, that the *Christian Religion* not only was at first attended with miracles, but even at this day cannot be believed by any reasonable person without one. Mere reason is insufficient to convince us of its veracity: and whoever is moved by *Faith* to assent to it, is conscious of a continued miracle in his own person, which subverts all the principles of his understanding, and gives him a determination to believe what is most contrary to custom and experience.

Source 10 from Paul-Henry Thiry, Baron d'Holbach, The System of Nature, *translated by H. D. Robinson (Boston: J. P. Mendum, 1853), pp. viii–ix, 12–13, 15, 19–23.*

10. From Paul-Henry Thiry, Baron d'Holbach, *The System of Nature*, 1770

Preface

The source of man's unhappiness is his ignorance of Nature. The pertinacity with which he clings to blind opinions imbibed in his infancy, which interweave themselves with his existence, the consequent prejudice that warps his mind, that prevents its expansion, that renders him the slave of fiction, appears to doom him to continual errour. He resembles a child destitute of experience, full of idle notions: a dangerous leaven mixes itself with all his knowledge: it is of necessity obscure, it is vacillating and false:—He takes the tone of his ideas on the authority of others, who are themselves in errour, or else have an interest in deceiving him. To remove this Cimmerian darkness,[30] these barriers to the improvement of his condition; to disentangle him from the clouds of errour that envelop him, that obscure the path he ought to tread; to guide him out of the Cretan labyrinth,[31] requires the clue of

---

30. **Cimmerian darkness:** in Greek mythology, the Cimmerians were a people inhabiting a land of perpetual darkness.
31. **Cretan labyrinth:** according to Greek mythology, there existed on the island of Crete a structure of winding passages leading to a monster with the body of a man and the head of a bull, the Minotaur. This monster was annually fed seven young men and seven young women from Athens as that city's tribute to the rulers of Crete.

Chapter 3

The Mind of an

Age: Science

and Religion

Confront

Eighteenth-

Century

Natural Disaster

Ariadne,[32] with all the love she could bestow on Theseus. It exacts more than common exertion; it needs a most determined, a most undaunted courage—it is never effected but by a persevering resolution to act, to think for himself; to examine with rigour and impartiality the opinions he has adopted. . . .

Man seeks to range out of his sphere: notwithstanding the reiterated checks his ambitious folly experiences, he still attempts the impossible; strives to carry his researches beyond the visible world; and hunts out misery in imaginary regions. He would be a metaphysician before he has become a practical philosopher. He quits the contemplation of realities to meditate on chimeras. He neglects experience to feed on conjecture, to indulge in hypothesis. He dares not cultivate his reason, because from his earliest days he has been taught to consider it criminal. He pretends to know his fate in the indistinct abodes of another life, before he has considered of the means by which he is to render himself happy in the world he inhabits: in short, man disdains the study of Nature, except it be partially. . . .

The most important of our duties, then, is to seek means by which we may destroy delusions that can never do more than mislead us. The remedies for these evils must be sought for in Nature herself; it is only in the abundance of her resources, that we can rationally expect to find antidotes to the mischiefs brought upon us by an ill-directed, by an over-powering enthusiasm. It is time these remedies were sought; it is time to look the evil boldly in the face, to examine its foundations, to scrutinize its super-structure: reason, with its faithful guide experience, must attack in their entrenchments those prejudices to which the human race has but too long been the victim. For this purpose reason must be restored to its proper rank,—it must be rescued from the evil company with which it is associated. . . .

Truth speaks not to these perverse beings [the enemies of the human race]:—her voice can only be heard by generous minds accustomed to reflection, whose sensibilities make them lament the numberless calamities showered on the earth by political and religious tyranny—whose enlightened minds contemplate with horrour the immensity, the ponderosity of that series of misfortunes with which errour has in all ages overwhelmed mankind. . . .

Of Nature

. . . The *civilized man,* is he whom experience and social life have enabled to draw from nature the means of his own happiness; because he has learned to oppose resistance to those impulses he receives from exterior beings, when experience has taught him they would be injurious to his welfare.

The *enlightened man,* is man in his maturity, in his perfection; who is capable of pursuing his own happiness; because he has learned to examine, to

---

32. **Ariadne:** a daughter of the King of Crete who fell in love with Theseus, an Athenian hero and one of the youths sent by Athens to be offered to the Minotaur. Ariadne gave Theseus a ball of thread, which he unwound as he penetrated the labyrinth and there killed the Minotaur. He then followed the thread back out of the labyrinth.

think for himself, and not to take that for truth upon the authority of others, which experience has taught him examination will frequently prove erroneous. . . .

It necessarily results, that man in his researches ought always to fall back on experience, and natural philosophy: These are what he should consult in his religion—in his morals—in his legislation—in his political government—in the arts—in the sciences—in his pleasures—in his misfortunes. Experience teaches that Nature acts by simple, uniform, and invariable laws. It is by his senses man is bound to this universal Nature; it is by his senses he must penetrate her secrets; it is from his senses he must draw experience of her laws. Whenever, therefore, he either fails to acquire experience or quits its path, he stumbles into an abyss, his imagination leads him astray. . . .

Man did not understand that Nature, equal in her distributions, entirely destitute of goodness or malice, follows only necessary and immutable laws, when she either produces beings or destroys them, when she causes those to suffer, whose organization creates sensibility; when she scatters among them good and evil; when she subjects them to incessant change—he did not perceive it was in the bosom of Nature herself, that it was in her abundance he ought to seek to satisfy his wants; for remedies against his pains; for the means of rendering himself happy: he expected to derive these benefits from imaginary beings, whom he erroneously imagined to be the authors of his pleasures, the cause of his misfortunes. From hence it is clear that to his ignorance of Nature, man owes the creation of those illusive powers under which he has so long trembled with fear; that superstitious worship, which has been the source of all his misery. . . .

The universe, that vast assemblage of every thing that exists, presents only matter and motion: the whole offers to our contemplation nothing but an immense, an uninterrupted succession of causes and effects; some of these causes are known to us, because they strike immediately on our senses; others are unknown to us, because they act upon us by effects, frequently very remote from their original cause. . . .

Of Motion and Its Origin

. . . Observation and reflection ought to convince us, that every thing in Nature is in continual motion. . . . Thus, the idea of Nature necessarily includes that of motion. But, it will be asked, from whence did she receive her motion? Our reply is, from herself, since she is the great whole, out of which, consequently, nothing can exist. . . .

If they [natural philosophers] had viewed Nature uninfluenced by prejudice, they must have been long since convinced, that matter acts by its own peculiar energy, and needs not any exterior impulse to set it in motion. They would have perceived, that whenever mixed bodies were placed in a capacity to act on each other, motion was instantly engendered, and that these mixtures acted with a force capable of producing the most surprising effects. If

Chapter 3
The Mind of an
Age: Science
and Religion
Confront
Eighteenth-
Century
Natural Disaster

filings of iron, sulphur and water be mixed together, these bodies thus capacitated to act on each other, are heated by degrees, and ultimately produce a violent combustion. If flour be wetted with water, and the mixture closed up, it will be found, after some little lapse of time, by the aid of a microscope, to have produced organized beings that enjoy life, of which the water and the flour were believed incapable: it is thus that inanimate matter can pass into life, or animate matter, which is in itself only an assemblage of motion. Reasoning from analogy, the production of a man, independent of the ordinary means, would not be more marvellous than that of an insect with flour and water. . . .

Those who admit a cause exterior to matter, are obliged to suppose, that this cause produced all the motion by which matter is agitated in giving it existence. This supposition rests on another, namely, that matter could begin to exist; a hypothesis that, until this moment, has never been demonstrated by any thing like solid proof. To produce from nothing, or the *Creation*, is a term that cannot give us the most slender idea of the formation of the universe; it presents no sense, upon which the mind can fasten itself.

Motion becomes still more obscure, when creation, or the formation of matter, is attributed to a *spiritual* being, that is to say, to a being which has no analogy, no point of contact, with it; to a being which has neither extent, nor parts, and cannot, therefore, be susceptible of motion, as we understand the term; this being only the change of one body relatively to another body, in which the body moved, presents successively different parts to different points of space. Moreover, as all the world are nearly agreed that matter can never be totally annihilated, or cease to exist, how can we understand, that that which cannot cease to be, could ever have had a beginning?

If, therefore, it be asked, whence came matter? it is a very reasonable reply to say, it has always existed. . . .

Let us, therefore, content ourselves with saying *that* which is supported by our experience, and by all the evidence we are capable of understanding; against the truth of which, not a shadow of proof such as our reason can admit, has ever been adduced; which has been maintained by philosophers in every age; which theologians themselves have not denied, but which many of them have upheld; namely, that *matter always existed; that it moves by virtue of its essence; that all the phenomena of Nature is ascribable to the diversified motion of the variety of matter she contains; and which, like the phenix,[33] is continually regenerating out of her own ashes.*

33. **phenix:** the common modern spelling is "phoenix." In Egyptian mythology, the phoenix was a large bird with a life span of 500 to 600 years, living in the Arabian desert. At the end of its life the phoenix was consumed in fire, and from its ashes a new phoenix arose.

QUESTIONS TO CONSIDER

The selections that you have read allow you to trace one of the major issues raised by the *philosophes* as they sought to use the discoveries of the Scientific Revolution to comprehend the physical world more completely. Your consideration of this issue—the relationship of God to the physical world—should give you some clear understanding of the thought of the *philosophes* and its implications.

Consider first the traditional views expressed by Catholic and Protestant theologians. What caused the Lisbon earthquake, according to Malagrida? Did he foresee further disaster overtaking the city? Can you find in his pamphlet possible remedies for the city's misery from which Lisbon residents might have derived comfort? Contrast Malagrida's view of the plight of Lisbon with that of John Wesley, bearing in mind, of course, the latter's Protestantism. To what cause did Wesley ascribe the earthquake? Did he see any way to avoid such disasters? Despite their obvious differences, do you find any similarity in outlook in Malagrida and Wesley?

Now move on to Enlightenment sources, which are arranged to permit you to trace the development of the *philosophes'* responses to the disaster and the implications of their thought. Voltaire's distillation of Newton's physics in Source 3 is fundamental to understanding the Enlightenment because Newton's work provided the basis for the *philosophes'* understanding of the world in which

they lived. Through what method did Newton propose to understand the physical world? What relationships did he find governing the physical world? In what way did Newton's ideas provide a governing theory to explain much of that physical world? Why might you expect those influenced by Newton to describe the physical world as a machine?

Source 4, Alexander Pope's "An Essay on Man," represents an early-eighteenth-century attempt to balance a belief in God with the new scientific discoveries of Newton and others. How does Pope reflect traditional religion? What elements of sixteenth- and seventeenth-century scientific thought do you find in Pope? Most important, what role does God play in the world, according to Pope? What effect does that divine role have on humankind?

Reconsider the entry on "Observation" from the *Encyclopedia*. What view of reason does the article offer to its readers? How does Buffon attempt to apply this vision in his discussion of earthquakes? What sort of causal pattern does he find for earthquakes? Despite his explanation of earthquakes, which is recognized today as incorrect, is there any room for a divine role in Buffon's explanation of these disasters? Whose view do you identify with more closely, Buffon's or Malagrida's?

Voltaire's "Poem on the Lisbon Disaster" is the reaction of the Enlightenment's most celebrated thinker to the earthquake. Contrast it with the account he had written earlier of Newton's science. How had Voltaire's

[77]

Chapter 3

The Mind of an

Age: Science

and Religion

Confront

Eighteenth-

Century

Natural Disaster

point of view changed during this interval? How does Voltaire respond to the views of his friend Alexander Pope? What response does he have to the theological explanation of the quake? Do you detect a growing skepticism in the thought of the older Voltaire? If so, in what ways? What response to Voltaire does Jean-Jacques Rousseau make in his letter? What similarities in thinking with earlier selections do you find in Rousseau?

Next examine Source 9, the selection by David Hume. Compare Voltaire's skepticism about a divine role in the world with the position Hume takes in "The Essay on Miracles." Also contrast Hume with Rousseau; how might intellectual differences have helped to cause their break? Where had Enlightenment skepticism, evident in Voltaire's later thought, led Hume? What religious implications of the Enlightenment's search to apply human reason to all issues do

you find in Hume's work? Is any room left here for a divine role in the natural order? Trace this tendency in the thought of Baron d'Holbach, whose ideas shocked even some *philosophes*. Where have the principles of the Enlightenment led in Holbach's *System of Nature*? As we noted earlier, some of Holbach's contemporaries called him an atheist. How else might you describe his thought?

Your answers as you carefully consider these questions should provide you with the basis for responding to the main questions in this chapter: Why did the Lisbon earthquake pose such an intellectual crisis for eighteenth-century thinkers? How did theologians explain the disaster? How did Enlightenment thinkers explain it? In what direction was their thought on the physical world and its relationship to divine forces leading them?

EPILOGUE

The difference in outlook between Malagrida and Wesley on the one hand and the older and skeptical Voltaire and Baron d'Holbach on the other is immense, and it represents a long intellectual journey for eighteenth-century thinkers. The culmination of this journey represented the success of the Scientific Revolution in modeling for the Western mind a method of searching for reasonable, scientific explanations of natural phenomena as well as imparting its faith in human ability to find these answers.

The Enlightenment, however, meant much more than even this. The implications of a movement that ultimately was unprepared, as we have seen, to accept traditional religion were tremendous beyond the fields of theology and natural science. Enlightenment skepticism in matters religious is controversial even to the present day. Its search for reasonable and comprehensible natural laws to govern all aspects of the human experience helped to change the Western world. Though a new and grander Lisbon arose from the old city's ruins, much else did not long survive the intellectual crisis of mid century that the earthquake embodied. The *philosophes'* search failed to uncover rational, natural laws to justify many human institutions of the eighteenth century. As a result, they called for sweeping changes of such existing institutions as divine right monarchy (see Chapter 2). In his *Social Contract,* for example, Rousseau argued for a new governing principle in which the general will of the people should govern. In the criminal justice practiced by governments of the day, the *philosophes* found a brutal system in which courts might employ torture to force defendants to testify against themselves and in which capital punishment was common. Many *philosophes* argued against the barbarism of such a system. In the work of the Italian thinker Cesare Bonesana, Marchese di Beccaria (1738–1794), the Enlightenment produced a strong statement against the death penalty and in favor of punishments based on prison terms graduated to fit the offense.

In religious matters, *philosophes* everywhere found an intolerance that to them seemed irrational, and Voltaire led their call for toleration and freedom of thought. Not even economic affairs escaped the attention of the *philosophes.* Eighteenth-century economic life was still dominated by guilds that set prices and government mercantilist policies that regulated trade. Adam Smith (1723–1790), a Scottish economist, led many Enlightenment thinkers in calling for a free economy. Let the natural laws of the economy work unimpeded and unregulated and the needs of all would be met, they argued. Everywhere the *philosophes* looked, they saw the need

for reform. The existence today in the modern West of much of what they called for testifies to the wide-ranging influence of their thought.

A further casualty of the earthquake in Portugal was the Society of Jesus, one of the great opponents of much of Enlightenment thought. The society fell victim to the Marquis of Pombal, chief minister of Portugal's weak-willed monarch, Joseph I, and the man who led the relief and rebuilding efforts in the devastated city. The Portuguese version of that eighteenth-century phenomenon described in your text as the "enlightened despot," Pombal wielded more and more royal power even though he never wore the crown.

Like a number of enlightened despots, including Frederick the Great of Prussia and Joseph II of Austria, Pombal had a vision of a government that was first of all absolute in power and only secondarily reforming in its policies. He found the great power of the Catholic church in Portugal a formidable obstacle to his hopes of building the secular strength of the state. Armed with greater prestige after the earthquake, Pombal attacked the greatest bastion of clerical power, the Society of Jesus, and expelled almost all of Portugal's Jesuits on September 1, 1759. In 1761 he ordered the execution of Gabriel Malagrida, the society's most visible Portuguese spokesman. Malagrida's ideas stood in the way of reconstruction because he preached a need for spiritual regeneration and focused people's attentions on the next life. Pombal, in contrast, required all of Portugal's energies for rebuilding in the here and now. Other Catholic

Chapter 3

The Mind of an

Age: Science .

and Religion

Confront

Eighteenth-

Century

Natural Disaster

countries duplicated the Portuguese expulsion of the Jesuits. Local political or theological issues were often at the root of such expulsions, but they resulted in the worldwide abolition of the Society of Jesus from 1773 to 1814.[34]

The postearthquake Western world, thanks to the natural forces of the Lisbon disaster and the intellectual forces of the Enlightenment, would be considerably transformed on a number of levels. The fruits of Enlightenment thought are still with us in many forms.

34. On the French experience, see Dale Van Kley, *The Jansenists and the Expulsion of the Jesuits from France* (New Haven, Conn.: Yale University Press, 1974).

CHAPTER FOUR

EUROPEAN MATERIAL LIFE, 1600–1800

Chapters 2 and 3 took us into the world of the political and intellectual elites of seventeenth- and eighteenth-century Europe. This is a world that historians long have known, because its inhabitants were almost uniformly literate and thus left abundant records of their lives and thoughts in letters, diaries, autobiographies, and works of literature and philosophy. From such records, historians have been able to describe in great detail the thought and daily life of Europe's elites, but no matter how much influence these groups wielded, they ultimately represented only a small minority of the population of early modern Europe.

The majority of seventeenth- and eighteenth-century Europeans were illiterate, or barely literate, and they left none of the conventional written records that long have given historians their raw material for reconstructing the lives of society's privileged orders. Only in recent decades, by creatively using records kept by literate Europeans about their ill-lettered

contemporaries, have historians developed the methodological skills to penetrate the world of these nonelites. As we will see, records kept by businessmen, clerics, legal officials, police officers, and tax agents can give us a very rich picture of the lives of these people. Rarely, however, can historians reconstruct the life of a single individual from such research. Rather, they abstract from their work something akin to a collective biography, frequently given validity by a quantitative expression of their research. In this chapter, we will examine some of the quantitative results of almost two generations of historical study of the economy, society, and culture of the long-silent majority of seventeenth- and eighteenth-century Europeans. In particular, we will examine their material lives, beginning with the most basic aspect of material existence: simply getting enough to eat. We will find that, at the beginning of our period, the majority of Europeans relied on a rather primitive agriculture that largely produced for local or regional needs. We also will discover that most people owned little more than the basic material necessities of life and that only the privileged orders, traditionally the upper clergy and the aristocracy, had sufficient resources to indulge in the consumption of exotic foods and to possess extensive furniture and large, elaborate wardrobes. Indeed, for early modern Europeans, such conspicuous material consumption was a visible sign of an individual's membership in a privileged order of society, and both social convention and formal regulations called *sumptuary laws* long forbad prosperous commoners to so indulge themselves.

We will find, too, that historians now can discern in northwestern Europe in the seventeenth and eighteenth centuries sweeping economic, social, and cultural changes that laid the foundations of our modern material world. Today most of us produce few, if any, of our own dietary needs; instead we rely on specialized producers around the world for our requirements in both food and durable goods. Moreover, unlike most women and men of an earlier age, many of today's Westerners derive at least a portion of their identities from the possession of certain goods. Our age has been called one of mass "conspicuous consumption," so different materially from the early modern West that one historian has described it as the result of a

"consumer revolution."[1] Such a term, of course, excites considerable debate among historians as to the magnitude of the changes that we have described, but historians concur that a profound cultural change in the seventeenth and eighteenth centuries seems to have reshaped how people expended their limited resources.

Our goal in this chapter is to trace the changes in Western material life over the seventeenth and eighteenth centuries by observing the variety of sources historians exploit in studying the existence of nonelite people and by following the two basic tasks performed by historians of the period: compiling statistical data and then analyzing them. Our goal will be to understand the material life of the majority of Europeans by formulating answers to the basic questions historians ask of relevant statistical data. What was the material existence of the majority of Europeans at the outset of our period? What changes occurred in their existence over time? What were the causes of these changes? What aspects of the modern, global economy can we discern in the period from 1600 to 1800?

1. Neil McKendrick, in Neil McKendrick, John Brewer, and J. H. Plumb, *The Birth of a Consumer Society: The Commercialization of Eighteenth-Century England* (Bloomington: Indiana University Press, 1982), p. 9.

SOURCES AND METHOD

The evidence in this chapter includes several images and literary sources and a variety of tables and graphs in which historians express the statistical results of their research. Analyzing these materials together will allow you to understand more fully the material existence of seventeenth- and eighteenth-century Europeans.

Source 1 is a primary record of early modern agricultural methods. It is an illustration from perhaps the most famous fifteenth-century book of hours, the *Très riches heures du duc de Berry* [*The Very Rich Hours of the Duke of Berry*]. Books of hours were manuscript devotional books containing biblical texts and prayers appropriate to the hours of the Christian devotional day, often supplemented by calendars of religious and secular events and, in copies produced for wealthy buyers, hand-colored illustrations of activities appropriate to the months or seasons of the year. The Duke of Berry (d. 1416) was the brother of the French king, Charles V, and possessed an opulent volume illustrated by the Limbourg brothers, Flemish artists known for their attention to detail. Thus the illustrations in the *Très riches heures* are valuable sources for historians in understanding the past, and in Source 1 we find a picture of the plowing activities of the month of March. Note, in particular, the cumbersome wheeled plow, used in much of northern Europe, whose design did not change for centuries. Constructed of wood, these early plows did not produce the deep plowing that is essential for productive agriculture, both to cut off and bury surface vegetation and to loosen the soil in preparation for seeding. What sort of furrow does this peasant plowman seem to be making? What sort of expenditure of human and animal labor was required to attain these results? This plowman would have been followed by another worker sowing seeds broadcast style, a highly inefficient way to plant by modern standards. Indeed, most early modern farmers understood little of modern farming techniques; even by the eighteenth century, only a very small number of affluent, educated landowners employed such techniques as crop rotation, fertilization of the soil, and selective livestock breeding. How productive do you think the peasant farmer in Source 1 was?

Source 2 presents modern historians' calculations of European agricultural productivity for wheat, rye, and barley, the grains that were the mainstays of the European diet during the seventeenth and eighteenth centuries. The data consist of *yield ratios* arranged by regions. Yield ratios are basic statistical constructs, derived by historians from farm records, that show the average number of bushels of grain harvested from one bushel of seed. Thus, from 1600 to 1649 in Zone I, one bushel of grain seed produced 6.7 bushels at harvest. To interpret these data, you need to understand that modern farming methods on amply watered wheat fields in the American Midwest produce yield ratios of at least 40:1. What do you conclude about the general productivity of agriculture across Europe in the period that is the subject of this chapter? Given such agricultural productivity, why might you conclude that the majority of the early modern population engaged in farming? Now examine each of the four zones for the evolution of productivity over time. Why might you not be surprised to find that farmers in late-seventeenth- and early-eighteenth-century England and the Low Countries led Europe in their adoption of modern agricultural techniques like crop rotation? Why might you agree with agricultural historians who have found that farmers in parts of France, Italy, and Spain began to apply such techniques somewhat later? In which countries did farmers not seem to have adopted new methods? What were the probable results in the food supply for late-seventeenth- and eighteenth-century residents of Zones I and II?

Even when we do note incremental improvement in agricultural output in parts of northwestern Europe like England and the Low Countries, farming, then as now, remained highly dependent on weather conditions, and agricultural produce was vulnerable to insects and diseases whose threats today have been diminished vastly by nineteenth- and twentieth-century advances in science. Thus, crops easily could fail, and famine was the result. In parts of northwestern Europe, as in England and the Low Countries, producers had access to cheap water transport so that bulky food cargoes could be shipped to areas beset by famine, either from other parts of the country or from foreign markets. In such areas, subsistence problems diminished early. But in areas like France, where the need for slow and costly land transport inhibited the movement of food supplies, real privation and even occasional starvation accompanied crop failures into the eighteenth century. Historians now understand these agricultural problems and their consequences thanks to their systematic collection of several

different sorts of data. They draw one body of data from records of grain and bread prices maintained by merchants and, in countries like France, by police agencies, which tracked prices in order to preempt food riots. Such price records are useful because they reflect the availability of food supplies; high prices for foodstuffs thus indicate shortages and, since wages varied little in the short term, real privation for those who lacked the means to purchase staples at elevated prices.

Historians' other source for understanding the experience of early modern populations, in the absence of modern government censuses, which date only from the nineteenth century, is the remarkable record of baptisms and burials systematically kept by Catholic and Protestant clergymen beginning in the sixteenth century. From their study of the parish registers maintained by the clergy, historians now can illustrate quantitatively the high birth and death rates of early modern Europeans and, importantly for our purpose, the effect of harvest failures on these rates.

Source 3 is a graph illustrating the effects of harvest failure and the resulting high wheat prices for people in the region of Amiens, France, in the 1690s. In the Amiens region the summer of 1693 was wet, a disastrous situation for ripening grain, and as a result the autumn harvest was very poor. What was the effect of such a harvest on the price of a container of wheat (a *septier* in Amiens)? What was the rate of this price increase before the larger harvest of 1694 began to come to market in August of that year and prices dropped? What do you think was the impact of such rising prices on people of limited means? Historians have found that when other factors, like illness, combined with food shortages, the result could be a demographic crisis, the highly abnormal situation in which a population group's deaths exceed its births. This is what occurred in Amiens. Food shortages there coincided in late 1693 with the onset of illnesses, perhaps in part spread by wandering poor searching for food, which often proved lethal for the very young and the very old. Other residents of Amiens perhaps consumed spoiled food products when they were unable to purchase their usual staples and also perished as a result. How are these circumstances represented on the graph? Given that malnutrition can produce various impediments to human conception, what effect did all of this have on the birthrate as measured in conceptions? Why might you conclude that the population of Amiens actually diminished in 1693 and 1694?

Source 4 illustrates a meal in a Dutch peasant household in 1653 that tells us much about the diet provided by the traditional agricultural methods that we have examined. The poverty of the household is evident; there is not even a table on which to place the meal. It rests on a three-legged stool. The meal is quite characteristic of the diet of most early modern Europeans, which was based largely on cereals and which was often deficient in proteins and other nutrients. The family is preparing to consume a gruel made by boiling oats or some other cereal with water or milk. What foods and nutrients do you find missing in such a diet? Since a balanced diet requires proteins essential for body growth, lipids (fats) to maintain body temperature, glucides (sugars) for muscular energy, and other nutrients, what do you think were the consequences of such a cereal-based diet?

Source 5 gives us further illustration of the material existence of early modern Europeans. It is a photograph of a museum reconstruction of a peasant cottage in the South Tyrol region of Austria. It is typical of many peasant dwellings of the early modern era in several ways. It is small, and like many dwellings it probably consisted of one room. Moreover, it seems to offer its residents a most unhealthy shelter. Many early modern Europeans shared their residences with livestock, and in this photograph, notice the wooden pen for chickens, with its feed trough, that serves as the base for the counter at the left of the room. The cooking arrangements also are worthy of note. This room lacks a fireplace with a chimney to draw out the smoke of the cooking fire that has blackened the wall in the room's right corner. The smoke, instead, slowly exited through an opening in the roof. What do you think were the health implications of such living conditions? If you combine such conditions with the dietary deficiencies that we have noted, what sort of health was probably the lot of many early modern Europeans? How do you think that contributed to demographic crises like that illustrated in Source 3?

[85]

The South Tyrol room in Source 5 also illustrates seventeenth- and eighteenth-century material life in another way. What sort of furniture do you find? The cupboard at the center of the photograph is a strictly utilitarian piece for holding various household possessions that would have been found in many early modern homes. Beyond that piece of furniture, there is none of the china, glassware, specialized cooking implements, and timepieces that we would find in modern homes; there are but a few metal pots and pans, and homemade items including a wooden box and a covered basket.

With Source 6, we return to an analysis of the European food supply. The growing agricultural productivity of England and the Low Countries, which we noted in Source 2, was one factor that permitted these areas to avoid large-scale famines after the seventeenth century. There were, however, other factors that also improved the food supply of much of northwestern Europe. By the eighteenth century, farmers in this area increasingly cultivated crops acquired by Europeans on their fifteenth- and sixteenth-century voyages of discovery in the Western Hemisphere. Chief among these was the potato, which produced five times more food output than did wheat planted on the same piece of soil. Moreover, in one corner of northwestern Europe, in the United Provinces (the present-day kingdom of the Netherlands), intense agricultural specialization developed, especially in dairying, that offered important supplements to traditional diets.

Because the Netherlands dominated trade with the lands of northern Europe around the Baltic Sea, Dutch farmers increasingly were able to specialize. In the sixteenth and seventeenth centuries, Dutch trade was especially great with East Prussia and the lands of the Polish-Lithuanian Commonwealth, which encompassed much of twenty-first-century Poland, Lithuania, Belarus, and Ukraine, as well as parts of western Russia. This region, largely part of Zone IV in Source 2, lagged behind the lands of northwestern Europe in agricultural productivity, but its great noble estates were worked at very low costs largely by the labor of serfs. The landowning aristocrats of the region found ready buyers in western Europe for their low-cost wheat and rye, and in the course of the sixteenth century the Dutch established control of the Baltic grain trade because they could undercut the freight rates of other maritime states with capacious freight vessels that were inexpensive to build and man. Thus, the produce of the Baltic states flowed through Amsterdam, both for local consumption and for transshipment to other northern European countries.

Historians can trace this trade quantitatively through remarkable records in Denmark. That nation charged tolls on all vessels sailing through the Sound, the narrow passage connecting the Baltic Sea to the Atlantic Ocean, from the early fifteenth century until 1857. These records noted the nationalities of ships and their cargoes, and they provide historians with a fairly accurate record of trade.

Various factors could diminish or interrupt this trade, like the bad harvests of the 1620s or the warfare of the 1630s. Source 6 illustrates the Dutch Baltic grain trade in the period from 1562 to 1650 expressed in *lasts* of grain shipped (one *last* was about 80 American gallons) and shows both the actual shipments and a moving average of shipments that demonstrates long-term trends. What is the trend in this trade through the mid-seventeenth century? Why do you think that such trade, combined with improved western European agricultural output, presaged the end of the sort of population crises illustrated in Source 3? What effect might this trade have had on Dutch agriculture? Why might you not be surprised to learn that many Dutch farmers abandoned grain production in the face of such low-priced competition to specialize in cash crops like vegetables and dairy products for local urban markets? Why might you also conclude that such farming exposed its practitioners to urban material culture?

Around the growing seventeenth- and eighteenth-century urban trading centers of northwestern Europe, like Amsterdam and London, many historians discern the beginnings of something akin to a modern consumer society, that is, a society in which significant numbers of people acquired goods and objects in excess of those necessary for mere subsistence and derived something of their identity from such consumption. Historians find such consumer behavior evident in Europeans' acquisition of both certain consumable products like foodstuffs and various more durable products like clothing, furniture, and household goods.

The first great change in consumer tastes in foodstuffs involved sugar. The main early modern source of sugar, sugar cane, is a difficult crop to cultivate. Requiring a tropical climate, a long growing season, abundant water, and a large labor force, sugar cane was impossible to cultivate in most of Europe, and sugar remained a relatively scarce and expensive luxury in the West until European conquest and colonization of the Western Hemisphere. There, in the course of the seventeenth century, the Dutch, English, French, Portuguese, and Spanish produced increasing quantities of sugar for European consumption by adopting a plantation system based on vast quantities of slave labor.

Because forced labor and European diseases early decimated the Native American population of the West Indian islands that became the chief centers of sugar production, Europeans soon turned to the enslavement of large numbers of Africans. Indeed, trade in slaves long was the central element of the so-called Atlantic "triangle trade" in which European merchants transported cloth and other manufactured products to West Africa and there exchanged these products for slaves. They then transported the slaves to European colonies in the Western Hemisphere, where planters purchased them largely for agricultural labor. In the Western Hemisphere the same ships then picked up sugar and other colonial produce for sale in Europe.

Source 7 summarizes data collected by historians on nearly 26,000 voyages by European and American slavers over more than three hundred years, until Britain (in 1807) and the United States (in 1808) began an international drive to outlaw this trade in human beings. Which nations' merchants engaged in this trade? Considering that Brazil was a Portuguese colony until 1822, which nation probably accounted for the largest number of slaves exported from Africa? Which country dominated the early slave trade prior to 1650? Remembering that the country designated on the table as the "United States" was a British colony through 1775, which country dominated the slave trade from 1650 until 1800? When did the slave trade reach its peak? Examining the average annual number of slaves transported in the column labeled "Annual Volume," calculate the rates of change in this trade by dividing the annual volume of each period by that of its predecessor (thus 10.1 divided by 3.3 yields a rate of average annual increase of 306 percent). Which periods experienced the greatest rates of increase?

The data in Source 8 detail the importation of sugar into Europe in the seventeenth and eighteenth centuries. They are the results of historians' research into trade records. Source 8A charts the quantities of sugar arriving in France in the eighteenth century. What trend do you observe in these data? Source 8B illustrates the effects in England and Wales of a rising West Indian sugar cane production attended by diminishing prices in processed sugar.

What do you observe about average per capita sugar consumption in England and Wales? What correlation between the transport of slaves and sugar production do you observe? Why might you conclude that tropical slave labor made it possible for this former luxury to become an item of everyday European consumption?

Europeans' early modern explorations brought them into contact with other tropical products for which they developed lasting tastes, especially the stimulants coffee and tea, which they sweetened with their growing supplies of sugar. Europeans first encountered coffee in the sixteenth century in the Middle East, where it was widely consumed, and the first source for European coffee was Mocha, in modern Yemen. But when coffee found ready acceptance in Europe in the course of the seventeenth century, merchants hastened to meet the demand. Thus, by the early eighteenth century the Dutch cultivated it on Java in the East Indies and the British and the Spanish produced it on the islands of the West Indies. Coffee became a commodity of mass consumption as coffee houses, establishments possessing the specialized equipment for preparing coffee, opened in great numbers in major cities. Indeed, by 1700 Paris had some 300 such establishments, and London may have had as many as 1,000.

The Chinese were the first to cultivate tea, and its production long remained a carefully guarded monopoly. They produced tea in the interior of their country and sold the leaves to Europeans chiefly through Canton, the sole port through which the Chinese government permitted trade with the early modern West. Trade with China further was limited because Europeans at first had little other than gold and silver that the Chinese sought in exchange for their tea. Thus, tea only appeared in very limited quantities at very high cost in Europe in the early seventeenth century. Nonetheless, the product was thought to have medicinal qualities, and demand for it slowly grew, especially in Britain and the United Provinces. It, too, became a commodity of mass consumption when its cost fell as the British East India Company developed a permanent trading operation in Canton in the early eighteenth century that ensured a reliable supply of Chinese tea.

Within a century of their introduction in the West, coffee, tea, sugar, and other products from the Western Hemisphere, like tobacco and chocolate, had become products of daily consumption for Europeans. Trade records demonstrate the rapid increase of imports of these goods that the eighteenth-century British called "groceries." The statistics in Source 9 illustrate trends in the grocery trade in England and Wales, and, like all such figures, they also reflect non-market factors that affected trade, like the American and French Revolutions of the 1780s and 1790s. Examine long-term trends. What part did groceries constitute in the total value of English and Welsh imports in 1559? When did the imports of groceries grow most greatly? Consider the chronology of the introduction of coffee and tea in Europe. How might you explain those large increases?

The introduction of these new, luxury goods had a wide-ranging impact on Europeans. Most immediately, perhaps, it set off a frenzy by consumers to acquire the specialized implements and tableware to prepare and consume coffee and tea. Historians document such acquisitions through the inventories that legal officials drew up in most Western countries at the time of a property owner's death. Although these probate records often fail to record the few possessions of the poor, they yield for scholars a representative sample of the goods owned by the middle class, which was the largest group of early modern consumers. Using such records, historians document the expanding consumption of tea, coffee, and even chocolate, finding that in 1695 only 10 percent of middle-class London households possessed implements for the preparation of these hot beverages, while almost all such homes had such equipment three decades later.

The widespread adoption of coffee and tea in the West had unexpected social consequences as well. The preparation of tea is a unique process; the beverage is prepared in the presence of those who will consume it, and tea long was at the center of social rituals in the East. Those rituals reappeared in Europe, as tea became the center of British sociability in a daily ritual usually presided over by the household's eldest female member. Fine Chinese porcelain ware that at first could not be duplicated in the West also was part of the consumption ritual. Some historians also have suggested that the delicate nature of

[89]

such Oriental tea services, and eventually their Western imitators, helped to instill more fastidious manners in some Europeans, since tea ware could easily break.

The large number of coffee houses in England and on the Continent also affected Western patterns of socialization. Such establishments sold coffee as well as a variety of other alcoholic and nonalcoholic drinks and meals, and they drew an often cosmopolitan, largely male clientele by offering newspapers, shipping journals, and sometimes books to their patrons. Indeed, they became central institutions in the forming of eighteenth-century middle-class opinion. Source 10 illustrates a London coffee house during the American War for Independence in 1781, at a time when the British sought to capture the Dutch West Indian island of Saint Eustatius, a main source of supplies for the rebels in North America. What is the central activity portrayed in this popular print? To what social class do you think the figures belonged?

As new drinks of tropical origin and the implements to prepare and consume them generated new trends in Western consumption, early modern Europeans began to consume greater quantities of other, more durable goods, too. Historians still debate their reasons. Some perhaps were attracted by the novelty of certain goods, like printed cotton textiles from India called calicoes. Others perhaps sought to imitate the material lives of their social betters, to acquire something of their superiors' respectability and social status. And many bought durable goods

because new sources for certain products increased their supply or new processes in their production lowered their purchase prices.

Clothing was the preeminent mass-consumed durable product, and until the seventeenth century most western European states in principle regulated its nature through sumptuary laws. Early modern society invested clothing with great significance, and rich dress was a visible mark of standing in the rigid hierarchy of traditional society. Thus a decree of the king of France in 1514 expressly linked aristocracy with dress by "prohibiting absolutely categorically all persons, commoners, non-nobles . . . from assuming the title of nobility either in their style or in their clothes."[2] By the same token, law or custom almost universally dictated sober dress for the middle classes, while according distinct costume to certain groups, like guild masters, as a sign of their social station. Religious tradition in both Catholic and Protestant lands reinforced all of this; Scripture, after all, associated materialism with the sins of greed, envy, and gluttony.

In the eighteenth century Europeans challenged established traditions of dress in a veritable revolution that reflected fundamental changes in European society. As population growth narrowed opportunities for many men in craft guilds with their identifying costumes, those men who made their marks in other fields sought to

2. Quoted in Daniel Roche, *The Culture of Clothing: Dress and Fashion in the 'Ancien Régime,'* translated by Jean Birrell (Cambridge: Cambridge University Press, 1994), p. 49.

display their success in distinctive dress. Women, whose role in the world of work outside the home had been closely circumscribed in the wake of the Protestant Reformation, also sought a new form of self-expression in clothing. Thus, probate inventories of the eighteenth century suggest that all social groups, even those with the most limited means, increased both the quantity and quality of the clothes in their wardrobes, reflecting a growing fashion consciousness that led many to reject traditional drab colors like black, brown, and gray and to clothe themselves in bright pastels and prints.

Source 10 affords us an image of these eighteenth-century trends in both the dress and grooming of European men. Several of the men quite obviously have abandoned the drab colors traditionally worn by men of their station; they wear suits of light, probably pastel, colors formerly worn only by aristocrats. Their suits themselves are elaborate, consisting of a coat, a waistcoat worn under the coat, and knee breeches and stockings that were fashioned of expensive fabrics like the rich, embroidered silks and calicoes often employed in waistcoats. Stockings often were made of silk, too, and the men's shoes often carried silver buckles. Such conspicuous consumption of rich materials made a statement about the economic status and social pretensions of men so garbed. No article of clothing, however, made as strong a statement about its wearer as did the wigs portrayed in this image. The wig, usually powdered to a pure

white color, enjoyed a long vogue in both men's and women's grooming in the seventeenth and eighteenth centuries, with monarchs setting the trend. Elizabeth I of England had worn a wig, as had the prematurely bald Louis XIII of France. The wig's popularity had little to do with utility, since it often covered a perfectly fine head of hair; rather, it made a statement about the wealth of its owner. A fine wig, made of human hair, could easily cost more than a fine suit of clothes, and proper professional care only added to its expense. Such a wig, therefore, alerted everyone to the economic and social status of its wearer, and the creator of Source 10 gives us a good sample of the forms wigs might take. But there is more, too, in Source 10. Note the pose and wig of the central figure. What about that figure suggests to you that the artist and some of his contemporaries might have looked askance at the social pretensions evident in such a conspicuous display? Women's costumes and wigs in certain social circles were even more elaborate than those of men, and they were the subject of even more satirical images.

Source 11 presents a table based on research into thousands of eighteenth-century Parisian inventories drawn up at the deaths of property owners, many of whom would have dressed like the men in Source 10. The table presents the average value of Parisian wardrobes and linens (underclothes, including shirts) according to the social status of their owners. The money value of Parisian wardrobes is expressed in the currency of the day, *livres tournois*, and since the buying power of that currency diminished over the course of the eighteenth century, the table also displays the values of clothing in terms of the number of *sétiers* of wheat they represented (in Paris the *sétier* equaled about 40 American gallons). What happened to the value of the wardrobes of all social classes over the period from 1700 to 1789? As in Source 7, calculate the rates of increase in the value of the wardrobes of each social group. What groups experienced the greatest increases in the values of their clothing? Compare the increases of wardrobe value among these groups with that among the privileged nobility. What can you conclude from these developments?

Such an upending of conventions in dress created considerable negative comment, which we sampled in Source 10, because it seemed to erode the established social order. Some thinkers, however, revealed a very modern understanding of the economic implications of the new rage for fashion, asserting that the satisfaction of the public's demand for ever-changing styles in clothing and durable goods created work for thousands of people who, in turn, spent their wages on products and services that created jobs for thousands of others. Such a thinker was Bernard Mandeville (1670–1733), a Dutch-born physician living in London who published a poem in 1705 that provoked great controversy. "The Grumbling Hive: or, Knaves Turn'd Honest" is economic theory presented as an allegory in which a large beehive represents England. In the poem, which is excerpted

in Source 12, Mandeville casts off the weight of tradition and even conventional morality to show how almost any activity can have a desirable economic result. Mandeville later wrote a lengthy explication of the poem in *The Fable of the Bees: or, Private Vices, Publick Benefits*, a work that only increased the controversy surrounding his ideas when the authorities twice charged him with publishing a "public nuisance." How would you describe the economic system portrayed by Mandeville in his poem? What economic role did Mandeville ascribe to the pursuit of fashionable luxury goods that more traditional thinkers would have seen as evidence of greed, envy, pride, and vanity? Why would many early-eighteenth-century readers, especially aristocratic legal and government officials whose wealth was in land and not commerce, reject his ideas? What do you think would be Mandeville's reception by twenty-first-century readers?

Consumers in the late seventeenth and eighteenth centuries also transformed their homes by acquiring many items that improved their lifestyles or demonstrated their material success. The sorts of homes illustrated in Sources 4 and 5 increasingly lodged only the most desperately poor, as growing numbers of people acquired more furniture, like chairs that replaced simple benches and stools and tables that often were quite elaborate in design. In kitchens, cooking implements grew in number, wooden bowls began to give way to earthenware and china thanks to technical improvements in their European manufacture as well as to a flood of Asian imports, and silverware became more common. Decorative items proliferated, too. Curtains became usual fixtures of life, at least in urban areas where the proximity of neighbors required them for privacy. Mirrors, whose price dropped in the late seventeenth century thanks to new techniques in their manufacture, increasingly lent sparkle to the walls of sometimes dank dwellings, just as pictures appeared on walls. Indeed, in the mid-seventeenth-century United Provinces, where perhaps eight hundred master painters were at work, some 3 million paintings, of varying quality, hung on Dutch walls. Timepieces and books also appeared with greater frequency in eighteenth-century households, in part the result of technical developments that lowered their prices. With the acquisition of all these articles, purchasers clearly attempted to define their status; inventories rather consistently show that owners displayed their new purchases in the rooms where they received guests.

Sources 13 and 14 illustrate this transformation with data from household inventories from Britain and regions of the United Provinces that had the sort of market-driven, specialized agriculture that we examined early in this chapter. What items increasingly became standard fixtures of Dutch household life between 1550 and 1750? What items assumed the same role in Britain between 1675 and 1725? In Britain, what areas were the trendsetters in consumer tastes?

Your task in this chapter is to assess the quantitative and qualitative evidence of change in western Europeans' material lives over two centuries. To do this, as we have noted, you first must seek answers in the data to several basic analytical questions. Begin by examining the data in Sources 2, 3, 6, 7, 8, 9, 11, 13, and 14 to ascertain the quantitative extent of change in production and consumption. Next, focus on consumption, seeking to understand through the data how and why it grew. Would farmers practicing subsistence agriculture, for example, have purchased the variety of consumer goods in Source 13? Weren't the purchases of rural Dutchmen facilitated by the cheap Baltic grain that allowed them to pursue the specialized, market-driven agriculture that drew them into the world of urban material culture? Finally, compare the images and texts in Sources 1, 4, 5, 10, and 12 to understand the magnitude of the qualitative change that took place in the material life of Europe. Contrast, for example the bare agricultural existence evident in Sources 1, 4, and 5 with the cosmopolitan group in the coffee house (Source 10) consuming a formerly exotic beverage. Pursuing such analyses, you should be able to answer the central questions of this chapter. What was the material existence of Europeans at the outset of the period? What changes occurred in their existence over time? What were the causes of these changes? What aspects of the modern, global economy can we discern in the period from 1600 to 1800?

Source 1 published in Georges Duby and Armand Wallon, editors, Histoire de la France rurale, vol. 2, L'âge classique, 1340–1789, by Hugues Neveux, Jean Jacquart, and Emmanuel Le Roy Ladurie (Paris: Éditions du Seuil, 1975), p. 184. Original picture source: Réunion des Musées Nationaux/Art Resource, NY.

1. Spring Agricultural Labor, from a Fifteenth-Century French Book of Hours of Jean, Duc de Berry

Source 2 from E. E. Rich and C. H. Wilson, editors, The Cambridge Economic History of Europe, vol. 5, The Economic Organization of Early Modern Europe (New York: Cambridge University Press, 1977), p. 81. Used by permission of Cambridge University Press.

2. Combined Yield Ratios of Wheat, Rye, and Barley, 1600–1820

Period	*Zone I*[a]	*Zone II*[b]	*Zone III*[c]	*Zone IV*[d]
1600–1649	6.7:1	—	4.5:1	4.0:1
1650–1699	9.3	6.2:1	4.1	3.8
1700–1749	—	6.3	4.1	3.5
1750–1799	10.1	7.0	5.1	4.7
1800–1820	11.1	6.2	5.4	—

a. Zone I: England, Low Countries.
b. Zone II: France, Spain, Italy.
c. Zone III: Germany, Switzerland, Scandinavia.
d. Zone IV: Russia, Poland, Czechoslovakia, Hungary.

Source 3 from Jacques Dupâquier, (ed.), Histoire du population française, Vol. 2: de la Renaissance à 1789, p. 208. © *Presses universitaires de France, 1988. Reprinted by permission.*

3. The Effects of Harvest Failure, 1690s

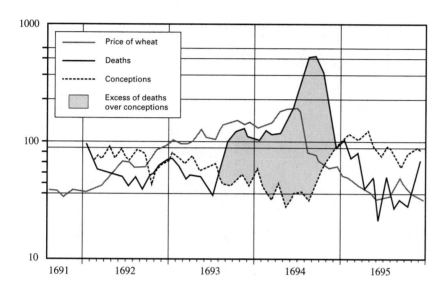

Source 4 published in Fernand Braudel, Civilization and Capitalism, 15th–18th Century, *vol. 1,* The structures of Everyday Life, *translated by Sian Reynolds (New York: Harper and Row, 1979), p. 138. Original picture source: engraving by A. Van Ostade in the Bibliothèque Nationale, Paris. Photograph: Bibliothèque Nationale.*

4. A Meal of Gruel in a Dutch Peasant Family, 1653

Source 5 published in Raffaella Sarti, Europe at Home: Family and Material Culture, *1500–1800 (New Haven, Conn.: Yale University Press, 2002). Original picture source: Sudtiroler Volkskunde Museum, Dietenheim/Teodone (Bolzano/Bozen).*

5. Peasant Kitchen with Open Fire in the South Tyrol

Source 6 from Milja van Tielhof, The "Mother of All Trades": The Baltic Grain Trade in Amsterdam from the Late 16th to the Early 19th Century *(Leiden and Boston: Brill, 2002), p. 43. Reprinted by permission of Brill.*

6. Baltic Grain Exports, 1562–1650

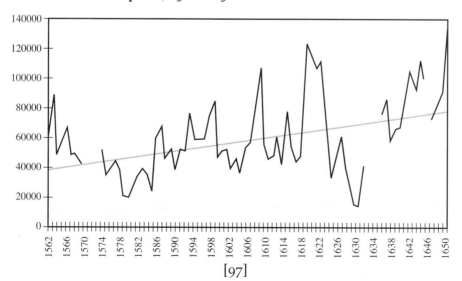

Source 7 from *The Atlantic Slave Trade*, Johannes Postma. Copyright 2003 by Johannes Postma. Reproduced with permission of Greenwood Publishing Group, Inc., Westport, CT.

7. Exports of Slaves from Africa by Nationality of Carrier, 1519–1867 (in thousands)

	Britain	France	Spain	Netherlands	USA & Br. Carib.	Denmark	Portugal & Brazil	All Nations	Annual Volume
1519–1600	2.0						264.1	266.1	3.3
1601–1650	23.0			39.9			439.5	502.4	10.1
1651–1675	115.2	5.9		59.5		0.2	53.7	234.5	9.4
1676–1700	243.3	34.1		97.4		15.4	161.1	551.3	22.1
1701–1725	380.9	106.3		74.5	11.0	16.7	378.3	967.7	38.7
1726–1750	490.5	253.9		76.4	44.5	7.6	405.6	1,278.5	51.2
1751–1775	859.1	321.5	1.0	118.2	89.1	13.4	472.9	1,875.2	75.0
1776–1800	741.3	419.5	8.6	34.2	54.3	30.4	626.2	1,914.5	76.6
1801–1825	257.0	217.9	204.8	1.3	81.1	10.5	871.6	1,644.2	65.8
1826–1850		94.1	279.2				1,247.7	1,621.0	64.8
1851–1867		3.2	23.4				154.2	180.8	10.6
All years	3,112.3	1,456.4	517	501.4	280	94.2	5,074.9	11,036.2	30.4
Percentage	28.2%	13.2%	4.7%	4.5%	2.5%	0.9%	46.0%	100.0%	

8. Sugar Statistics, 1663–1799

8A. Sugar Arriving in France, 1730–1790 (in millions of pounds)

Dates	Average	Maximum	Minimum	Increase over Previous Period
1730–35	59	64	53	
1736–43	86	100	71	+46%
1749–55	114	135	90	+33%
1764–76	138	164	111	+21%
1784–90	178	200	149	+29%

8B. Sugar Imports for Home Consumption: England and Wales, 1663–1799

Years	Sugar: lbs per capita (annual average)
1663, 1669	2.13
1690, 1698–99	4.01
1700–09	5.81
1710–19	8.23
1720–29	12.02
1730–39	14.90
1740–49	12.73
1750–59	16.94
1760–69	20.20
1770–79	23.02
1780–89	21.14
1790–99	24.16

9. Imports of Groceries as a Percentage of the Total Value of Imports into England and Wales, 1559–1800

Year	% in groceries
1559[a]	8.9
1663–9[a]	16.6
1700	16.9
1750	27.6
1772	35.8
1790	28.9
1800	34.9

[a]Calculated from Port of London figures, assuming that London's imports represented 80% of the total for the country, and that 5% of the value of imports in the outports were groceries in 1559 and that 10% were in 1663–1669.

Source 10 by W. Dickinson, "The Coffeehouse Patriots; or News from St. Eustatia"(London, 15 October 1781), stipple; no. 12 of a series (11 3/4 x 14 in.). BM Sat., 5923; HL, print 216/4. Huntington Library, San Marino, California. Published in Brian W. Cowan, The Social Life of Coffee: The Emergence of the British Coffeehouse *(New Haven, Conn.: Yale University Press, 2005), p. 83. Library of Congress.*

10. "The Coffee House Patriots; or News from St. Eustatia," 1781

Source 11 from Daniel Roche. La culture des apparences: Une histoire dn vêtement (XVII–XVIII siècle), *1989, p. 96.*

11. Nominal and Real Value of Wardrobes and Linen in Paris, 1700–1789

	c. 1700		c. 1789	
	Nominal Value (in livres)	Value in Wheat (in sétiers)[a]	Nominal Value (in livres)	Value in Wheat (in sétiers)[b]
Nobilities	1,800	97.6	6,000	254.0
Wage earners	27	1.4	85	3.6
Domestics	55	2.9	293	12.4
Artisans and shopkeepers	344	18.5	587	24.8
Office-holders, commoners and the professions	148	7.9	694	29.2
Total	2,374	128.3	7,659	324.0

[a]Calculated on the basis of the decennial average price in the Paris market, 1695–1704; one *sétier* of corn = 18.61 *livres.*

[b]Calculated on the basis of the decennial average price in the Paris market, 1780–9; one *sétier* of the corn = 23.61 *livres.*

Source 12 from Bernard Mandeville. The Fable of the Bees; or, Private Vices, Publick Benefits, *edited by F. B. Kaye, 2 vols. (Oxford: Clarendon Press, 1924), 1:17–20, 25–26.*

12. Bernard Mandeville, "The Grumbling Hive: or, Knaves Turn'd Honest," 1705

Spacious Hive well stockt with Bees,
That liv'd in Luxury and Ease;
And yet as fam'd for Laws and Arms,
As yielding large and early Swarms;
Was counted the great Nursery
Of Sciences and Industry.
No Bees had better Government,
More Fickleness, or less Content:
They were not Slaves to Tyranny,
Nor rul'd by wild *Democracy;*
But Kings, that could not wrong, because
Their Power was circumscrib'd by Laws.

THESE Insects liv'd like Men, and all
Our Actions they perform'd in small:

They did whatever's done in Town,
And what belongs to Sword or Gown:
Tho' th' Artful Works, by nimble Slight
Of minute Limbs, 'scap'd Human Sight;
Yet we've no Engines, Labourers,
Ships, Castles, Arms, Artificers,
Craft, Science, Shop, or Instrument,
But they had an Equivalent:
Which, since their Language is unknown,
Must be call'd, as we do our own. . . .

VAST Numbers throng'd the fruitful Hive;
Yet those vast Numbers made 'em thrive;
Millions endeavoring to supply
Each other's Lust and Vanity;
While other Millions were employ'd,
To see their Handy-works destory'd;
They furnish'd half the Universe;
Yet had more Work than Labourers.
Some with vast Stocks, and little Pains,
Jump'd into Business of great Gains;
And some were damn'd to Sythes and Spades,
And all those hard laborious Trades;
Where willing Wretches daily sweat,
And wear out Strength and Limbs to eat:
(*A*.)[3] While others follow'd Mysteries,
To which few Folks bind 'Prentices;[4]
That want no Stock, but that of Brass,[5]
And may set up without a Cross;[6]
As Sharpers,[7] Parasites, Pimps, Players,
Pick-pockets, Coiners, Quacks, South-sayers,[8]
And all those, that in Enmity,
With downright Working, cunningly
Convert to their own Use the Labour
Of their good-natur'd heedless Neighbour.

3. Letters refer to sections of the author's explication of the poem in *The Fable of the Bees: or, Private Vices, Publick Benefits*, which is not excerpted here.

4. **'Prentices:** apprentices.

5. **Brass:** a largely archaic term meaning "nerve," "brashness," or "gall."

6. **Cross:** a small coin.

7. **Sharper:** a swindler or a professional gambler.

8. **South-sayers:** an archaic spelling of *soothsayer*, that is, someone who professes to be able to predict the future, usually for a fee.

(B.) These were call'd Knaves, but bar the Name,
The grave Industrious were the same:
All Trades and Places knew some Cheat,
No Calling was without Deceit. . . .

   (1.) THE ROOT OF EVIL, Avarice,
That damn'd ill-natur'd baneful Vice,
Was Slave to Prodigality,
(K.)That noble Sin; (L.) whilst Luxury
Employ'd a Million of the Poor,
(M.)And odious Pride a Million more:
(N.) Envy it self, and Vanity,
Were Ministers of Industry;
Their darling Folly, Fickleness,
In Diet, Furniture and Dress,
That strange ridic'lous Vice, was made
The very Wheel that turn'd the Trade.
Their Laws and Clothes were equally
Objects of Mutability;
For, what was well done for a time,
In half a Year became a Crime;
Yet while they alter'd thus their Laws,
Still finding and correcting flaws,
They mended by Inconstancy
Faults, which no Prudence could foresee.

   THUS Vice nurs'd Ingenuity,
Which join'd with Time and Industry,
Had carry'd Life's Conveniencies,
(O.) Its real Pleasures, Comforts, Ease,
(P.) To such a Height, the very Poor
Liv'd better than the Rich before,
And nothing could be added more. . . .

Source 13 from Jan de Vries. The Dutch Rural Economy in the Golden Age, 1500–1700 *(New Haven, Conn.: Yale University Press, 1974), p. 219. Copyright © 1974. Reprinted by permission of the publisher, Yale University Press.*

13. Percentage of Rural Households Possessing Certain Consumer Goods, 1550–1750

Region	Period	Number of Inventories[a]	Books	Clocks	Mirrors	Silver
Hennaarderadeel	1550–62	42	9.5	0	9.5	23.7
Leeuwarderadeel	1566–74	40	2.5	0	7.5	2.5
Leeuwarderadeel	1583–99	64	3.1	0	18.7	14.6
Idaarderadeel	1611–23	20	5.0	0	15.0	—
Leeuwarderadeel and Wonscradeel	1616–41	83	29.0	0	53.0	36.0
Hennaarderadeel	1646–54	40	22.5	0	95.0	67.5
Barradeel	1651–61	21	38.0	0	—	38.0
Woerden area	1651–61	21	10.0	0	38.0	33.0
Leeuwarderadeel	1677–86	50	32.0	2.0	86.0	46.0
Idaarderadeel	1676–1702	26	19.0	—	46.0	31.0
Barradeel	1679–92	15	53.0	—	—	53.0
Leeuwarderadeel	1711–50	49	55.7	70.5	94.0	63.2

[a]Occasionally, omissions in the sources require that certain inventories be excluded in the calculation of the above averages.

Source 14 from Lorna Weatherill, Consumer Behaviour and Material Culture in Britain, 1660–1760 p. 88, published by Routledge. Copyright © 1998. Reprinted by permission of Thomson Publishing Services, on behalf of Taylor & Francis Books (UK), and the author.

14. Changing Frequencies of Ownership of Selected Goods in Towns and Country Areas, 1675–1725

Saucepans (%)

	1675	1685	1695	1705	1715	1725
London	11	36	43	57	55	73
Major town	3	3	8	10	13	35
Other town	2	7	5	8	31	37
Rural/village	1	2	5	5	9	12

Earthenware (%)

	1675	1685	1695	1705	1715	1725
London	14	19	33	52	59	75
Major town	37	26	39	44	54	74
Other town	36	38	35	26	54	74
Rural/village	26	26	34	34	43	51

Books (%)

	1675	1685	1695	1705	1715	1725
London	18	17	19	41	34	56
Major town	23	23	16	13	23	30
Other town	18	22	24	23	23	42
Rural/village	18	18	16	16	17	13

Clocks (%)

	1675	1685	1695	1705	1715	1725
London	11	15	19	24	52	51
Major town	7	3	8	28	33	26
Other town	17	16	19	15	31	43
Rural/village	8	8	13	19	29	31

Pictures (%)

	1675	1685	1695	1705	1715	1725
London	9	26	21	57	60	60
Major town	30	20	32	49	60	48
Other town	21	24	21	6	43	47
Rural/village	2	3	3	5	9	10

Looking Glasses (%)

	1675	1685	1695	1705	1715	1725
London	58	74	79	81	91	80
Major town	50	59	47	67	62	61
Other town	36	45	49	51	69	74
Rural/village	11	16	20	25	30	28

Window Curtains (%)

	1675	1685	1695	1705	1715	1725
London	23	30	43	39	60	62
Major town	20	20	13	31	33	52
Other town	6	13	17	11	29	26
Rural/village	4	5	5	6	7	10

China (%)

	1675	1685	1695	1705	1715	1725
London	0	0	0	7	33	35
Major town	0	0	11	13	13	9
Other town	0	7	8	8	17	11
Rural/village	0	1	1	2	2	4

Utensils for Hot Drinks (%)

	1675	1685	1695	1705	1715	1725
London	0	0	2	7	22	60
Major town	0	0	3	3	12	22
Other town	0	0	2	0	17	16
Rural/village	0	0	0	1	3	6

QUESTIONS TO CONSIDER

Each of the sources that you considered in this chapter may be read like a piece of a puzzle that, when assembled with other pieces, presents a picture of the material life of the vast majority of Europeans in the seventeenth and eighteenth centuries. The assembled pieces will also reveal a Europe increasingly engaged with the world beyond its shores. Let us now begin to fit those pieces together.

Consider first the basic food supplies available to Europeans. How did agricultural productivity prior to the eighteenth century compare to that of our own era? What sort of diet did it provide the majority of Europeans? Why would you not be surprised to learn that modern scientists have found that nutritionally based ailments like rickets abounded among these people? How did reliance on rather primitive agricultural techniques leave Europeans vulnerable to crises like that in Amiens? How did contact with a world beyond western Europe begin to change this diet? What did cheap, Baltic wheat permit Dutch farmers to do? What new crops did Europeans discover in the New World? How did the European diet become more varied with new, imported beverages and sugar by the eighteenth century? Some historians argue that Europeans gained these products, and eventually many others, at tremendous cost to non-Western peoples. What validity, if any, do you see in their point of view?

Next, let us move beyond diet to the durable goods that are part of everyday life: clothing, furniture, household decorations, and the like. Certainly, Sources 4 and 5 present us with striking examples of families in the United Provinces and Austria living with the barest necessities. Do you see in either source any consumer articles beyond the barest necessities? Next, consult the records of material possessions in Sources 11, 13, and 14. What became of the wardrobe of even the humblest Parisian between 1700 and 1789? What sort of possessions entered Dutch and English households between 1550 and 1725? Considering that many inventories reported that buyers placed their new acquisitions in the "public" areas of their homes, why do you think some people purchased so many things beyond the bare necessities?

Finally, consider the new European cosmopolitanism revealed by these changes. What sort of transformation did this new age of consumption reveal in Europe? What can you read into the fact that, by the eighteenth century, many Europeans no longer worried about their next meal, but instead regarded formerly exotic commodities like coffee, tea, and sugar as daily necessities? What significance might you find in men gathering in coffee houses to learn the news of trade and conflicts in far corners of the non-European world? Why might you conclude that Europe realized the full impact of the discoveries of the sixteenth century in the seventeenth and eighteenth centuries by becoming part of a global community and economy?

As you form answers to these questions that transcend the lessons of the individual pieces of evidence and that lead you to general conclusions, you should be on your way to putting together the pieces of the puzzle. As you do so, you should be able to answer this chapter's fundamental questions. What was the material existence of Europeans at the outset of the period? What changes occurred in their existence over time? What were the causes of these changes? What aspects of the modern, global economy can we discern in the period from 1600 to 1800?

EPILOGUE

At first glance, our sources may seem to portray a consumer society far removed from our own, in which crowds sometimes line up for the opportunity to be among the first to acquire some new electronic wonder. How significant, we may think, was the development of a Western taste for sugar, coffee, or tea, or the increasing purchases of mirrors and clocks? The implications of the developments that we have traced, nonetheless, are tremendous, because they still shape our world today.

We have examined the transformation of a world with a largely static economy, widespread privation, and a rigidly hierarchical society whose outlook was still defined by traditional religious precepts into something quite

new. By the late eighteenth century the West was part of a global economy defined and driven by the spending of citizens who in part expressed their individuality in the patterns of their consumption. Indeed, in an economic sense, the era was even more creative than the present chapter suggests. We have concentrated, after all, only on the commodities of consumption. Had we also examined the means by which businesses satisfied consumer desires, we would have found that, in countries like Britain and the United Provinces, a retail distribution network had emerged in the towns and cities that presaged that of the the modern world. At first much distribution was concentrated in the hands of merchants whom the English called *mercers*, retailers who sold a little bit of everything, dry goods as well as foodstuffs. These and more specialized merchants, moreover, were numerous; there were more shops per capita in Britain in 1750 than there were a century later, and their proprietors and those whose wares they sold understood modern marketing principles. Like their twenty-first-century counterparts, eighteenth-century manufacturers and merchants realized that they could expand consumer demand with various strategies. Manufacturers like Josiah Wedgwood, a pioneering English dinnerware manufacturer, began to track new trends in consumer taste so that he could increase his firm's sales by catering to them. At the retail level, merchants soon developed special pricing strategies to increase sales, such as the promotion of a "loss leader," that is, a product intentionally priced below the retailer's own cost in order to attract buyers, who might then be expected to purchase other, undiscounted goods. Shopkeepers also encouraged purchases by offering credit, advertising their shops with elaborate signs, and publicizing their wares in newspapers. In addition, fashion magazines, appearing in France as early as the 1670s, generated consumer interest in new clothing styles.

All of these factors contributed by the eighteenth century to a growing demand for consumer articles with which purchasers sought to establish their identity and status. This suggests that there existed tremendous demand for a plethora of consumer goods well before the industrial processes of mass production emerged in the Industrial Revolution that began in Britain after about 1750. In a sense, the growth of consumer consumption, and the concomitant development of distribution networks for goods, prepared the way for marketing and consumption on an even larger scale once the factory system that we will examine in Chapter 6 developed. The factory would transform merchandising from eighteenth-century mercers' shops first into nineteenth-century department stores and finally into twenty-first-century megastores supplied with wares from around the world.

CHAPTER FIVE

A DAY IN

THE FRENCH REVOLUTION:

JULY 14, 1789

Tuesday, July 14, 1789, dawned cool and cloudy in Paris. Leaden skies threatening heavy rainfall cast little light into the narrow, crowded streets of the capital. But the rain held off until evening, thereby providing the opportunity for events to occur in the city's streets and squares that set off a fundamental change in the political history of France and the West as a whole. When rain finally fell, sending Parisians scurrying home, the forces of King Louis XVI had lost control of the capital, and, ultimately, much more. The French Revolution initiated by the events of July 14 eventually would destroy the royal absolutism that we examined in Chapter 2 and replace it with a government founded on the principle of popular sovereignty, that is, that political authority rests with the people, not the king. We can better understand this revolution if we examine which Parisians took part in the events of July 14 and why they did so.

On that Tuesday, the people of Paris seized the great fortress and prison on the city's eastern edge known as the Bastille. Construction of the Bastille had begun in 1370 as part of the eastern defenses of Paris. The fortress had eight towers, set in walls about 80 feet high and 10 feet thick. Its only entrance was by two drawbridges across a moat that was dry in 1789; by that date the Bastille had been obsolete as a fort for several centuries. Developments in modern artillery had rendered its walls vulnerable, and the growth of Paris meant that the Bastille was no longer on the city's periphery, but instead was surrounded by the streets of the suburb known as the Faubourg Saint-Antoine.

As early as the fifteenth century, the monarchy had confined prisoners in the Bastille, but the systematic use of the old fort as a prison began during the ministry of Cardinal Richelieu in the early seventeenth century. The Bastille confined persons whose offenses were not punishable under the regular criminal laws of France, and received political prisoners held without trial under royal orders known as *lettres de cachet*. Religious dissenters joined the prison's inmates during the reign of Louis XV (1715–1774). The nature of this prison made it a symbol of despotism in the eighteenth century, but such notoriety was little warranted by 1789. Although the Bastille had a capacity for forty-two prisoners in cells, with room for additional inmates in a dungeon that had been unused for twenty years, it held only seven prisoners on July 14, 1789. These seven—four forgers, two noblemen locked away at the behest of their families for immoral behavior, and one murder suspect—hardly seemed victims of royal injustice. Indeed, the monarchy was considering plans to demolish this outdated structure when the Paris crowd captured it.

The origins of the crowd's storming of the Bastille, the first—but not the last—mass action of its kind in Paris during the revolution, may be found in a political and economic crisis that had kept France in turmoil during the preceding thirty months. As a consequence of the costly wars of the eighteenth century and a system of taxation that largely exempted the clergy and nobility from fiscal obligations, the French monarchy faced bankruptcy by 1787.[1] Several finance ministers struggled with the crown's fiscal problems, but all eventually arrived at the same solution:

fundamental financial reform that would tax the Church and the nobility, not simply the commoners.] In proposing such changes, however, the royal ministers encountered constitutional problems. The proposed reforms violated traditional rights of the clergy and nobility, and the king was forced to call for the meeting of a French representative body—the Estates General, which had not met since 1614—to consider reform.[2]

The election campaign for the Estates General stirred up the country, creating expectations of change. Election regulations enfranchised almost all male taxpayers, and these voters did not select a legislature prepared simply to approve tax reform and go home. Some representatives of the clergy and nobility resisted any change. More seriously, the monarchy confronted the defiant members of the Third Estate, representing the commoners, who demanded tax reform and greater political equality. They declared themselves a National Assembly, the rightful representatives of the French people, and then, on June 20, 1789, in their Tennis Court oath, called for a constitution to limit royal power. This defiance of royal authority really had been the first act of revolution.

The king vacillated at first in the face of such defiance but then resolved on

---

1. France's successful intervention in the American War of Independence played no small part in this situation. The American war cost France 2 billion livres, a figure about four times the government's tax receipts in 1788. By that year, interest payments on the government's debts consumed 51 percent of its receipts.

2. Royal failure to call the Estates General was deliberate; the body was an obstacle to royal absolutism.

3. Representatives of the clergy constituted the First Estate of the Estates General; representatives of the nobility made up the Second Estate of what had been traditionally a three-house legislature. In 1789 the king required this traditional style of meeting, which gave great voice to the small minority of the population who were clerics and nobles.

two steps. On June 22, 1789, he signed orders for the movement of troops into the region of Paris and Versailles to regain control of events. Those assigned were largely foreign soldiers (Swiss and German regiments especially) in French service, who presumably would be more willing to use force on civilians than would French soldiers. Such troop movements, however, could not be kept secret. There was growing fear in Versailles and Paris of a royal coup in early July directed against the defiant National Assembly and its supporters in the capital.

The king's second step was the dismissal of Jacques Necker as royal finance minister on July 11, 1789. Popular opinion regarded Necker as a liberal financial genius whose skills kept the government solvent, stabilized financial markets, and kept Paris supplied with food. But he and the ministers associated with him were replaced with officials more fully committed to Louis's impending use of force to reestablish royal authority.

Political events of the preceding months and a rapid rise in bread prices caused by recent bad harvests had heightened tension in Paris even before the king reached this decision. The concurrence of political and

economic unrest already had led to large-scale rioting on April 27–28, 1789, when rumors spread that a wallpaper manufacturer, Reveillon, had advocated reduction of workers' wages.[4] Troops had been needed to restore order in the capital in April. News of Necker's firing reached Paris about 9:00 A.M. on July 12, a Sunday, when the population's release from normal weekday duties favored the spread of rumor and political agitation. One of the agitators, the demagogic Camille Desmoulins, effectively directed the thoughts of many Parisians to action when he said to his listeners at the popular gathering place, the Palais Royal:

Citizens, you know that the Nation had asked for Necker to be retained, and he has been driven out! Could you be more insolently flouted? After such an act they will dare anything, and they may perhaps be planning and preparing a Saint-Bartholomew massacre of patriots for this very night! . . . To arms! To arms![5]

Demonstrations broke out in Paris by the middle of the day on July 12, bolstered by the adherence of the French Guards, a unit charged with keeping order in the city, to the cause of the crowds. By evening, fighting was taking place between demonstrators and units of the foreign troops ordered to Paris by the king, and their commanders withdrew royal forces from the city. Unrest continued through the night without opposition. At about

---

4. Reveillon was one of Paris's largest manufacturers; his wallpaper works employed about 300 persons. He had not, however, precisely advocated a reduction of wages in a speech he gave at his local assembly to elect representatives to the Estates General. On April 23, Reveillon had said that if the price of bread could be reduced, workers' wages would follow, resulting in a lower cost for the goods they produced. Sources vary widely on the human cost of the rioting. Jacques Godechot, *The Taking of the Bastille: July 14, 1789,* trans. Jean Stewart (New York: Scribner's, 1970, p. 147), accepts a figure of 300 dead.

5. Quoted by Godechot, pp. 187–188. **Saint-Bartholomew Massacre:** on August 24, 1572, Catholic forces killed several thousand Protestants all over France during the French wars of religion.

1:00 A.M. on July 13, crowds began to burn the tax stations along the wall surrounding Paris, since the majority of the commoners blamed the tax on goods entering the capital for higher food prices. At 6:00 A.M., crowds attacked a monastery where they believed food was stored.

As disorder grew in the capital, on the morning of July 13, the men who had served as electors of the Parisian deputies to the Estates General assembled at the Paris city hall and implemented two important decisions.[6] First, they constituted a committee from their ranks to administer the city, in effect creating a revolutionary municipal government; second, they called for the founding of a "civic militia." The militia's stated purpose was to keep order in the capital, but the formation of such an armed force, obeying the orders of the electors rather than the king, was another revolutionary act.

The creation of the militia, soon to be called the *National Guard,* required arms, and the search for guns and ammunition became the next object of crowd action. On the morning of

6. Rules for Estates General elections in Paris required that voters in each of the city's sixty electoral districts select electors, who in turn would vote for representatives to the Estates General.

July 14, a crowd estimated at 80,000 persons forced its way into the *Invalides,* an old soldiers' home/barracks, and seized all of the 32,000 muskets stored there. Muskets were of little value without gunpowder and musket balls, however, and the crowd found few of these commodities at the Invalides. They surged on that morning to the Bastille, to which royal officers earlier had transferred 250 barrels of powder for safekeeping as Paris grew restive. Defending the fortress against a growing crowd were eighty-two *invalides* (older or partially disabled soldiers fit only for garrison duty) and thirty-two soldiers of the Swiss regiments in French service. After two deputations from the crowd failed to secure the commander's surrender, the attack began around 1:30 P.M. By 5:00 P.M. the Bastille and its supplies had fallen to the crowd.

You now have a summary of what the crowd did on July 14, 1789. Such mass actions were common in early modern Europe. Your task in this chapter is to analyze the evidence presented here to answer basic questions about the crowd. Why were the people of Paris angry in mid-July 1789? How were Parisians mobilized for action? Who made up the crowd that stormed the Bastille?

SOURCES AND METHOD

This chapter presents a variety of evidence to assist you in answering the basic questions about the atmosphere in Paris in July 1789 that produced the attack on the Bastille. Source 1 is a selection by an eighteenth-century attorney, political theorist, and journalist, Simon-Nicolas-Henri Linguet (1736–1794). Unlike *philosophes* (see Chapter 3), who advocated limits on royal power, Linguet believed that modern society was characterized by a conflict pitting the wealthy and powerful against the poor and powerless, and he called for a stronger monarchy to protect the rights of the masses against the greed and pretensions of the rich and influential. This point of view led Linguet to persistently criticize persons and institutions of influence in prerevolutionary France, especially the *parlements*, the powerful law courts, dominated by aristocratic judges, that claimed the right to block the implementation of royal decrees. Such criticism earned Linguet powerful enemies who secured his disbarment by the Parlement of Paris and his dismissal as editor of a prominent French journal. As a result, he left France and eventually settled in London, where he published a political journal that continued his criticism from 1777 to 1788. When Linguet returned to France in 1780 to deal with business aspects of his journal, however, his enemies secured his arrest on charges of criminal libel under a *letter de cachet*. The authorities held Linguet, without trial and largely in solitary confinement, in the Bastille from September 1780 until May 1782. When finally freed, Linguet returned to London and resumed publication of his journal, in which he first published the *Memoires* of his captivity that constitute Source 1. This source represents your first opportunity to analyze the work of a journalist, and on one level the meaning and value of this source may seem obvious: this is a journalist's firsthand account of his experiences. But the critical historian must analyze such sources on other levels to ascertain their full meaning. What sort of language did this journalist use to express his ideas, and most importantly, how many people encountered his writings and perhaps were influenced by them?

One of the foremost historians of eighteenth-century French journalism noted that "more than any other prerevolutionary writer, Linguet demonstrated the power of journalism to move and stir readers, to appeal to their passions as well as their minds."[7] Linguet made early use of a technique well known to modern journalists, that of employing language chosen for its shock effect, and thus its ability to draw readers' attention. Linguet's influence rested on more that his writing style, however. Historians identify the eighteenth century as a period marked by a rapidly expanding "public sphere" in which the middle class, growing in numbers as well as literacy, read more widely and discussed ideas and events in new venues of socialization like coffee houses (see Chapter 4). Paris was one of the centers of such discourse, because in the eighteenth century it had free elementary schools, at least for boys, in every parish, and therefore a very high literacy rate. Thus many Parisians read a wide variety of pamphlets and newspapers, while even more listened to public readings and discussions of such sources of news and opinion in cafés and other places.

7. Jeremy Popkin, "The Prerevolutionary Origins of Political Journalism," in Jack R. Censer, ed., *The French Revolution in Intellectual History* (Chicago: Borsey Press, 1989), p. 127.

Linguet's journal took on added general significance in such a city because its press runs were extraordinarily large; in an age in which few French newspapers printed more than 10,000 copies, Linguet's journal counted 20,000 subscribers. Moreover, the specific issue in which Linguet printed his *Memoires* must have generated considerable Parisian attention because it addressed a subject of proven interest in Paris, the Bastille. Since the late seventeenth century French readers had consumed lurid tales of the royal prison's brutal treatment of its inmates, including a man in an iron mask. As a consequence, the Bastille had come to be a symbol to many of the nature of royal justice. What did Linguet suggest was the cause of confinement for prisoners of state like him? How did conditions of his confinement contradict the thought of enlightened, eighteenth-century jurists like Cesare Bonnesana, the marquis of Beccaria (1738–1794), who condemned the confinement of suspects without benefit of trial? How did Linguet's language, particularly that conveying irony, strengthen his negative characterization of the Bastille? What conclusions about royal justice must Parisians have drawn from Linguet's account and tales like his?

The next pieces of evidence you encounter in the chapter are visual. You already have analyzed such sources in Chapter 2, and you should examine the pictures presented in this chapter to reconstruct the physical setting for the events of 1789. In analyzing the evidence, your objective should be to derive answers to this question: What features of the physical layout of Paris were conducive to the spread of rumors and agitation?

Source 2 offers a view of the Palais Royal, the property of the Duke of Orléans, a member of the royal family. On the grounds of this palace, the duke developed a commercial and entertainment area lined with shops and cafés. The palace and its grounds were outside of police jurisdiction because they belonged to the duke and so attracted political agitators, prostitutes, and criminals such as pickpockets. Much of the politically active population of Paris would have been familiar with the grounds of the Palais Royal. What role might such a site have played on July 14, 1789? Why might the significance of the Palais Royal for the political climate of 1789 have been so great that a few historians have seen it as evidence of a plot by its owner to foment a revolution that might benefit his own political ambitions?

Source 3 shows the rue du Fer-à-Moulin, a street typical of many of those of eighteenth-century Paris at the time of the Revolution. In 1789 much of the Parisian population of about 600,000 still lived in such streets, crowded inside the boundaries set by the city's former medieval fortifications. To accommodate this dense population, residential buildings were six or seven stories high and crowded, with an average of almost thirty residents in each one. Try to imagine life in these buildings and streets. Do you think people would have spent a great deal of time in the streets? Why? What sorts of exchanges of information might have occurred in streets like these?

Source 4 introduces a new form of evidence, architectural drawings of residential buildings, to enhance your understanding of the physical aspect of Paris in 1789. The floor plan for 18, rue Contrescarpe is of a house very near the Bastille. Such multi-storied structures typically had a ground floor that was rented out to a merchant or craftsman who maintained a shop that opened on the street. A craftsman might also have rented a workshop behind the shop on the ground floor. Access to the residential upper floors was through the gate opening onto the street at the end of the passage leading to the interior courtyard. Each building's numerous residents would cross the courtyard daily going in and out or fetching water from the well. All would have needed to mount the staircase to rooms whose prices decreased as the number of steps separating them from the ground increased. As a consequence of this pricing procedure, a master craftsman might occupy a large apartment on the first floor up these stairs; his employees, the tiny rooms in the attic. Reflect on this living situation. How might news and rumor have spread in such a setting? How might a crowd be mobilized there? Why might the economic power of an employer and his residential proximity to his workers in such buildings permit an employer who was committed to a political cause to draw his workers along with him?

This chapter also presents quantitative data in the form of graphs, tables, and a map. The information presented here is essential to understanding which social groups participated in the events of July 14, 1789, and why. The majority of pre-nineteenth-century Europeans left few conventional written records, like letters and diaries, that might allow historians to interpret their thought. Historians' ingenuity, however, has allowed them to understand these people through other sources. In constructing the data sets on food prices in this chapter, historians drew on a rich source for understanding seventeenth- and eighteenth-century life. Because early modern governments recognized a correlation between high food prices during periods of dearth on one hand and riots and other acts of public disorder on the other, they kept close watch on such prices. Their effort generated excellent records of food prices, especially of the cost of wheat, the essential ingredient for the bread that was the staple of early modern diets. Look at the graphs numbered 5 and 6 among the evidence for this chapter. Although the two researchers used slightly different measures of wheat in assembling their data, you are presented with significant price trends: Long-term trends in wheat prices for France as a whole are in Source 5 and short-term trends for Paris alone are in Source 6. Analyze the price trends presented here. Between the 1730s and mid-1780s, the highest prices were the result of failed harvests in the early 1770s. During that period, the rural poor in some regions of the country resorted at times to eating boiled grass or acorns when bread became too scarce and costly. The high food prices resulting from harvest failures also generated popular fear that the elevated cost of food was the result not of dearth, but of speculators unscrupulously hoarding large quantities of grain to artificially drive up prices and increase their own profits. Such fears, indeed, earlier had caused widespread rioting in the Paris region in the 1770s. How did prices in 1789 in Paris and France compare with those of the 1770s? Imagine yourself a Frenchman aged forty in 1789. What would your memory of food prices be? How would those of 1789 strike you? Consult Source 7, a table. How would price trends in 1788–1789 have affected your family's income? Reflect, too, on the fact that women did their families' marketing in the eighteenth century. Why would you not be surprised to find women protesting food prices and other issues? Why might you have been concerned about the preservation of order in Paris in July 1789 if you had been a police official?

Historians drew on a second kind of source—tax data—in formulating the map presenting the composition of the various Paris sections by income (Source 8). These data are your basis for understanding the economic structure of Paris's population and, most important for our purposes, the economic background of the crowd members who stormed the Bastille. For centuries, historians and government officials held that the lowest and most criminal elements comprised these crowds. Indeed, eighteenth-century French police records use a phrase that may be translated as "the

scum of the people" in describing the composition of crowds. What do we find about the Bastille crowd, however? Notice that the map in Source 8 provides data on the taxes paid by residents of the forty-eight sections into which early revolutionary Paris was divided. From those data we may judge each section's relative wealth because, of course, wealthier citizens paid more taxes. To completely analyze the data you need to know that "active" citizens under the 1791 constitution were adult males who could vote by virtue of paying taxes worth three days' labor (nationally, 41 percent of citizens did not meet this minimum standard). "Eligible" citizens were "active" citizens qualified for administrative office by paying taxes worth at least ten days' labor. Using this information, ascertain from the table in Source 8 the sections of Paris that housed those who made up the Bastille crowd. Why do you think that the police would have erred had they characterized that crowd in their usual manner?

Other data might also allow historians further to identify the members of the crowd, if not by name, at least by social group. Police records of those arrested in unsuccessful rebellions that provide personal data on participants have been systematically exploited only recently by historians. But the Bastille attack began a successful revolution, and the crowd members became heroes and heroines who received the title *Vainqueurs de la Bastille* ("Conquerors of the Bastille") and state pensions if they had been disabled in the attack. The list of these persons is one among

[117]

many functions of the administrative and fiscal record keeping of a modern state, but it provides you, in the table that is Source 9, with an occupational listing of the Bastille's conquerors. From a distance of two hundred years, it is probably impossible to reconstruct the precise income of each conqueror. Moreover, each trade, like the cabinetmaking common in the Faubourg Saint-Antoine, would have shown a variety of incomes within the ranks of its practitioners—another frustration. We do know, however, that in skilled trades the self-employed tended to be masters of their trades and therefore were probably more affluent than journeymen wage earners or apprentices employed by others. Examine the table. What were the most common trades of the Bastille's attackers? Who predominated, wage earners or the self-employed? What conclusion do you draw from the fact that most of the conquerors had definite trades and were not unskilled or poor?

Written sources can supplement quantitative evidence and supply historians with information on public opinion in Paris during the month of July 1789. This chapter presents several types of such evidence, which you have not previously analyzed. Source 10 is another part of the massive bureaucratic record generated by modern states, in this case a petition addressed to the French national legislature by a woman seeking compensation for herself and her husband as conquerors of the Bastille. In reading her petition, ask yourself how her account further contributes to your knowledge of the crowd's composition. Remember that

the division of household labor in the eighteenth century gave housewives the major marketing responsibility. Why might women be involved in crowd actions in 1789 or at other points in the revolution, even though late-eighteenth-century political practice deprived them of the vote?

Next you will read a travel account, a literary form very common in the early modern period. Europe's curiosity about the outside world grew with the Age of Exploration during the sixteenth century, and a large reading audience developed for accounts by European travelers. The usefulness of such works in reconstructing a society varies, however, according to the intelligence and observational skills of their authors. In the case of Arthur Young, whose Paris report is excerpted as Source 11, we have the work of a master of the travel genre.

Arthur Young (1741–1820) was a wealthy and educated Englishman who sought out and publicized the latest agricultural techniques. Before visiting France to examine French farming, a journey that produced the selection here, Young, who was well known as an agricultural expert and as an economist, published descriptions of his travels through England, Wales, and Ireland. The record of his travels in France is valuable, therefore, for several reasons. Young's fame and his knowledge of the French language gained him access to many prominent Frenchmen. The observational skills he had honed on earlier trips allowed him quickly to appreciate the economic problems of France and to assess public reaction to them. Finally, as luck would have it, his journey took him through France in the years 1787, 1788, and 1789, so that he was present in the country during the early days of the revolution. His account, consequently, is extremely useful in understanding the events of the year 1789. Young tells us a great deal about modern politics and the spread of revolution. Thanks to the parish schools, the population of Paris was much more literate than the rural population of France. How did Young find this literacy affecting politics in the capital? How did political news spread to provincial cities like Metz? Do you find in any of this description a political life that in some ways presages that of our modern age? Recall, too, the fears many Frenchmen had about having adequate food supplies in the eighteenth century. Why did Young believe that troop movements would renew such fears?

The third kind of written evidence presented in this chapter is diplomatic correspondence. The letters of ambassadors to their home governments long have been useful sources for historians. Their utility derives from the very functions of ambassadors. Since the posting of the first permanent ambassadors by Italian Renaissance states, these officials performed several roles. First, they represented their country's interests to foreign courts, and thus we can identify the policies of their states in ambassadors' correspondence with

their superiors. Additionally, from their earliest days ambassadors kept their governments informed of conditions in their host countries that might affect international relations; they functioned almost like spies, gathering all available information for use by their governments. In this regard, the British ambassador's reports to his superiors in the Foreign Office are extremely important. In 1789 France was a major power that had long been in conflict with England and one most influential in achieving American victory over the English in the War of Independence. As a result, information on political events in France was crucial to English policymakers, and their ambassador supplied detailed reports on France. As with all sources, however, the historian must ap-proach such correspondence with a critical eye. Was the ambassador writing from firsthand knowledge of events? Is his information verified by other sources? How would you assess the reliability of the Duke of Dorset, the English ambassador to France, whose letters are presented as Source 12? What do they tell you about events in Paris?

All these sources should fit together in your mind like the pieces of a puzzle, allowing you to reconstruct the state of public opinion in Paris in July 1789, to determine how crowds were mobilized, and to understand who stormed the Bastille on July 14.

THE EVIDENCE ·

Source 1 from Simon-Nicolas-Henri Linguet, Mémoires sur al Bastille, et la détention de l'auteur dans ce château royal depuis le 20 Septembre 1780 jusqu'au 19 mai 1782 *(London: Thomas Spilsbury, 1783), pp. 53bis, 54bis, 67, 96. Translated by Julius R. Ruff.*

1. The Bastile as a Symbol: The *Mémoires* of Simon-Nicolas-Henri Linguet, 1783

The cells are all located in towers whose walls are thirty feet thick at their bases and at least twelve feet thick at their upper reaches. Each cell has a single air hole piercing this wall, but each of these is covered by three iron grates, one on the inside of the wall, one in its center, and the third on its outer side. The bars cross each . . . and thanks to the ingenuity of their designer, the bars of each grate align precisely with the openings in the others, so that there is only a two-inch wide opening for the inmate to see beyond the wall.

Formerly each of these vault-like cells had three or four of these small openings . . . but since this multiplicity of small windows aided the circulation of air, diminished humidity, and prevented infectious disease, etc., a humane warden had all but one per cell closed up. On nice days, that remaining openings admits just enough light to allow one to better discern the gloom.

Thus, in winter, these cells are iceboxes because they are lofty enough for the cold to pervade them, while in summer they are suffocating, humid ovens because the thickness of the walls prevents the heat from ever drying them out. . . .

In such an atmosphere the prisoner passes his days, and many of his nights, pressed against the interior grate that I have described . . . in order to draw a bit of fresh air and to see a little daylight. . . .

The prisoner of state in the Bastille, that is to say, a man who displeased a minister, a clerk, or one of their valets, is delivered without resources of any kind . . . to absolute silence . . . , to a nonexistence more cruel than death. . . . There he wears himself out fruitlessly begging for legal redress, notification of the charges against him, the intervention of his friends. He utters his prayers, laments, and supplications in vain, and his jailers tell him so as the only knowledge that they share with him. . . .

Thus I was held without charges, trial and the right to confront the evidence against me, or verdict of guilt. . . . Is this not the utmost abuse of power and one of the greatest proofs of the inhumanity against citizens practiced in the Bastille?

Source 2 from Musée Carnavalet, Paris. © Photothèque des Musées de la Ville de Paris.

2. Henri Monnier, *The Palais Royal*

Source 4 adapted from David Garrioch, Neighborhood and Community in Paris, 1740–1790 (New York: Cambridge University Press, 1986), p. 222. Reprinted by permission.

4. Plan of a Typical Parisian Residential Building, 18, Rue Contrescarpe, Faubourg St.-Antoine

Source 3 from Musée Carnavalet, Paris. © Photothèque des Musées de la Ville de Paris.

3. Rue du Fer-à-Moulin, 1870

Source 5 adapted from Ernest Labrousse, Ruggiero Romano, and F.-G. Dreyfus, Le prix du froment en France au temps de la monnaie stable (1726–1913) *(Paris: Ecole des Hautes Études en Sciences Sociales, 1970), p. xiv.*

5. Average Price of a Hectoliter (100 liters) of Wheat in France, 1730–1790

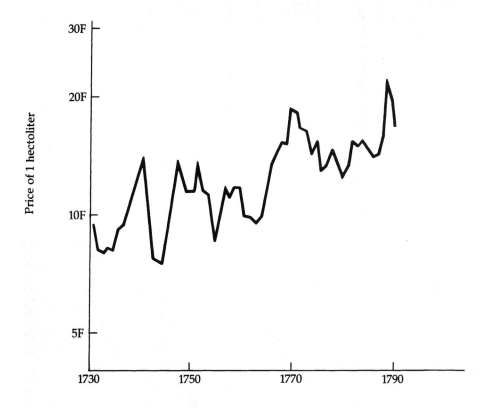

Source 6 from Jacques Godechot, The Taking of the Bastille, July 14, 1789 *(New York: Scribner's, 1970), p. 13. Used by permission.*

6. Price of 100 Kilograms of Wheat in Paris, 1770–1790

Source 7 from George Rudé, "Prices, Wages and Popular Movements in Paris During the French Revolution," Economic History Review, *2nd ser., vol. 6 (1953), p. 248. Used by permision of Basil Blackwell Ltd.*

7. Bread and the Wage Earner's Budget[a]

Occupation	Effective Daily Wage in Sous (s)[b]	Expenditure on Bread as Percentage of Income with Bread at	
		9s (Aug 1788)	14½s (Feb–July 1789)
Laborer in Reveillon wallpaper works	15	60	97
Builder's laborer	18	50	80
Journeyman mason	24	37	60
Journeyman, locksmith, carpenter, etc.	30	30	48
Sculptor, goldsmith	60	15	24

[a]The price of the 4-pound loaf consumed daily by a workingman and his family as the main element in their diet.
[b]"Effective" wage represents the daily wage adjusted for 111 days of nonwork per calendar year for religious observation, etc.

Source 8 map from Marcel Reinhard, Nouvelle histoire de Paris: La Révolution *(Paris: Distributed by Hachette for the Association pour la publication d'une Histoire de Paris, 1971), pp. 66–67. Key and table from George Rudé,* The Crowd in the French Revolution *(New York: Oxford University Press, 1959), pp. 244–245. Copyright © 1959. Used by permission of Oxford University Press.*

8. Map of Paris by Economic Circumstances of Residents, 1790

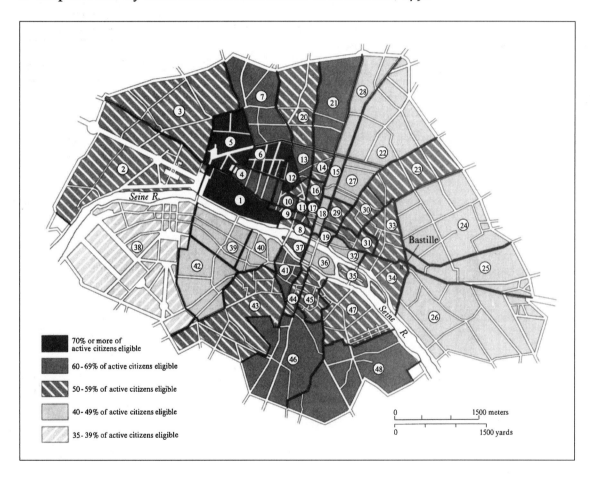

Section[a]	Bastille July[b]	Section	Bastille July	Section	Bastille July
1. Tuileries	2	17. Marché des Innocents	6	34. Arsenal	23
2. Champs Élysées	—	18. Lombards	5	35. Île Saint-Louis	—
3. Roule	2	19. Arcis	3	36. Notre Dame	1
4. Palais Royal	1	20. Faubourg Montmartre	—	37. Henri IV	2
5. Vendôme	1	21. Poissonière	1	38. Invalides	5
6. Bibliothèque	2	22. Bondy	4	39. Fontaine de Grenelle	2
7. Grange Batelière	2	23. Temple	9	40. Quatre Nations	6
8. Louvre	1	24. Popincour	87	41. Théâtre Français	6
9. Oratoire	2	25. Montreuil	139	42. Croix Rouge	2
10. Halle au Blé	6	26. Quinze Vingts	193	43. Luxembourg	7
11. Postes	4	27. Gravilliers	3	44. Thermes de Julien	3
12. Louis XIV	—	28. Faubourg St. Denis	1	45. Sainte-Geneviève	10
13. Fontaine Montmorency	—	29. Beaubourg	5	46. Observatoire	3
14. Bonne Nouvelle	—	30. Enfants Rouges	2	47. Jardin des Plantes	3
15. Ponceau	3	31. Roi de Sicile	3	48. Gobelins Outside Paris	3
16. Mauconseil	4	32. Hôtel de Ville	18		
		33. Place Royale	17	*Total*	602

[a]Names of sections are as in 1790–1791.
[b]Numbers arrested, killed, wounded, or participated in the attack on the Bastille.

Source 9 from George Rudé, The Crowd in the French Revolution *(New York: Oxford University Press, 1959), pp. 246–248. Copyright © 1959. Used by permission of Oxford University Press.*

9. Trades of the Bastille Insurgents, 1789

Trade	Participants (no.)	Trade	Participants (no.)	Trade	Participants (no.)
1. Food, Drink		Cabinet makers	48 (9)	**9. Leather**	
Bakers	5	Chandlers	—	Curriers	—
Brewers	2 (1)ᵃ	Fancy ware	9 (1)	Leather, skin dressers	2
Butchers	5 (3)	Joiners	49 (8)	**10. Print and Paper**	
Cafés, restaurants	4	Upholsterers	4 (1)	Bookbinders	—
Chocolate	—	**5. Transport**		Booksellers	—
Cooks	2 (2)	Bargemen	3 (3)	Papermakers	1
Fruit vendors	—	Blacksmiths	—	Printers	8 (4)
Grocers	—	Carters	5 (5)	**11. Glass, Pottery**	
Innkeepers	2	Coachmen	2 (1)	Earthenware	1
Pastry chefs	4	Farriers	4 (1)	Potters	7
Tobacco	—	Harness, saddlers	5	Royal Glass factory	1 (1)
Wine merchants	11	Porters	16 (16)	**12. Miscellaneous**	
2. Building, Roads		Riverside workers	5 (5)	Actors, artists, musicians, etc.	—
Carpenters	3	Shipyard workers	5 (5)	Beggars	—
Glaziers	—	Wheelwrights	—	Bourgeois	—
Locksmiths	41 (8)	**6. Metal**		Businessmen	4
Monumental masons	9 (1)	Braziers	7 (1)	Charcoal burners	3
Navvies	2 (2)	Buttonmakers	3	Civil servants	—
Painters	4	Cutlers	—	Clerks	5
Paviors	—	Edge-tool makers	2	Domestic servants, cleaners	—
Plasterers	—	Engravers, gilders	13	Deputies	—
Quarrymen	—	Founders	9 (2)	Fishermen	2 (1)
Sawyers	4 (1)	Goldsmiths	6 (1)	Housewives	—
Sculptors	20 (1)	Instrument makers	—	Journalists, publishers	—
Stonecutters	4 (4)	Jewelers	5	Laborers	2 (2)
Stonemasons	7 (5)	Mechanics	—	Launderers	3 (1)
Surveyors	—	Nailsmiths	9 (1)	Newsagents, vendors	—
Tilers	—	Pewterers	2	Peasants	—
3. Dress		Stovemakers	5 (3)	Priests	—
Beltmakers	—	Tinsmiths	5 (2)	Professional (lawyers, doctors)	—
Boot and shoe	28 (5)	Watchmakers	3	Shopkeepers, assistants	22 (1)
Dressmakers	—	**7. Wood**		"Smugglers"	—
Dyers, cleaners	3	Coopers	3 (1)	Teachers	1
Florists, gardeners	6 (3)	Turners	10	Trades	56 (1)
Furriers	2 (1)	**8. Textiles**		Army, police, National Guard:	
Hairdressers	10	Cotton	—	a. Officers	—
Hatters	9 (4)	Gauze	22 (22)	b. Others	77
Ribbon weavers	3 (3)	Silk	1 (1)		
Stocking weavers	4 (4)	Weavers	1	*Total*	662 (149)
Tailors	7 (1)				
4. Furnishing					
Basketmakers	2				
Boxmakers	1				

ᵃFigures in parentheses represent insurgents who probably were wage-earners (i.e., not self-employed).

Source 10 from selected documents translated with notes and commentary by Darline Gay Levy, Harriet Branson Applewhite, and Mary Durham Johnson, from Women in Revolutionary Paris, 1789–1795 *(Urbana: University of Illinois Press, 1979), pp. 29–30. Copyright © 1979 by the Board of Trustees of the editors of the University of Illinois. Used with permission of the editors of the University of Illinois Press.*

10. Petition Addressed by Marguerite Pinaigre to the French National Assembly

Legislators:

The person named here, Margueritte Piningre [*sic*], wife of Sieur Bernard Vener, one of the Vainqueurs de la Bastille, has the honor of appearing today before your august assembly to reclaim the execution of the decree issued by the Constituent Assembly in his [her husband's] favor in 1789. This intrepid citizen, who has the misfortune of being crippled for the rest of his days without ever being able to work again in his life because of wounds received on all parts of his body, yes, Legislators, not only has this dear citizen fought in the conquest of the Bastille with the greatest courage, but furthermore, his *citoyenne*[8] wife, who is present here, worked equally hard with all her might, both of them having resolved to triumph or to die. It is she who ran to several wineshops to fill her apron with bottles, both broken and unbroken, which she gave to the authorities to be used as shot in the cannon used to break the chain on the drawbridge of the Bastille. Therefore, by virtue of these legitimate claims the petitioner believes herself justified in coming before the National Assembly today to advise it concerning the nonexecution of laws relative to conquerors who were severely maimed, as was the petitioner's husband. This law awards a pension to those who are really crippled and without the means for earning their living. Such is the situation of the latter, who is offering to provide evidence in the form of authentic statements. Nevertheless, he still has not been awarded this pension which he so richly deserves, he as well as his wife, as a consequence of the dangers they faced. The only gratification which this citizen has received is a small sum of four hundred *livres,* which since 1789 has barely sufficed to care for him and to help him get over the severe wounds he suffered.

Under these circumstances, and in the light of such a compelling account, the petitioner dares hope, Messieurs, for your justice and your usual generosity. May you be willing to take under urgent consideration the object of a request which is becoming as pressing as it is urgent—assuming that surely you would not allow one of the most zealous and

8. *citoyenne:* citeness. As an expression of revolutionary equality, during the revolution, the terms of address "citizen" and "citeness" replaced the traditional "Monsieur" and "Madame," based as they were on "My Lord" and "My Lady."

intrepid Vainqueurs de la Bastille to languish any longer bent under the weight of the indigence to which he is presently reduced, along with his wife and his children, who expect his every minute to be his last—because from this period [July 14, 1789] on he has always been ill and continues to suffer cruelly every day. The petitioner expects the favor of the representatives of the French nation, to whom she will never cease to offer her most heart-felt gratitude.

[signed] Marguerite Pinaigre

Source 11 from Arthur Young, Travels in France During the Years 1787, 1788 and 1789, *edited by Jeffry Kaplow (Gloucester, Mass.: Peter Smith, 1976), pp. 104–105, 130, 145–146.*

11. Arthur Young's Report from France

[June 1789 (in Paris)]

THE 9TH.—The business going forward at present in the pamphlet shops of Paris is incredible. I went to the Palais Royal to see what new things were published, and to procure a catalogue of all. Every hour produces something new. Thirteen came out to-day, sixteen yesterday, and ninety-two last week. We think sometimes that Debrett's or Stockdale's shops at London are crouded, but they are mere deserts, compared to Desenne's, and some others here, in which one can scarcely squeeze from the door to the counter. The price of printing two years ago was from 27 liv. to 30 liv.[9] per sheet, but now it is from 60 liv. to 80 liv. This spirit of reading political tracts, they say, spreads into the provinces, so that all the presses of France are equally employed. Nineteen-twentieths of these productions are in favour of liberty, and commonly violent against the clergy and nobility; I have to-day bespoken[10] many of this description, that have reputation; but enquiring for such as had appeared on the other side of the question, to my astonishment I find there are but two or three that have merit enough to be known. Is it not wonderful,[11] that while the press teems with the most levelling and even seditious principles, which put in execution would overturn the monarchy, nothing in reply appears, and not the least step is taken by the court to restrain this extreme licentiousness of publication? It is easy to conceive the

---

9. **livre:** the main unit of Old Regime currency, made up of 20 sous (s). Each sou contained 12 deniers (d); 6 livres equaled 1 écu.

10. **bespoken:** Young employs an archaic usage of this word, whose meaning here may most clearly be rendered as "encountered."

11. **wonderful:** another older usage. Young does not state approval here but indicates that the contents of the press were surprising.

spirit that must thus be raised among the people. But the coffee-houses in the Palais Royal present yet more singular and astonishing spectacles; they are not only crouded within, but other expectant crouds are at the doors and windows, listening *à gorge déployée*[12] to certain orators, who from chairs or tables harangue each his little audience: the eagerness with which they are heard, and the thunder of applause they receive for every sentiment of more than common hardiness or violence against the present government, cannot easily be imagined. I am all amazement at the ministry permitting such nests and hot-beds of sedition and revolt, which disseminate amongst the people, every hour, principles that by and by must be opposed with vigour, and therefore it seems little short of madness to allow the propagation at present.

THE 10TH.—Every thing conspires to render the present period in France critical: the want of bread is terrible: accounts arrive every moment from the provinces of riots and disturbances, and calling in the military, to preserve the peace of the markets. The prices reported are the same as I found at Abbeville and Amiens 5s. (2½d.) a pound for white bread, and 3½s. to 4s. for the common sort, eaten by the poor: these rates are beyond their faculties, and occasion great misery.

THE 26TH.—Every hour that passes seems to give the people fresh spirit: the meetings at the Palais Royal are more numerous, more violent, and more as-sured; and in the assembly of electors, at Paris, for sending a deputation to the National Assembly, the language that was talked, by all ranks of people, was nothing less than a revolution in the government, and the establishment of a free constitution: what they mean by a free constitution, is easily understood— *a republic*; for the doctrine of the times runs every day more and more to that point; yet they profess, that the kingdom ought to be a monarchy too; or, at least, that there ought to be a king. In the streets one is stunned by the hawkers of seditious pamphlets, and descriptions of pretended events, that all tend to keep the people equally ignorant and alarmed. The supineness, and even stu-pidity of the court, is without example: the moment demands the greatest deci-sion—and yesterday, while it was actually a question, whether he should be a Doge of Venice,[13] or a King of France, the King went a hunting! The spectacle of the Palais Royal presented this night, till eleven o'clock, and, as we afterwards heard, almost till morning, is curious. The croud was prodigious, and fire-works of all sorts were played off, and all the building was illuminated: these

---

12. *à gorge déployée:* enthusiastically.

13. **Doge of Venice:** in principle the head of Venetian government, the Doge in reality was a figurehead.

were said to be rejoicings on account of the Duc d'Orléans[14] and the nobility joining the commons; but united with the excessive freedom, and even licentiousness of the orators, who harangue the people; with the general movement which before was threatening, all this bustle and noise, which will not leave them a moment tranquil, has a prodigious effect in preparing them for whatever purposes the leaders of the commons shall have in view; consequently they are grossly and diametrically opposite to the interests of the court;—but all these are blind and infatuated.

[*July 1789 (on the road at Metz, a city
    about 150 miles east of Paris)*]

THE 14TH.—They have a *cabinet littéraire*[15] at Metz, something like that I described at Nantes, but not on so great a plan; and they admit any person to read or go in and out for a day, on paying 4*s*. To this I eagerly resorted, and the news from Paris, both in the public prints, and by the information of a gentleman, I found to be interesting. Versailles and Paris are surrounded by troops: 35,000 men are assembled, and 20,000 more on the road, large trains of artillery collected, and all the preparations of war. The assembling of such a number of troops has added to the scarcity of bread; and the magazines[16] that have been made for their support are not easily by the people distinguished from those they suspect of being collected by monopolists. This has aggravated their evils almost to madness; so that the confusion and tumult of the capital are extreme.

14. **Duc d'Orléans:** Louis Philippe Joseph, Duke of Orléans (1747–1793), was a member of the royal family who played an equivocal role in the Revolution's early years. As a member of the Assembly of Notables, he opposed new royal taxing authority. On June 25, 1789, the duke answered the call of the Third Estate of the Estates General for noblemen to join it, in defiance of royal order, as the National Assembly. This is the event celebrated in Young's account. The duke's ownership of the Palais Royal has led generations of historians to accuse him of inciting the revolutionary agitation that took place there. Before his death in the Reign of Terror, he served as a member of the legislature and in 1792 cast his vote for the death of Louis XVI.
15. *cabinet littéraire:* reading room.
16. **magazines:** storage depots.

Source 12 from Keith Michael Baker, editor, Readings in Western Civilizations, *vol. 7*, The Old Regime and the Revolution *(Chicago: University of Chicago Press, 1987), pp. 193–196.*

12. Report of the British Ambassador, the Duke of Dorset, to the Foreign Office in London

(25th June, 1789.) The reports concerning the scarcity of corn[17] in the neighbourhood of Paris have but too much foundation: the deficiency of this material article extends to the distance of 15 leagues[18] round the City and is so severely felt that Administration has been obliged to supply the different great Markets, by sending corn from the Magazines of the *Ecole Militaire*[19] originally intended for the consumption of the Capital: in regard to the other Provinces of the Kingdom there is no further apprehension, as they are sufficiently supplied 'till the ensuing harvest which has every appearance of being very plentifull. . . .

The French Guards have, in some few instances within these few days, shewn a great reluctance to act and some of the men have declared that if they should be called upon to quell any disturbance they will, if compelled to fire, take care not to do any mischief. The Archbishop of Paris was very ill-treated last night by the mob at Versailles: his coach was broke to pieces and his horses much bruised: if the Guards had not protected him he must himself have been inevitably destroyed.

The people now are disposed to any desperate act of violence in support of the *Assemblée Nationale.*[20] I shall not fail to send Your Grace immediate intelligence of any momentous occurrence during this critical state of affairs. . . .

(16th July, 1789.) I wrote to Your Grace on the 12th Inst. by a messenger extraordinary to inform you of the removal of M. Necker from His Majesty's Councils: I have now to lay before Your Grace an account of the general revolt, with the extraordinary circumstances attending it, that has been the immediate consequence of that step. On Sunday evening a slight skirmish happened in the Place de Louis XV, in which two Dragoons[21] were killed, and two wounded of the Duc de Choiseuil's Regiment: after which all the troops left the Capital, and the populace remained unmolested masters of everything: much to their credit however, uncontrouled as they now were, no

---

17. **corn:** in British usage, this word refers to grain, not American corn, or maize.
18. **league:** a unit of distance equal to 2.764 miles in English-speaking countries.
19. *Ecole Militaire:* the Military School in Paris.
20. *Assemblée Nationale:* the National Assembly.
21. **Dragoon:** cavalryman equipped with both a sabre and a short musket and therefore capable of fighting either mounted or on foot.

material mischief was done; their whole attention being confined to the burning of some of the Barriers. Very early on Monday morning the Convent of St. Lazare was forced, in which, besides a considerable quantity of corn, were found arms and ammunition supposed to have been conveyed thither as a place of security, at different periods from the Arsenal: and now a general consternation was seen throughout the Town: all shops were shut; all public and private works at a stand still and scarcely a person to be seen in the Streets excepting the armed *Bourgeoisie,* a temporary police for the protection of private property, to replace the established one which no longer had any influence.

In the morning of Tuesday the Hospital of Invalids was summoned to surrender and was taken possession of after a very slight resistance: all the cannon, small arms and ammunition were immediately seized upon, and every one who chose to arm himself was supplied with what was necessary . . . in the evening a large detachment with two pieces of cannon went to the Bastille to demand the ammunition that was there, the *Gardes Bourgeoises*[22] not being then sufficiently provided: a flag of truce was sent on before and was answered from within, notwithstanding which the governor (the Marquis de Launay) contrary to all precedent fired upon the people and killed several: this proceeding so enraged the populace that they rushed to the very gates with a determination to force their way through if possible: upon this the Governor agreed to let in a certain number of them on condition that they should not commit any violence: these terms being acceded to, a detachment of about 40 in number advanced and were admitted, but the drawbridge was immediately drawn up again and the whole party instantly massacred: this breach of honor aggravated by so glaring an act of inhumanity excited a spirit of revenge and tumult such as might naturally be expected: the two pieces of cannon were immediately placed against the Gate and very soon made a breach which, with the disaffection that as is supposed prevailed within, produced a sudden surrender of that Fortress: M. de Launay, the principal gunner, the tailer, and two old invalids who had been noticed as being more active than the rest were seized and carried to the *Hôtel de Ville*[23] where, after a very summary trial before the tribunal there, the inferior objects were put to death and M. de Launay had also his head cut off at the Place de Grève, but with circumstances of barbarity too shocking to relate. . . . In the course of the same evening the whole of the *Gardes Françoises*[24] joined the Bourgeoisie with all their cannon, arms and ammunition: the Regiments that were encamped in the *Champ de Mars,*[25] by an Order from Government left the ground at 2 o'Clock yesterday morning and fell back to Sêve, leaving all their camp

22. *Gardes Bourgeoises:* the civic militia formed by the Parisian electors on July 13.
23. *Hôtel de Ville:* the Paris city hall.
24. *Gardes Françoises:* the French Guards, the unit normally charged with Parisian security, whose loyalty to the king had begun to erode as early as June 18, 1789.
25. *Champ de Mars:* the large parade ground in Paris in front of the Military School (Ecole Militarie).

equipage behind them; the magazines of powder and corn at the *Ecole Mili-taire* were immediately taken possession of and a *Garde Bourgeoise* appointed to protect them. Nothing could exceed the regularity and good order with which all this extraordinary business has been conducted: of this I have myself been a witness upon several occasions during the last three days as I have passed through the streets, nor had I at any moment reason to be alarmed for my personal safety.

QUESTIONS TO CONSIDER

Crowd violence was not uncommon in early modern Europe, and historians have recently shown that such violence, rather than reflecting blind rage, often represented the expression of very definite ideas. Recall the political crisis of June and July 1789. The National Assembly was defying the king, and many Parisians supported this stand. Both the legislators at Versailles and the people of Paris knew that royal troops were moving in the latter's direction. They correctly connected these military steps with Necker's dismissal and believed that the king was beginning a coup to suppress demands for change in France. How might political problems coinciding with other difficulties have helped to produce the Bastille attack? Your problem in this chapter is to reconstruct the nature and spread of certain ideas in Paris on July 14, 1789, by bringing together the various pieces of evidence presented here.

Consider first the symbolic significance of the Bastille for eighteenth-century Parisians. Why might this underused prison have been a natural target for those hostile to the monarchy? Next consider the physical setting of this historical drama. Examine the picture of the Palais Royal. How many people could congregate here in fair weather like that experienced on July 12–14? What effect might Camille Desmoulins have had on such a crowd? If political agitation and rumors spread beyond the Palais Royal, what physical features of Paris, visible in the city's streets and residences, would have been conducive to their dispersion throughout the city? What conditions did Parisians encounter in the streets? How would these conditions affect the spread of news? What features of the floor plans of typical Parisian houses might have permitted the mobilization of all residents in a political cause? Combine all these facts and you should have an idea of the nature of political activity in the city in 1789.

Next, consider the prices for wheat in Paris. You need to know what these prices represented to Parisians in terms of daily survival. How might food prices have inspired the agitation made possible by the city's physical layout? Examine both national and Parisian trends in wheat prices. What impact did rising bread prices have on the budgets of even skilled workers like journeymen masons and locksmiths? What do you suppose their response to such prices might have been? Remember that Jacques Necker, who was widely regarded as an important factor in keeping Paris supplied with food, was dismissed on July 11.

Examine next the social background of the Bastille's attackers. Refer to the map and the table showing the trades and residences of Bastille insurgents to determine which groups felt the problems of 1789 most acutely. What social groups were represented in the crowd? What was their economic standing? What parts of the city did they come from? Why do you suppose such groups, rather than other residents of the city, were moved to action? What factors conducive to the mobilization of the insurgents would you expect to find among them? Why would you expect them to be accustomed to organization in trades still governed by guilds? Why would you expect them to have been involved in the business activities of Parisian streets and markets?

As you complete this analysis, you should have an understanding of the composition of the Bastille crowd, how it was mobilized, and why the population might be agitated by food problems in 1789. Remember that the food price crisis coincided with a political crisis. Consult the written sources to understand the conjunction of these problems. How does Arthur Young show the response of Parisian public opinion to all of this? Were the effects of the crisis felt beyond Paris? Look at the report of the British ambassador. What does he tell us about developments in Paris? Considering that the Bastille fell to a group of armed rebels, how do you account for the ambassador's assurances that he felt safe? Refer to your findings on the crowd's composition in answering this question and remember the creation of a civil guard made up of middle-class citizens. What social group controlled Paris by the time rain fell on July 14?

By combining these sources, both the traditional written accounts long used by historians and the sociological material that establishes the composition of the crowd, you should be able now to answer the central questions of this chapter. What stirred Parisians to mass action? Who was in that crowd on July 14, 1789?

EPILOGUE

The fall of the Bastille to a popular attack whose genesis you have analyzed in this chapter was an event charged with both practical and symbolic significance. On the practical level, capturing the Bastille provided the crowd with the gunpowder it sought and made regaining control of Paris virtually impossible for the royal army. In consequence, the king's resolve to oppose the National Assembly evaporated along with his hopes of controlling Paris. Louis XVI announced to the National Assembly on July 15 that troops would be removed from the region of the capital; on July 16 he recalled Necker as finance minister. On the following day, July 17, the king went to Paris, where his actions publicly confirmed royal recognition and acceptance of the events of the preceding days. First he received the keys to the city from its new mayor, Jean-Sylvan Bailly, representative of the electors of Paris who now controlled the capital. At the city hall he affixed to his hat the blue, white, and red cockade,[26] composed of the blue and red of the Paris coat of arms and the white of the monarchy. That cockade would become the symbol of the Revolution, and its colors would come to form a new national flag.

With these actions, Louis XVI effectively surrendered control of events to the citizen rebels of Paris. Although we now know that his private sentiments remained steadfastly opposed to the widening Revolution, his public acquiescence was plain to Frenchmen of all political persuasions. The king's brother, the Count of Artois, left the country on the evening of July 16, the first of thousands who would flee the growing Revolution out of fear or hatred for what it represented. At the same time, towns and cities all over France imitated Paris by forming revolutionary governments and National Guards to consolidate the overthrow of the old regime in municipal administration. Disorder spread among peasants in the countryside, prompting the National Assembly on August 4, 1789, to end the distinct privileges of the nobility and clergy; henceforth, all citizens would be equal before the law, pay taxes, and enjoy equal rights and opportunities. The Revolution had won its first great victory, a fact that even the king later recognized. Planning an escape in 1792, Louis said that, in hindsight, he should have fled Paris on July 14, 1789, to rally his forces and undo the revolution.

He stated, "I know I missed my opportunity: that was on July 14th. I ought to have gone away then. . . . I missed my opportunity, and I've never found it again."[27]

The symbolic importance of the Bastille's fall also was great. Despite its small prisoner census by 1789, the old fortress-prison symbolized royal power to eighteenth-century Frenchmen. The Paris government conferred the job of physically smashing this symbol of the Old Regime on a patriotic contractor, Pierre-François Palloy (1755–1834). In his hands, the transformation of the Bastille into another sort of symbol began. Palloy demolished the prison and transformed its remains into physical symbols of liberty's victory. In 1790 he had stones of the prison carved into eighty-three small replicas of the Bastille and sent one to each of France's new administrative units, the *départements*. In 1793 he sent stones from the Bastille to the 544 districts of France and a number of political clubs and prominent citizens. He also had the prison's irons struck into commemorative medals and sponsored festivals celebrating the prison's fall. Others followed his lead. Masonry taken from the prison was used in a Parisian bridge so that citizens could tread on the "stone of tyranny." Lafayette sent a key to the Bastille to George Washington as a symbol of the victory of liberty. This key hangs today at Mount Vernon. And on July 14, 1790, the city of Paris honored 954 citizens who had taken

26. **cockade:** a rosette of ribbons of ten worn on the hat as a wind of badge in the eighteenth century

27. Quoted in Godechot, p. 257.

part in the prison's capture as conquerors of the Bastille.

Eighteenth-century Frenchmen recognized the great symbolic importance of July 14, 1789, and France commemorated the anniversary of the Bastille's fall throughout its Revolution. Future generations recognized the event's importance, too. In 1880 the Third Republic made July 14 the great national holiday, observed in France with as much patriotic fervor as Americans observe July 4.

CHAPTER SIX

LABOR OLD AND NEW:

THE IMPACT OF

THE INDUSTRIAL REVOLUTION

The main difficulty did not . . . lie so much in the invention of a proper self-acting mechanism for drawing and twisting cotton as in the distribution of the different members of the apparatus into one cooperative body, in impelling each organ with its appropriate delicacy and speed, and above all, in training human beings to renounce their desultory habits of work, to identify themselves with the unvarying regularity of work of the complex automation. It requires in fact a man of Napoleonic nerve and ambition to subdue refractory tempers of work people accustomed to irregular spasms of diligence, and to urge on his multifarious and intricate constructions in the face of prejudice, passion, and envy.

This is how Andrew Ure, an early and enthusiastic analyst of the Industrial Revolution, characterized the problems of industrial management in his book *The Philosophy of Manufacturers* (1835). In these few sentences, Ure identified the essence of the Industrial Revolution. As most Western Civilization courses correctly emphasize, the period of history this label describes did indeed represent an economic and technological revolution of the greatest magnitude. The manner in which the West produced its goods changed more in the century from 1750 to 1850 than in all the previous centuries of human history, making necessary, as Ure says, the solution of tremendous problems of technology and integration of industrial processes.

But the Industrial Revolution had another impact, one that Ure did not neglect, though he approached it from the managerial point of view in emphasizing the manager's need to train his employees. That Ure thought the disciplining of the work force was perhaps the manager's chief problem suggests the broad social impact of industrialization. The first generations of factory laborers

[138]

encountered a world of work dramatically transformed from that of their fathers and mothers, a laboring situation with which most were totally unfamiliar.

The work life of the preindustrial laborer certainly was not easy. Workdays were long, typically dawn to dusk, six days per week, and it was common for wives and children to labor alongside their husbands and fathers as part of a household economy. Indeed, for agricultural workers and craftsmen alike, labor took up so much of their time that little remained for other daily activities. The material rewards of labor often were meager, too. But preindustrial work, however long, hard, and unrewarding, had characteristics that distinguished it from early industrial labor.

Preindustrial work usually was conducted in and around the worker's residence. Such labor afforded the worker occasional variety and, in some instances, a measure of control over the pace of work. We may see this effect if we examine the various types of preindustrial workers. Agricultural workers certainly experienced periods of intensive labor, especially at spring plowing and at harvest time, but periods of less intensive labor, especially in the winter months, punctuated their work year and brought them a bit of respite from their duties.

Many of the skilled craftsmen who produced the consumer goods of preindustrial Europe were organized by trade into local, professional groups known as guilds. Guilds performed many functions for their members. By controlling the size of their membership, guilds could limit the number

of practitioners of a trade in their cities because practice of a trade often required guild membership. Such limitation of membership aimed at protecting the livelihoods of guild members by ensuring that there would be sufficient work, and thus income, for each one. Guilds set prices for their products as well, always at a level that would ensure an adequate income to guild members and prevent ruinous price competition. Guilds gave the consumer a measure of protection, too. Guilds regulated the quality of their members' output and, through a system of training known as *apprenticeship,* guaranteed consumers that producers had sufficient skills in their trades to produce a fine product. Apprenticeship gave a craftsman the essential skills of his trade, and most men followed apprenticeship with employment as *journeymen,* that is, as workers who were sufficiently skilled to command a daily wage in the shop of a guild master. Full guild membership, and the right to open one's own production unit in his trade, was reserved for those journeymen who completed a *masterpiece,* a fine example of their skills in their chosen profession, which won for them the title of guild master.

The production unit of a guild master afforded him some measure of freedom in plying his trade within guild regulations. The master supervised a production unit that often included members of his family, apprentices, and sometimes journeymen. The master set the pace for himself and his workers, who, particularly in Catholic countries, might look forward to a number of religious holidays, civic

Chapter 6

Labor Old

and New:

The Impact of

the Industrial

Revolution

festivals, and fairs to interrupt their year's labor.

In the later centuries of the preindustrial age, another kind of labor began to emerge. Called the *putting-out system*, this form of employment became common in textile production. A merchant would purchase raw material, often wool, and deliver it to various rural workers, who would spin, weave, dye, and finish the cloth, using traditional methods. Often workers were farm families who took in textile work to supplement their incomes. Merchants sought such rural workers because they worked cheaply and because they were beyond the jurisdiction of urban authorities, who limited textile production to guild members. The putting-out system allowed merchants to gather large numbers of workers under their control and thus organize production more efficiently. Even workers in this more disciplined mode of production enjoyed some freedom in organizing their work, however, despite the low wages that often kept them in poverty. For example, consider a weaver employed as part of the putting-out system. The weaver might enjoy "holy Monday," that is, a prolongation of the Sabbath, by taking the first day of the week off. The weaver might also take a few hours off on Tuesday and Wednesday as well, completing the week's required production only by working all night Thursday and Friday. No matter how he or she scheduled his or her work time, however, the choice was the weaver's. The worker had some control over the labor.

Indeed, all these factors that somewhat lessened the intensity of preindustrial labor have led some historians to idealize preindustrial work. It is important that we do not follow their example. By perhaps the most important measure of a laborer's work life—the standard of living it supports—it is by no means certain that early industrial employment represented an overall worsening of workers' living conditions. Historians continue to debate the issue of standard of living, examining diverse data on wages, diet, and housing; the problem clearly is a complex one. Whereas the preindustrial skilled craftsman was generally well rewarded for his work, the agricultural laborer and putting-out worker usually were not, and peasant families on the Continent sometimes lived a subsistence existence. For some rural workers, early industrial labor may actually have improved their standard of living.

Industrial labor, however, definitely brought all those employed in the new mills, factories, and mines a new style of work. Hours in the new establishments remained long, and the work year was interrupted by fewer holidays because factory owners could maximize returns on their massive investments in plants and machines only by using them to their fullest. Labor by whole families often continued, too, but the factory system separated them from their homes, and the tasks and workplaces of family members were very different. Husbands endured the heaviest labor in textile mills or mines. Their wives, research has shown, most often remained at home, keeping house, caring for young children, and often laboring many hours in low-paying tasks that could be done at home— "slop work," that is, needle trades, bookbinding, millinery, or other such occupations. Only a minority of married women worked in early mills and mines. Children and unmarried women, however, went out to work in mills, where their hands were better suited to intricate machinery than men's, or in mines, where their small statures allowed them to move through low mine tunnels more easily than men. Their wages always were very low.

Most significantly, perhaps, the worker lost control over the pace of his or her work. Modern factory production dictated that workers serve these new machines that had taken over the productive role. Barring breakdowns, the machine's pace never varied; the new work was monotonous. Workers found themselves endlessly repeating the same tasks in the production process with little autonomy. In addition, industrial work imposed a new punctuality on workers. For the factory system to function smoothly, all had to be at their work stations on time and remain there except during scheduled breaks. "Holy Monday" and unscheduled leisure time threatened the smooth operation of an industrial establishment. Early mines and factories posed significant safety problems, too, as we will see.

How did the first generations of industrial workers respond to such fundamental changes? Some adapted. Others proved incapable of adjusting

to the new working conditions, and absenteeism (especially on Mondays), chronic tardiness, and workers' inability to keep pace with machines plagued many early mills. Many other workers experienced a growing inner alienation, identified by such observers of industrialism as Karl Marx, that manifested itself in various forms of asocial behavior. When economic conditions were good and jobs were plentiful, early mills had problems with frequent employee resignations. Some mills experienced as much as 100 percent annual employee turnover.

Other new social problems also accompanied industrialization. Urban expansion accompanied the factory system (see Chapter 8), reflecting the movement of many rural families to growing cities in search of factory employment. Such moves separated the new arrivals from friends and from the social controls of village life. In the city they often found not only the poverty of early industrial work but also the anonymity of urban life and the wealth of modern society displayed by the privileged classes. The result was a rapid rise of crimes against property accompanying urban growth. Older social problems persisted, too. Preindustrial workers frequently consumed alcohol in excess as an escape from their tedious work lives. Indeed, "holy Monday" often reflected the effects of a worker's weekend of alcohol abuse. The early industrial age was little different. One English clergyman described to a committee of Parliament the sight of twelve-year-old coal miners staggering with drink.

Chapter 6

Labor Old

and New:

The Impact of

the Industrial

Revolution

The human response to this fundamental change in work thus assumed many forms; however, these did not include organized resistance to the machine age by industrial workers. Those employed in early mills and mines often were illiterate and consequently difficult to mobilize for collective actions such as strikes. Moreover, laws like the English Combination Acts (1799, 1800) and the French Le Chapelier Law (1791) actually forbade worker organizations; the few early unions were illegal and secretive. The only overt resistance to industrialization, therefore, came not from industrial workers but from one group of preindustrial laborers, namely, the artisans. Members of this class had a high rate of literacy and thus were aware that the new machines ultimately threatened both their livelihoods and their work autonomy. They lashed out with acts of machine smashing. English machine smashers were called *Luddites* after one Ned Ludd, who supposedly originated their movement, but such efforts to forestall the use of machinery were not uniquely English. Machine smashing occurred in western Continental Europe at least through 1848.

Machine smashing, of course, could not stop industrialization, and workers in early mines and mills became the objects of an increasingly stringent discipline aimed at forcing their acceptance of the new labor. Overseers beat child laborers. Managers fined or dismissed adults and sometimes blacklisted particularly difficult workers to deny them any employment.

In this chapter you will be asked to contrast the working conditions of the preindustrial and industrial ages. How did industrial labor differ from preindustrial work? How did such labor evolve? What effects did the new labor have on the first generations of men, women, and children in Europe's mills and mines?

SOURCES AND METHOD

The central questions of this chapter require your analysis of both preindustrial and industrial labor. As an aid to this analysis, the evidence for this chapter is accordingly divided into two groups, one relating to the preindustrial age (the "old labor") and the other to the industrial era (the "new labor").

Let us begin our consideration of the old labor with its most traditional form, agricultural labor. Source 1 is the work of Sébastien Le Prestre de Vauban

(1633–1707). Vauban was a brilliant military engineer whose skill in designing fortifications and conducting sieges for the army of Louis XIV of France propelled him to the highest rank in the army, Marshal of France. But Vauban's interests were not narrowly military in scope. This highly intelligent and observant man wrote extensively on a variety of problems; he was the author of treatises on agriculture, construction, and the need for religious toleration in an age of widespread persecution of religious minorities. The selection from Vauban's writings presented in Source 1 is drawn from one of his last works, a proposal for reforming the tax system of early eighteenth-century France with the goals of both greater equity in assessing the tax burden and increased revenues to balance the royal budget. To adequately present his ideas, Vauban undertook a description of the economic situations of his fellow Frenchmen in this work, which gives the student of the eighteenth century a number of insights into the lot of common people who left little other record of their activities. In reading this source, pay particular attention to the agricultural workers Vauban describes. This group owned little property, but instead worked the lands of others. Lacking land of their own, this group of workers possessed a certain mobility, which would lead many of their number to factory employment a century after Vauban's analysis of their situation. How long was the agricultural work year of this group? Why were the earnings of such people from agriculture insufficient? What sort of nonagricultural employment did members of the family unit undertake?

In Source 2, you encounter further evidence on agricultural labor, this time on working conditions of farm workers in England almost a century and a half after Vauban wrote. Source 2 offers you for the first time a type of evidence you will analyze several times in this chapter, the record of hearings on early industrial working conditions conducted by legislative committees. From such records, committee members drew up recommendations, which often resulted in legislation to improve working conditions in early mills, factories, and mines. These records have a great advantage for the historian

because they also offer a glimpse into the world of the illiterate laboring poor of an earlier age. Secretaries to the investigating committees often took down the testimony of witnesses verbatim, providing an enduring record of all the difficulties of labor in the early industrial era. Mrs. Britton labored in the old style as an agricultural worker, but she brought a unique perspective to her testimony to a committee of the British Parliament because she once had worked in a factory also. What were the work conditions and the standard of living of agricultural workers like Mrs. Britton and her husband? How did agricultural labor compare with factory labor for Mrs. Britton?

With Source 3 we turn to the labor of the preindustrial craftsman. The evidence on craftsmen's labor opens with a summary of holidays in a textile-producing city, Lille, France, in the seventeenth century. How would you characterize the pace of labor in Lille, a city whose work calendar was not unusual in Catholic Europe?

Source 4 presents excerpts from guild regulations in the Prussian woolen industry. The Industrial Revolution began in England in the mid-eighteenth century but affected the Continent much later, only in the first decades of the nineteenth century. Thus, these guild regulations dating from 1797 describe the traditional labor of many Europeans. In reading them, ask yourself what sort of labor conditions these regulations sustained. A worker's demonstration of his mastery of all the processes of producing wool cloth won him the "freedom of the guild" and its privileges. The latter involved the right to establish his

Chapter 6

Labor Old

and New:

The Impact of

the Industrial

Revolution

own production unit and market his goods, as well as guild assistance when old age or illness prevented work. What sort of limits on the activities of guild members accompanied these freedoms? What do you think were the reasons for these restrictions? What efforts to protect both the consumer and the guild members' market can you discern in these restrictions? Why was the putting-out system explicitly forbidden to guild members? What specifically in all these restrictions seems intended to create a protected monopoly for producers?

Source 5 describes another facet of the old style of labor in textile production, namely, the putting-out system. It is the work of François-Alexandre Frédéric, Duke of La Rochefoucauld-Liancourt (1747–1827), an astute observer of the social and economic problems of his day who applied his energy and wealth to various reform schemes, including experimental farms and an early cotton mill. La Rochefoucauld wrote persuasively on the need for improved poor relief and better education for all Frenchmen. Here, to support his call for social change, La Rochefoucauld provides a good description of the putting-out system in his travel account of 1781 to 1783, based on his visit to Rouen, the capital of the northern French province of Normandy. Who was employed in textiles in Rouen? What does the duke tell you about the quantity of production in Rouen, despite the continued use of hand looms? How did the organization of this work, the quantity of production, and the

destinations of its products foreshadow certain features of the industrial age?

Next, consider the evidence on the new labor, that is, the work of the industrial age. Source 6 presents pictorial evidence, which, as we have seen in Chapter 2, can constitute an important source for the historian. Source 6A is a sixteenth-century woodcut of a German weaver that tells us much about traditional textile labor. In what sort of a structure do you think this loom was located? Why do you think that this sort of loom produced only limited quantities of cloth? Why do you think that the weaver probably required considerable training to operate his loom? What do you suppose was the relationship of the male weaver to the spinner who is handing him the thread (his raw material)? Source 6B is an engraving of the weaving process carried on in an English mill in 1833. A large, central steam engine turned the shafts along the room's ceiling from which ran belts that powered the looms. How much skilled human labor seems to have been required to produce cloth with such machinery? How do you think the price of fabric produced in such mills would compare with that of the weaver in Source 6A? What are the genders and roles of the workers shown in this source? What do you think would have been the economic consequences of this new mode of production for men like the weaver in Source 6A?

Source 7 is dramatic evidence that sweeping changes in the work life of the West provoked protest, in this case an unsuccessful attack by an armed mob of some one hundred men against a water-powered textile finishing plant in the West Riding district of the English county of Yorkshire in 1812. Our source is a selection from an account of a criminal trial of eleven of these Luddites. Such accounts sold widely in the eighteenth and nineteenth centuries to an increasingly literate public hungry for sensational news, and they offer the historian a rather unique window into the past. The sentences in criminal cases permit the historian to gauge the gravity of the offense for the society in which it occurred, but most importantly the testimony in them provides students of the past with another valuable written source for studying the activities of common people, who left scant written records of their lives. As with other sources, the historian must be a critical reader of trial records, asking first of all if they are accurate. Fortunately, accounts like that in Source 7 were the work of reporters employed by publishers to attend important trials, to record key testimony verbatim, and to summarize other aspects of cases. Historians also must assess the roles of those whose testimony they read; plaintiffs, for example, usually aim to sway the court in their favor by presenting a version of the facts favorable to their position. In Source 7, the testimony is that of the crime's victim, the mill owner, but other witnesses confirmed the veracity of the account he provided here. What do you conclude about the gravity of the threat the mill's attackers saw in the new technology it contained? The court found eight of these men guilty under a statute that required the death penalty

for anyone attempting to destroy a mill. What gravity do you think eighteenth- and nineteenth-century property owners and lawmakers ascribed to the activities described in Source 7?

Sources 8 and 9 are regulations governing the conditions of work in early industrial enterprises. In using this material, the historian must remember that such regulations describe the behavior prescribed by persons in authority; they may not describe the actual comportment of those whose behavior the statutes aimed to control. Indeed, we can assume that there was frequent conflict between the prescribed rules and the actual behavior of working people as workers adapted to the new conditions of industrial work.

Examine the work code for the foundry and engineering works in Moabit, an industrial suburb of Berlin, Germany, in 1844 (Source 8). What sort of habits did these regulations seek to inculcate in the foundry workers? Notice also the pay practices described in paragraph 18. Why would management have adopted these? What disadvantages did they represent for the worker?

The apprenticeship agreement for girls as silk workers in rural Tarare, France (Source 9), retains the terminology of the old labor in designating new workers as apprentices, but it lays down industrial-age work rules for the young women. Examine the agreement carefully, noting its disciplinary features. How long was the apprenticeship? When were wages paid? What happened if a girl left before the completion of her apprenticeship? What were the work hours?

Chapter 6

Labor Old

and New:

The Impact of

the Industrial

Revolution

In what ways did management seek to increase production? Such mills as this were established in rural areas, away from cities like Lyons, where male preindustrial silk weavers had a centuries-long history of guild organization (and of unrest). Given that information, can you discern why the mill's location was chosen and why a female work force was sought? What attractions did the mill, with its long workday, offer unmarried rural women who otherwise would have been reluctant to seek industrial employment away from home?

The testimony of William Cooper to the Sadler Committee of the British Parliament (Source 10) provides dramatic evidence about the conditions of industrial labor in early textile mills. What effect did mill labor have on Cooper? What were the hours of work? How did overseers enforce punctuality and a faster work pace by young workers? Were conditions within the mills conducive to good health? Compare Cooper's height to that of his father. What could have accounted for Cooper's shorter stature? When he had health problems and was unable to work, what recourse did Cooper have?

Source 11 also describes the condition of labor in the textile industry, but it records the lot of women fifty or more years after William Cooper's experiences in the mills. Had working conditions improved very much since Cooper's day? How long was the workday? Did the work demand exceptional energy or skill from the workers? How did management impose discipline in such matters as punctuality?

With the selections brought together as Source 12, you will once more analyze the records of English parliamentary inquiries, but this time the committees examined coal mine labor in the 1840s. Read first the testimony of Joseph Staley. Note his position in the mine. How might this have affected his conclusion about his miners' health? How many boys did he employ, and what ages were they? What sort of labor did the boys do? What were their hours? Analyze the testimony of William Jagger. What age was he? How long had he worked in the mine? What were his hours? What do his testimony and the comment by the investigator following that testimony tell you about work conditions and mine safety?

With the testimony of Patience Kershaw we have a record of women's labor in the mines. What sort of labor did Kershaw do? What weight of coal did she move daily? What health effects did such labor have on women like Kershaw and her sisters? What impression did she make on the parliamentary investigator, as indicated in his comment following her testimony?

Industrialization transformed the Western world in many ways, and we will examine aspects of its consequences in other chapters of this book as well (see especially Chapters 8 and 13). Your analysis of the evidence presented here should aid you in understanding one aspect of that transformation: the emergence of a new world of industrial labor and how it affected men and women of the eighteenth and nineteenth centuries.

THE EVIDENCE

THE OLD LABOR

Source 1 from Sébastien Le Prestre de Vauban, Project d'une Dixme royale, *ed. by E. Coornaert (Paris: Alcan, 1933) reprinted in Pierre Goubert,* The Ancien Régime: French Society, 1600–1750, *trans. by Steve Cox (New York: Harper and Row, 1974), pp. 116–118. Copyright © 1973 by George Weidenfield & Nicholson Ltd. Reprinted with the permission of Steve Cox.*

1. Agricultural Labor Described by Vauban, About 1700

. . . It only remains to take stock of two million men[1] all of whom I suppose to be day-laborers or simple artisans scattered throughout the towns, *bourgs*[2] and villages of the realm.

What I have to say about all these workers . . . deserves serious attention, for although this sector may consist of what are unfairly called the dregs of the people, they are nonetheless worthy of high consideration in view of the services which they render to the State. For it is they who undertake all the great tasks in town and country without which neither themselves nor others could live. It is they who provide all the soldiers and sailors and all the serving women; in a word, without them the State could not survive. It is for this reason that they ought to be spared in the matter of taxes, in order not to burden them beyond their strength. . . .

Among the smaller fry, particularly in the countryside, there are any number of people who, while they lay no claim to any special craft, are continually plying several which are most necessary and indispensable. Of such a kind are those we call *manoeuvriers*, who, owning for the most part nothing but their strong arms or very little more, do day- or piece-work for whoever wants to employ them. It is they who do all the major jobs such as mowing, harvesting, threshing, woodcutting, working the soil and the vineyards, clearing land, ditching, carrying soil to vineyards or elsewhere, labouring for builders and several other tasks which are all hard and laborious. These men may well find this kind of employment for part of the year, and it is true that they can usually earn a fair day's wage at haymaking, harvesting and grape-picking time, but the rest of the year is a different story. . . .

---

1. Vauban wrote in an age that had no modern census data for accurately assessing the size of a population. His figures here, at best, are an estimate. Indeed, modern demographic historians generally find Vauban's population data highly inaccurate.

2. *bourgs:* market towns.

Chapter 6

Labor Old

and New:

The Impact of

the Industrial

Revolution

It will not be inappropriate [to give] some particulars about what the country day-laborer can earn.

I shall assume that of the three-hundred and sixty-five days in the year, he may be gainfully employed for one hundred and eighty, and earn nine *sols*[3] a day. This is a high figure, and it is certain that except at harvest and grape-picking time most earn not more than eight *sols* a day on average, but supposing we allow the nine *sols*, that would amount to eighty-five *livres* and ten *sols*, call it ninety *livres*, from which we have to deduct his liabilities (taxes plus salt[4] for a family of four, say 14l. 16s.) . . . leaving seventy-five *livres* four *sols*.

Since I am assuming that his family . . . consists of four people, it requires not less than ten *septiers*[5] of grain, Paris measure, to feed them. This grain, half wheat, half rye . . . commonly selling at six *livres* per *septier* . . . will come to sixty *livres*, which leaves fifteen *livres* four *sols* out of seventy-five *livres* four *sols*, out of which the labourer has to find the price of rent and upkeep for his house, a few chattels, if only some earthenware bowls, clothing and linen, and the needs of his entire family for one year.

But these fifteen *livres* four *sols* will not take him very far unless his industry[6] or some particular business supervenes and his wife contributes to their income by means of her distaff,[7] sewing, knitting hose or making small quantities of lace . . . also by keeping a small garden or rearing poultry and perhaps a calf, a pig or a goat for the better-off . . . ; by which means he might buy a piece of larding bacon and a little butter or oil for making soup. And if he does not additionally cultivate some small allotment, he will be hard pressed to subsist, or at least he will be reduced, together with his family, to the most wretched fare. And if instead of two children he has four, that will be worse still until they are old enough to earn their own living. Thus however we come at the matter, it is certain that he will always have the greatest difficulty in seeing the year out. . . .

---

3. *sol:* sou.

4. Salt was subject to a form of tax in France before 1789. Tax farmers purchased the exclusive right to sell this dietary necessity to the public. The public was required by law to buy a certain amount of salt per year from these monopolists; in paying the price of the salt, buyers also paid a salt tax, the *gabelle,* to the tax farmers, who turned the proceeds of this over to the government. This form of taxation kept salt prices artificially high in much of France and was deeply resented by many taxpayers.

5. *septier:* a unit of measure in use in France prior to the Revolution of 1789. Its precise size varied from one district to another; hence here Vauban must specify that he is using the Parisian *septier.* Ten Parisian *septiers* would have equaled about 15.5 hectoliters, or 43 bushels.

6. Many rural workers would have been employed in some phase of textile production, such as weaving.

7. **distaff:** a staff that holds unspun flax or wool during the process of spinning such material into thread. The word can also refer to women's work or interests, because spinning was women's work.

Source 2 from British Parliamentary Papers: Reports of Special Assistant Poor Law Commissioner on the Employment of Women and Children in Agriculture *(London: William Clowes and Sons for Her Majesty's Stationery Office, 1843), pp. 66–67.*

2. Testimony of an Agricultural Worker's Wife and Former Factory Worker, 1842[8]

Mrs. *Britton,* Wife of _____ *Britton,* of *Calne, Wiltshire,* Farm-labourer, examined.

I am 41 years old; I have lived at Calne all my life. I went to school till I was eight years old, when I went out to look after children. At ten years old I went to work at a factory in Calne, where I was till I was 26. I have been married 15 years. My husband is an agricultural labourer. I have seven children, all boys. The oldest is fourteen, the youngest three-quarters of a year old. My husband is a good workman, and does most of his work by the lump, and earns from 9s. to 10s. a-week pretty constantly, but finds his own tools,—his wheelbarrow, which cost 1l., pickaxe, which cost 3s., and scoop, which cost 3s.[9]

I have worked in the fields, and when I went out I left the children in the care of the eldest boy, and frequently carried the baby with me, as I could not go home to nurse it. I have worked at hay-making and at harvest, and at other times in weeding and keeping the ground clean. I generally work from half-past seven till five, or half-past. When at work in the spring I have received 10d. a-day, but that is higher than the wages of women in general; 8d. or 9d. is more common. My master always paid 10d. When working I never had any beer, and I never felt the want of it. I never felt that my health was hurt by the work. Hay-making is hard work, very fatiguing, but it never hurt me. Working in the fields is not such hard work as working in the factory. I am always better when I can get out to work in the fields. I intend to do so next year if I can. Last year I could not go out, owing to the birth of the baby. My eldest boy gets a little to do; he don't earn more than 9d. a-week; he has not enough to do. My husband has 40 lugs[10] of land, for which he pays

8. This testimony was delivered before a parliamentary committee studying the employment of women and children in British agriculture.

9. **by the lump:** Mr. Britton was paid by the job rather than by the hour or day. English coinage mentioned in this and following selections (with the abbreviations for each denomination where appropriate) includes:
   £ or l.: pound sterling.
   s.: shilling; 20 shillings to 1 pound sterling.
   d.: pence (from Latin *denari*); 12 pence to 1 shilling.
   crown: a coin worth 5 shillings.
   groat: a coin worth 4 pence.

10. **lug:** an old English measure of area equal to 49 square yards. The Brittons' 40 lugs would, therefore, have equaled 1,960 square yards, less than half of a full acre, which is 4,840 square yards.

Chapter 6

Labor Old

and New:

The Impact of

the Industrial

Revolution

10s. a-year. We grow potatoes and a few cabbages, but not enough for our family; for that we should like to have forty lugs more. We have to buy potatoes. One of the children is a cripple, and the guardians[11] allow us two gallons of bread a-week for him.[12] We buy two gallons more, according as the money is. Nine people can't do with less than four gallons of bread a-week. We could eat much more bread if we could get it; sometimes we can afford only one gallon a-week. We very rarely buy butcher's fresh meat, certainly not oftener than once a-week, and not more than sixpenny worth. I like my husband to have a bit of meat, now he has left off drinking. I buy $\frac{1}{2}$ lb. butter a-week, 1 oz. tea, $\frac{1}{2}$ lb. sugar. The rest of our food is potatoes, with a little fat. The rent of our cottage is 1s. 6d. a-week; there are two rooms in it. We all sleep in one room, under the tiles. Sometimes we receive private assistance, especially in clothing. Formerly my husband was in the habit of drinking, and everything went bad. He used to beat me. I have often gone to bed, I and my children, without supper, and I have had no breakfast the next morning, and frequently no firing.[13] My husband attended a lecture on teetotalism one evening about two years ago, and I have reason to bless that evening. My husband has never touched a drop of drink since. He has been better in health, getting stouter, and has behaved like a good husband to me ever since. I have been much more comfortable, and the children happier. He works better than he did . . .

Source 3 from Alain Lottin, Chavatte, ouvrier lillois. Un contemporain de Louis XIV *(Paris: Flammarion, 1979), pp. 323–324. Reprinted with permission.*

3. The Work Year in Seventeenth-Century Lille, France

Holidays in Seventeenth-Century Lille

January	Monday following Epiphany (January 6)
22 January	Feast of St. Vincent
25 January	Feast of St. Paul's Conversion
February	Ash Wednesday

11. **guardian:** Poor Law official.

12. **two gallons of bread:** the gallon as a gauge of wheat and other dry material is an archaic English measure, the weight of which was far from standard in the British Isles. Sources refer to gallons of wheat weighing anywhere from 8 to almost 10 pounds. If we assume a gallon to have been 9 pounds in the case of the Brittons, we find that the family claims to have required a minimum of 36 pounds of bread per week. For this time, in which bread was the basic dietary element of the poor, demographic historians assume an adult to have consumed 2 pounds per day. Even if the family comprised only two adults and the rest children, these were extremely short rations.

13. **firing:** that is, no morning hearth fire for want of the cost of fuel.

22 February	Feast of the Chair of St. Peter
March or April	Tuesday of Holy Week until the Thursday after Easter (eight working days)
3 May	Feast of the Finding of the True Cross
9 May	Feast of St. Nicholas
May or June	Feast of Pentecost (seventh Sunday after Easter): Pentecost eve through the following Thursday (five days)
5 June	Corpus Christi
9 June or second Sunday in June	Municipal procession accompanied by banquets
11 June	Feast of St. Barnabas
June	Thursday after municipal procession is a holiday
2 July	Feast of the visitation of the Virgin
1 August	Feast of St. Peter in Chains
3 August	Feast of St. Stephen
29 August	Feast of the Beheading of St. John the Baptist, followed by five days off
1 October	Feast of St. Remy
18 October	Feast of St. Luke
1 November	All Saints Day
24–31 December	Christmas (eight days)

This represents a total of forty-four days off, in addition to Sundays.

Sources 4 and 5 from Sidney Pollard and Colin Holmes, editors, Documents in European Economic History, *vol. 1,* The Process of Industrialization, 1750–1870 *(New York: St. Martin's, 1968), pp. 45–48; pp. 91–92. Copyright © 1968 by St. Martin's Press. Reprinted with permission of St. Martin's Press, Inc., and Sidney Pollard.*

4. Guild Regulations in the Prussian Woolen Industry, 1797

§ 760

Although it is laid down in the General Privilege (8 Nov. 1734) that it shall not be necessary to produce a masterpiece in order to gain the master's freedom; yet it was ruled afterwards: that anyone aspiring to the freedom of the gild, shall (22 November 1772) apart from being examined by the Inspector of Manufactures and the Gild Master whether he be properly experienced in sorting and fulling, wool shearing and preparing and threading the looms, also weave a piece of cloth of mixed colour from wool dyed by himself.

Chapter 6

Labor Old

and New:

The Impact of

the Industrial

Revolution

§ 765–§ 771

The woollen weavers may sell by retail and cutting-up home produced cloths and baizes[14] on condition that they and their fellow gild members may not only sell in their own town the goods made locally, but may also offer them for sale at fairs and annual markets. The latter, however, is limited to this extent (1772 and 1791): that a gild member may not take part in any market or fair unless he has at least 12 pieces of cloth for sale, though it is permissible (18 December 1791) for two of them to enter a fair and to offer cloth for sale if they have at least 12 pieces of cloth between them; at the same time, this privilege is extended also to weavers (1772) who are no longer practising their trade themselves.

The woollen weavers of Salzwedel, however, may not sell the cloths produced by themselves, by retail and cutting-up, even in their own town, because the local cloth cutters' and tailors' gild enjoys, according to its old privilege (1233, 1323 and last confirmed on 26 January 1715) the sole right of cutting up woollen and similar cloth for sale, so that neither the local merchants, nor the mercers, nor the woollen weavers of the town, whose rights were recently confirmed, have the right to cut up woollen cloth for sale.

Woollen weavers may not trade in woollen cloths made outside their own town, unless they have been specially granted this right, because this would infringe the privileges granted to the merchants. . . .

Neither finishers nor croppers,[15] dyers or other craftsmen (1772) are permitted to trade in woollen cloths or undertake putting-out agencies on pain of losing their craft privileges.

In the countryside (28 August 1723, 14 November 1793) neither linen (?) weavers, nor vergers[16] or schoolmasters, nor husbandmen themselves, are permitted to manufacture woollen or worsted cloth not even for their own use. Neither are town linen weavers permitted to make goods wholly of wool.

Woollen weavers are permitted to dye their own cloths, but neither they nor the merchants are permitted to have the cloths made in the Electoral Mark finished or dyed in foreign towns, on pain of confiscation of the goods. While the export of unfinished and undyed cloths is permissible (1772), merchants and woollen weavers should be persuaded (26 October and 10 November 1791) to export only dyed and finished cloths.

Woollen weavers may not (1772) keep their own tenting frame and stretch their own cloths, but must leave this finishing process to the cloth finishers. They have however the concession (28 October and 11 November 1773) that they may keep 10–12 frames, but on these they may only stretch 3/4 widths, and twill flannels. . . .

---

14. **baize:** a soft woolen fabric.

15. **cropper:** a craftsman who sheared the nap from woolen cloth.

16. **verger:** a parish official generally charged with care of the interior of a church.

§ 798

On pain of requisition and, for repeated offences, on pain of loss of the freedom of the gild, better yarn may not be used for the ends of pieces of cloth than is used for the middle. No weaver is permitted to keep frames of his own, on pain of loss of his gild freedom, and he is obliged to take his cloths to the master shearmen; tanned wool and wool-fells may not be woven into pieces, but must be made only into rough goods and horse blankets. Finally it is laid down in detail how each type of woollen and worsted cloth shall be manufactured; and weavers have been advised several times to observe closely the detailed rules and regulations of the woollen and worsted order (20 September 1784, 9 September and 8 October 1787). . . .

§ 800

It is further laid down as a general rule, that all cloths shall be viewed by sworn aulnagers,[17] of whom eight shall be elected in large companies, six in medium sized ones, and two to four among small ones, and they shall be viewed three times, and sealed accordingly after each time. The first viewing shall determine that the piece is woven with sufficient and satisfactory yarn, woven sufficiently closely and without flaws, and of the correct length and width. The second, held on the frame, shall determine whether the cloth is overstretched, and has wholly pure wool, is fulled cleanly and free of errors in fulling, and the third, held on the frame after dyeing, whether it has suffered by the dyeing.

5. La Rochefoucauld Describes the Putting-Out System in Rouen, France, 1781–1783

I then saw the material called cotton check (*cotonnades*). There are all sorts of cotton manufacture made up at Rouen and in the area 15 leagues[18] around it. The peasant who returns to the plough to work his fields, sits at his cotton frame and makes either *siamoises*[19] or ticking or even white, very fine, cotton cloth. One must admire the activity of the Normans. This activity does not interfere at all with their daily work. Land is very dear and consequently very well cultivated. The farmer works on the land during the day and it is in the evening by the light of the lamp that he starts his other task. His workers and his family have to help. When they have worked all week they come into the town with horses or carts piled up with material. Goods are sold in the Hall, which is all that remains of the palace of the former Dukes of Normandy, on

17. **aulnager:** an official charged with measuring and inspecting woolen cloth.
18. **league:** a league equals 2.764 miles.
19. *siamoises:* common cotton goods.

Chapter 6

Labor Old

and New:

The Impact of

the Industrial

Revolution

Thursdays. It is a truly wonderful sight. It takes place at a surprising speed. Almost 800,000 francs worth of business is transacted between 6.00 and 9.00 in the morning. Among those who do the buying there are many agents who buy for merchants and then the goods pass to America, Italy and Spain. The majority goes to America. I have seen many pieces destined to become shirts for negroes; but their skin will be seen through the material, since the cloth is thin and almost sufficiently coarse to make ticking. It costs 17, 20 and even 25 francs per aune[20] in the Hall.

20. **aune:** an old French measurement unit for textiles; equal to 45 inches.

THE NEW LABOR

Source 6A from Jost Amman and Hans Sachs, The Book of Trades (New York: Dover Publications, 1973), p. 56.
Source 6B has two sources: Time Life Pictures/Getty Images and the Granger Collection, New York.

6B. Weaving: An English Cotton Mill, 1833

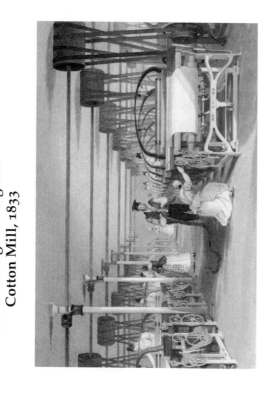

6A. Weaving: A Sixteenth-Century German Weaver and His Loom

[155]

Chapter 6

Labor Old

and New:

The Impact of

the Industrial

Revolution

Source 7 from An Historical Account of the Luddites of 1811, 1812, and 1813 with Report of Their Trials at York Castle from the 2nd to the 12th of January, 1813 . . . *(Huddersfield: John Cowgill, 1862), pp. 94–95.*

7. Labor Protest: Luddite Attack on a Water-Powered Textile Mill in the West Riding of Yorkshire, April 11, 1812

Mr. William Cartwright examined by Mr. Topping. He stated, that on the 11th April last, he was in possession of a mill at Rawfolds, in the township of Liversedge, in the West-Riding. Had been in possession of it nearly three years. It was a Water Mill, erected for the express purpose of finishing cloth by machinery. Previous to the 11th of April he had been apprehensive, or rather he expected an attack being made upon it, and in consequence of this expectation he had taken such measures for its security and protection as he thought best adapted to the purpose. He had slept in the mill for six weeks previous to the attack, and had procured musketry and ammunition, and several of his workmen slept in the mill for the week immediately preceding the attack. Witness had beds in the mill, and himself slept in the counting house. On the 11th of April last, which was Saturday, he had in the mill five soldiers and four of his own people besides himself. Witness retired to bed twenty-five minutes past twelve o'clock; in a quarter of an hour he heard the dog bark furiously; it was on the ground floor, and had been placed there for the purpose of giving the alarm, on the approach of any person in the nighttime. He got out of bed supposing the dog had given a false alarm, because he expected the first alarm to proceed from the watch at the outside of the building. As soon as he opened the door he was astonished by a heavy fire of musketry, accompanied by a violent breaking of the windows on the ground-floor; the crash was considerable; a violent hammering was at the same moment commenced at the door, and a part of the assailants went round to the other door at the end of the building. . . . Mr. Cartwright proceeded to state that they flow to their arms instantly, which had been piled the night before; they had not time to put on any of their clothes, nor did he think of it, but commenced a brisk firing.

. . . They fired through loop-holes which were in an oblique direction with respect to the interior of the building, but which commanded the front of the building. The firing was kept up regularly by the people out of doors for a considerable time. . . . Mr. Cartwright said he heard distinctly the expressions, "In with you, lads." "D—them, kill them every one." The number of people appeared considerable. A constant firing on both sides continued for some time, he could not form a correct opinion as to the time, but from the number of shots fired by them he supposed it must have occupied as much as twenty minutes. After the firing from without had slackened, they abated theirs within, with a view to save the effusion of blood. He then heard a confused alarm on one side as if an attempt was making to carry off the wounded men. After the firing had ceased he heard the cries of the wounded men. The people in going off appeared to divide and take different roads, but both of them leading ultimately towards Huddersfield.

Source 8 from Sidney Pollard and Colin Holmes, editors, Documents in European Economic History, *vol. 1,* The Process of Industrialization, 1750–1870 *(New York: St. Martin's Press, 1968), pp. 534–536. Copyright © 1968 by St. Martin's Press. Reprinted with permission of St. Martin's Press, Inc., and Sidney Pollard.*

8. Rules for Workers in the Foundry and Engineering Works of the Royal Overseas Trading Company, Berlin, 1844

In every large works, and in the co-ordination of any large number of workmen, good order and harmony must be looked upon as the fundamentals of success, and therefore the following rules shall be strictly observed.

Every man employed in the concern named below shall receive a copy of these rules, so that no one can plead ignorance. Its acceptance shall be deemed to mean consent to submit to its regulations.

(1) The normal working day begins at all seasons at 6 a.m. precisely and ends, after the usual break of half an hour for breakfast, an hour for dinner and half an hour for tea, at 7 p.m., and it shall be strictly observed.

Five minutes before the beginning of the stated hours of work until their actual commencement, a bell shall ring and indicate that every worker employed in the concern has to proceed to his place of work, in order to start as soon as the bell stops.

The doorkeeper shall lock the door punctually at 6 a.m., 8.30 a.m., 1 p.m. and 4.30 p.m.

Workers arriving 2 minutes late shall lose half an hour's wages; whoever is more than 2 minutes late may not start work until after the next break, or at least shall lose his wages until then. Any disputes about the correct time shall be settled by the clock mounted above the gatekeeper's lodge.

These rules are valid both for time- and for piece-workers, and in cases of breaches of these rules, workmen shall be fined in proportion to their earnings. The deductions from the wage shall be entered in the wage-book of the gatekeeper whose duty they are: they shall be unconditionally accepted as it will not be possible to enter into any discussions about them.

Chapter 6

Labor Old

and New:

The Impact of

the Industrial

Revolution

(2) When the bell is rung to denote the end of the working day, every work-man, both on piece- and on day-wage, shall leave his workshop and the yard, but is not allowed to make preparations for his departure before the bell rings. Every breach of this rule shall lead to a fine of five silver groschen to the sick fund. Only those who have obtained special permission by the overseer may stay on in the workshop in order to work.—If a workman has worked beyond the closing bell, he must give his name to the gatekeeper on leaving, on pain of losing his payment for the overtime.

(3) No workman, whether employed by time or piece, may leave before the end of the working day, without having first received permission from the overseer and having given his name to the gatekeeper. Omission of these two actions shall lead to a fine of ten silver groschen payable to the sick fund.

(4) Repeated irregular arrival at work shall lead to dismissal. This shall also apply to those who are found idling by an official or overseer, and refuse to obey their order to resume work.

(5) Entry to the firm's property by any but the designated gateway, and exit by any prohibited route, e.g., by climbing fences or walls, or by crossing the Spree, shall be punished by a fine of fifteen silver groschen to the sick fund for the first offences, and dismissal for the second.

(6) No worker may leave his place of work otherwise than for reasons connected with his work.

(7) All conversation with fellow-workers is prohibited; if any worker requires information about his work, he must turn to the overseer, or to the particular fellow-worker designated for the purpose.

(8) Smoking in the workshops or in the yard is prohibited during working hours; anyone caught smoking shall be fined five silver groschen for the sick fund for every such offence.

(9) Every worker is responsible for cleaning up his space in the workshop, and if in doubt, he is to turn to his overseer.—All tools must always be kept in good condition, and must be cleaned after use. This applies particularly to the turner, regarding his lathe.

(10) Natural functions must be performed at the appropriate places, and whoever is found soiling walls, fences, squares, etc., and similarly, whoever is found washing his face and hands in the workshop and not in the places assigned for the purpose, shall be fined five silver groschen for the sick fund.

(11) On completion of his piece of work, every workman must hand it over at once to his foreman or superior, in order to receive a fresh piece of work. Pattern makers must on no account hand over their patterns to the foundry without express order of their supervisors. No workman may take over work from his fellow-workman without instruction to that effect by the foreman.

(12) It goes without saying that all overseers and officials of the firm shall be obeyed without question, and shall be treated with due deference. Disobedience will be punished by dismissal.

(13) Immediate dismissal shall also be the fate of anyone found drunk in any of the workshops.

(14) Untrue allegations against superiors or officials of the concern shall lead to stern reprimand, and may lead to dismissal. The same punishment shall be meted out to those who knowingly allow errors to slip through when supervising or stocktaking.

(15) Every workman is obliged to report to his superiors any acts of dishonesty or embezzlement on the part of his fellow workmen. If he omits to do so, and it is shown after subsequent discovery of a misdemeanour that he knew about it at the time, he shall be liable to be taken to court as an accessory after the fact and the wage due to him shall be retained as punishment. Conversely, anyone denouncing a theft in such a way as to allow conviction of the thief shall receive a reward of two Thaler, and, if necessary, his name shall be kept confidential.—Further, the gatekeeper and the watchman, as well as every official, are entitled to search the baskets, parcels, aprons etc. of the women and children who are taking the dinners into the works, on their departure, as well as search any worker suspected of stealing any article whatever. . . .

(18) Advances shall be granted only to the older workers, and even to them only in exceptional circumstances. As long as he is working by the piece, the workman is entitled merely to his fixed weekly wage as subsistence pay; the extra earnings shall be paid out only on completion of the whole piece contract. If a workman leaves before his piece contract is completed, either of his own free will, or on being dismissed as punishment, or because of illness, the partly completed work shall be valued by the general manager with the help of two overseers, and he will be paid accordingly. There is no appeal against the decision of these experts.

(19) A free copy of these rules is handed to every workman, but whoever loses it and requires a new one, or cannot produce it on leaving, shall be fined $2\frac{1}{2}$ silver groschen, payable to the sick fund.

Moabit, August, 1844.

Chapter 6

Labor Old

and New:

The Impact of

the Industrial

Revolution

Source 9 from Erna Olafson Hellerstein, L. P. Hume, and K. M. Offen, editors, Victorian Women: A Documentary Account of Women's Lives in Nineteenth-Century England, France, and the United States *(Stanford, Calif.: Stanford University Press, 1981), pp. 394–396. Used by permission of Stanford University Press.*

9. Apprenticeship Contract for Young Women Employed in the Silk Mills of Tarare, France, 1850s

MILLING, REELING, AND WARP-PREPARATION OF SILKS

Conditions of Apprenticeship

Art. 1. To be admitted, young women must be between the ages of thirteen and fifteen, of good character and in good health, intelligent and industrious, and must have been vaccinated. They must present their birth certificate, a certificate of vaccination, and a trousseau.

Art. 2. Girls who are accepted by the establishment will be placed in milling, reeling, or warp[21] preparation by the director, according to the needs of the establishment and their intelligence.

Art. 3. During the apprenticeship period, the pupil will be paid wages, fed, lodged, given heat and light, and laundry *for her body linen only;* she will also be furnished with aprons.

Art. 4. The pupil promises to be obedient and submissive to the mistresses charged with her conduct and instruction, as well as to conform to the rules of the establishment.

Art. 5. In case of illness the director will notify the father or guardian of the sick apprentice, and if her state necessitates a leave, it will be granted until her recovery.

Art. 6. If the sick pupil remains in the establishment, every care necessitated by her condition will be given to her.

Art. 7. In case of illness or any other serious cause that warrants her leaving, the apprentice who must absent herself from the establishment will be obligated to prolong her apprenticeship during a time equal to that of her absence.

Art. 8. The director alone has the right to authorize or refuse leaves. They will be granted only on the request of the father or guardian of the pupil.

Art. 9. Apprenticeship is for three consecutive years, *not including an obligatory trial month.* In order to encourage the pupil, she will be paid:

1st year:	a wage of 40 to 50 francs
2nd year:	" " " 60 to 75 "
3rd year:	" " " 80 to 100 "

21. **warp:** in the weaving process, threads placed lengthwise in the loom. They were woven with threads called the *weft* or *woof* placed perpendicularly to them.

After the apprenticeship the wage will be established according to merit.

At the end of the apprenticeship, a gratuity of 20 francs will be given to the apprentice to reward her for her exactitude in fulfilling her engagements.

Art. 10. The effective work time is twelve hours. Summer and winter, the day begins at 5 o'clock and ends at 7:15.

Breakfast is from 7:30 to 8:15; lunch is from 12:00 to 1:00; snack is from 5:00 to 5:30; supper is at 7:15.

After the second year, pupils will receive lessons in reading, writing, and arithmetic. They will be taught to sew and do a little cooking.

Art. 11. As a measure of encouragement and with no obligation, it is established that at the end of each month the young people will be graded as follows:

1st class, gift for the month 1 fr. 50 c.
2nd class   1 " —
3rd class   50 c.
4th class   —[22]

Each month a new classification will take place, and the young person will rise or fall according to her merit. This classification will be based on an overall evaluation of conduct, quantity and quality of work, docility and diligence, etc.

Art. 12. Wages are not due until the end of the year. They will be paid during the month following their due date. Gifts, incentive pay, and compensation for extra work will be paid each month.

Art. 13. Any apprentice who leaves the establishment before the end of her term, or who has been dismissed for bad conduct, conspiracy, rebellion, laziness, or a serious breach of the rules loses her rights to wages for the current year; beyond this, in such a case, the father or guardian of the pupil agrees to pay the director of the establishment the sum of one hundred francs to indemnify him for the non-fulfillment of the present agreement: half of this sum will be given to the *bureau de bienfaisance*[23] in the pupil's parish.

Art. 14. If, during the first year, apprentice is recognized as unfit, despite the agreement and in the interest of both parties the director reserves the right to send her away without indemnity.

Art. 15. The apprentice who leaves the establishment at the end of the first month under the pretext that she cannot get used to the place, will pay 50 centimes per day toward the costs she has occasioned, as well as her travel expenses . . .

22. Abbreviations for French currency:
   fr.: franc.
   c.: centime; 100 centimes to 1 franc.
23. *bureau de bienfaisance:* Catholic social welfare organization.

Chapter 6

Labor Old

and New:

The Impact of

the Industrial

Revolution

Source 10 from British Parliamentary Papers: Reports from Committees, *vol. 15*, Labour of Children in Factories *(London: House of Commons, 1832), pp. 6–13.*

10. Report of the Sadler Committee, 1832[24]

William Cooper, called in; and Examined.

What is your business?—I follow the cloth-dressing at present.

2. What is your age?—I was eight-and-twenty last February.

3. When did you first begin to work in mills or factories?—When I was about 10 years of age.

4. With whom did you first work?—At Mr. Benyon's flax[25] mills, in Meadowland, Leeds.

5. What were your usual hours of working?—We began at five, and gave over at nine; at five o'clock in the morning.

6. And you gave over at nine o'clock?—At nine at night.

7. At what distance might you have lived from the mill?—About a mile and a half.

8. At what time had you to get up in the morning to attend to your labour?—I had to be up soon after four o'clock.

9. Every morning?—Every morning.

10. What intermissions had you for meals?—When we began at five in the morning, we went on until noon, and then we had 40 minutes for dinner.

11. Had you no time for breakfast?—No, we got it as we could, while we were working.

12. Had you any time for an afternoon refreshment, or what is called in Yorkshire your "drinking?"—No; when we began at noon, we went on till night; there was only one stoppage, the 40 minutes for dinner.

13. Then as you had to get your breakfast, and what is called "drinking" in that manner, you had to put it on one side?—Yes, we had to put it on one side; and when we got our frames doffed, we ate two or three mouthfuls, and then put it by again.[26]

---

24. **Sadler Committee:** the Committee on the Bill to Regulate the Labour of Children in the Mills and Factories of the United Kingdom.

25. **flax:** a plant whose fiber is manufactured into linen for thread or weaving into fabrics.

26. Vocabulary of the textile mill:
    frame: the water frame, an early spinning machine.
    doff: the task, in the industrial spinning process, of removing spindles filled with yarn from the spinning machine.
    bobbin: a reel, cylinder, or spoollike apparatus on which thread is wound.
    card: a tool used to comb out textile fibers (wool, flax, etc.) in preparation for spinning them into thread.
    gigger: a person who worked in the gigging process, a step in dressing wool cloth in which loose fibers are drawn off the fabric and in which the fabric's nap is raised. The process used **teasles,** thistlelike plants that hooked the fabric and raised it.
    boiler: part of the processing of wool involved boiling and scrubbing to remove oils.
    primmer, brusher: workers involved in the final preparation of woolen cloth.

14. Is there not considerable dust in a flax mill?—A flax mill is very dusty indeed.

15. Was not your food therefore frequently spoiled?—Yes, at times with the dust; sometimes we could not eat it, when it had got a lot of dust on.

16. What were you when you were ten years old?—What is called a bobbin-doffer; when the frames are quite full, we have to doff them.

17. Then as you lived so far from home, you took your dinner to the mill?—We took all our meals with us, living so far off.

18. During the 40 minutes which you were allowed for dinner, had you ever to employ that time in your turn in cleaning the machinery?—At times we had to stop to clean the machinery, and then we got our dinner as well as we could; they paid us for that.

19. At these times you had no resting at all?—No.

20. How much had you for cleaning the machinery?—I cannot exactly say what they gave us, as I never took any notice of it.

21. Did you ever work even later than the time you have mentioned?—I cannot say that I worked later there: I had a sister who worked up stairs, and she worked till 11 at night, in what they call the card-room.

22. At what time in the morning did she begin to work?—At the same time as myself.

23. And they kept her there till 11 at night?—Till 11 at night.

24. You say that your sister was in the card-room?—Yes.

25. Is not that a very dusty department?—Yes, very dusty indeed.

26. She had to be at the mill at five, and was kept at work till eleven at night?—Yes.

27. During the whole time she was there?—During the whole time; there was only 40 minutes allowed at dinner out of that.

28. To keep you at your work for such a length of time, and especially towards the termination of such a day's labour as that, what means were taken to keep you awake and attentive?—They strapped us at times, when we were not quite ready to be doffing the frame when it was full.

29. Were you frequently strapped?—At times we were frequently strapped.

30. What sort of strap was it?—About this length [*describing it*].

31. What was it made of?—Of leather.

32. Were you occasionally very considerably hurt with the strap?—Sometimes it hurt us very much, and sometimes they did not lay on so hard as they did at others.

33. Were the girls strapped in that sort of way?—They did not strap what they called the grown-up women.

34. Were any of the female children strapped?—Yes; they were strapped in the same way as the lesser boys. . . .

44. Were your punishments the same in that mill as in the other?—Yes, they used the strap the same there.

45. How long did you work in that mill?—Five years.

[163]

Chapter 6

Labor Old

and New:

The Impact of

the Industrial

Revolution

46. And how did it agree with your health?—I was sometimes well, and sometimes not very well.

47. Did it affect your breathing at all?—Yes; sometimes we were stuffed.

48. When your hours were so long, you had not any time to attend to a day-school?—We had no time to go to a day-school, only to a Sunday-school,[27] and then with working such long hours we wanted to have a bit of rest, so that I slept till the afternoon, sometimes till dinner, and sometimes after.

49. Did you attend a place of worship?—I should have gone to a place of worship many times, but I was in the habit of falling asleep, and that kept me away; I did not like to go for fear of being asleep.

50. Do you mean that you could not prevent yourself from falling asleep, in consequence of the fatigue of the preceding week?—Yes. . . .

85. After working at a mill to this excess, how did you find your health at last?—I found it very bad indeed; I found illness coming on me a long time before I fell down.

86. Did you at length become so ill as to be unable to pursue your work?—I was obliged to give it up entirely.

87. How long were you ill?—For six months.

88. Who attended?—Mr. Metcalf and Mr. Freeman.

89. What were you told by your medical attendants was the reason of your illness?—Nothing but hard labour, and working long hours; and they gave me up, and said no good could be done for me, that I must go into the country.

90. Did this excessive labour not only weaken you, but destroy your appetite?—It destroyed the appetite, and I became so feeble, that I could not cross the floor unless I had a stick to go with; I was in great pain, and could find ease in no posture.

91. You could drink in the meantime, if you could not eat?—Yes, I could drink.

92. But you found that did not improve your health?—No.

93. Has it been remarked that your excessive labour from early life has greatly diminished your growth?—A number of persons have said that such was the case, and that I was the same as if I had been made of iron or stone.

94. What height are you?—About five feet. It is that that has hindered me of my growth.

95. When you were somewhat recovered, did you apply for labour?—I applied for my work again, but the overlooker said I was not fit to work; he was sure of that, and he would not let me have it. I was then obliged to throw myself on the parish.[28]

27. **Sunday-school:** churches often ran schools for mill children on their day off (Sunday) to teach the rudiments of reading and writing along with religious instruction.

28. **on the parish:** under existing English laws, poor relief was the responsibility of the local parish.

96. Have you subsisted on the parish ever since?—Yes.

97. Have you been always willing and anxious to work?—I was always willing and anxious to work from my infancy.

98. Have you been on the parish since your severe illness?—Yes.

99. How long is that ago?—Six months. When I was ill I got something from the Society; they relieved me then, but when I became better I received no benefit from it.

100. Yours is not what is called a Friendly Society?—No, it is what we call Odd Fellows.[29]

101. And they do not extend relief after a certain period?—Not after you get better. . . .

124. You say that you had no time to go to school during the week, but that you went on Sunday?—I went on Sunday; I had no time to go to a day-school.

125. Can you read or write?—I can read, but I cannot write. . . .

184. How did you contrive to be awake so early in the morning?—My father used to call me up.

185. Did he get up so early as that for his own business?—He got up on purpose to call me.

186. How many hours did he work in a day at his own business?—Sometimes from five in the morning till eight at night.

187. You say he was a shoemaker?—Yes.

188. Then, according to this, he worked more hours than you did?—I think not so long.

189. Did your father take his regular intervals for his meals?—I should think so.

190. And walked about to market for his family; had he not many pauses in his labour?—He worked at home, and therefore could do as he pleased. . . .

198. Has your health improved since you left off working long hours?—I am a deal better than I was; but I believe that if I could have got work, and have had something to support me, I should have recruited my health better. I have been very poorly kept for these last six months, having been out of work. I have only half a crown a week allowed from the parish for my wife and myself. . . .

217. Do you think you would be able to stand your work?—I should like to try; I cannot bear to go wandering about the streets. . . .

220. Is being a gigger harder than the others?—Yes, gigging is very hard work; the fleeces are so heavy and full of water, and you have to stand in this position [*describing it*] to support them and turn the fleece over; if you are not over strong it makes you rather deformed in your legs.

---

29. **Friendly Society, Odd Fellows Society:** organizations founded to benefit workers through "self-help." They took up small weekly sums from their members and used the funds thus collected to aid sick or injured members who were unable to work, or to assist the widows and orphans of members.

Chapter 6

Labor Old

and New:

The Impact of

the Industrial

Revolution

221. At what age do people generally begin gigging?—Some begin about 15, 16 or 17, and some lads begin when about 14.

222. At what age did your father die?—He was 60 when he died.

223. Have you seen the man lately who is doing your work at Mr. Brown's?—Yes.

224. Is he in good health?—I do not know; I must not say a thing that I do not know; it is a good while since I saw him.

225. Was your father a tall or a short man?—He stood about five feet seven.

226. And you are five feet?—Yes.

227. Have you any brothers or sisters?—Two brothers and a sister.

228. Do they work in the same trade?—I have a brother working now at the same trade; he was seventeen the 14th of last February.

229. Has he good health?—He had not over good health when I came from Leeds.

Source 11 from Sidney Pollard and Colin Holmes, editors, Documents in European Economic History, *vol. 2,* Industrial Power and National Rivalry *(New York: St. Martin's, 1972), pp. 322–323. Copyright © 1972 by St. Martin's Press. Reprinted with permission of St. Martin's Press, Inc., and Sidney Pollard.*

11. Working Conditions of a Female Textile Worker in Germany, 1880s and 1890s

In the weaving sheds the girls work in an atmosphere which, on the third day of my work there, gave me bad lung catarrh; tiny flakes of the twisted wool fill the air, settle on dress and hair, and float into nose and mouth; the machines have to be swept clean every two hours; the dust is breathed in by the girls, since they are not allowed to open the windows. To this has to be added the terrible nerve-racking noise of the rattling machines so that no one can hear himself speak. No communication with one's neighbour is possible except by shouting on the top of one's voice. In consequence, all the girls have screeching, irritating voices: even when the shop has gone quiet, at the end of the working day, on the street, at home, they never converse quietly like other people, their conversation is a constant yelling, which produces the impression among outsiders that they are quarrelling.

It is truly a miracle that so many girls still look fresh and blooming, and that they still feel like singing at work, usually sentimental folk songs. . . .

The girls work hard, very hard, and quite a few told me how they collapsed with the exertion of the first four weeks of work, and how most of them suffer for months with irritations of the lung and throat until they get used to the dust. To this has to be added the poor, miserable food, the short periods of rest in rooms which don't deserve the name of "dwelling"—and yet the girls remain cheerful, healthy, lively and enterprising.

I have always watched this with admiration; I could not have stood this for long. I could not take anything in the morning beside coffee; only in the evening I hurried, totally exhausted, to my hotel, to swallow some nourishing food with great difficulty. . . .

No one would dream of stopping work and taking a rest even when suffering from violent headache or toothache, not even a quarter of an hour of being late was tolerated without a substantial fine at the end of the week. . . .

The work of the carpet weavers should not be underrated, it is anything but monotonous or repetitive. When working the complex Turkish patterns, the weaver has to catch the exact moment for changing the different coloured reels. She has to think and coordinate, calculate and pay attention and concentrate all her thoughts. This work requires far more mental activity and sense of responsibility than the crochet work and needlework done by hundreds of girls of society, year after year, in expectation of the shining knight who would one day come and rescue them.

Most factories start work at half past six, pause for breakfast from 8 to 8.30, dinner 12–1; at 4 there are 20–30 minutes for tea, and work goes on until 7. On Saturdays work ends at 5.30, in order to give time to the workers to clean the machines thoroughly and to oil them by 6; Mondays, work starts half an hour later probably because all the girls have a hangover from Sunday.

Source 12 from British Parliamentary Papers: Reports from Commissioners: Children's Employment (Mines), vol. 17, Appendix to the First Report of the Commissioners (Mines) (London: William Clowes for Her Majesty's Stationery Office, 1842), pp. 39, 103, 107–108.

12. Report on the Employment of Children in British Mines, 1841–1842

May 14, 1841:

No. 49. Mr. *Joseph Staley,* Managing Partner in Coal-works at Yate Common, in the parish of Yate (Two Pits), carried on under the firm of *Staley* and *Parkers.*

Employ from 30 to 35 hands; not more than five or six boys under 13; the two youngest are from eight to nine years old, who work with their father; perhaps three boys not more than 10 years of age; they assist in cutting and carting out the coal from a one-foot seam; no doorboys employed, because there is sufficient ventilation without being particular about closing them; the carters generally manage the doors as they pass; the boys earn from 6s. to 9s. per week when they get handy at cutting; have not more than three or four

Chapter 6

Labor Old

and New:

The Impact of

the Industrial

Revolution

under 18; all over 15 are earning nearly men's wages—say 15s. per week; the men earn from 18s. to 20s.; considers two tons a fair day's work; wages paid in money every Saturday; the older boys receive their own; the boys, in carting out the coals from the *googs* [narrow inclined planes up which the coal is pulled by a chain and windlass], when short distances, draw by the *girdle* or *lugger, i.e.* a rope round the waist, with an iron hook depending in front, to which a chain, passing between the legs, is attached; if for longer distances, they use wheeled-carriages on a railway; no horses are employed under ground at present; the smaller boys do not tug more than 1 cwt.[30] at a time; the carts generally hold about 2 cwt. each; the thickest vein is two feet six inches, and is worked by the young men; the boys cart through a two feet six inches passageway; the young men have four feet, there being a bed of soft stuff above the coal, to cut away before they come to the roof; the shaft is 45 fathoms,[31] worked by a steam-engine, and strong-plaited rope; thinks rope decidedly safer than chain, as it gives more timely notice of any defect, by a strand or two giving way, whereas a link of iron is sometimes near breaking, a good while before it is discovered, and then separates on a sudden. . . .

MESSRS. WILLSON, HOLMES, AND STOCKS, QUARRY-HOUSE PIT.

No. 6. *William Jagger,* aged 11.   May 6:

I am a hurrier[32] for my father, Benjamin Jagger; have been in here four years and upwards; I come to work at seven o'clock, and go home at four, five, and six; I get breakfast afore I come down; I get my dinner down here, I get it about one o'clock; I don't know how long I am taking it; I get it as I can; I go to work directly after; I get currant-cake and buttered cake sometimes, never any meat; I get a bit of meat for supper when I go up. I went to day-school often; I comed to work about half a year; I go to Sunday-school now at church; I cannot read or write. I have got to hurry a corve 400 yards; I don't know what weight it is [$2\frac{1}{2}$ cwt.]; it runs upon rails; I push the corves; some of the boys push when there is no rail. I do not oft hurt my feet; I never met with an accident. The men serve me out sometimes—they wallop me; I don't know what for, except 'tis when I don't hurry fast enough; I like my work very well; I would rather hurry than set cards.

The mainway of this pit is 3 feet 6 inches high and 400 yards in length; seams 17 inches thick; gear in good order; shaft not walled up. At the moment of stepping out

30. **cwt.:** hundredweight, i.e., 100 pounds.

31. **fathom:** a fathom equals 6 feet; the shaft of 45 fathoms thus extended 270 feet below the earth's surface.

32. Mining vocabulary:
    hurrier: a person who drew a wagon loaded with coal through mine tunnels to the shaft up which the load would be raised to the earth's surface.
    corve: small wagon for carrying coal or ore in a mine.

of the corve at the pit's bottom, a stone weighing from five to seven pounds fell in the water close by my feet from the unlined shaft near the top, or from the bank, a circumstance at once illustrative of the importance of protecting persons in their descent, by walling up the sides of the shaft, and thereby preventing loose measures from falling.

MR. JOSEPH STOCKS, BOOTH TOWN PIT, HALIFAX.

No. 26. *Patience Kershaw*, aged 17.   May 15:

My father has been dead about a year; my mother is living and has ten children, five lads and five lasses; the oldest is about thirty, the youngest is four; three lasses go to mill; all the lads are colliers, two getters and three hurriers; one lives at home and does nothing; mother does nought but look after home.

All my sisters have been hurriers, but three went to the mill, Alice went because her legs swelled from hurrying in cold water when she was hot. I never went to day-school; I go to Sunday-school, but I cannot read or write; I go to pit at five o'clock in the morning and come out at five in the evening; I get my breakfast of porridge and milk first; I take my dinner with me, a cake, and eat it as I go; I do not stop or rest any time for the purpose; I get nothing else until I get home, and then have potatoes and meat, not every day meat. I hurry in the clothes I have now got on, trousers and ragged jacket; the bald place upon my head is made by thrusting the corves; my legs have never swelled, but sisters' did when they went to mill; I hurry the corves a mile and more under ground and back; they weigh 3 cwt.; I hurry 11 a-day; I wear a belt and chain at the workings to get the corves out; the getters[33] that I work for are *naked* except their caps; they pull off all their clothes; I see them at work when I go up; sometimes they beat me, if I am not quick enough, with their hands; they strike me upon my back; the boys take liberties with me sometimes, they pull me about; I am the only girl in the pit; there are about 20 boys and 15 men; all the men are naked; I would rather work in mill than in coal-pit.

> This girl is an ignorant, filthy, ragged, and deplorable-looking object, and such a one as the uncivilized natives of the prairies would be shocked to look upon.[34]

33. **getter:** a person who cut the coal from the seam. Young male hurriers, who often suffered stunted growth because of their excessive labor in moving coal as children, often graduated to the occupation of getter. Short stature was an asset in the restricted spaces of mine tunnels. The mining commission report from which this testimony is drawn notes that getters described themselves as "mashed up."

34. This comment by the mine commissioners is amplified elsewhere in their report, where they note that Kershaw worked in a mine whose tunnels contained 3 or 4 inches of water at all times and that she moved her corve 1,800 to 2,000 yards on each trip.

Chapter 6

Labor Old

and New:

The Impact of

the Industrial

Revolution

QUESTIONS TO CONSIDER

Let us bring together your findings on the old and new labor of European working men and women. Your goal is to understand the changes affecting them in the late eighteenth and nineteenth centuries and how these changes came about. You may want to review the questions in Sources and Method before continuing your study of the evidence.

First, consider the length of time workers devoted to labor. Was the preindustrial workday much different in length from the early-industrial-age workday? Note especially the findings of the Sadler Committee on the workdays of William Cooper, employed in industrial labor, and his father, a craftsman of the old school. Next, consider the number of workdays per year. Both old and new labor generally required a six-day work-week. But reexamine the holidays at Lille, remembering to punctuate the work year with a liberal number of "holy Mondays." On how many days per year did Vauban estimate his workers were employed in agriculture? Compare this quantity of work with that demanded of William Cooper. Like many nineteenth-century miners, this textile worker could probably have looked forward to holidays only on Christmas, Easter Monday, and the Monday after Pentecost. What other time off from work could he have expected? What effect did the Industrial Revolution have on the annual quantity of work for many laborers?

Those employed in both old and new styles of labor certainly worked hard. But the quality, pace, and discipline of their respective work situations certainly varied. Let us first consider the quality or nature of the old labor. What sort of variety characterized the work of agricultural workers like those described by Vauban and Mrs. Britton? Where was much of their work carried on? Where did most industrial-age labor take place? Why do you think Mrs. Britton testified that she preferred physically taxing agricultural work to factory labor? Why do you think William Cooper would have preferred the craftsman's work of his father to industrial labor? How do you think the necessity of working with machinery would have shaped Cooper's opinion? What basic qualitative differences distinguished the old from the new labor?

Consider the pace of work. Who set the pace for guild members? Who set the pace in the putting-out system, the factory, and the mine? Notice the discipline of the industrial-era workplace, too. What sort of punishments and incentives prodded employees to work quickly? Considering the conditions of preindustrial labor, why do you think the specific regulations in Source 9 were necessary? Recall the statement by Andrew Ure that opened this chapter. What were management's goals in imposing this kind of discipline?

Other changes in labor also accompanied the Industrial Revolution. What do the testimonies from the coal miners and the records of French and German textile workers tell us about the labor of women in the industrial age? Reexamine Mrs. Britton's testimony. In what setting did she labor after her marriage? What effect might female and child industrial labor have had on the family? What educational opportunities existed for boys and girls in industrial labor?

Finally, let us consider the health and safety of workers under both the old and the new systems. Which style of labor do you think Mrs. Britton and William Cooper would have considered more healthful? What hazards awaited textile workers like Cooper and miners like William Jagger and Patience Kershaw?

In other ways, old and new labor were not quite so different. Ideally, any job should provide some security of continuing employment. How did the Prussian guild regulations seek to protect the markets and incomes of the textile workers? Did any other workers, old or new, benefit from such efforts to protect job security? Consider the problems of Mr. Britton and Vauban's workers, as well as the effect of cycles of economic prosperity and depression on William Cooper and his fellow textile workers. Did any of them have hopes of continuing employment opportunity?

Consider, too, the problems all these workers confronted when illness, injury, or economic conditions denied them employment. What recourse did Mrs. Britton and her family have in the face of poverty? Did William Cooper have any additional resources to draw on when illness struck? Were they sufficient for his needs?

Your comparative analysis of this chapter's sources provides one more insight into the industrialization of western Europe. Economic historians speak of *proto-industrialization,* a process that paved the way for industrialization by organizing production into larger units employing traditional technologies. Industrial capitalists later combined experience in such organization with new machines to produce the Industrial Revolution. To understand this process, consider what the factory system meant: large units of production, controlled by capitalists who were prepared to organize labor and resources for a profit, and competition among producers who sought worldwide markets. What evidence of modern industrial organization do you find in the putting-out system? In what ways did it occupy a transitional role? Were its methods of production old or new? Was its organization of production old or new? How were its labor-management relations similar to those of the industrial age? What do the events in Source 7 suggest about the effect of work changes on those accustomed to the old style of labor?

Now you are ready to provide detailed answers to the main questions of this chapter: What was the nature of the new labor? How did it evolve? How did it differ from the old labor? Be sure to base your responses on the evidence you have assessed.

Chapter 6

Labor Old

and New:

The Impact of

the Industrial

Revolution

EPILOGUE

A combination of developments served to improve conditions for later generations of workers. Early industrial workers won such improvements in their lot only slowly and with considerable struggle, however. The right to take part in government by voting was one common demand of nineteenth-century workers in a Europe that accorded a political voice only to the wealthy and privileged, if it accorded one to anyone at all. Workers in England began to win the vote only in 1867 after considerable agitation; a revolution in France in 1848 established the right of universal suffrage for men. Elsewhere the vote came more slowly, and Russian workers lacked voting rights until 1906.

In the more democratic western European nations, a widened right to vote in the nineteenth century made political institutions more responsive to workers' needs. During that century, several European parliaments passed legislation that sought to regulate working conditions for women and children, to establish minimum safety standards, and to begin to provide the accident, health, and old age insurance plans that protect modern workers. Real improvements, however, often lagged behind such legislation. Early wage, hour, and safety regulations ran counter to an important political philosophy of the nineteenth century, liberalism (see Chapter 7), which viewed such legislation as interference in freedom of management. Thus, when early regulations were passed, there frequently

were not enough officials to enforce them by comprehensive factory inspections. If you refer to William Cooper's testimony, you will find him completely unaware of a parliamentary act to regulate work hours, eloquent proof of this early lack of enforcement. Governments were slow to create the machinery necessary to enforce these rules.

The nineteenth century also witnessed an often bitter struggle by workers to form their own organizations promoting their common welfare. Because unions and strikes, as we have seen, were illegal in many countries, the first worker organizations of the early nineteenth century often were self-help groups such as the one that aided William Cooper. Only after much struggle did governments in countries like England and France legalize labor unions and the right to strike.

The legalization of unions, however, allowed industrial workers to take collective action in strikes to win better wages and conditions. Early strikes often produced bloody conflict between labor on one side and management, sometimes backed by police or the army in the name of keeping order, on the other. The first major victory for a noncraft union, however, occurred in the London dockworkers' strike of 1889. Twentieth-century developments have improved the lot of workers in other ways, especially through increased leisure time, realized in the forty-hour workweek and paid vacations.

Improvements in wages and working conditions, however, did not change the basic nature of modern factory labor. In the industrial workplace, the pace of work continued to be set by machines, granting little independence to the individual worker, who remained a human cog in the greater modern industrial machine. Though most workers adjusted to this kind of labor, manifestations of their discontent have not disappeared entirely. In 1968, as you will see in Chapter 13, millions of French workers went on strike and occupied their factories. One of their chief demands was for a concept they called *autogestion*, that is, some voice in the workplace decisions that governed their lives on the job.

Such demands by employees have not gone entirely unheeded by man-agement. There have been efforts to reintroduce some worker input into the production process through such practices as quality circles, in which workers engaged in the same phases of production meet periodically to discuss their jobs and to make suggestions for improving the production process. Other experiments in such industries as automobile assembly have sought to involve individual workers in several phases of the production process as a way of mitigating the monotony of assembly-line work. Nevertheless, the basic nature of industrial employment, as symbolized by the production line, remains unchanged.

CHAPTER SEVEN

TWO PROGRAMS FOR

SOCIAL AND POLITICAL

CHANGE: LIBERALISM

AND SOCIALISM

THE PROBLEM

"Workingmen of all countries unite!" proclaimed Karl Marx and Friedrich Engels in *The Communist Manifesto* of 1848, urging working people to overthrow the capitalist system and end the working conditions of the early Industrial Revolution, which we explored in Chapter 6. Marx and Engels were partisans in a nineteenth-century ideological clash in which they and other proponents of socialism opposed liberalism, the dominant doctrine among the rising class of factory owners and managers. Nineteenth-century liberals and socialists differed greatly in their views on such issues as the definition of freedom and democracy, the role of government, and their visions of the future.

We must be careful in this chapter to understand liberalism in its nineteenth- and not its twenty-first-century sense.

For most twenty-first-century Americans, *liberalism* describes an ideology that calls for an activist role for government in ensuring the basic needs of its citizens in a variety of areas, including civil rights, material wants, and health and safety protection. In the nineteenth century, liberals sought to maximize the freedom of the individual from government control. Drawing on traditions restricting royal authority that dated back to medieval times, many liberals saw in the French Revolution the essential victory they sought to win all over Europe. In destroying the Old Regime, with its absolute monarchy and privilege for the aristocratic few, the Revolution had created a new political order based on individual freedom. Everywhere, liberals sought to draft constitutions that would limit royal authority and ensure basic individual rights. The citizen was to be safe from arbitrary arrest and was to enjoy freedom of speech, assembly, religion, and the press.

For the early or classical liberals, however, individual freedom did not mean political democracy, a voice for all in government. The constitutional arrangements created by liberals usually included some sort of property qualification for voting. Most liberals were members of the middle classes and believed that to exercise the right to vote, a citizen had to have some stake in the existing social and economic order in the form of property. The majority lacked sufficient wealth to vote in all early-nineteenth-century countries under liberal rule. But one liberal French minister, François Guizot, noted that the poor possessed full freedom to increase their wealth so that they could acquire property and participate in political life! Extreme as this view may seem to us, it does express the liberal faith that peaceful political change was possible. The key to the success of such a system of government was the establishment of a society of laws protecting individual freedoms.

Liberal economic thought was also a doctrine of absolute freedom. Liberals opposed the guild and aristocratic privileges that had limited career opportunities in Old Regime Europe. Thus, individual economic opportunity, embodied in the opening of all careers to citizens on the basis of their talents, not their titles, became the central liberal economic tenet. But liberals' faith in economic freedom had far greater implications.

Liberals believed that immutable natural laws, like supply and demand, regulated economic life. Government interference in economic life, they believed, violated not only these laws but individual freedom as well. Based in large part on the writings of such classical liberal economists as the Englishmen Adam Smith (1723–1790), Thomas Malthus (1766–1834), and David Ricardo (1772–1823), liberal economic thought defended the right of early industrial employers to be free of government regulation. Their doctrine was summed up in the French phrase *laissez-faire* (literally, "leave it alone").

Socialists differed from liberals in that they saw the French Revolution of 1789 as simply the first step in revamping Europe's old order. The revolution had established individual freedom but not political democracy. More important for socialists, the revolution had not brought social democracy. To achieve this goal, they advocated a more equitable distribution of society's wealth. Their message, as you might imagine, had considerable appeal to those workers employed in the mills, factories, and mines of the early Industrial Revolution whose lot we explored in Chapter 6.

Some early socialist thinkers expressed the view that economic equality could be realized by peaceful evolutionary change. Karl Marx applied the label "utopian" to those thinkers because of the impracticality, in his view, of their schemes. Charles Fourier (1771–1837) advocated a restructuring of society around essentially agricultural communities that represented an attempt to turn the clock back to a preindustrial economy. Louis Blanc (1811–1882) advocated state assistance in the creation of worker-owned units of production, which was difficult to imagine in a Europe dominated by

Chapter 7

Two Programs

for Social

and Political

Change:

Liberalism

and Socialism

the liberal ideology of government noninterference in economic life. But some utopian socialists, notably Robert Owen (1771–1858), who created a model industrial town around his textile mills in New Lanark, Scotland, achieved real improvements for working people.

Utopian socialism did not transform society. Some of its ideas, however, did influence other socialist thinkers, including Karl Marx, who advocated a revolutionary transformation of society. Indeed, revolutionary socialism gained large numbers of working-class followers and by the middle and late nineteenth century threatened western Europe's liberal political

leaders with the possibility of a complete overhaul of society in the name of political and social democracy.

Nineteenth-century liberalism and socialism both produced important thinkers who analyzed the ills of their society and advanced not only plans for change but critiques of the opposing ideology. What visions of the future did liberals and socialists propose? How did they hope to realize their ideals? How did their ideologies differ? Your task in this chapter is to answer these questions by examining the ideas of two nineteenth-century political and social theorists.

SOURCES AND METHOD

Liberalism and socialism each had large numbers of eloquent proponents in the nineteenth century. This chapter presents you with samples of liberal and socialist thought in the nineteenth century drawn from the writings of but one advocate of each cause. Your sources in this chapter are the works of the liberal Alexis de Tocqueville and the revolutionary socialist Karl Marx. These two thinkers have been selected because they expressed strikingly different views on similar subjects: the historical development of the West, the nature of democracy, and the role of revolution. Tocqueville and Marx also analyzed the French Revolution of 1848, a topic you may wish to review in your textbook. Their contrasting views on the same issues will provide the

basis for your answers to the general questions on liberalism and socialism.

In analyzing the works of Tocqueville and Marx, you must understand that these works were polemic in character—that is, they were all written to advocate the causes espoused by their authors. All such works may be expected to emphasize their authors' viewpoints and summarily dismiss opposing points of view that may have considerable validity. Because each theorist was an eloquent advocate of his cause, some examination of their separate backgrounds and viewpoints is necessary to permit you to analyze their ideas fruitfully.

Alexis Charles Henri Clérel de Tocqueville was born in 1805, the son of an aristocratic father who hoped for the restoration of the French monarchy destroyed by the Revolution of 1789. When Napoleon's fall from power finally brought a restored monarchy, the Tocquevilles rose to positions of importance in government. Alexis de Tocqueville's talents gained early recognition with his appointment as a judge at the youthful age of twenty-one. It was not as a jurist that Tocqueville gained fame, however, but rather as a liberal political theorist and as an early student of what we would call today sociology and political science.

In 1831 Tocqueville and his long-time friend Gustave de Beaumont undertook a fact-finding tour in the United States to study that country's pioneering penitentiary system. For nine months Tocqueville and Beaumont traveled through the United States, observing prisons and much more. The fruit of their trip was twofold: a study of prisons based largely on Beaumont and Tocqueville's observations and Tocqueville's own study of American society and government published as *Democracy in America* (1835–1840). Tocqueville's keen analysis of American society in this work gained him immediate international recognition, and he received an honor unusual for a person of his age: election to the French Academy in 1841.[1]

After election in 1839 to the French Chamber of Deputies, Tocqueville also assumed an active role in French politics. He joined the opposition to the government of King Louis Philippe and rejected especially the monarchy's restriction of the right to vote to wealthy Frenchmen. As a deputy, Tocqueville wrote a report on slavery that contributed to its abolition in France's colonies. Further, in a speech to the Chamber of Deputies in January 1848 during a period of apparent political calm, his analysis of social conditions led him to predict the imminence of revolution. Indeed, revolution broke out less than four weeks later.

Despite his opposition to Louis Philippe, Tocqueville long had criticized revolution, perceiving a danger that individual liberty could be lost in revolutionary enthusiasm. Nevertheless, he was elected to the legislature of the new Second Republic created by the Revolution of 1848 and took part in the drafting of its constitution, arguing unsuccessfully against a directly elected president. He correctly foresaw the possibility that an ambitious demagogue could sway the people to gain election and threaten democracy. In December 1848, the victor in the presidential elections was Louis-Napoleon Bonaparte. This nephew of Emperor Napoleon I destroyed the republic in favor of an authoritarian empire, naming himself Emperor Napoleon III.[2] Tocqueville

1. **French Academy:** an association of scholars, writers, and intellectual leaders founded in 1635 to maintain the purity of the French language and establish standards of correct usage. The Academy has only forty members, called the "immortals," who vote to fill vacancies in their ranks caused by deaths of members. The dignity of such election is usually confined to persons of advanced years and long-proven merit.

2. **Emperor Napoleon III:** Bonapartists recognize the son of Emperor Napoleon I (r. 1804–1814, 1815) as Napoleon II. But Napoleon II never actually ruled France. Aged three years when his father abdicated, he was taken to Vienna by his maternal grandfather, the emperor of Austria, and spent his brief life there until his death in 1832.

Chapter 7

Two Programs

for Social

and Political

Change:

Liberalism

and Socialism

retired permanently from public life after Bonaparte's seizure of power, unable to support the new, undemocratic regime.

Returning to writing, Tocqueville produced two more important works before his death from tuberculosis in 1859. The first was his *Recollections* of the Revolution of 1848 and the Second Republic, based on his experiences in Paris in 1848 and 1849; the second was a study of the French Revolution of 1789, *The Old Regime and the Revolution.* Both works demonstrate again Tocqueville's liberal ideology and political astuteness.

In reading the selections by Tocqueville, you should ascertain the nature of his liberal thought. In Source 1, what does Tocqueville identify as the main trend in historical development? What implications did this trend, which he found strong in America, have for Europe's existing class structure? What problems does Tocqueville, in Source 2, find - accompanying American democracy? What threatened the individual? What danger did centralized authority pose? In Source 3, Tocqueville treats revolution. Why does he see the danger of revolution diminishing with the advance of political democracy? Does he find revolution justified at times?

Sources 3 and 4 provide you with summations of Tocqueville's political thought and his view of the future. Under what sort of government had he spent his youth? What did it contribute to his political thought?

Born in Germany in 1818, thirteen years after Tocqueville, Karl Marx was the advocate of a very different political order, one of socialist revolution. The son of a successful attorney, Marx enjoyed an excellent education. He studied law first and then philosophy, a field in which he completed the doctoral degree that normally would have led to an academic career. Young Marx, however, was an advocate of political and economic democracy whose growing radicalism and atheism precluded such a career. When he turned instead to journalism, his ideas quickly offended the Prussian censors, who suppressed his newspaper.

Marx left Germany in 1843 for Paris, a city in which there was considerable discussion of utopian socialist ideas. Perhaps the greatest single event in Marx's two-year stay in Paris was his meeting with a young businessman, Friedrich Engels, with whom he was to enjoy a lifelong friendship. Engels shared Marx's socialist ideas, gave him intellectual support, and provided financial aid that allowed Marx to devote his life to writing.

French authorities expelled Marx for his radical political ideas in 1845. He moved to Brussels, Belgium, where he and Engels wrote *The Communist Manifesto,* an abstract declaration of war between the working class and its capitalist exploiters. Belgian authorities ultimately also expelled Marx. Back in Paris by March 1848, Marx, like Tocqueville, based his writings on some firsthand experience of the French Revolution of 1848. He also returned to Germany during 1848 before settling in England in 1849, where he spent the rest of his life.

Marx's poor command of spoken English and his illegible handwriting precluded his employment in white-collar jobs, and he and his family often lived in poverty when there were delays in Engels's generosity. In England, Marx drew on his own excellent education, his knowledge of French socialist thought from his Paris days, and his daily research in the British Museum Library to refine his views on socialist revolution. He wrote studies of contemporary events, including *Class Struggles in France* and *The Eighteenth Brumaire of Louis Bonaparte,* which dealt with the French Revolution of 1848 and its aftermath. The final product of his labors was the first volume of *Capital* (1867), a work Engels completed after Marx's death in 1883.

Marx was not to witness the implementation of his ideals during his life. His chief attempt at revolutionary organization, the International Workingmen's Association, or First International, founded in 1864, broke up as a result of ideological disputes in 1876. In those disputes, the always irascible Marx found his viewpoints challenged by another revolutionary activist, Mikhail Bakunin (1814–1876). Marx, who prided himself on what he believed was the scientific certainty of his ideas, found Bakunin insufficiently "scientific" and ruptured socialist unity in securing the latter's expulsion from the association. Bakunin went on to become one of the founders of modern anarchism, a movement advocating the destruction of all institutions of modern society. Marx spent the few years remaining

before his death in 1883 drained and embittered by his struggle in the International and by family problems. He died believing that his ideas would have little impact. Nevertheless, his writings became the basis for the international socialist movement.

As you read the selections by Marx, you should answer a number of questions to aid you in formulating your responses to the central problems of this chapter. Marx, like Tocqueville, had a definite view of history. Examine Source 5, a selection from *The Communist Manifesto.* What basic event, according to Marx, has characterized and shaped all historical development? Why does Marx find the latest phase of history, modern middle-class ("bourgeois") capitalism, particularly oppressive? What is Marx's view of the free economy advocated by nineteenth-century liberals?

In Source 6, Marx deals with the French Revolution of 1848. That revolution, of course, failed to bring the working classes to power. Whom did it bring to power in France? In Source 7 we have Marx's statement of his ideals in government. Marx proclaims that he advocates democracy. How does that democracy differ from the kind of democracy acceptable to liberals like Tocqueville?

Now you are ready to read the selections with an eye to answering the main questions of this chapter: What were Tocqueville's and Marx's separate political visions? How did they hope to see their visions realized? How did these two thinkers and their liberal and socialist ideologies differ?

Chapter 7

Two Programs

for Social

and Political

Change:

Liberalism

and Socialism

THE EVIDENCE

ALEXIS DE TOCQUEVILLE

Sources 1 and 2 from Alexis de Tocqueville, Democracy in America, *edited by J. P. Mayer and Max Lerner, translated by George Lawrence (New York: Harper & Row, 1965), pp. 3–5, 610–611, 613, 618; pp. 231–233, 665, 667–669. English translation copyright © 1965 by Harper & Row Publishers, Inc. Copyright renewed. Reprinted by permission of HarperCollins Publishers, Inc.*

1. Tocqueville's View of History

No novelty in the United States struck me more vividly during my stay there than the equality of conditions. It was easy to see the immense influence of this basic fact on the whole course of society. It gives a particular turn to public opinion and a particular twist to the laws, new maxims to those who govern and particular habits to the governed.

I soon realized that the influence of this fact extends far beyond political mores and laws, exercising dominion over civil society as much as over the government; it creates opinions, gives birth to feelings, suggests customs, and modifies whatever it does not create.

So the more I studied American society, the more clearly I saw equality of conditions as the creative element from which each particular fact derived, and all my observations constantly returned to this nodal point.

Later, when I came to consider our own side of the Atlantic, I thought I could detect something analogous to what I had noticed in the New World. I saw an equality of conditions which, though it had not reached the extreme limits found in the United States, was daily drawing closer thereto; and that same democracy which prevailed over the societies of America seemed to me to be advancing rapidly toward power in Europe. . . .

A great democratic revolution is taking place in our midst; everybody sees it, but by no means everybody judges it in the same way. Some think it a new thing and, supposing it an accident, hope that they can still check it; others think it irresistible, because it seems to them the most continuous, ancient, and permanent tendency known to history. . . .

Running through the pages of our history, there is hardly an important event in the last seven hundred years which has not turned out to be advantageous for equality.

The Crusades and the English wars decimated the nobles and divided up their lands. Municipal institutions introduced democratic liberty into the heart of the feudal monarchy; the invention of firearms made villein and noble equal on the field of battle; printing offered equal resources to their minds; the post brought enlightenment to hovel and palace alike; Protestantism maintained

[180]

that all men are equally able to find the path to heaven. America, once discovered, opened a thousand new roads to fortune and gave any obscure adventurer the chance of wealth and power.

If, beginning at the eleventh century, one takes stock of what was happening in France at fifty-year intervals, one finds each time that a double revolution has taken place in the state of society. The noble has gone down in the social scale, and the commoner gone up; as the one falls, the other rises. Each half century brings them closer, and soon they will touch.

And that is not something peculiar to France. Wherever one looks one finds the same revolution taking place throughout the Christian world.

WHY GREAT REVOLUTIONS
WILL BECOME RARE

When a people has lived for centuries under a system of castes and classes, it can only reach a democratic state of society through a long series of more or less painful transformations. These must involve violent efforts and many vicissitudes, in the course of which property, opinions, and power are all subject to swift changes.

Even when this great revolution has come to an end, the revolutionary habits created thereby and by the profound disturbances thereon ensuing will long endure.

As all this takes place just at the time when social conditions are being leveled, the conclusion has been drawn that there must be a hidden connection and secret link between equality itself and revolutions, so that neither can occur without the other.

On this point reason and experience seem agreed.

Among a people where ranks are more or less equal, there is no apparent connection between men to hold them firmly in place. None of them has any permanent right or power to give commands, and none is bound by his social condition to obey. Each man, having some education and some resources, can choose his own road and go along separately from all the rest.

The same causes which make the citizens independent of each other daily prompt new and restless longings and constantly goad them on.

It therefore seems natural to suppose that in a democratic society ideas, things, and men must eternally be changing shape and position and that ages of democracy must be times of swift and constant transformation.

But is this in fact so? Does equality of social conditions habitually and permanently drive men toward revolutions? Does it contain some disturbing principle which prevents society from settling down and inclines the citizens constantly to change their laws, principles, and mores? I do not think so. The subject is important, and I ask the reader to follow my argument closely.

Almost every revolution which has changed the shape of nations has been made to consolidate or destroy inequality. Disregarding the secondary causes which have had some effect on the great convulsions in the world, you will

Chapter 7

Two Programs

for Social

and Political

Change:

Liberalism

and Socialism

almost always find that equality was at the heart of the matter. Either the poor were bent on snatching the property of the rich, or the rich were trying to hold the poor down. So, then, if you could establish a state of society in which each man had something to keep and little to snatch, you would have done much for the peace of the world. . . .

Such men are the natural enemies of violent commotion; their immobility keeps all above and below them quiet, and assures the stability of the body social.

I am not suggesting that they are themselves satisfied with their actual position or that they would feel any natural abhorrence toward a revolution if they could share the plunder without suffering the calamities; on the contrary, their eagerness to get rich is unparalleled, but their trouble is to know whom to despoil. The same social condition which prompts their longings restrains them within necessary limits. It gives men both greater freedom to change and less interest in doing so.

Not only do men in democracies feel no natural inclination for revolutions, but they are afraid of them.

Any revolution is more or less a threat to property. Most inhabitants of a democracy have property. And not only have they got property, but they live in the conditions in which men attach most value to property. . . .

Therefore the more widely personal property is distributed and increased and the greater the number of those enjoying it, the less is a nation inclined to revolution.

Moreover, whatever a man's calling and whatever type of property he owns, one characteristic is common to all.

No one is fully satisfied with his present fortune, and all are constantly trying a thousand various ways to improve it. Consider any individual at any period of his life, and you will always find him preoccupied with fresh plans to increase his comfort. Do not talk to him about the interests and rights of the human race; that little private business of his for the moment absorbs all his thoughts, and he hopes that public disturbances can be put off to some other time.

This not only prevents them from causing revolutions but also deters them from wanting them. Violent political passions have little hold on men whose whole thoughts are bent on the pursuit of well-being. Their excitement about small matters makes them calm about great ones. . . .

There are also other, and even stronger, reasons which prevent any great change in the doctrines of a democratic people coming about easily. I have already indicated them at the beginning of this book.

Whereas, in such a nation, the influence of individuals is weak and almost nonexistent, the power of the mass over each individual mind is very great. . . .

Whenever conditions are equal, public opinion brings immense weight to bear on every individual. It surrounds, directs, and oppresses him. The basic constitution of society has more to do with this than any political laws. The more alike men are, the weaker each feels in the face of all. Finding nothing that raises him above their level and distinguishes him, he loses his self-confidence when he comes into collision with them. Not only does he mistrust his own strength, but even comes to doubt his own judgment, and he is brought very near to recognizing that he must be wrong when the majority hold the opposite view. There is no need for the majority to compel him; it convinces him.

Therefore, however powers within a democracy are organized and weighted, it will always be very difficult for a man to believe what the mass rejects and to profess what it condemns.

This circumstance is wonderfully favorable to the stability of beliefs.

2. Tocqueville on the Problems of Democracy

TYRANNY OF THE MAJORITY

I regard it as an impious and detestable maxim that in matters of government the majority of a people has the right to do everything, and nevertheless I place the origin of all powers in the will of the majority. Am I in contradiction with myself?

There is one law which has been made, or at least adopted, not by the majority of this or that people, but by the majority of all men. That law is justice.

Justice therefore forms the boundary to each people's right.

A nation is like a jury entrusted to represent universal society and to apply the justice which is its law. Should the jury representing society have greater power than that very society whose laws it applies?

Consequently, when I refuse to obey an unjust law, I by no means deny the majority's right to give orders; I only appeal from the sovereignty of the people to the sovereignty of the human race. . . .

Omnipotence in itself seems a bad and dangerous thing. I think that its exercise is beyond man's strength, whoever he be, and that only God can be omnipotent without danger because His wisdom and justice are always equal to His power. So there is no power on earth in itself so worthy of respect or vested with such a sacred right that I would wish to let it act without control and dominate without obstacles. So when I see the right and capacity to do all given to any authority whatsoever, whether it be called people or king, democracy or aristocracy, and whether the scene of action is a monarchy or a republic, I say: the germ of tyranny is there, and I will go look for other laws under which to live.

My greatest complaint against democratic government as organized in the United States is not, as many Europeans make out, its weakness, but rather its irresistible strength. What I find most repulsive in America is not the extreme freedom reigning there but the shortage of guarantees against tyranny.

[183]

Chapter 7

Two Programs

for Social

and Political

Change:

Liberalism

and Socialism

When a man or a party suffers an injustice in the United States, to whom can he turn? To public opinion? That is what forms the majority. To the legislative body? It represents the majority and obeys it blindly. To the executive power? It is appointed by the majority and serves as its passive instrument. To the police? They are nothing but the majority under arms. A jury? The jury is the majority vested with the right to pronounce judgment; even the judges in certain states are elected by the majority. So, however iniquitous or unreasonable the measure which hurts you, you must submit.[3]

But suppose you were to have a legislative body so composed that it represented the majority without being necessarily the slave of its passions, an executive power having a strength of its own, and a judicial power independent of the other two authorities; then you would still have a democratic government, but there would be hardly any remaining risk of tyranny.

WHAT SORT OF DESPOTISM
DEMOCRATIC NATIONS HAVE TO FEAR

I noticed during my stay in the United States that a democratic state of society similar to that found there could lay itself peculiarly open to the establishment of a despotism. And on my return to Europe I saw how far most of our princes had made use of the ideas, feelings, and needs engendered by such a state of society to enlarge the sphere of their power. . . .

3. [Tocqueville's note:] At Baltimore during the War of 1812 there was a striking example of the excesses to which despotism of the majority may lead. At that time the war was very popular at Baltimore. A newspaper which came out in strong opposition to it aroused the indignation of the inhabitants. The people assembled, broke the presses, and attacked the house of the editors. An attempt was made to summon the militia, but it did not answer the appeal. Finally, to save the lives of these wretched men threatened by the fury of the public, they were taken to prison like criminals. This precaution was useless. During the night the people assembled again; the magistrates having failed to bring up the militia, the prison was broken open; one of the journalists was killed on the spot and the others left for dead; the guilty were brought before a jury and acquitted.

I once said to a Pennsylvanian: "Please explain to me why in a state founded by Quakers and renowned for its tolerance, freed Negroes are not allowed to use their rights as citizens? They pay taxes; is it not right that they should vote?"

"Do not insult us," he replied, "by supposing that our legislators would commit an act of such gross injustice and intolerance."

"So, with you, Negroes do have the right to vote?"

"Certainly."

"Then how was it that at the electoral college this morning I did not see a single one of them in the meeting?"

"That is not the fault of the law," said the American. "It is true that Negroes have the right to be present at elections, but they voluntarily abstain from appearing."

"That is extraordinarily modest of them."

"Oh! It is not that they are reluctant to go there, but they are afraid they may be maltreated. With us it sometimes happens that the law lacks force when the majority does not support it. Now, the majority is filled with the strongest prejudices against Negroes, and the magistrates do not feel strong enough to guarantee the rights granted to them by the lawmakers."

"What! The majority, privileged to make the law, wishes also to have the privilege of disobeying the law?"

Our contemporaries are ever a prey to two conflicting passions: they feel the need of guidance, and they long to stay free. Unable to wipe out these two contradictory instincts, they try to satisfy them both together. Their imagination conceives a government which is unitary, protective, and all-powerful, but elected by the people. Centralization is combined with the sovereignty of the people. That gives them a chance to relax. They console themselves for being under schoolmasters by thinking that they have chosen them themselves. Each individual lets them put the collar on, for he sees that it is not a person, or a class of persons, but society itself which holds the end of the chain.

Under this system the citizens quit their state of dependence just long enough to choose their masters and then fall back into it.

A great many people nowadays very easily fall in with this brand of compromise between administrative despotism and the sovereignty of the people. They think they have done enough to guarantee personal freedom when it is to the government of the state that they have handed it over. That is not good enough for me. I am much less interested in the question who my master is than in the fact of obedience. . . .

Subjection in petty affairs is manifest daily and touches all citizens indiscriminately. It never drives men to despair, but continually thwarts them and leads them to give up using their free will. It slowly stifles their spirits and enervates their souls, whereas obedience demanded only occasionally in matters of great moment brings servitude into play only from time to time, and its weight falls only on certain people. It does little good to summon those very citizens who have been made so dependent on the central power to choose the representatives of that power from time to time. However important, this brief and occasional exercise of free will will not prevent them from gradually losing the faculty of thinking, feeling, and acting for themselves, so that they will slowly fall below the level of humanity.

I must add that they will soon become incapable of using the one great privilege left to them. Those democratic peoples which have introduced freedom into the sphere of politics, while allowing despotism to grow in the administrative sphere, have been led into the strangest paradoxes. For the conduct of small affairs, where plain common sense is enough, they hold that the citizens are not up to the job. But they give these citizens immense prerogatives where the government of the whole state is concerned. They are turned alternatively into the playthings of the sovereign and into his masters, being either greater than kings or less than men. When they have tried all the different systems of election without finding one to suit them, they look surprised and go on seeking for another, as if the ills they see did not belong much more to the constitution of the country itself than to that of the electoral body.

It really is difficult to imagine how people who have entirely given up managing their own affairs could make a wise choice of those who are to do that for them. One should never expect a liberal, energetic, and wise government to originate in the votes of a people of servants.

[185]

Chapter 7

Two Programs

for Social

and Political

Change:

Liberalism

and Socialism

First document in Source 3 from Alexis de Tocqueville, Democracy in America, *edited by J. P. Mayer and Max Lerner, translated by George Lawrence (New York: Harper & Row, 1965), pp. 674–675. English translation copyright © 1965 by Harper & Row Publishers, Inc. Copyright renewed. Reprinted by permission of HarperCollins Publishers, Inc. Second document from* The Recollections of Alexis de Tocqueville *by Alexis de Tocqueville, (1893; tr. by Alexander Teixeira de Mattos, 1896; complete ed. by J. P. Mayer, 1949).*

3. Tocqueville on Revolution

[*The general danger of revolution*]

There are some habits, some ideas, and some vices which are peculiar to a state of revolution and which any prolonged revolution cannot fail to engender and spread, whatever may be in other respects its character, object, and field of action.

When in a brief space of time any nation has repeatedly changed its leaders, opinions, and laws, the men of that nation will in the end acquire a taste for change and grow accustomed to see all changes quickly brought about by the use of force. Then they will naturally conceive a scorn for those formalities of whose impotence they have been daily witnesses, and they will be impatient to tolerate the sway of rules which they have so often seen infringed.

As ordinary ideas of equity and morality are no longer enough to explain and justify all the innovations daily introduced by revolution, men fall back on the principle of social utility, political necessity is turned into a dogma, and men lose all scruples about freely sacrificing particular interests and trampling private rights beneath their feet in order more quickly to attain the public aim envisaged.

Such habits and ideas, which I call revolutionary since all revolutions give rise to them, are seen as much in aristocracies as among democratic peoples. But in the former case they are often less powerful and always less permanent, because there they come up against habits, ideas, faults, and eccentricities which are opposed to them. They therefore vanish of their own accord when the revolution is at an end and the nation recovers its former political ways. However, that is not always the case in democratic countries, for in them there is always a danger that revolutionary instincts will mellow and assume more regular shape without entirely disappearing, but will gradually be transformed into mores of government and administrative habits.

Hence, I know of no country in which revolutions are more dangerous than in a democracy, because apart from the accidental and ephemeral ills which they are ever bound to entail, there is always a danger of their becoming permanent, and one may almost say, eternal.

I think that resistance is sometimes justified and that rebellion can be legitimate. I cannot therefore lay it down as an absolute rule that men living in times of democracy should never make a revolution. But I think that they, more than others, have reason to hesitate before they embark on such an enterprise and that it is far better to put up with many inconveniences in their present state than to turn to so dangerous a remedy.

[*Tocqueville on the Revolution of 1848
in France*]

*My Explanation of the 24th of February and My Thoughts as to Its
Effects upon the Future*[4]

And so the Monarchy of July[5] was fallen, fallen without a struggle, and before rather than beneath the blows of the victors, who were as astonished at their triumph as were the vanquished at their defeat. . . .

I had spent the best days of my youth amid a society which seemed to increase in greatness and prosperity as it increased in liberty; I had conceived the idea of a balanced, regulated liberty, held in check by religion, custom and law; the attractions of this liberty had touched me; it had become the passion of my life; I felt that I could never be consoled for its loss, and that I must renounce all hope of its recovery.

I had gained too much experience of men to be able to content myself with empty words; I knew that, if one great revolution is able to establish liberty in a country, a number of succeeding revolutions make all regular liberty impossible for very many years.

I could not yet know what would issue from this last revolution, but I was already convinced that it could give birth to nothing that would satisfy me; and I foresaw that, whatever might be the lot reserved for our posterity, our own fate was to drag on our lives miserably amid alternate reactions of licence and oppression. . . .

I spent the rest of the day with Ampère, who was my colleague at the Institute,[6] and one of my best friends. He came to discover what had become of me in the affray, and to ask himself to dinner. I wished at first to relieve myself by making him share my vexation. . . .

I saw that he not only did not enter into my view, but that he was disposed to take quite an opposite one. Seeing this, I was suddenly impelled to turn against Ampère all the feelings of indignation, grief and anger that had been accumulating in my heart since the morning; and I spoke to him with a violence of language which I have often since recalled with a certain shame, and which none but a friendship so sincere as his could have excused. I remember saying to him, *inter alia*.[7]

"You understand nothing of what is happening; you are judging like a poet or a Paris cockney.[8] You call this the triumph of liberty, when it is its final

---

4. On Thursday, February 24, 1848, King Louis Philippe abdicated the throne in the face of the Paris revolution and fled the capital for England.

5. **Monarchy of July:** the term often used for the regime of King Louis Philippe because that government came to power in July 1830.

6. **Institute:** Institut de France, the cultural institution including the French Academy, of which Tocqueville was a member. **Jean-Jacques Ampère** (1800–1864): a philologist and professor of French literature.

7. *inter alia:* Latin, "among other things."

8. **cockney:** generally a person of the lower classes born in London's East End. In this context, it refers to someone from that same class in Paris.

Chapter 7

Two Programs

for Social

and Political

Change:

Liberalism

and Socialism

defeat. I tell you that the people which you so artlessly admire has just succeeded in proving that it is unfit and unworthy to live a life of freedom. Show me what experience has taught it! Where are the new virtues it has gained, the old vices it has laid aside? No, I tell you, it is always the same, as impatient, as thoughtless, as contemptuous of law and order, as easily led and as cowardly in the presence of danger as its fathers were before it. Time has altered it in no way, and has left it as frivolous in serious matters as it used to be in trifles."

After much vociferation we both ended by appealing to the future, that enlightened and upright judge who always, alas! arrives too late.

Source 4 from Roger Boesche, editor, James Toupin and Roger Boesche, translators, Alexis de Tocqueville: Selected Letters on Politics and Society *(Berkeley: University of California Press, 1985), pp. 112–113. Copyright © 1985 The Regents of the University of California. Reprinted with permission.*

4. Tocqueville's Ideals of Government (Letter to Eugène Stoffels)[9]

I do not think that in France there is a man who is less revolutionary than I, nor one who has a more profound hatred for what is called the revolutionary spirit (a spirit which, parenthetically, is very easily combined with the love of an absolute government). What am I then? And what do I want? Let us distinguish, in order to understand each other better, between the end and the means. What is the end? What I want is not a republic, but a hereditary monarchy. I would even prefer it to be legitimate rather than elected like the one we have, because it would be stronger, especially externally. What I want is a central government energetic in its own sphere of action. Energy from the central government is even more necessary among a democratic people in whom the social force is more diffused than in an aristocracy. Besides our situation in Europe lays down as imperative law for us in what should be a thing of choice. But I wish that this central power had a clearly delineated sphere, that it were involved with what is a necessary part of its functions and not with everything in general, and that it were forever subordinated, in its tendency, to public opinion and to the legislative power that represents this public opinion. I believe that the central power can be invested with very great prerogatives, can be energetic and powerful in its sphere, and that at the same time provincial liberties can be well developed. I think that a government of this kind can exist, and that at the same time the majority of the nation itself

---

9. **Eugène Stoffels** (1805–1852): an official in Metz, France, and a friend of Tocqueville from their days together in secondary school.

can be involved with its own affairs, that political life can be spread almost everywhere, the direct or indirect exercise of political rights can be quite extensive. I wish that the general principles of government were liberal, that the largest possible part were left to the action of individuals, to personal initiative. I believe that all these things are compatible; even more, I am profoundly convinced that there will never be order and tranquility except when they are successfully combined.

As for the means: with all those who admit that we must make our way gradually toward this goal, I am very much in accord. I am the first to admit that it is necessary to proceed slowly, with precaution, with legality. My conviction is that our current institutions are sufficient for reaching the result I have in view. Far, then, from wanting people to violate the laws, I profess an almost superstitious respect for the laws. But I wish that the laws would tend little and gradually toward the goal I have just indicated, instead of making powerless and dangerous efforts to turn back. I wish that the government would itself prepare mores and practices so that people would do without it in many cases in which its intervention is still necessary or invoked without necessity. I wish that citizens were introduced into public life to the extent that they are believed capable of being useful in it, instead of seeking to keep them away from it at all costs. I wish finally that people knew where they wanted to go, and that they advanced toward it prudently instead of proceeding aimlessly as they have been doing almost constantly for twenty years.

KARL MARX

Source 5 from Karl Marx and Friedrich Engels, The Communist Manifesto, *translated by Samuel Moore (New York: Penguin, 1977), pp. 79–83, 85–92, 95–96.*

5. Marx's View of History

1

BOURGEOIS AND PROLETARIANS[10]

The history of all hitherto existing society is the history of class struggles.

Freeman and slave, patrician and plebeian, lord and serf, guild-master[11] and journeyman, in a word, oppressor and oppressed, stood in constant opposition to one another, carried on an uninterrupted, now hidden, now open fight, a fight that each time ended, either in a revolutionary reconstitution of society at large, or in the common ruin of the contending classes.

10. **bourgeois, proletarian:** "By bourgeoisie is meant the class of modern Capitalist, owners of the means of social production and employers of wage labour. By proletariat, the class of modern wage-labourers who, having no means of production of their own, are reduced to selling their labour power in order to live" (note by Engels to the English edition, 1888).
11. **guild-master:** "that is, a full member of a guild, a master within, not a head of a guild" (note by Engels to the English edition, 1888).

Chapter 7

Two Programs

for Social

and Political

Change:

Liberalism

and Socialism

In the earlier epochs of history, we find almost everywhere a complicated arrangement of society into various orders, a manifold gradation of social rank. In ancient Rome we have patricians, knights, plebeians, slaves; in the Middle Ages, feudal lords, vassals, guild-masters, journeymen, apprentices, serfs; in almost all of these classes, again, subordinate gradations.

The modern bourgeois society that has sprouted from the ruins of feudal society has not done away with class antagonisms. It has but established new classes, new conditions of oppression, new forms of struggle in place of the old ones.

Our epoch, the epoch of the bourgeoisie, possesses, however, this distinctive feature: it has simplified the class antagonisms. Society as a whole is more and more splitting up into two great hostile camps, into two great classes directly facing each other: Bourgeoisie and Proletariat.

From the serfs of the Middle Ages sprang the chartered burghers of the earliest towns. From these burgesses the first elements of the bourgeoisie were developed.

The discovery of America, the rounding of the Cape, opened up fresh ground for the rising bourgeoisie. The East-Indian and Chinese markets, the colonization of America, trade with the colonies, the increase in the means of exchange and in commodities generally, gave to commerce, to navigation, to industry, an impulse never before known, and thereby, to the revolutionary element in the tottering feudal society, a rapid development.

The feudal system of industry, under which industrial production was monopolized by closed guilds, now no longer sufficed for the growing wants of the new markets. The manufacturing system took its place. The guild-masters were pushed on one side by the manufacturing middle class; division of labour between the different corporate guilds vanished in the face of division of labour in each single workshop.

Meantime the markets kept ever growing, the demand ever rising. Even manufacture no longer sufficed. Thereupon, steam and machinery revolutionized industrial production. The place of manufacture was taken by the giant, Modern Industry, the place of the industrial middle class, by industrial millionaires, the leaders of whole industrial armies, the modern bourgeois.

Modern industry has established the world market, for which the discovery of America paved the way. This market has given an immense development to commerce, to navigation, to communication by land. This development has, in its turn, reacted on the extension of industry; and in proportion as industry, commerce, navigation, railways extended, in the same proportion the bourgeoisie developed, increased its capital, and pushed into the background every class handed down from the Middle Ages.

We see, therefore, how the modern bourgeoisie is itself the product of a long course of development, of a series of revolutions in the modes of production and of exchange.

Each step in the development of the bourgeoisie was accompanied by a corresponding political advance of that class. An oppressed class under the sway of the feudal nobility, an armed and self-governing association in the medieval commune;[12] here independent urban republic (as in Italy and Germany), there taxable "third estate" of the monarchy (as in France), afterwards, in the period of manufacture proper, serving either the semi-feudal or the absolute monarchy as a counterpoise against the nobility, and, in fact, corner-stone of the great monarchies in general, the bourgeoisie has at last, since the establishment of Modern Industry and of the world market, conquered for itself, in the modern representative State, exclusive political sway. The executive of the modern State is but a committee for managing the common affairs of the whole bourgeoisie.

The bourgeoisie, historically, has played a most revolutionary part.

The bourgeoisie, wherever it has got the upper hand, has put an end to all feudal, patriarchal, idyllic relations. It has pitilessly torn asunder the motley feudal ties that bound man to his "natural superiors," and has left remaining no other nexus between man and man than naked self-interest, than callous "cash payment." It has drowned the most heavenly ecstasies of religious fervour, of chivalrous enthusiasm, of philistine sentimentalism, in the icy water of egotistical calculation. It has resolved personal worth into exchange value, and in place of the numberless indefeasible chartered freedoms, has set up that single, unconscionable freedom—Free Trade. In one word, for exploitation, veiled by religious and political illusions, it has substituted naked, shameless, direct, brutal exploitation.

The bourgeoisie has stripped of its halo every occupation hitherto honoured and looked up to with reverent awe. It has converted the physician, the lawyer, the priest, the poet, the man of science, into its paid wage-labourers.

The bourgeoisie has torn away from the family its sentimental veil, and has reduced the family relation to a mere money relation. . . .

The bourgeoisie cannot exist without constantly revolutionizing the instruments of production, and thereby the relations of production, and with them the whole relations of society. Conservation of the old modes of production in unaltered form, was, on the contrary, the first condition of existence for all earlier industrial classes. Constant revolutionizing of production, uninterrupted disturbance of all social conditions, everlasting uncertainty and agitation distinguish the bourgeois epoch from all earlier ones. All fixed, fast-frozen relations, with their train of ancient and venerable prejudices and opinions are

12. **commune:** "the name taken, in France, by the nascent towns even before they had conquered from their feudal lords and masters local self-government and political rights as the 'Third Estate.' Generally speaking, for the economical development of the bourgeoisie, England is here taken as the typical country; for its political development, France" (note by Engels to the English edition, 1888). "This was the name given their urban communities by the townsmen of Italy and France, after they had purchased or wrested their initial rights of self-government from their feudal lords" (note by Engels to the German edition, 1890).

Chapter 7

Two Programs

for Social

and Political

Change:

Liberalism

and Socialism

swept away, all new-formed ones become antiquated before they can ossify. All that is solid melts into air, all that is holy is profaned, and man is at last compelled to face with sober senses, his real conditions of life, and his relations with his kind.

The need of a constantly expanding market for its products chases the bourgeoisie over the whole surface of the globe. It must nestle everywhere, settle everywhere, establish connexions everywhere. . . .

Modern bourgeois society with its relations of production, of exchange and of property, a society that has conjured up such gigantic means of production and of exchange, is like the sorcerer, who is no longer able to control the powers of the nether world whom he has called up by his spells. For many a decade past the history of industry and commerce is but the history of the revolt of modern productive forces against modern conditions of production, against the property relations that are the conditions for the existence of the bourgeoisie and of its rule. It is enough to mention the commercial crises that by their periodical return put on its trial, each time more threateningly, the existence of the entire bourgeois society. In these crises a great part not only of the existing products, but also of the previously created productive forces, are periodically destroyed. In these crises there breaks out an epidemic that, in all earlier epochs, would have seemed an absurdity—the epidemic of over-production. . . .

And how does the bourgeoisie get over these crises? On the one hand by enforced destruction of a mass of productive forces; on the other, by the conquest of new markets, and by the more thorough exploitation of the old ones. That is to say, by paving the way for more extensive and more destructive crises, and by diminishing the means whereby crises are prevented.

The weapons with which the bourgeoisie felled feudalism to the ground are now turned against the bourgeoisie itself.

But not only has the bourgeoisie forged the weapons that bring death to itself; it has also called into existence the men who are to wield those weapons—the modern working class—the proletarians.

In proportion as the bourgeoisie, i.e., capital, is developed, in the same proportion is the proletariat, the modern working class, developed—a class of labourers, who live only so long as they find work, and who find work only so long as their labour increases capital. These labourers, who must sell themselves piecemeal, are a commodity, like every other article of commerce, and are consequently exposed to all the vicissitudes of competition, to all the fluctuations of the market.

Owing to the extensive use of machinery and to division of labour, the work of the proletarians has lost all individual character, and, consequently, all charm for the workman. He becomes an appendage of the machine, and it is only the most simple, most monotonous, and most easily acquired knack, that is required of him. Hence, the cost of production of a workman is restricted,

almost entirely, to the means of subsistence that he requires for his maintenance, and for the propagation of his race. . . .

Modern industry has converted the little workshop of the patriarchal master into the great factory of the industrial capitalist. Masses of labourers,
crowded into the factory, are organized like soldiers. As privates of the industrial army they are placed under the command of a perfect hierarchy of officers and sergeants. Not only are they slaves of the bourgeois class, and of the
bourgeois State; they are daily and hourly enslaved by the machine, by the
overlooker, and, above all, by the individual bourgeois manufacturer himself.
The more openly this despotism proclaims gain be its end and aim, the more
petty, the more hateful and the more embittering it is. . . .

The proletariat goes through various stages of development. With its birth
begins its struggle with the bourgeoisie. At first the contest is carried on by
individual labourers, then by the work-people of a factory, then by the opera-
tives of one trade, in one locality, against the individual bourgeois who
directly exploits them. They direct their attacks not against the bourgeois conditions of production, but against the instruments of production themselves;
they destroy imported wares that compete with their labour, they smash to
pieces machinery, they set factories ablaze, they seek to restore by force the
vanished status of the workman of the Middle Ages.

At this stage the labourers still form an incoherent mass scattered over the
whole country, and broken up by their mutual competition. If anywhere they
unite to form more compact bodies, this is not yet the consequence of their
own active union, but of the union of the bourgeoisie, which class, in order to
attain its own political ends, is compelled to set the whole proletariat in motion, and is moreover yet, for a time, able to do so. At this stage, therefore, the
proletarians do not fight their enemies, but the enemies of their enemies, the
remnants of absolute monarchy, the landowners, the non-industrial bourgeois, the petty bourgeoisie. Thus the whole historical movement is concentrated in the hands of the bourgeoisie; every victory so obtained is a victory
for the bourgeoisie.

But with the development of industry the proletariat not only increases in
number; it becomes concentrated in greater masses, its strength grows, and it
feels that strength more. The various interests and conditions of life within the
ranks of the proletariat are more and more equalized, in proportion as machinery obliterates all distinctions of labour, and nearly everywhere reduces
wages to the same low level. The growing competition among the bourgeois,
and the resulting commercial crises, make the wages of the workers ever more
fluctuating. The unceasing improvement of machinery, ever more rapidly developing, makes their livelihood more and more precarious; the collisions between individual workmen and individual bourgeois take more and more the
character of collisions between two classes. Thereupon the workers begin to
form combinations (Trades Unions) against the bourgeois; they club together

Chapter 7
Two Programs
for Social
and Political
Change:
Liberalism
and Socialism

in order to keep up the rate of wages; they found permanent associations in order to make provision beforehand for these occasional revolts. Here and there the contest breaks out into riots.

Now and then the workers are victorious, but only for a time. The real fruit of their battles lies, not in the immediate result, but in the ever-expanding union of the workers. This union is helped on by the improved means of communication that are created by modern industry and that place the workers of different localities in contact with one another. It was just this contact that was needed to centralize the numerous local struggles, all of the same character, into one national struggle between classes. But every class struggle is a political struggle. And that union, to attain which the burghers of the Middle Ages, with their miserable highways, required centuries, the modern proletarians, thanks to railways, achieve in a few years. . . .

Of all the classes that stand face to face with the bourgeoisie today, the proletariat alone is a really revolutionary class. The other classes decay and finally disappear in the face of modern industry; the proletariat is its special and essential product.

The lower middle class, the small manufacturer, the shopkeeper, the artisan, the peasant, all these fight against the bourgeoisie, to save from extinction their existence as fractions of the middle class. They are therefore not revolutionary, but conservative. Nay more, they are reactionary, for they try to roll back the wheel of history. . . .

In the conditions of the proletariat, those of old society at large are already virtually swamped. The proletarian is without property; his relation to his wife and children has no longer anything in common with the bourgeois family relations; modern industrial labour, modern subjection to capital, the same in England as in France, in America as in Germany, has stripped him of every trace of national character. Law, morality, religion, are to him so many bourgeois prejudices, behind which lurk in ambush just as many bourgeois interests.

All the preceding classes that got the upper hand sought to fortify their already acquired status by subjecting society at large to their conditions of appropriation. The proletarians cannot become masters of the productive forces of society, except by abolishing their own previous mode of appropriation, and thereby also every other previous mode of appropriation. They have nothing of their own to secure and to fortify; their mission is to destroy all previous securities for, and insurances of, individual property.

All previous historical movements were movements of minorities, or in the interest of minorities. The proletarian movement is the self-conscious, independent movement of the immense majority, in the interest of the immense majority. The proletariat, the lowest stratum of our present society, cannot stir, cannot raise itself up, without the whole superincumbent strata of official society being sprung into the air.

2
PROLETARIANS AND COMMUNISTS

In what relation do the Communists stand to the proletarians as a whole?

The Communists do not form a separate party opposed to other working-class parties.

They have no interests separate and apart from those of the proletariat as a whole.

They do not set up any sectarian principles of their own, by which to shape and mould the proletarian movement.

The Communists are distinguished from the other working-class parties by this only: 1. In the national struggles of the proletarians of the different countries, they point out and bring to the front the common interests of the entire proletariat, independently of all nationality. 2. In the various stages of development which the struggle of the working class against the bourgeoisie has to pass through, they always and everywhere represent the interests of the movement as a whole.

The Communists, therefore, are on the one hand, practically, the most advanced and resolute section of the working-class parties of every country, that section which pushes forward all others; on the other hand, theoretically, they have over the great mass of the proletariat the advantage of clearly understanding the line of march, the conditions, and the ultimate general results of the proletarian movement.

The immediate aim of the Communists is the same as that of all the other proletarian parties: formation of the proletariat into a class, overthrow of the bourgeois supremacy, conquest of political power by the proletariat.

The theoretical conclusions of the Communists are in no way based on ideas or principles that have been invented, or discovered, by this or that would-be universal reformer.

They merely express, in general terms, actual relations springing from an existing class struggle, from a historical movement going on under our very eyes. The abolition of existing property relations is not at all a distinctive feature of Communism.

All property relations in the past have continually been subject to historical change consequent upon the change in historical conditions.

The French Revolution, for example, abolished feudal property in favour of bourgeois property.

The distinguishing feature of Communism is not the abolition of property generally, but the abolition of bourgeois property. But modern bourgeois private property is the final and most complete expression of the system of producing and appropriating products, that is based on class antagonisms, on the exploitation of the many by the few.

In this sense, the theory of the Communists may be summed up in the single sentence: Abolition of private property.

Chapter 7

Two Programs

for Social

and Political

Change:

Liberalism

and Socialism

Source 6 from Karl Marx, The Class Struggles in France (1848–1850), *edited by C. P. Dutt (New York: International Publishers, 1964), pp. 33–34, 39–40, 50–52, 55, 56, 58–59. Used by permission of International Publishers.*

6. Marx on the Revolution of 1848 in Paris

1
FROM FEBRUARY TO JUNE 1848

With the exception of a few short chapters, every important part of the annals of the revolution from 1848 to 1849 carries the heading: Defeat of the revolution!

But what succumbed in these defeats was not the revolution. It was the pre-revolutionary traditional appendages, results of social relationships, which had not yet come to the point of sharp class antagonisms—persons, illusions, conceptions, projects, from which the revolutionary party before the February Revolution was not free, from which it could be freed, not by the victory of February, but only by a series of defeats.

In a word: revolutionary advance made headway not by its immediate tragi-comic achievements, but on the contrary by the creation of a powerful, united counter-revolution, by the creation of an opponent, by fighting whom the party of revolt first ripened into a real revolutionary party.

To prove this is the task of the following pages.

I. THE DEFEAT OF JUNE 1848

After the July Revolution, when the Liberal banker, Laffitte, led his godfather, the Duke of Orleans, in triumph to the Hôtel de Ville,[13] he let fall the words: "From now on the bankers will rule." Laffitte had betrayed the secret of the revolution. . . .

It was not the French bourgeoisie that ruled under Louis Philippe, but a fraction of it, bankers, Stock Exchange kings, railway kings, owners of coal and iron works and forests, a section of landed proprietors that rallied around them—the so-called finance aristocracy. It sat on the throne, it dictated laws in the Chambers, it conferred political posts from cabinet portfolios to the to-bacco bureau.

The real industrial bourgeoisie formed part of the official opposition, *i.e.,* it was represented only as a minority in the Chambers. . . .

The petty bourgeoisie of all degrees, and the peasantry also, were com-pletely excluded from political power. Finally, in the official opposition or

---

13. **Hôtel de Ville:** City Hall. The Duke of Orleans emerged from the July Revolution as King Louis Philippe.

entirely outside the *pays légal*,[14] there were the ideological representatives and spokesmen of the above classes, their savants, lawyers, doctors, etc., in a word: their so-called talents. . . .

The Provisional Government which emerged from the February barricades, necessarily mirrored in its composition the different parties which shared in the victory.[15] It could not be anything but a compromise between the different classes which together had overturned the July throne, but whose interests were mutually antagonistic. A large majority of its members consisted of representatives of the bourgeoisie. . . . The working class had only two representatives, Louis Blanc and Albert. . . .

Up to noon on February 25, the republic had not yet been proclaimed; on the other hand, the whole of the Ministries had already been divided among the bourgeois elements of the Provisional Government and among the generals, bankers and lawyers of the *National*. But the workers were this time determined not to put up with any swindling like that of July 1830. They were ready to take up the fight anew and to enforce the republic by force of arms. With this message, Raspail betook himself to the Hôtel de Ville. In the name of the Parisian proletariat he commanded the Provisional Government to proclaim the republic; if this order of the people were not fulfilled within two hours, he would return at the head of 200,000 men. The bodies of the fallen were scarcely cold, the barricades were not yet cleared away, the workers not yet disarmed, and the only force which could be opposed to them was the National Guard. Under these circumstances the prudent state doubts and juristic scruples of conscience of the Provisional Government suddenly vanished. The interval of two hours had not expired before all the walls of Paris were resplendent with the tremendous historical words:

République française! Liberté, Egalité, Fraternité![16]. . .

The proletariat, by dictating the republic to the Provisional Government and through the Provisional Government to the whole of France, stepped into the foreground forthwith as an independent party, but at the same time challenged the whole of bourgeois France to enter the lists against it. What it won

14. *pays légal:* literally, "legal country." Here Marx refers to the fact that the monarchy established by the July Revolution created a very limited right to vote. One had to possess a substantial amount of property to qualify for the right to vote, with the result that only 170,000 men, out of a population of about 30,000,000, qualified to vote for the Chamber of Deputies in the 1830s.

15. In his work *The Eighteenth of Brumaire of Louis Bonaparte* (New York: International Publishers, 1935), p. 101, Marx referred to the participation of a broad spectrum of social groups in the February Revolution as the "Universal brotherhood swindle." This means that, in his view, the lower classes were seduced into revolutionary action by bourgeois promises of democracy that were unfilled in the postrevolutionary government.

16. *République française! Liberté, Egalité, Fraternité:* "The French Republic: Liberty, Equality, Fraternity," the motto of the Revolution of 1789.

Chapter 7

Two Programs

for Social

and Political

Change:

Liberalism

and Socialism

was the terrain for the fight for its revolutionary emancipation, but in no way this emancipation itself! . . .

A hundred thousand workers thrown on the streets through the crisis and the revolution were enrolled by the Minister Marie in so-called National *Ateliers*![17] Under this grand name was hidden nothing but the employment of the workers on tedious, monotonous, unproductive earthworks at a wage of 23 sous.[18] English *workhouses* in the open—that is what these National *Ateliers* were. . . .

All the discontent, all the ill humour of the petty bourgeois was simultaneously directed against these National *Ateliers,* the common target. With real fury they reckoned up the sums that the proletarian loafers swallowed, while their own situation became daily more unbearable. A state pension for sham labour, that is socialism! they growled to themselves. They sought the basis of their misery in the National *Ateliers,* the declarations of the Luxembourg,[19] the marches of the workers through Paris. And no one was more fantastic about the alleged machinations of the Communists than the petty bourgeoisie who hovered hopelessly on the brink of bankruptcy.[20] . . .

In the National Assembly all France sat in judgment on the Paris proletariat. It broke immediately with the social illusions of the February Revolution; it roundly proclaimed the bourgeois republic, nothing but the bourgeois republic. It at once excluded the representatives of the proletariat, Louis Blanc and Albert, from the Executive Commission appointed by it; it threw out the proposal of a special Labour Ministry,[21] and received with stormy applause

---

17. **atelier:** workshop. The National Ateliers were government-funded projects to provide work to the unemployed.

18. **23 sous:** The sou was a French coin worth 5 centimes (100 centimes to 1 franc). Thus Marx cites a wage of a little over 1 franc per day for the labor. Initially, wages in the workshops were 2 francs per day for laborers and 1 franc per day for those unemployed for whom labor could not be found. Even 2 francs per day was less than the usual wage for skilled artisans like tailors and shoemakers.

19. **the Luxembourg:** the revolutionary government established a commission to study labor problems; chaired by the socialist Louis Blanc and composed of representatives of various trades, it was headquartered in the Luxembourg Palace. The commission secured the government's enactment of a ten-hour workday in Paris and a twelve-hour workday in the provinces. This reform would have reduced most workers' hours of labor had it been enforced by government supervision.

20. One of the causes of the Revolution of 1848 was a general European economic crisis in 1846–1848 that had its origins in agricultural problems. Potato harvests were disastrously deficient in Ireland and other countries in 1845–1848 because of a blight. Weather factors conspired to reduce wheat harvests in these same years, creating rising food prices and general distress in the economies of most European countries.

21. The National Assembly, elected by universal manhood suffrage in April 1848, had a moderate to conservative majority: Of the 900 members, about 500 were moderate republicans and 300 were monarchists. In such a chamber, proposals for a Ministry of Labor and for a guaranteed right to work, proposed by Louis Blanc, gained little support.

the statement of the Minister Trélat: "The question is merely one of bringing labour back to its old conditions."

But all this was not enough. The February republic was won by the workers with the passive support of the bourgeoisie. The proletarians regarded themselves, and rightly, as the victors of February, and they made the proud claims of victors. They had to be vanquished on the streets, they had to be shown that they were worsted as soon as they fought, not with the bourgeoisie, but against the bourgeoisie. Just as the February republic, with its socialist concessions, required a battle of the proletariat, united with the bourgeoisie, against monarchy, so a second battle was necessary in order to sever the republic from the socialist concessions, in order to officially work out the bourgeois republic as dominant. The bourgeoisie had to refute the demands of the proletariat with arms in its hands. And the real birthplace of the bourgeois republic is not the February victory; it is the June defeat. . . .

The Executive Commission began by making entry into the National *Ateliers* more difficult, by turning the day wage into a piece wage, by banishing workers not born in Paris to Sologne, ostensibly for the construction of earthworks. These earthworks were only a rhetorical formula with which to gloss over their expulsion, as the workers, returning disillusioned, announced to their comrades. Finally, on June 21, a decree appeared in the *Moniteur*,[22] which ordered the forcible expulsion of all unmarried workers from the National *Ateliers*, or their enrolment in the army.

The workers were left no choice: they had to starve or start to fight. They answered on June 22 with the tremendous insurrection in which the first great battle was joined between the two classes that split modern society. It was a fight for the preservation or annihilation of the bourgeois order. The veil that shrouded the republic was torn to pieces.

It is well known how the workers, with unexampled bravery and talent, without chiefs, without a common plan, without means and, for the most part, lacking weapons, held in check for five days the army, the Mobile Guard, the Parisian National Guard, and the National Guard that streamed in from the provinces. It is well known how the bourgeoisie compensated itself for the mortal anguish it underwent by unheard of brutality, and massacred over 3,000 prisoners.[23] . . .

By making its burial place the birth place of the bourgeois republic, the proletariat compelled the latter to come out forthwith in its pure form as the state whose admitted object is to perpetuate the rule of capital, the slavery of labour. With constant regard to the scarred, irreconcilable, unconquerable

22. *Moniteur:* a journal that published parliamentary debate and government decrees.

23. Marx does not wildly exaggerate the losses here. Casualties in the actual fighting and in the retribution following it were high.

Chapter 7

Two Programs

for Social

and Political

Change:

Liberalism

and Socialism

enemy—unconquerable because its existence is the condition of its own life—bourgeois rule, freed from all fetters, was bound to turn immediately into bourgeois terrorism. With the proletariat removed for the time being from the stage and bourgeois dictatorship recognised officially, the middle sections, in the mass, had more and more to side with the proletariat as their position became more unbearable and their antagonism to the bourgeoisie became more acute. Just as earlier in its upsurge, so now they had to find in its defeat the cause of their misery. . . .

Only through the defeat of June, therefore, were all conditions created under which France can seize the initiative of the European revolution. Only after baptism in the blood of the June insurgents did the tricolour[24] become the flag of the European revolution—the red flag.

And we cry: *The revolution is dead!—Long live the revolution!*

Source 7 *from Karl Marx and Friedrich Engels,* The Communist Manifesto, *translated by Samuel Moore (New York: Penguin, 1977), pp. 104–105.*

7. Marx's Ideals of Government and Economy

We have seen above, that the first step in the revolution by the working class, is to raise the proletariat to the position of ruling class, to win the battle of democracy.

The proletariat will use its political supremacy to wrest, by degrees, all capital from the bourgeoisie, to centralize all instruments of production in the hands of the State, i.e., of the proletariat organized as the ruling class; and to increase the total of productive forces as rapidly as possible.

Of course, in the beginning, this cannot be effected except by means of despotic inroads on the rights of property, and on the conditions of bourgeois production; by means of measures, therefore, which appear economically insufficient and untenable, but which, in the course of the movement, outstrip themselves, necessitate further inroads upon the old social order, and are unavoidable as a means of entirely revolutionizing the mode of production.

These measures will of course be different in different countries.

Nevertheless, in the most advanced countries, the following will be pretty generally applicable:

1. Abolition of property in land and application of all rents of land to public purposes.

2. A heavy progressive or graduated income tax.

24. **tricolour:** the three-colored flag, composed of vertical stripes of blue, white, and red, adopted in the 1789 Revolution and today the flag of France.

[200]

3. Abolition of all right of inheritance.

4. Confiscation of the property of all emigrants and rebels.

5. Centralization of credit in the hands of the State, by means of a national bank with State capital and an exclusive monopoly.

6. Centralization of the means of communication and transport in the hands of the State.

7. Extension of factories and instruments of production owned by the State; the bringing into cultivation of wastelands, and the improvement of the soil generally in accordance with a common plan.

8. Equal liability of all to labour. Establishment of industrial armies, especially for agriculture.

9. Combination of agriculture with manufacturing industries; gradual abolition of the distinction between town and country, by a more equable distribution of the population over the country.

10. Free education for all children in public schools. Abolition of children's factory labour in its present form. Combination of education with industrial production, &c., &c.

When, in the course of development, class distinctions have disappeared, and all production has been concentrated in the whole nation, the public power will lose its political character. Political power, properly so called, is merely the organized power of one class for oppressing another. If the proletariat during its contest with the bourgeoisie is compelled, by the force of circumstances, to organize itself as a class, if, by means of a revolution, it makes itself the ruling class, and, as such, sweeps away by force the old conditions of production, then it will, along with these conditions, have swept away the conditions for the existence of class antagonisms and of classes generally, and will thereby have abolished its own supremacy as a class.

In place of the old bourgeois society, with its classes and class antagonisms, we shall have an association, in which the free development of each is the condition for the free development of all.

QUESTIONS TO CONSIDER

Tocqueville and Marx pose different responses to many of the same issues in the selections presented in this chapter. Your basic task in answering the main questions of this chapter is to compare their ideas.

Central to the thought of both men is a certain vision of historical evolution. Indeed, Marx called himself a "scientific socialist" because, in his view, he had discovered the immutable course of historical development. What was this historical process for Marx? What patterns of history did Tocqueville identify? As you continue your study of modern Western history in this course, consider which of these thinkers' ideas seem most adequately to have predicted the political and economic development of the West.

Chapter 7

Two Programs

for Social

and Political

Change:

Liberalism

and Socialism

Both Marx and Tocqueville address the problem of revolution in the selections that you have read. First consider Tocqueville. What threats to democracy did he see emerging in the West? Why did he believe that revolution was not likely to be a threat to democracy? What dangers, according to Tocqueville, did revolution pose when it did erupt? Did Tocqueville's liberal principles admit any circumstances under which society should resort to revolution as a means of change? Recall Tocqueville's attitude toward the government of King Louis Philippe in Source 3. Why did Tocqueville oppose the Revolution of 1848 despite this view?

Now analyze Marx's ideas on revolution. Examine the historical role for revolution that Marx believed he had found. Why did Marx see the middle class, those who owned the factories and embraced liberal ideas, as revolutionary? In what ways, according to Marx, was capitalism sowing the seeds of its destruction? What class would challenge the factory owners in revolution? What vision of the future did that class have, according to Marx? Did they want the political democracy Tocqueville was prepared to accept or a broader reorganization of society? How did Marx and Tocqueville differ in their views of the desirability of revolution?

Both authors also wrote on the same revolution, the French uprising of 1848, providing us a further opportunity to contrast their views. As your study of the 1848 revolutions no doubt has demonstrated, it is impossible to consider the uprisings of that year a success. Whether revolutionaries' goals were nationalist or liberal, the revolutions ended in defeat everywhere. This was certainly the case in France, where the conflict of June 1848 between the government of the Second Republic and the Parisian unemployed created the political climate for the election of Louis-Napoleon Bonaparte.

How did each author view the Revolution of 1848? What guiding emotion do you detect in Tocqueville's *Recollections* of February 24, 1848? What was its source? In formulating your answer, consult the selection in which Tocqueville discusses general aspects of revolution and expresses his ideals of government. What was Marx's view of the failure of the June 1848 revolt? Why was the victory that emerged in 1848 an essential step for Marx toward the final revolution?

Finally, let us compare the political and economic ideals advocated by the liberal Tocqueville and the socialist Marx. Your task here is made more challenging by the assertion of both these political thinkers that they advocated democracy. To understand the differences between them, review their writings to determine how each defined "democracy." Is Tocqueville's conception of democracy expressed primarily in terms of political participation? Is there any room in his thought for social democracy, that is, a more egalitarian distribution of society's wealth? How does Tocqueville characterize his political thought in Source 4? Recall France's history of recurring revolution. Why might he accept a monarch in Europe and an elected head of government in America?

Sources 5 through 7 express especially clearly Marx's democratic philosophy. Does Marx believe in political democracy? How is he concerned with social democracy? Who would control property, credit, and the means of production in his ideal society? What answers does Marx have to such abuses of industrialization as child labor? What impact would his system have on the lives of its citizens?

Finally, consider the two thinkers' views on the role of government. What role in the lives of its citizens does Tocqueville assign to the government? How does that view mark him as a nineteenth-century liberal? What sort of postrevolutionary government does Marx envision? How does it differ from Tocqueville's ideal? Are there areas where Marx and Tocqueville might agree?

With answers to these fairly specific questions in mind, you are now ready to answer the general questions presented earlier in this chapter: What visions of the future did liberals and socialists propose? How did they hope to realize their ideals? How did their ideologies differ?

EPILOGUE

The selections in this chapter present two contrasting nineteenth-century visions of Western society. Most of what you have read appeared around the middle of the nineteenth century, much of it in the midst of the West's last general outbreak of revolution in 1848. Because both authors wrote about that event and had a definite view of revolution, perhaps it is appropriate to examine briefly how their predictions fared after 1848.

The events of 1848 shook Tocqueville's faith in the growth of democracy founded on limited government and increasing equality of property as well as in political stability and evolutionary change based on respect for the rule of law. Indeed, in 1850 he wrote to his friend Eugène Stoffels of events in France with considerable despair:

What is clear to me is that for sixty years we have fooled ourselves by believing that we could see the end of revolution. The revolution was thought to have finished at 18 *brumaire*, the same was thought in 1814; I thought myself in 1830 that it could well be at an end . . . I was wrong. It is clear today . . . not only that we have not seen the end of the immense revolution which started before our time, but that today's child will probably not see it.[25]

25. Tocqueville to Eugène Stoffels, quoted in Jack Lively, *The Social and Political Thought of Alexis de Tocqueville* (Oxford: Clarendon Press, 1962), p. 211. The radical leaders of the French Revolution of 1789–1799 had sought to break with the traditional Western calendar and its Christian observances. Thus they created a new calendar devoid of Christian holidays and with renamed months. The date 18 *brumaire* was the day in 1799 that marked Napoleon's seizure of power in France; 1814 was the year of the restoration of the French monarchy after Napoleon's fall; 1830, of course, was the year King Louis Philippe came to power.

Chapter 7

Two Programs

for Social

and Political

Change:

Liberalism

and Socialism

Tocqueville died in 1859 questioning his vision of the future, and Marx lived on until 1883, also disillusioned, as we have noted, by his own apparent failure decisively to affect the socialist movement. Events after their deaths would have surprised both men. Political change in much of Europe proved to be far more evolutionary than revolutionary in the years after 1848, thanks to several developments predicted neither by Tocqueville nor by Marx.

The liberal ideology represented by Tocqueville became less and less a narrow doctrine of individual freedom. Later liberals, such as the Englishman John Stuart Mill (1806–1873), emphasized that economic liberty reached its limits when it allowed employers to abuse their employees with the low wages and poor working conditions we examined in Chapter 6. Consequently, they supported legislation to rectify many of the worst abuses of industrial employment. Such liberals also believed in political democracy and won extended franchises in countries like England and Italy.

Communist revolution occasionally did break out, as Marx had predicted. But he utterly misjudged the historical developments that produced such revolutions. Writing from the vantage point of the early Industrial Revolution, Marx assumed that working-class misery would intensify and produce communist revolution only in the most industrialized nations. Instead, Marx's revolution broke out in places where he never would have expected it. Peasant populations in countries either on the threshold of industrialization, like Russia in 1917, or not yet industrialized, like China and Vietnam in the 1940s and 1950s, have been the chief adherents of communist revolution. Marx had believed peasants incapable of such ideological mobilization, counting them a politically inert "sack of potatoes." And, contrary to Marx's prediction that communism would constitute the final stage of human development, such regimes, like that in the former Soviet Union, were breaking down by the early 1990s.

In much of the industrialized West, the widened right to vote, in fact, engendered a new kind of evolutionary socialism quite distinct from Marx's revolutionary socialism. The German Eduard Bernstein (1850–1932) was among the first to recognize that working-class voting rights eliminated the need for Marx's class warfare and revolution. Armed with the vote, Bernstein emphasized, workers could elect parliaments favoring their needs and peacefully win a better life through legislation. The need for revolution was at an end.

In the twenty-first century, socialist parties committed to political democracy, sometimes allied with liberals, have been instrumental in bringing greater social equality for working people in much of Western Europe. In modern England, France, Italy, Germany, and other nations, legislation improving working conditions and wages as well as establishing the protection of health and unemployment insurance and old age pensions stands as a monument to the widened vote created by liberals and the use of that vote by democratic so-cialists. The consequent improvement in working-class conditions ultimately resulted in the decline in the broad popular appeal of Marxian revolutionary socialists in much of the West.

CHAPTER EIGHT

VIENNA AND PARIS,

1850–1930:

THE DEVELOPMENT OF

THE MODERN CITY

The nineteenth century was a period of great change in Europe. Just as the Industrial Revolution transformed the Continent's mode of production and, as we have seen in Chapter 6, its patterns of work, it also greatly accelerated the urbanization of the West. Individual cities grew rapidly as large numbers of immigrants from rural areas came in search of industrial jobs, and society was transformed as urban rather than rural life became the lifestyle of the majority. By the second half of the nineteenth century, over half of the population of England and Wales, the original centers of the Industrial Revolution, dwelt in cities, and Germany and other countries reached that level of urban concentration of population within several decades.

Unfortunately for the residents of Europe's growing nineteenth-century cities, living conditions in these centers often were very difficult. This is how one French author described Paris in 1848:

If you contemplate from the summit of Montmartre or any other hill in the neighborhood, the congestion of houses piled up at every point of a vast horizon, what do you observe? Above, a sky that is always overcast, even on the finest day. Clouds of smoke, like a vast floating curtain, hide it from view. A forest of chimneys with black or yellowish chimneypots renders the sight singularly monotonous. . . . Looking at it, one is tempted to wonder whether this is Paris; and, seized with sudden fear, one is reluctant to venture into this vast maze, in which a million beings jostle each other, where the air, vitiated by unhealthy effluvia, rising in a poisonous cloud, almost obscures the sun. Most of the streets in this wonderful Paris are nothing but filthy alleys forever damp from a reeking flood.

[206]

Hemmed in between two rows of tall houses, they never get the sun; it reaches only the tops of the chimneys dominating them. To catch a glimpse of the sky you have to look straight up above your head. A haggard and sickly crowd perpetually throngs these streets, their feet in the gutter, their noses in infection, their eyes outraged by the most repulsive garbage at every street corner. The best-paid workmen live in these streets. There are alleys, too, in which two cannot walk abreast, sewers of ordure and mud, in which the stunted dwellers daily inhale death. These are the streets of old Paris, still intact.[1]

Rapid population growth overwhelmed the capacity of early-nineteenth-century municipal governments to provide for the needs of their new citizens. The problems described in the quotation were almost universal. Many cities in Continental Europe remained hemmed in by medieval or early modern fortifications designed to protect much smaller populations from military attack. Even without this obstacle to expansion, however, urban spread was limited by the almost complete absence of cheap, public transportation. People had to live close to their jobs because they walked to them, and essentially medieval residential patterns persisted in which craftsmen and merchants dwelled behind or above their places of business and poorer persons occupied the upper floors of the same buildings.

The growth in the urban population within the old walls led to an increasingly dense pattern of residence. Landlords added additional floors to existing buildings, cut up once spacious apartments into many smaller living units, erected inferior dwellings in courtyards and other open spaces, and rented basement and attic rooms. Sunlight and fresh air disappeared as building heights increased along narrow, medieval streets. Basements were particularly unhealthy dwellings; they often leaked and seldom received sunlight or ventilation. With little but musty, stale air available to them, it was a custom of basement residents to get an occasional "airing" out of doors.

Simple movement of people was a problem in the streets of such cities. Lacking sidewalks, pedestrians competed with horse-drawn vehicles for the opportunity to move through cramped streets wet with household waste water and soiled by horse droppings. A trip across a major city, which today would require a matter of minutes by subway, consumed considerably more time in the early nineteenth century. Many cities were almost strangled by such transportation difficulties within their old walls.

Rapid population growth in the limited spaces of many cities produced serious health and social problems. Extremely primitive methods for disposal of human wastes often led to pollution of water supplies, and in the first decades of the nineteenth century, sewers in Paris and other cities emptied into the very rivers that

1. H. Lecouturier, *Paris incompatible avec la République, plan d'un nouveau Paris où les révolutions seront impossibles* (Paris: 1848), quoted in Louis Chevalier, *Laboring Classes and Dangerous Classes in Paris during the First Half of the Nineteenth Century*, trans. by Frank Jellinek (Princeton, N.J.: Princeton University Press, 1981), p. 155. Montmartre is the highest point in Paris.

Chapter 8

Vienna

and Paris,

1850–1930:

The Development

of the Modern

City

were the main sources of municipal water. Under such conditions, disease spread rapidly, and life could be short. Epidemics of cholera, a disease often transmitted by polluted drinking water, struck many cities in the nineteenth century; 20,000 persons died in one outbreak of the disease in Paris in 1832. Indeed, well into the nineteenth century, most cities retained an age-old urban demographic pattern in which death rates among their citizens exceeded birth rates. The limited urban population growth that occurred prior to about 1850 was almost entirely the result of immigration to the cities from rural areas.

A rapidly rising crime rate was probably the most vexing of the social consequences of urban growth. Urban life often plunged unskilled immigrants of rural origin into deep poverty. Though crime sometimes stemmed from poverty, certain features of urban life encouraged it. The social controls of rural village life largely were absent in the cities, where the anonymity of the individual in the urban mass facilitated lawbreaking. Police resources for controlling such behavior were limited or nonexistent during the first half of the nineteenth century, too. The pioneering effort at urban crime control, the London Metropolitan Police Force, was created only in 1829, and was imitated widely only after 1850.

In fact, only after about 1850 can we find Western society systematically attempting to solve the real problems of urban living. Collectively, these responses transformed city life and produced our modern pattern of urban living. Several nineteenth-century

developments made possible this important transformation. We should note first that the power of central governments grew everywhere. The state's ability to command resources in the form of taxes financed many improvements. Its growing bureaucracy also provided the personnel to undertake the first modern urban planning. And its need to maintain order in growing cities led to improved police services and better street lighting to inhibit crime, wider streets to allow for troop movements in case of urban rebellion, and better sanitation to protect the health of its citizens and taxpayers.

The Industrial Revolution played a major role in the urban transformation, too. It created new technologies whose application to city life would improve conditions, and it produced wealth, increasingly shared by more and more persons, which could finance private projects of urban building and improvement. Industrialization also sustained a new consumer-oriented economy characterized by the mass distribution of the products of the new factories to large urban markets. Modern science played a part in urban improvements, too. The work of Louis Pasteur (1822–1895) and other scientists made possible purer water and food to protect public health.

The combination of these nineteenth-century developments would transform the Western city by 1930. Your problem in this chapter is to examine the physical expressions and social consequences of this transformation in two major cities: Paris, France, and Vienna, Austria. How were these cities physically reshaped in response to early-nineteenth-century problems? How did this physical transformation affect the lifestyle of urban dwellers?

SOURCES AND METHOD

In order to analyze this chapter's sources, you will require some specific information on nineteenth-century Paris and Vienna. In the 1870s, Paris and Vienna, respectively, were Europe's second- and third-largest cities; only the population of Greater London was larger. As the political capitals of their nations and as major cultural, commercial, and industrial centers, they experienced rapid growth during much of the period from 1850 to 1930. The population of Paris grew from 547,000 persons in 1800 to 2,714,000 persons a century later, a growth rate of 496 percent. For the same period, Vienna's population grew even more rapidly: from 247,000 persons to 1,675,000 persons, for a growth rate of 678 percent.[2] With such rapid growth, Paris and Vienna experienced the full range of urban problems we examined earlier in this chapter. The two cities' responses to these problems are typical of those of most Continental European cities in our period. But to analyze our evidence on these changes, some background on Paris and Vienna is necessary.

Unlike English cities, which early abandoned their defensive walls because of the protection from attack afforded all of England by its surrounding seas, most Continental European cities retained their walls into the nineteenth century because of the probability of military assault. Thus, Paris traditionally had been confined by fortifications against attackers and by barriers erected to enforce the collection of taxes on goods entering the city. Within those confines, the city described at the beginning of this chapter developed. Only in the 1850s did major improvements of the central city begin. But these improvements in Paris were centrally planned because the national government administered the French capital through its prefect of the Seine Department.[3] As a result, change in Paris could come about rapidly, since the financial resources of the national government could be brought to the process, and the prestige of that government aided private investment schemes for civic improvements like new housing.

From 1852 to 1870, Emperor Napoleon III governed France. He personally drafted detailed plans for the improvement of Paris and entrusted these to his energetic prefect of the Seine, Baron Georges Eugène Haussmann (1809–1891). Haussmann's projects

2. B. R. Mitchell, *European Historical Statistics 1750–1970*, abridged edition (New York: Columbia University Press, 1978), pp. 12–15. This is the source for all population statistics through 1970 in this chapter.

3. In 1791 the Legislative Assembly divided France into eighty-three departments for administrative purposes. Paris was the Department of the Seine until twentieth-century reforms subdivided the metropolitan area into a number of new departments in the interest of efficiency. Napoleon I instituted the office of the prefect as the central government's administrator in each department.

Chapter 8

Vienna

and Paris,

1850–1930:

The Development

of the Modern

City

combined government initiative and money with private capital, and his results were sweeping and rapid. He cut new boulevards through the warren of narrow, medieval streets in the city's center and began the construction of peripheral boulevards along the line of the tax wall of 1784 that once enclosed the city. The new boulevards were wide. Indeed, some of them were almost 400 feet in width. Such street-building efforts eased movement of goods and persons through the city and improved health standards by opening the center of Paris to more light and fresh air. At the same time, the city's physical appearance changed dramatically as private investors erected new apartment buildings along Haussmann's broad boulevards.

Matters of public health also occupied Haussmann. The government greatly expanded the Paris sewer system and built aqueducts to bring clean drinking water into the city. Haussmann's work also added to the cityscape of Paris parks where residents could enjoy recreational opportunities and unrestricted sunlight and fresh air. Former royal hunting preserves at the western and eastern borders of the city, the Bois de Boulogne (the Boulogne Wood) and the Bois de Vincennes (the Vincennes Wood), became great new public parks, and Haussmann added major new inner-city parks: the Buttes-Chaumont, Monceau, and Montsouris parks.

Urban improvements continued in Paris after Haussmann. More major new thoroughfares opened, including the Avenue de l'Opéra in 1877, and public transportation soon flowed on the new boulevards. Paris had had slow-moving and rather expensive

horse-drawn buses called omnibuses since 1828. But the new boulevards permitted the city to lead Europe in the introduction of horse-drawn tramcars running much more quickly on steel tracks. By the end of the nineteenth century, electrification of trams provided increasingly efficient and inexpensive public transportation. And in 1900 the city opened a subway system, the Métropolitain, which many urban transportation specialists regard as the world's most comprehensive public transportation system.

The twentieth century also witnessed greater attention to solving the housing problems of working people in Paris. The apartment buildings constructed along Haussmann's boulevards, built at private expense, were intended to provide real estate investors a good return on their capital. These new buildings housed the middle- and upper-class Parisians, who, like their counterparts throughout Continental Europe, preferred the city to the suburbs, which were already drawing affluent English people and Americans out of their cities. These new buildings and Haussmann's boulevards, however, destroyed much old working-class housing, and Paris's near suburbs, like those of many European cities, became zones of cheap worker housing as well as home to industries too large for the city itself.

Much of this housing for workers was of poor quality, however, because building expenses had to be kept low to keep rents affordable. Also to keep prices low, such housing was densely built; in Paris, working-class suburbs often had greater population densities than the central city. Worse still, there was an increasing shortage of low-cost housing in the early twentieth century in Paris. Rent controls, made necessary by World War I (1914–1918), continued until after World War II (1939–1945) and made private construction of low-cost housing unprofitable. As a result, French national and city governments cooperated to construct low-cost housing called HBM (Habitation de Bon Marché, that is, inexpensive housing). Built as multi-storied apartment buildings, some of this new housing arose in the zone that had been occupied by Paris's most recent city wall, which was built in 1841–1845 and which the government razed after World War I.

Vienna, like Paris, sustained a rapid and planned transformation from a congested, walled city to a modern metropolis in the nineteenth century. As in Paris, the initiative came from the central government. In December 1857, Emperor Francis Joseph ordered the destruction of Vienna's fortifications and the implementation of a plan for his capital's expansion into the area of the old walls and the open spaces, called the *glacis*, surrounding them.[4] Moreover, in 1860 the emperor granted Vienna full municipal self-government, an act that encouraged local initiatives in developing this

zone. Soon, just as Haussmann had promoted the construction of peripheral boulevards along the old tax wall of Paris, Viennese planners mapped out a broad system of boulevards, collectively called the *Ringstrasse*, along the old defense lines. As in Paris, this new boulevard system was grand: the Ringstrasse's builders made it 2.5 miles long and 185 feet wide. Along it rose new public buildings and privately financed apartment buildings.

Just as in Paris, such construction affected the human geography of Vienna. The old city within the walls had been densely populated before 1857, but it had never been squalid. The Imperial Court resided within the walls, and many of Austria's great nobles maintained residences nearby. Most of Vienna's suburbs, on the other hand, had long contained the residences of the economically disadvantaged: densely built tenements of two- and three-room apartments, structures that Viennese called "rent barracks" and "bedbug castles." The construction of the Ringstrasse reinforced this segregation, as its new apartment buildings became the residences of affluent families whose wealth was derived from new industries or service in the expanding governmental institutions of nineteenth-century Austria-Hungary. Even though the city of Vienna annexed numerous suburbs in 1867 and again in 1890, many neighborhoods just beyond the Ringstrasse retained their working-class character.

A new street system encouraged the development of public transportation in Vienna as it did in Paris. Horse-drawn trams began to run in 1868, and these were electrified at the turn of the

4. Early modern fortifications customarily were surrounded by a *glacis,* an unbuilt area intended to provide free-fire zones for the fortifications' defenders. By the nineteenth century, as artillery ranges increased, these zones often had become quite broad indeed. In Vienna's case, the glacis was 1,485 feet wide. Destruction of constraining fortifications was a common feature of urban development in the nineteenth and early twentieth centuries. The following cities tore down their defensive walls in the years indicated: Brussels (1830s), Geneva (1851), Barcelona (1854), Basel (1860–1867), Madrid (1868), and Bologna (1902).

Chapter 8

Vienna

and Paris,

1850–1930:

The Development

of the Modern

City

century. Also at the century's end, in 1894, the city began construction of a peripheral railroad, the Stadtbahn (or S-Bahn), that ran in tunnels for about a quarter of its 16.5-mile route. A true subway system was planned, too, but World War I prevented its construction, and Vienna opened its subway system only in 1980.

Late-nineteenth-century Viennese planners effected many other improvements in their city. They initiated a system providing pure water to the city in 1860 and rechanneled the Danube in 1870–1875 to prevent dangerous flooding. Other public services improved, too, as the elected municipal government assumed control of gas and electric power and extended these utilities into working-class districts. Most importantly, Viennese planners, like Haussmann, opened parks to provide healthful recreation opportunities for citizens. The Ringstrasse itself included a great deal of green space, but the most important park opened to citizens in the 1880s when Emperor Francis Joseph turned a former hunting preserve on the Danube River over to the city. This new park, the Prater, had some 3,200 acres and by the end of the nineteenth century offered something for almost everyone. It had paths for walking, riding, or bicycling; lakes for boating; soccer fields; an amusement park with a large Ferris wheel; and Europe's largest outdoor theater.

Such development made Vienna a much more attractive city by the outbreak of World War I in 1914. But that war drastically changed the city. Austria-Hungary broke up at the war's end, and Vienna found itself not the political and cultural center of a cosmopolitan empire of 54 million, but the capital of a republic of 6 million, with one-third of those living in Vienna. The capital of the small Republic of Austria faced great problems. Population growth outstripped the construction of new, privately owned housing even before World War I, and wartime rent controls, as in Paris, ended most private construction during and after the war. Thus the city found itself with a major housing shortage at the war's end, when soldiers returned from the army to marry and establish families, and refugees from the former empire's territories crowded the city.

In Vienna, as in Paris and many other cities, the government sought to address this and other problems. The postwar constitution of Austria gave Vienna the status of a province, with authority to raise and spend substantial revenues. The government of this city was in the hands of the Socialist party until 1934, and that party used public funds for the construction of 63,924 low-cost housing units to meet the housing shortage and to provide better residences for those dwelling in Vienna's tenements. Other projects improved recreational opportunities; these included public swimming pools and a 60,000-seat stadium in the Prater.

Now let us use this background material on Paris and Vienna to consider the evidence. Your sources for answering the questions posed in this chapter are of two chief types. You first encounter pictorial evidence, a type of historical source that you have analyzed in earlier chapters. In the present chapter, you will wish to examine this evidence carefully to discern the solutions to the urban problems that the pictures present. The pictures also present various architectural answers to the problems of living in the city. You should consider carefully the solutions posed by architects and builders to society's needs, because architecture is an important source for the historian. Architects do not design for themselves, but at the commission of their customers. As a result, their designs generally reflect the needs and values of their employers.

This chapter presents a second kind of evidence, one which so far you have not analyzed extensively: maps and city plans. Maps are important records of human activity that often are underused by historians. Many historians simply employ maps to illustrate their narratives, as a military historian frequently does when he or she presents a map to describe a battle. Other social scientists, like sociologists and human geographers, make more extensive use of maps. Their study of maps as primary sources allows them to discover basic elements of human activity, such as residential patterns. It is in this fashion that you should view the maps.

Let us now apply these general guidelines to analysis of specific pieces of evidence. Sources 1 through 3 provide pictorial evidence on the pre-industrial city. Observe the pictures carefully, recalling our description of such cities in the Problem section of this chapter. Source 1 is a picture of Vienna in 1850, before the Ringstrasse development, showing the city walls and the glacis. What is your impression of the city within those walls? In which direction have

buildings grown because of the city's confinement within these walls? What sort of opportunities did the glacis offer urban planners?

Sources 2 and 3 take us within early-nineteenth-century Paris. Consider Source 2, a photograph of the rue Bernard de Palissy. What kind of housing did such a street seem to offer? What do you think the population density in such a neighborhood would have been? Consider health conditions. How much sunlight probably reached the residences on this street? Given the city's lack of sewers in the early nineteenth century, what function do you think the central gutter performed? Why do you think such a street would offend your senses and prove unhealthful? Source 3 is a photograph of leather workshops along the Bièvre River. This district was in a densely populated area of the city on a river flowing into the Seine River, from which Parisians drew much of their drinking water in the early nineteenth century. Leather processing produces strong chemical odors and much toxic waste. Why do you think the workshops were built along the Bièvre? What sort of health impact do you suppose these workshops had?

Sources 4 and 5 present a map and photograph of Vienna's Ringstrasse. Study the map in Source 4. It shows central Vienna, with the Danube Canal curving across the lower right of the map near building Number 13. What evidence of deliberate planning efforts do you see in the development? Does the Ringstrasse, which intermingled new apartment buildings with both public and commercial buildings, seem to have certain functional zones? Why might you conclude that commerce

Chapter 8

Vienna

and Paris,

1850–1930:

The Development

of the Modern

City

occupied one zone? Moving along the Ringstrasse, what sort of functional change do you observe at the area's first building, the Votivkirche, a church built in the 1850s in thanksgiving for the emperor's escape from an assassination attempt? What sort of institutions surround the Hofburg, or imperial palace?

Source 5 offers you a photograph of key Ringstrasse buildings. Do you find any harmony of architectural styles in the public buildings? Why do you think architects adopted classical Greek architecture for the houses of Parliament? Why might they have adopted Gothic architecture for the city hall? Do you think such tactics heightened the sense of different functional zones within the Ringstrasse? Consider the scale of the boulevard. How might its great width have improved communications and public health?

In Sources 6 through 9, you must analyze evidence on Paris. The map in Source 6 is particularly rich in detail on the city improvements wrought by Baron Haussmann during the Second French Empire. How has Haussmann improved Paris streets? What other transportation improvements do you find on the map? Consider, too, the impact Haussmann's work had on the quality of life for Parisians. How many new parks were opened during Haussmann's tenure in office? What problems dictated the aqueducts in the lower center of the map and in its upper right? What do you notice about the city's growth? What suburbs did it annex to provide for growth?

Sources 7 through 9 illustrate a major project in Paris's nineteenth-century improvements, the Avenue de l'Opéra. Source 7 is a map showing the creation of the avenue. Haussmann began this broad avenue in the 1850s to provide better communication in western Paris, but it was completed only in 1878, after he left office. The complexities of property acquisition for the new street played a major role in its delayed completion. What was the street pattern in this area of the city before the avenue's construction? What effects do you think the avenue had on its district? Refer to Source 8 as well now. How does this photograph affect your opinion of the complexity of this project? How would knowing that street builders had to level a large hill, the Butte Saint-Roch, to provide a level path for the avenue change your assessment of the project's difficulty? What sort of housing, judging by Source 8, was removed to make way for the avenue? Refer to Source 9 at this juncture, a photograph of the completed avenue looking toward the new opera house, which opened in 1875. How did the avenue improve communications in the city? What health benefits probably resulted from its construction? What sort of housing seems to surround the avenue?

Sources 10 through 12 provide you with detailed examples of the housing built along the Ringstrasse and Haussmann's new streets. Examine Source 10, paying particular attention to the ornamentation around the windows and their size in this building constructed in the late nineteenth century, before elevators came into widespread use. What about the building's façade suggests to you that the building's upper floors might contain less prestigious, cheaper, and smaller apartments than the lower floors? Why might you conclude that, in the absence of elevators, some former patterns of social segregation by floor persisted?

Source 11 is an engraving of a building typical of those that arose along Haussmann's new boulevards in Paris. Such structures usually had shops facing the street on the ground floor with apartments on upper floors. Access to the buildings' residential sections often was through a large double door (at lower left in the picture) leading past the lodging of a *concièrge,* who controlled access to the building and kept it clean, to an inner courtyard.

Source 12 illustrates an architect's plan for another such apartment building. Such plans, showing the building literally as it would look if you removed its roof and looked down into it, are easy to read when you know a few rules. On this plan, doorways are shown as openings in the dark outline of the building, and windows are shown as white, narrower areas in the building's outline. The rest of the features of the building may be analyzed through the keys.

Remember that architects design buildings with a definite clientele in mind. Examine the apartment on the ground floor and the two apartments found on each of the first, second, and third floors (floors above the third contained smaller apartments and servants' quarters). How many rooms do these apartments contain? Consider, too, other features like service staircases, stables, and coach houses. What do these features of the building floor plan suggest to you about the types of residents expected for these apartments? Compare your conclusions with those you derived from analyzing the exterior decoration of the Vienna apartment building in Source 10. Why might you conclude that the same class of resident lived in both the Vienna and Paris buildings?

Sources 13 and 14 present examples of the recreational areas added to nineteenth-century cities. Source 13 is a photograph of the Prater in the late nineteenth century. What sort of diversions did this part of the great park offer? What developments in nineteenth-century urban life would have made such a place more accessible to citizens of all classes? Source 14 illustrates Haussmann's Buttes-Chaumont Park, constructed in 1864–1867 near Belleville, one of the nineteenth-century worker suburbs annexed by Paris. On an area formerly occupied by quarries and dumps, Haussmann's engineers created a lake surrounded by a dramatically landscaped park with a view of the entire Paris area. Note that a multitrack railroad line traverses a corner of the park and that the smokestacks of industrial enterprises cluster around its periphery. What does the presence of these activities suggest to you about the suburbs of cities like Paris and Vienna?

Sources 15 through 17 focus on the near suburbs of both cities. Source 15 is a photograph of the working-class neighborhood of Belleville. What sort of concentration of people might you imagine inhabited a narrow street such as this one? Having examined the landscape around Buttes-Chaumont

Chapter 8

Vienna

and Paris,

1850–1930:

The Development

of the Modern

City

Park in Source 14, examine Source 16, a picture of a suburban factory that opened in 1873 at Ivry. Why might you conclude that such suburbs would have been rather unhealthy places of residence? Turn to Source 17, which illustrates Viennese worker housing. Why do you find late-nineteenth-century conditions in Vienna little different from those in Paris?

Sources 18 and 19 illustrate the impact of the Industrial Revolution on urban life, particularly by the new modes of transportation made possible by industrialization. The Stadtbahn, or S-Bahn, encircled Vienna, and buses and electric trolleys like those of Paris appeared on the streets of all European cities. The fares on such vehicles were low at all times and often were discounted for workers at rush hours. What impact might the availability of such transportation have had on worker living patterns? Since public transportation ran seven days per week, why do you think recreational opportunities for workers increased?

Our final sources illustrate post–World War I answers to the problems of city life, whose growing complexity dictated state rather than private action. Almost all major European cities built public, low-cost housing for workers after World War I. Source 20 illustrates the largest such Viennese housing project, the Karl Marx Hof, which provided homes for 5,000 persons in 1,382 apartments. Such projects really were small cities, equipped with common laundries, child-care facilities, and parklike courtyards. Contrast this block of apartments with the tenements in Source 17. Why would you think that such large complexes would have been more healthful for workers than the old tenements?

Source 21 is a floor plan of a Parisian low-cost housing project with two apartments sharing a common stair. The Parisian solution to the housing shortage differed in detail, but not in substance, from the Viennese apartments of the Karl Marx Hof. Observe the floor plans carefully. What common late-twentieth-century amenities are missing? Floor plans always show placement of radiators. Do you find any? Indeed, do you find any heat source for multi-room apartments other than fireplaces? While each apartment has a toilet, does each have a shower? Notice the sizes of the rooms. How do they compare with those to which you are accustomed? For what class of residents do you think such apartments were designed?

Source 22 is a photo of Vienna's Kongressbad swimming pool. It was one of the largest pools in Europe, measuring 66 feet × 330 feet. Built at public expense, such a pool represented the culmination of many trends. Why would such projects as this pool, which attracted 450,000 bathers in 1930, have been virtually impossible without developments in public transportation during our period? How do the pool and public housing developments reflect a government attitude toward the solution of urban problems different from that of the earlier nineteenth century?

As you examine the evidence that follows, you should be able to formulate answers to this chapter's central questions. How were these cities physically reshaped in response to the problems of the early nineteenth century? How did this physical transformation affect the lifestyles of urban dwellers?

Source 1 from Donald J. Olsen, The City as a Work of Art (New Haven, Conn.: Yale University Press, 1986), p. 61. Photograph: Historisches Museum der Stadt Wien.

1. Vienna in 1850

Source 2 from Donald J. Olsen, The City as a Work of Art *(New Haven, Conn.: Yale University Press, 1986), p. 222. Photograph: © Photothèque des Musées de la Ville de Paris/Cliché Lauros-Giraudon by SPADEM.*

2. A Paris Street in the 1850s: The Rue Bernard de Palissy

Source 3 from Mark Girouard, Cities and People: A Social and Architectural History (New Haven, Conn.: Yale University Press, 1985), p. 298. Photograph: © Photothèque des Musées de la Ville de Paris/Cliché Lauros-Giraudon by SPADEM.

3. **Leather Workshops on the Bièvre River in Paris in the Mid-Nineteenth Century**

Source 4 from Wolfgang Braunfels, translated by Kenneth J. Northcott, Urban Design in Western Europe: Regime and Architecture, 900–1900 *(Chicago: University of Chicago Press, 1988), p. 304.*

4. Schematic Drawing of the Viennese Ringstrasse and Its Major Buildings

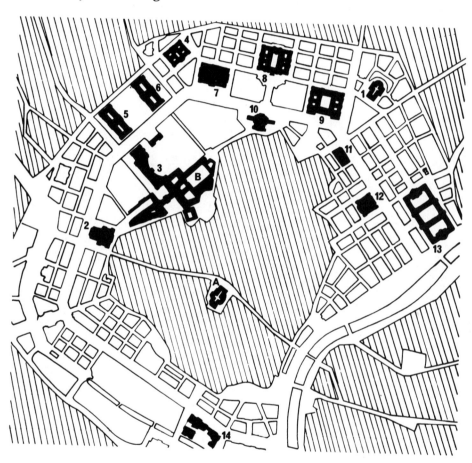

Key

Pre-1857 Buildings
A St. Stephen's Cathedral
B *Hofburg* (Imperial Palace)

Post-1857 Buildings
1 Votivkirche (the Votive Church or Church of the Divine Savior)
2 Opera House
3 New Hofburg
4 Courthouse
5 Art History Museum
6 Natural History Museum
7 Parliament

8 City Hall
9 University
10 Burgtheater
11 Banking Union
12 Stock Exchange
13 Army Barracks
14 School of Arts and Crafts

Chapter 8

Vienna

and Paris,

1850–1930:

The Development

of the Modern

City

Source 5 from William M. Johnston, Vienna, Vienna: The Golden Age, 1815–1914 *(New York: Clarkson N. Potter, 1981), p. 128. Photograph courtesy of Mondadori Press.*

5. Vienna Ringstrasse in the Late Nineteenth Century

The Parliament building is in the foreground; city hall is the spired building in the upper left; the university is the domed building right of center; and the Burgtheater appears in the upper right.

Source 6 from Thomas F. X. Noble et al., Western Civilization: The Continuing Experiment, *second edition (Boston: Houghton Mifflin, 1998), p. 859.*

6. Paris, 1850–1870

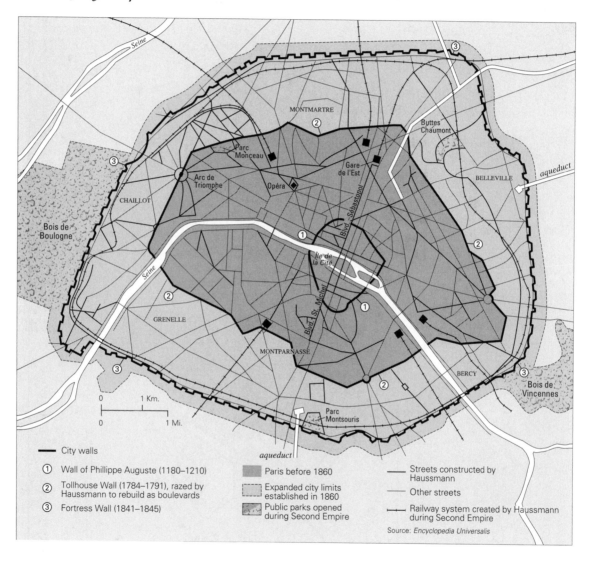

City walls

1. Wall of Phillippe Auguste (1180–1210)
2. Tollhouse Wall (1784–1791), razed by Haussmann to rebuild as boulevards
3. Fortress Wall (1841–1845)

Paris before 1860

Expanded city limits established in 1860

Public parks opened during Second Empire

Streets constructed by Haussmann

Other streets

Railway system created by Haussmann during Second Empire

Source: *Encyclopedia Universalis*

Chapter 8

Vienna

and Paris,

1850–1930:

The Development

of the Modern

City

Source 7 from Anthony Sutcliffe, The Autumn of Central Paris: The Defeat of Town Planning, 1850–1870 (Montreal: McGill-Queens University Press, 1971), p. 48.

7. The Completion of the Avenue de l'Opéra, Paris, 1876–1877

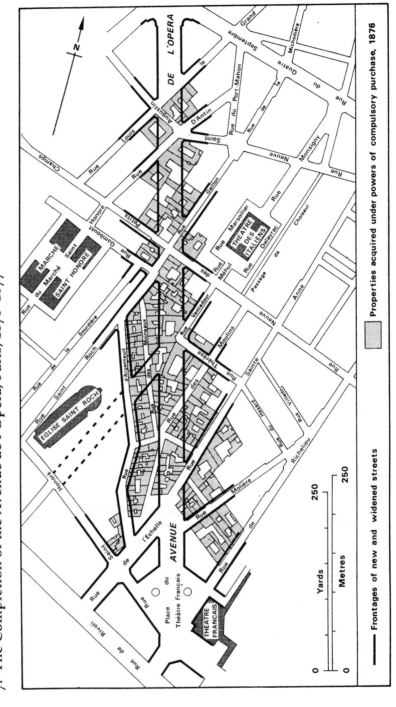

8. Clearing Old Neighborhoods for the Avenue de l'Opéra, Paris, 1876

Chapter 8

Vienna

and Paris,

1850–1930:

The Development

of the Modern

City

Source 9 from F. Roy Willis, Western Civilization, *vol. 4,* From the Seventeenth Century to the Contemporary Age *(Lexington, Mass.: D. C. Heath, 1985), fourth edition, p. 269. Photograph by H. Roger-Viollet.*

9. Avenue de l'Opéra, Paris, Late Nineteenth Century

Source 10 from Donald J. Olsen, The City as a Work of Art *(New Haven, Conn.: Yale University Press, 1986), p. 156. Original source: Kunstgeschichte Institut Universität Wien. Photograph by Johanna Fiegl.*

10. Ringstrasse Apartment Building, Schottenring 25

Chapter 8

Vienna

and Paris,

1850–1930:

The Development

of the Modern

City

Source 11 from David H. Pinkney, Napoleon III and the Rebuilding of Paris *(Princeton, N.J.: Princeton University Press, 1958), Plate 16. Original Source:* The Builder *(London), 16 (March 6, 1858).*

11. A Paris Apartment Building, Late Nineteenth Century

Source 12 from Donald J. Olsen, The City as a Work of Art *(New Haven, Conn.: Yale University Press, 1986), p. 118. Original source:* Revue générale d'architecture, *18 (1860), p. 41.*

12. Floor Plan of Apartment Building at 39, Rue Neuve des Mathurins, Paris

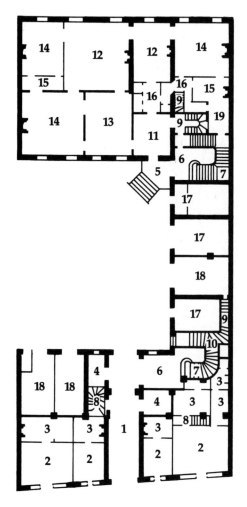

Ground floor

1 Passage from carriage entrance
   to courtyard
2 Shops
3 Shop backrooms
4 Concierge residence and kitchen
5 Entry steps
6 Grand staircase vestibule
7 Grand staircase

8,9,10 Service staircases
   11 Antechamber
   12 Parlors
   13 Dining rooms
   14 Bedrooms
   15 Bathrooms
   16 Cloakroom
   17 Stables
   18 Coach house
   19 Light/air shafts

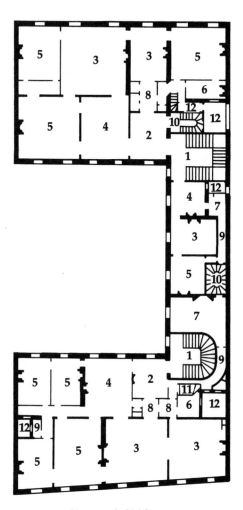

First, second, third floors

   1 Grand staircase
   2 Antechambers
   3 Parlors
   4 Dining rooms
   5 Bedrooms
   6 Bathrooms
   7 Kitchens
   8 Cloakrooms
   9 Corridors
10,11 Service stairs
   12 Light/air shafts

Chapter 8

Vienna

and Paris,

1850–1930:

The Development

of the Modern

City

Source 13 from William M. Johnston, Vienna, Vienna: The Golden Age, 1815–1914 *(New York: Clarkson N. Potter, 1981), p. 228. Photograph courtesy of Raccolta delle Stampe Bertarelli, Milan, Italy.*

13. The Prater, Vienna

Source 14 from Maurice Agulhon et al., Histoire de la France urbaine, *vol. 4,* La ville de l'âge industriel: Le cycle haussmannien *(Paris: Éditions du Seuil, 1983), p. 48. Photograph from Bibliothèque Historique de la Ville de Paris/Seuil.*

14. The Buttes-Chaumont Park, Paris

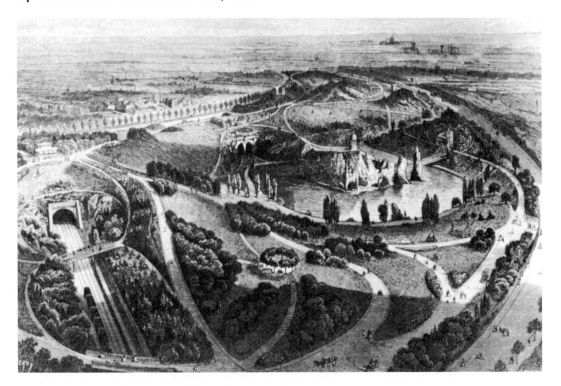

Chapter 8
Vienna
and Paris,
1850–1930:
The Development
of the Modern
City

Source 15 from Lapi-Viollet.

15. A Nineteenth-Century Parisian Working-Class Suburb in Belleville

Source 16 from Maurice Agulhon et al., Histoire de la France urbaine, *vol. 4,* La ville de l'age industriel: Le cycle haussmannien *(Paris: Éditions du Seuil, 1983), p. 202. Photograph courtesy of Archives Seuil, Paris.*

16. The Lemoine Forges at Ivry, 1881

Chapter 8

Vienna

and Paris,

1850–1930:

The Development

of the Modern

City

Source 17 from Helmut Gruber, Red Vienna: Experiment in Working-Class Culture, 1919–1934 *(New York: Oxford University Press, 1991), p. 47. Original source: Verein für Geschichte der Arbeiterbewegung, Vienna.*

17. Vienna Workers' Tenement, Early Twentieth Century

Source 18 from William M. Johnston, Vienna, Vienna: The Golden Age, 1815–1914 *(New York: Clarkson N. Potter, 1981), p. 240. Photograph courtesy of Mondadori Press.*

18. The Vienna S-Bahn and Its Schönbrunn Station, Built Between 1894 and 1897

Source 19 from Maurice Agulhon et al., Histoire de la France urbaine, *vol. 4,* La ville de l'âge industriel: Le cycle haussmannien *(Paris: Éditions du Seuil, 1983), p. 350. Photograph by Harlingue/Viollet.*

19. The Gare de l'Est Bus and Tramway Stop in 1936

Source 20 from Paul Hoffmann, Viennese: Splendor, Twilight, and Exile *(New York: Doubleday, 1988). Photograph from Austrian Press and Information Service.*

20. The Karl Marx Hof, Erected 1927–1929

Chapter 8

Vienna

and Paris,

1850–1930:

The Development

of the Modern

City

Source 21 from Norma Evenson, Paris: A Century of Change, 1878–1978 *(New Haven, Conn.: Yale University Press, 1979), p. 219. Original source:* La vie urbaine *(Published by the Institut d'Urbanisme de Paris), no. 18, November 15, 1933.*

21. Floor Plan of Parisian HBM (Low-Cost Housing) Apartments, 1933

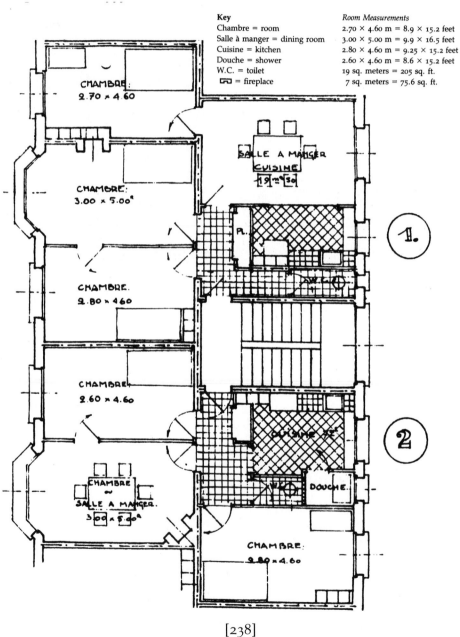

Key

Chambre = room
Salle à manger = dining room
Cuisine = kitchen
Douche = shower
W.C. = toilet
🔲 = fireplace

Room Measurements

2.70 × 4.60 m = 8.9 × 15.2 feet
3.00 × 5.00 m = 9.9 × 16.5 feet
2.80 × 4.60 m = 9.25 × 15.2 feet
2.60 × 4.60 m = 8.6 × 15.2 feet
19 sq. meters = 205 sq. ft.
7 sq. meters = 75.6 sq. ft.

Source 22 from Helmut Gruber, Red Vienna: Experiment in Working-Class Culture, 1919–1934 *(New York: Oxford University Press, 1991), p. 122. Original source: Verein für Geschichte der Arbeiterbewegung, Vienna.*

22. Kongressbad, Vienna, One of Europe's Largest Pools, About 1930

Chapter 8

Vienna

and Paris,

1850–1930:

The Development

of the Modern

City

QUESTIONS TO CONSIDER

In the previous sections of this chapter, we considered each city individually. To answer the chapter's central questions, we now need to study the cities jointly, drawing general trends from their individual experiences in urban development.

Consider first the core of the cities. Notice the street patterns and recall the problems that faced early-nineteenth-century cities. What common approaches to street building do you find in Paris and Vienna? Notice how the ring boulevards of Vienna connect every area of the city with the riverfront. Notice how Haussmann's boulevards facilitate direct north-south and east-west movement in Paris. Why did city and national governments lay out such streets? What facilities for recreation do you find incorporated into many of the cities? Consult especially the maps of Paris and Vienna. Why do you think a Parisian or Viennese of 1800 would have had difficulty recognizing his or her city in 1900?

Improvements in the urban cores of cities benefited all to some extent. Let us look more deeply into these physical improvements, however, to discern whether one class, at least initially, benefited more than others from private and government initiatives for municipal improvements. Consult the sources to determine the kinds of buildings arising in the central cities in the late nineteenth century. Paris and Vienna continued to employ a large part of their central cores for residential use. What classes seem to have occupied the new buildings constructed along Haussmann's boulevards and the Ringstrasse boulevards in Vienna? Where do the sources for Paris and Vienna suggest that persons of lower income were forced to live when the wealthy appropriated much of the central city for residential purposes? Why do you find an economically segregated housing pattern evolving? How might transportation developments have supported residential segregation?

Reflect also on the buildings erected at public expense in the second half of the nineteenth century, remembering all the while that universal, free public education became a reality only in the late nineteenth or early twentieth century in most countries. The opera in Paris, completed in 1875, typifies such buildings, as do the museums and theaters built in Vienna in the same period. What social groups do you think initially benefited most from such institutions? What does this tell you about the groups most influencing late-nineteenth-century politics? Why would you perhaps agree with those historians who call the nineteenth century the century of the middle class?

The right to vote became increasingly universal among European males in the late nineteenth and early twentieth centuries. Indeed, in many countries all women also gained the vote after World War I. At the same time, political parties addressing working-class needs arose in many countries. What evidence of such new political empowerment do you see in Parisian and Viennese urban development in the early twentieth century? Why do you think improved, low-cost public transport would have allowed lower-income groups an improved lifestyle by the early twentieth century?

Finally, consider whether the developments reflected in your sources, including the construction projects, railroads, sewers, and water supply systems, would have been possible without the advances of industrialization. Why can you say with some justice that in the second half of the nineteenth century, the Industrial Revolution helped to solve some of the problems it created in the first half?

After considering the sources as a unit, you should be ready to formulate answers to the chapter's main questions. How were the cities physically reshaped in response to the problems of the first decades of the early nineteenth century? How did this physical transformation affect the lifestyle of urban dwellers?

EPILOGUE

The development of Paris and Vienna after our period typifies one major trend in twentieth-century urban affairs: the end of urban growth in much of the West. Northern Europe led the way, as its rapid nineteenth-century population growth ended by the first decades of the twentieth century. The dramatic growth of urban populations characteristic of the nineteenth century ended as overall population growth rates diminished. Indeed, many cities had an actual decline in population in the twentieth century, and this was the case with Paris and Vienna.

The chief cause of Vienna's population decline was Austria-Hungary's defeat in World War I. The peace treaties ending that war left Vienna the capital of a truncated Austria, a city with the buildings for imperial glory, but without the old imperial territory and population. Vienna's population growth ended with the empire, and the city's population actually shrank. The 1910–1911 population was 2,031,000 people; the city's population in 1981 was 1,504,200.

Paris better illustrates trends in modern urban life because twentieth-century warfare less seriously affected that city. Paris continues to be a major cultural hub, and twentieth-century improvements have made it a bit more livable, although modern ecological problems like air pollution from large concentrations of motor vehicles are posing new problems for solution. Nevertheless, Paris reached its population peak in 1920–1921 at 2,907,000 persons and was inhabited by 2,152,423 in 1992.[5]

Urban growth in Paris and many other cities ceased in the twentieth century in large part because of a suburbanization that was much more extensive than that of the nineteenth century. In the nineteenth century, as we've seen, suburban growth

5. Other major cities reached their population peaks as follows: Amsterdam, 1960–1961; Birmingham, 1950–1951; Glasgow, 1940–1941; London, 1940–1941; Manchester, 1930–1931; Rotterdam, 1960–1961; Stockholm, 1960–1961.

[241]

Chapter 8

Vienna

and Paris,

1850–1930:

The Development

of the Modern

City

followed the roads, railroads, and later subways. In the twentieth and twenty-first centuries, limited-access highways also have abetted suburban sprawl. However, the social divisions of the nineteenth century persist. Paris continues to have a greater portion of its population ranked among economically and professionally higher status groups than the rest of France, but its suburbs still have a marked working-class complexion. Improved transportation has carried the working classes to communities more distant from the capital. The often drab working-class outer districts of Paris and its near suburban communities until recently have reflected their social composition at election time, voting so heavily for socialist or communist candidates committed to

workers' causes that they have been nicknamed "the Red Belt."

In fact, suburbanization has become so extensive that modern planners in Western Europe are being forced to direct its course the way nineteenth-century planners tried to shape urban development. In the late twentieth century, French planners, for example, began to lay out large population centers on the distant periphery of Paris. Such centers, like Cergy-Pontoise, northeast of Paris, are suburban in their location and connected to the city by train and highway, but are almost urban in their population density. The modern city thus continues as the locus of Western civilization, but it is now a smaller city influencing a much broader area.

CHAPTER NINE

EXPANSION AND PUBLIC
OPINION: ADVOCATES OF
THE "NEW IMPERIALISM"

From the 1870s until around 1905, Western nations engaged in a brief but extremely intense period of imperial expansion. In one sense, of course, this was not entirely a new phenomenon. From the sixteenth through the eighteenth centuries, the emerging nations of western Europe had struggled over possession of the New World. Between roughly 1815 and 1871, the West, beset with internal problems, had engaged in only limited attempts at colonialism, but some nations, principally England, nevertheless had sought to expand their economic spheres of influence. In some ways, then, the "new imperialism" of the late nineteenth century was not dramatically different from the old.

Yet to many living at the time (as well as to a number of later historians), the imperialism of the late nineteenth and early twentieth centuries seemed markedly different from earlier forms of territorial expansion. For one thing, the number of contestants for empire had increased with the addition of the newly formed nations of Germany and Italy. Indeed, even the United States, itself a nation composed of former European colonies, joined in the headlong scramble for new territories. The increased number of empire-seeking nations probably contributed to the speed with which unclaimed areas were brought under Western control.

Another factor that made the colonial expansion of the late nineteenth and early twentieth centuries appear "new" was that many people believed that this was their nation's last opportunity to build or enlarge an empire. Only Africa and parts of Asia remained vulnerable to imperialistic ventures. Awareness of this fact filled the nations of the West with a sense of urgency: If a nation did not acquire colonies quickly, other nations would do so. This feeling of urgency doubtless contributed to the speed of empire building as well as to

Chapter 9

Expansion

and Public

Opinion:

Advocates of

the "New

Imperialism"

the heightened sense of national competition for greatness. So powerful was this sentiment that by the turn of the century almost all of Africa and parts of Asia had fallen under Western control, and the West, accurately or not, could boast of itself as the master of much of the world.

A third factor that made the "new imperialism" seem different from the old was that advocates and opponents of colonial expansion felt the need to sway public opinion. Before the late eighteenth century, public opinion was not considered a crucial factor when monarchs or bodies representing a limited electorate decided what policies their respective governments should pursue. To be sure, certain powerful interest groups had to be consulted or appealed to, but the opinion of the general public was rarely heeded. The expansion of the electorate,[1] however, together with increased educational opportunities and literacy, the corresponding mass circulation of newspapers, and the evolution of modern political campaign techniques, served to make the general public more aware of the government's policies and even to give them a limited voice in the shaping of those policies. Hence, supporters or opponents of particular policies were obliged to appeal to—and, in some cases, manipulate—public opinion. Thus, the new imperialism also appeared different in that it was warmly debated not only in palaces and parliaments but also in the streets, the press, the workingmen's halls, and the public houses ("pubs") of the Western nations.

No historical trend such as the new imperialism takes place in a vacuum, unaffected by other trends and events that precede and parallel it and, in some cases, help to cause it. In the West, several important developments in the second half of the nineteenth century not only acted to create the new imperialism but also helped impart to that movement its particular shape and character.

One of the most important occurrences in the West preceding and paralleling the new imperialism was that of rapid population growth. Between 1850 and 1900, the population of Europe (including Russia) increased 54 percent, from approximately 274 million to 423 million. Germany's population jumped over 62 percent, Great Britain's 41 percent, Italy's around 41 percent, and Belgium's 48 percent. This population boom was primarily the result of falling death rates, in turn caused by the controlling of epidemic diseases, increased food production, and improvements in transportation that allowed food supplies to reach cities and regions of local famines. In the United States, where massive immigration from Europe supplemented the large natural increase, the population increased an astounding 227 percent.[2]

This dramatic jump in population, especially in the cities of Europe, created a serious need for jobs, particularly in the nonagricultural sector. The pressure for greater employment in turn increased Europe's demand for raw materials for industrial production and markets for those manufactured

1. The expansion of the electorate took place in the United Kingdom in 1867–1884, in Germany in 1871, in France in 1875, and in Italy in 1913.

2. Between 1846 and 1900, the number of emigrants from Europe to the United States and Latin America probably exceeded 30 million.

goods. Moreover, in some areas of Europe (notably Italy), the rise in rural population put a heavy strain on land and agricultural resources, which resulted in increased emigration. It is easy to imagine how these problems, caused by population pressures, might be linked to calls for expansionism.

A second important trend during this time was the spread and apparent peaking of the Industrial Revolution. By the latter part of the nineteenth century, much of the West had joined in the Industrial Revolution and thus (as noted earlier) needed raw materials and, equally important, markets for manufactured goods. A severe depression struck Europe and the United States in 1873 and lasted into the 1890s, making it impossible for the West to consume all the manufactured goods it could produce. Unless industries were to shut down, bringing on massive unemployment, new markets would have to be found. With most of the Western countries erecting protective tariff barriers to keep out each other's manufactured goods, these new markets would have to be found outside the West, in areas that could be exploited almost at will.

The Industrial Revolution not only provided an incentive for a new upsurge of imperialism, but also gave the West the means to accomplish this expansion. Technological improvements, especially in transportation and communications, allowed Western mercantile and financial houses gradually to draw much of the world into an integrated global market dominated by Western merchants and financiers. As English economist Stanley Jevons boasted in 1866:

The several quarters of the globe are our willing tributaries. The plains of North America and Russia are our cornfields; Chicago and Odessa our granaries; Canada and the Baltic our forests; Australia contains our sheep farms, and in South America are our herds of oxen . . . the Chinese grow tea for us; and coffee, sugar and spice arrive from East Indian plantations. Spain and France are our vineyards, and the Mediterranean our fruit garden.[3]

Advances in medicine and in weapons technology made it further possible for Westerners to subdue non-Western peoples and live for extended periods in non-Western climates. Great Britain, for example, acquired the Upper Nile River area in 1898, but only after slaughtering 20,000 tribesmen at Omdurman, thanks to the newly invented machine gun. As Hilaire Belloc's "Modern Traveler" would sing,

Whatever happens, we have got
The Maxim gun; and they have not.[4]

A third important trend that contributed to late-nineteenth-century imperialism was that of intensified competition among Western nations. It was obvious at the time to many people that Western nations did not have to seize non-Western territories

3. Quoted in R. R. Palmer and Joel Colton, *A History of the Modern World* (New York: Alfred A. Knopf, 1965), pp. 574–575.
4. Quoted in Roland Oliver and G. N. Sanderson, *The Cambridge History of Africa* (Cambridge: Cambridge University Press, 1985), vol. 6, p. 98. The Maxim gun was the brainchild of British engineer Sir Hiram Maxim, who in 1889 perfected the machine gun.

Chapter 9
Expansion
and Public
Opinion:
Advocates of
the "New
Imperialism"

in order to dominate them economically. Moreover, some of the territories that Western nations colonized could offer no immediate profits to their conquerors. Yet in this era of intensified rivalry, colonies were widely regarded as assets that could be exploited in the increased competition among Western nations and also as potential military bases to protect the extraction of raw materials and the maintenance of trade lanes. Safe harbors and coaling stations for a modern steam-powered navy were seen as critically important to each Western nation's power and survival. At the same time, no single country could be allowed to gain an advantage over others in the rush for colonies and the establishment of national "greatness." Thus U.S. president William McKinley justified taking the Philippine Islands partly to keep them out of the hands of any other national competitor seeking to exploit Asia and the Pacific. Truly, heightened national competition, along with other trends, helped renew the spirit of imperialism in the West. With the new nations of Germany and Italy and the newly imperialistic United States added to the race, the scramble for colonies at times seemed almost frantic.

Finally, in the West two extremely important, albeit in some ways contradictory intellectual trends preceded and paralleled the "new imperialism" and thus provided an ideological foundation for expansion. The first of these was Social Darwinism, a system of ideas that spread rapidly throughout the West in the second half of the nineteenth century. An application of the theories of biological evolution to human affairs, Social Darwinism taught that peoples, like species, were engaged in a life-or-death struggle to determine the "survival of the fittest." Those classes or nations that emerged triumphant in this struggle were considered the most fit, and hence best suited to carry on the evolution of the human race. Therefore the subjugation of weak peoples by strong ones not only was in accordance with the laws of nature, but was bound to result in a more highly civilized world as well. Most celebrated among the Social Darwinists was the Englishman Herbert Spencer, a diminutive and eccentric writer who became a worldwide celebrity through his writings. (A letter was once addressed to him, "Herbert Spencer. England. And if the postman doesn't know the address, he ought to." It was delivered.)

Although Spencer himself disapproved of imperialism, it is easy to see how his writings could be used as a justification for empire building. At the conclusion of the Spanish-American War in 1898, whereby the United States acquired its empire from Spain, Senator Henry Cabot Lodge justified the transfer of colonies by asserting that "Spain . . . has proved herself unfit to govern, and for the unfit among nations there is no pity in the relentless world-forces which shape the destinies of mankind."[5]

At the same time that many in the West embraced this notion of a struggle for survival between the "fittest" and the "unfit" (a doctrine with strong racist overtones), they also adopted the concept of the "White Man's

5. Henry Cabot Lodge, *The War with Spain* (New York: Harper and Brothers, 1899), p. 2.

Burden." This concept held that it was the duty of the "fittest" not so much to destroy the "unfit" as to "civilize" them; white people, according to this view, had a responsibility to educate the rest of the world to the norms of Western society. As racist as Social Darwinism, the belief in the White Man's Burden downplayed the idea of a struggle for survival between peoples and emphasized the "humanitarian" notion of bringing the benefits of "civilization" to the "uncivilized." Using this argument, many in the West justified imperialism as an obligation, a sacrifice that God had charged the "fittest" to make. In his 1876 speech to the International Conference of Geographers, King Leopold II of Belgium declared:

> The matter which brings us together today is one most deserving the attention of the friends of humanity. For bringing civilization to the only part of the earth [Africa] which it has not yet reached and lightening the darkness in which whole peoples are plunged is, I venture to say, a crusade worthy of this century of progress. . . .[6]

6. From Henri Brunschwig, *French Colonialism 1871–1914: Myths and Realities* (New York: Praeger, 1966), p. 35.

Although the doctrine of the White Man's Burden differed in tone from that of Social Darwinism, one can see that its practical results might well be the same.

Thus, a number of important trends preceded and paralleled the rising imperialist tide in the West in the late nineteenth and early twentieth centuries. As we shall see, not only did these demographic, economic, technological, diplomatic, and intellectual trends profoundly alter the lives and attitudes of most Westerners, but they also gave power to the expansionist surges of the new imperialism.

Your task in this chapter is to analyze the writings of important advocates of imperialism from four of the most active expansionist nations: Germany, Great Britain, France, and Italy. What were the main arguments used by each spokesperson in favor of colonial expansion? How did each attempt to appeal to public opinion? Finally, how can their speeches and writings help us identify the principal motives and justifications for the new imperialism?

SOURCES AND METHOD

One of the most significant currents in the West during the last half of the nineteenth century was the popular identification of the common people with the symbols and traditions of their respective nations. Although

roots of this modern sense of nationalism can be found in Napoleonic France, this tendency gained enormous strength and momentum in the latter part of the nineteenth century, fueled by national holidays and celebrations (Bastille Day in France, begun in 1880; Queen Victoria's jubilees in Great Britain in 1887 and 1897; the

Chapter 9

Expansion

and Public

Opinion:

Advocates of

the "New

Imperialism"

massive funerals of King Victor Emmanuel II of Italy in 1878 and of Tsar Alexander III of Russia in 1894), the erection of enormous monuments to the nation (the Eiffel Tower in France, the Washington Monument in the United States, the national monument to William I of Germany), the renovation of capital cities on magnificent scales (London, Paris, Berlin, Vienna, Rome, and Washington, D.C.), the commemoration of national heroes and historical events on postage stamps, and the creation or re-creation of international athletic competitions (the Davis Cup in tennis, begun in 1900; the Olympic Games, revived in 1896). This new sense of popular nationalism in which people of different classes, religions, and ethnic groups identified with the nation itself rather than with its monarch or government or with their own particular groups was a crucial step in the creation of the modern nation-state. Against the powerful force of modern nationalism, competing ideas such as Marxism had little initial effect.[7]

And yet, if the people were expected to identify with their nation, it seemed logical that their opinions about that nation and the policies of its government ought to be heard. And although few advocated actual rule by "the people," the prevailing sentiment was that their opinions should at least be heeded. Indeed, the few remaining autocrats, like the stubborn Nicholas II of Russia, would ignore this impulse at their peril—and to

7. For an excellent discussion of this trend, see Eric Hobsbawm and Terence Ranger, eds., *The Invention of Tradition* (Cambridge: Cambridge University Press, 1983), especially pp. 263–307.

their ultimate destruction. Therefore, when some political leaders in the West began to embrace imperialist ideas and ventures, they had to appeal to the populace for their support.

The evidence in this chapter, selections from five writings and one speech, is arranged in chronological order. Source 1 is from the extremely popular short book *Bedarf Deutschland der Kolonien?* (*Does Germany Need Colonies?*) by Friedrich Fabri (1824–1891), a longtime inspector of the Barmen Rhine Mission in German Southwest Africa. Originally published in 1879, the book was so popular that it ran through numerous editions in the late nineteenth and early twentieth centuries (the edition you will be reading was the original one, published in 1879).

Source 2 is from an 1883 letter written by John Gibson Paton (1824–1907) to James Service, governor-general of Australia. Paton was a Scotsman who in 1857 was ordained by the Reformed Presbyterian Church of Scotland and sent to be a missionary in the New Hebrides Islands (east of Australia). Missionaries such as Paton at first glance may not appear to be very important or influential. Yet their writings and occasional lectures during visits home had an enormous impact on churchgoers, and most of the men in the congregation were voters. For example, in 1889 fear of Scottish Presbyterian voters prompted Lord Salisbury to alter Great Britain's policy toward Nyasaland in southeast Africa. In 1889, Paton's autobiography (actually written by his brother from Paton's notes and letters) was published and was an extremely popular volume (a children's edition appeared in 1892).

Source 3 is a selection from an 1890 work by Jules Ferry (1832–1893). Born into a solidly bourgeois and well-to-do family (his father was a lawyer), Ferry had enough money to travel, study, take up painting, and write. He was a Republican who approved of the overthrow of Napoleon III (although he winced at the fact that the emperor's downfall had been brought on by Prussia) and served as the premier of France's Third Republic twice between 1880 and 1885. Although Ferry came late to his advocacy of imperialism, his popularity made him an important figure in appealing to the people of France to support the building of the second colonial empire. He was responsible for the French annexation of Tunisia.

Source 4 is from a speech made by Joseph Chamberlain (1836–1914), a wealthy manufacturer and member of the British Parliament since 1876, to a city relief association on January 22, 1894. Chamberlain, a former mayor of Birmingham (1873–1875) who was an advocate of social reforms to aid the working class, was invited to speak at the meeting, which was called to discuss widespread unemployment and hard times in Birmingham.

The fifth piece of evidence is taken from a book that gained wide circulation in Italy, *Cose affricane* (*Concerning Africa*) (Milan, 1897), by Ferdinando Martini. Martini (1841–1928) was a well-known author, playwright, theater producer, and government official (he was governor of the Italian colony Eritrea from 1897 to 1900). *Cose affricane* was written in the wake of the

Italian defeat by Ethiopia when Italy attempted to seize that African nation. This was a major humiliation for Italy.

The final piece of evidence (Source 6) is a selection from the enormously popular book *With Kitchener to Khartum* (1898) by British journalist and war correspondent George Warrington Steevens (1869–1900). In 1884, General Charles Gordon was sent by the British government to suppress a rebellion in the Sudan that threatened the stability of Egypt. Surrounded at Khartoum, Gordon and his force were wiped out on January 25, 1885, before relief could reach them (the reaction in Great Britain was about the same as the shock Americans felt when they learned of the "last stand" of General George Armstrong Custer in 1876). When Major General Horatio Herbert Kitchener was ordered to smash the rebellion and avenge Gordon, Steevens went along as a war correspondent for the London *Daily Mail*. His vivid dispatches were read avidly throughout Great Britain and later collected into the book *With Kitchener to Khartum*. Steevens died of typhoid fever during the siege of Ladysmith (in Natal) during the Boer War.

All the pieces of evidence presented here were designed to influence or sway public opinion on imperialistic ventures. To help you answer the central questions in this chapter, you will want to examine each piece of evidence for the following points: (1) Does the author identify a problem or problems which he thinks imperialism can solve? What are they? If more than one, which is the most

Chapter 9
*Expansion
and Public
Opinion:
Advocates of
the "New
Imperialism"*

important? How will imperialism solve it? (2) How (if at all) does the author regard the "host populations" in the regions to be colonized? What adjectives, if any, are used to describe them? Does the author mention what effect Western imperialism will have on the "host populations"? (3) How does the author deal (if at all) with opponents of imperialism? How are they characterized? (4) How (if at all) does the author connect imperialism with one or more of the parallel trends and events? (5) In what other ways does the author attempt to influence public opinion?

Remember that each piece of evidence may include more than one reason to undertake imperialistic ventures. It would be helpful to take notes as you examine the evidence.

Keep the central questions in mind: What were the main arguments in favor of colonial expansion used by the six advocates of imperialism? How did each spokesman attempt to appeal to public opinion? How can these selections aid in identifying the principal motives and justifications for the new imperialism?

THE EVIDENCE

Source 1 from Friedrich Fabri, Bedarf Deutschland der Kolonien? *(Gotha: Friedrich Andreas Berthes, 1879), pp. 106–108. Translated by David E. Lee.*

1. Friedrich Fabri's *Bedarf Deutschland der Kolonien?*, 1879

But the German nation, which is fundamentally seaworthy and adept both commercially and industrially, which is more skillful at agricultural colonization than others, and is provided with a workforce more abundant and available than that of any other civilized people, should that nation not now successfully set off on this new path? We doubt this all the less the more we are convinced that today the colonial question has already become a vital question for the development of Germany. Dealing thoughtfully but also forcefully with this question will have profitable results for our economic situation and for our entire national development. Just the fact that we are dealing with a new question, whose multifaceted importance for the German people represents still untrodden virgin soil, can prove beneficial in many ways. In the new German Reich many things are already so embittered and soured and poisoned by sterile partisan squabbles that opening up a new, promising path of national development could have a liberating effect in many areas because it could be a powerful stimulant to the spirit of the people, propelling them in new directions. That too would be a joy and a plus. Of greater consequence is the consideration that a people guided to the height of its political power can maintain its historical position successfully only as long as it can both recognize itself as and prove itself to be *the bearer of a cultural mission*. At the same time this is the only course that guarantees the durability and growth of national prosperity, the necessary basis of a lasting development of power. The times in which Germany contributed to the challenges of our century only through intellectual and literary activity are past. We have become political and we have also become powerful. But political power, when it pushes itself into the foreground of our national ambitions as an end in itself, leads to harshness, even to barbarity, if it is not ready and willing to serve the spiritual and the moral as well as the economic cultural missions of its time. The French national economist Leroy Beaulieu ends his work on colonization with these words: "The greatest nation in the world is the one that colonizes the most; if it is not that today, it will be tomorrow." No one can deny that in this regard England is far superior to all other states. During the last decade, of course, we often heard people, especially in Germany, talking about "England's declining power." The person who knows how to calculate the relative power of a state only according to the number of troops prepared to fight a war—as has become almost customary in our iron age—may think that such a position can be easily justified. Whoever lets his eye wander round the globe, however, and takes in the constantly growing, powerful colonial possessions of Great Britain, whoever mulls over the power that it draws from these possessions, the skill with which it administers them, and indeed the dominant position that the anglo-saxon people assume in all overseas lands, for such a person that sort of talk will seem to be the reasoning of a philistine. England maintains its worldwide possessions, its suzerainty over all the oceans with a troop strength that hardly equals one quarter the army of a single one of our continental military states. This is not only a great economic boon but also at the same time the ultimate proof of the solid power, the cultural strength of England. Certainly England will stay as far away from the mass wars of the Continent as it can, or it will only enter the action together with allies; and none of this will bring any harm to the position of power occupied by the island empire. In any case it would be good if we Germans would begin to learn from the colonial skill of our anglo-saxon cousins. Centuries ago, when the German Reich stood at the head of the states of Europe, it was the leading commercial and maritime power. If the new German Reich wants to justify and maintain its power, then it will have to grasp it as a cultural mission and no longer hesitate to renew once again its colonial calling.

Chapter 9

Expansion

and Public

Opinion:

Advocates of

the "New

Imperialism"

Source 2 from John G. Paton (Senior Missionary, New Hebrides Mission) to the Hon. James Service (Governor-General of Australia), August 1883, quoted in Louis L. Snyder, editor, The Imperialism Reader *(Princeton, N.J.: D. Van Nostrand, 1962), pp. 295–297. Reprinted by permission.*

2. Letter from John G. Paton to James Service Urging British Possession of the New Hebrides, 1883

The Hon. James Service,
Premier

Sir:

For the following reasons we think the British government ought now to take possession of the New Hebrides group of the South Sea islands, of the Solomon group, and of all the intervening chain of islands from Fiji to New Guinea.

1. Because she has already taken possession of Fiji in the east, and we hope it will soon be known authoritatively that she has taken possession of New Guinea at the northwest, adjoining her Australian possessions, and the islands between complete this chain of islands lying along the Australian coast. Taking possession of the New Hebrides would not add much to her expenses, as her governments on Fiji and New Guinea with the visits of her men-of-war passing through the group of the New Hebrides and intervening islands on their way to New Guinea, would almost be sufficient for all her requirements on the islands between.

2. The sympathy of the New Hebrides natives are all with Great Britain, hence they long for British protection, while they fear and hate the French, who appear eager to annex the group, because they have seen the way the French have treated the native races in New Caledonia, the Loyalty Islands, and other South Sea islands.

3. Till within the past few months almost all the Europeans on the New Hebrides were British subjects, who long for British protection.

4. All the men and all the money (over £140,000) used in civilizing and Christianizing the New Hebrides have been British. Now fourteen missionaries and the Dayspring mission ship, and about 150 native evangelists and teachers are employed in the above work on this group, in which over £6000 yearly of British and British-colonial money is expended; and certainly it would be unwise to let any other power now take possession and reap the fruits of all this British outlay.

5. Because the New Hebrides are already a British dependency in this sense—all its imports are from Sydney and Melbourne and British colonies, and all its exports are also to British colonies.

6. The islands of this group are generally very rich in soil and in tropical products so that if a possession of Great Britain, and [if] the labour traffic stopped so as to retain what remains of the native populations on them, they would soon, and for ages to come, become rich sources of tropical wealth to these colonies, as sugar cane is extensively cultivated on them by every native of the group, even in his heathen state. For natives they are an industrious, hard-working race, living in villages and towns, and, like farmers, depending on the cultivation and products of the ground for their support by their plantations. The islands also grow maize, cotton, coffee, arrowroot, and spices, etc., and all tropical products could be largely produced on them.

7. Because if any other nation takes possession of them, their excellent and spacious harbors, as on Efate, so well-supplied with the best fresh water, and their near proximity to Great Britain's Australasian colonies, would in time of war make them dangerous to British interests and commerce in the South Seas and her colonies.

8. The thirteen islands of this group on which life and property are now comparatively safe, the 8,000 professed Christians on the group, and all the churches formed among them, are by God's blessing the fruits of the labours of British missionaries, who, at great toil, expense, and loss of life, have translated, got printed, and taught the natives to read the Bible in part or in whole in nine different languages of this group, while 70,000 at least are longing and ready for the gospel. On this group twenty-one members of the mission families died or were murdered by the savages in beginning God's work among them, not including good Bishop Peterson, of the Melanesian mission, and we fear all this good work would be lost if the New Hebrides fall into other than British hands.

9. Because we see no other way of suppressing the labour traffic in Polynesia, with all its many evils, as it rapidly depopulates the islands, being attended by much bloodshed, misery, and loss of life.[8] It is an unmitigated evil to the natives, and ruinous to all engaged in it, and to the work of civilizing and Christianizing the islanders, while all experience proves that all labour laws and regulations, with government agents and gunboats, cannot prevent such evils, which have always been the said accompaniments of all such traffic in men and women in every land, and because this traffic and its evils are a sad stain on our British glory and Australasian honor, seeing Britain has done so much to free the slave and suppress slavery in other lands.

For the above reasons, and others that might be given, we sincerely hope and pray that you will do all possible to get Victoria and the other colonial

---

8. For decades the South Sea Islands had been plagued by unscrupulous men known as "blackbirders" who abducted laborers and sold them as slaves to work in the cotton fields of Fiji and Queensland, the sugar fields of New Caledonia, and the sheep stations of Australia. See Cyril S. Belshaw, *Changing Melanesia: Social Economics and Cultural Contact* (London: Oxford University Press, 1954), pp. 17–19.

Chapter 9

Expansion

and Public

Opinion:

Advocates of

the "New

Imperialism"

governments to help and unite in urging Great Britain at once to take possession of the New Hebrides group. Whether looked at in the interests of humanity, or of Christianity, or commercially, or politically, surely it is most desirable that they should be at once British possessions; hence we plead for your judicious and able help, and remain, your humble servant,

> JOHN G. PATON
> Senior Missionary
> New Hebrides Mission

Source 3 from Jules Ferry, Tonkin et la Mère-Patrie *(1890), translated by and quoted in Harvey Goldberg, editor,* French Colonialism *(New York: Rinehart and Co., 1959), pp. 3–4.*

3. Jules Ferry's Appeal to the French to Build the Second Colonial Empire, 1890

Colonial policy is the child of the industrial revolution. For wealthy countries where capital abounds and accumulates fast, where industry is expanding steadily, where even agriculture must become mechanized in order to survive, exports are essential for public prosperity. Both demand for labor and scope for capital investment depend on the foreign market. Had it been possible to establish, among the leading industrial countries, some kind of rational division of production, based on special aptitudes and natural resources, so that certain of them engaged in, say, cotton and metallurgical manufacture, while others concentrated on the alcohol and sugar-refining industries, Europe might not have had to seek markets for its products in other parts of the world. . . . But today every country wants to do its own spinning and weaving, forging and distilling. So Europe produces, for example, a surplus of sugar and must try to export it. With the arrival of the latest industrial giants, the United States and Germany; of Italy, newly resurrected; of Spain, enriched by the investment of French capital; of enterprising little Switzerland, not to mention Russia waiting in the wings, Europe has embarked on a competitive course from which she will be unable to turn back.

All over the world, beyond the Vosges and across the Atlantic, the raising of high tariffs has resulted in an increasing volume of manufactured goods, the disappearance of traditional markets, and the appearance of fierce competition. Countries react by raising their own tariff barriers, but that is not enough. . . . The protectionist system, unless accompanied by a serious colonial policy, is like a steam engine without a safety valve. An excess of capital invested in industry not only reduces profits on capital but also arrests the rise of wages. This phenomenon cuts to the very core of society, engendering passions and countermoves. Social stability in this industrial age clearly depends on outlets for industrial goods. The beginning of the economic crisis, with its prolonged, frequent strikes—a crisis which has weighed so heavily on Europe since 1877—coincided in France, Germany, and England with a marked and persistent drop in exports. Europe is like a commercial firm whose business turnover has been shrinking for a number of years. The European consumer-goods market is saturated; unless we declare modern society bankrupt and prepare, at the dawn of the twentieth century, for its liquidation by revolution (the consequences of which we can scarcely foresee), new consumer markets will have to be created in other parts of the world. . . . Colonial policy is an international manifestation of the eternal laws of competition.

Without either compromising the security of the country or sacrificing any of its past traditions and future aspirations, the Republicans have, in less than ten years, given France four kingdoms in Asia and Africa. Three of them are linked to us by tradition and treaty. The fourth represents our contribution to peaceful conquest, the bringing of civilization into the heart of equatorial Africa. Suppose the Republic had declared, with the doctrinaires of the Radical school, that the French nation ends at Marseilles. To whom would Tunisia, Indochina, Madagascar, and the Congo belong today?

Source 4 from Joseph Chamberlain, M. P., Foreign & Colonial Speeches *(London: George Routledge and Sons, 1897), pp. 131–139.*

4. Joseph Chamberlain, Speech to the West Birmingham Relief Association, January 22, 1894

We must look this matter in the face, and must recognise that in order that we may have more employment to give we must create more demand. (Hear, hear.) Give me the demand for more goods and then I will undertake to give plenty of employment in making the goods; and the only thing, in my opinion, that the Government can do in order to meet this great difficulty that we are considering, is so to arrange its policy that every inducement shall be given to the demand; that new markets shall be created, and that old markets shall be effectually developed. (Cheers.) You are aware that some of my opponents please themselves occasionally by finding names for me—(laughter)—and among other names lately they have been calling me a Jingo.[9] (Laughter.) I am no more a Jingo than you are. (Hear, hear.) But for the reasons and arguments I have put before you tonight I am convinced that it is a necessity as

9. **Jingo:** a belligerent patriot; a chauvinist.

Chapter 9

Expansion

and Public

Opinion:

Advocates of

the "New

Imperialism"

well as a duty for us to uphold the dominion and empire which we now possess. (Loud cheers.) For these reasons, among others, I would never lose the hold which we now have over our great Indian dependency—(hear, hear)—by far the greatest and most valuable of all the customers we have or ever shall have in this country. For the same reasons I approve of the continued occupation of Egypt; and for the same reasons I have urged upon this Government, and upon previous Governments, the necessity for using every legitimate opportunity to extend our influence and control in that great African continent which is now being opened up to civilisation and to commerce; and, lastly, it is for the same reasons that I hold that our navy should be strengthened—(loud cheers)—until its supremacy is so assured that we cannot be shaken in any of the possessions which we hold or may hold hereafter.

Believe me, if in any one of the places to which I have referred any change took place which deprived us of that control and influence of which I have been speaking, the first to suffer would be the working-men of this country. Then, indeed, we should see a distress which would not be temporary, but which would be chronic, and we should find that England was entirely unable to support the enormous population which is now maintained by the aid of her foreign trade. If the working-men of this country understand, as I believe they do—I am one of those who have had good reason through my life to rely upon their intelligence and shrewdness—if they understand their own interests, they will never lend any countenance to the doctrines of those politicians who never lose an opportunity of pouring contempt and abuse upon the brave Englishmen, who, even at this moment, in all parts of the world are carving out new dominions for Britain, and are opening up fresh markets for British commerce, and laying out fresh fields for British labour. (Applause.) If the Little Englanders[10] had their way, not only would they refrain from taking the legitimate opportunities which offer for extending the empire and for securing for us new markets, but I doubt whether they would even take the pains which are necessary to preserve the great heritage which has come down to us from our ancestors. (Applause.)

When you are told that the British pioneers of civilisation in Africa are filibusters,[11] and when you are asked to call them back, and to leave this great continent to the barbarism and superstition in which it has been steeped for centuries, or to hand over to foreign countries the duty which you are unwilling to undertake, I ask you to consider what would have happened if 100 or 150 years ago your ancestors had taken similar views of their responsibility? Where would be the empire on which now your livelihood depends? We should have been the United Kingdom of Great Britain and Ireland; but those vast dependencies, those hundreds of millions with whom we keep up

10. **Little Englanders:** Britain's anti-imperialists.

11. **filibuster:** a person engaged in a private military action against a foreign government.

a mutually beneficial relationship and commerce would have been the subjects of other nations, who would not have been slow to profit by our neglect of our opportunities and obligations. (Applause.)

Let me give you one practical illustration, in order to show what ought to be done, and may be done, in order to secure employment for our people. I will take the case of a country called Uganda, of which, perhaps, you have recently heard a good deal. A few years ago Uganda was only known to us by the reports of certain enterprising and most venturesome travellers, or by the accounts which were given by those self-denying missionaries who have gone through all these wild and savage lands, endeavouring to carry to the people inhabiting them the blessings of Christianity and civilisation. (Applause.) But within very recent times English authority has been established in Uganda, and an English sphere of influence has been declared. Uganda is a most fertile country. It contains every variety of climate; in a large portion of it European colonisation is perfectly feasible; the products are of the utmost richness; there is hardly anything which is of value or use to us in our commerce which cannot be grown there; but in spite of these natural advantages, during the past generation the country has been desolated by civil strife and by the barbarities of its rulers, barbarities so great that they would be almost incredible if they did not come to us on the authority of thoroughly trustworthy eyewitnesses.

All that is wanted to restore this country to a state of prosperity, to a commercial position which it has never attained before, is settled peace and order. (Hear, hear.) That peace and order which we have maintained for so long in India we could secure by a comparatively slight exertion in Uganda, and, when this is proposed to us, the politicians to whom I have referred would repudiate responsibility and throw back the country into the state of anarchy from which it has only just emerged; or they would allow it to become an appendage or dependency of some other European nation, which would at once step in if we were to leave the ground free to them. I am opposed to such a craven policy as this. (Applause.) I do not believe it is right. I do not believe it is worthy of Great Britain; and, on the contrary, I hold it to be our duty to the people for whom at all events we have for the time accepted responsibility, as well as to our own people, even at some cost of life, some cost of treasure, to maintain our rule and to establish settled order, which is the only foundation for permanent prosperity. When I talk of the cost of life, bear in mind that any cost of life which might result from undertaking this duty would be a mere drop in the ocean to the bloodshed which has gone on for generations in that country before we ever took any interest in it.

But I will go further than that. This rich country should be developed. It is at the present time 800 miles from the sea, and unless we can reach a country by the sea we cannot obtain its products in a form or at a cost which would be likely to be of any use to us, nor can we get our products to them. Therefore

[257]

Chapter 9

Expansion

and Public

Opinion:

Advocates of

the "New

Imperialism"

what is wanted for Uganda is what Birmingham has got—an improvement scheme. (Laughter.) What we want is to give to this country the means of communication by a railway from the coast which would bring to that population—which is more intelligent than the ordinary populations in the heart of Africa—our iron, and our cloths, and our cotton, and even our jewelry, because I believe that savages are not at all insensible to the delights of personal adornment. (Laughter.) It would bring to these people the goods which they want and which they cannot manufacture, and it would bring to us the raw materials, of which we should be able to make further use.

Now, it is said that this is the business of private individuals. Private individuals will not make that railway for fifty years to come, and for the good reason that private individuals who go into investments like railways want to see an immediate prospect of a return. They cannot afford to go for ten or twenty years without interest on their money, and accordingly you will find that in undeveloped countries no railway has ever been made by private exertion, but has always been made by the prudence and foresight and wisdom of a government. . . .

Source 5 from Ferdinando Martini, Cose affricane: da Saati ad Abba Carmina: discoursi e scritti *(Milan: Fratelli Treves, 1897), pp. 122, 136, 140. Translated by Gina Pashko.*

5. Ferdinando Martini, from *Cose affricane*, 1897

Italy has 108 inhabitants per square kilometer; France has only 73. In proportion to its territory, only three countries in Europe surpass Italy in population density: Belgium, Holland, and Great Britain. If we continue at this rate, Italy will soon take the lead: in the decade of 1871–1881, the birth rate exceeded the death rate by seven percent, and in the following years, by eleven percent. Every year 100,000 farmers and agricultural laborers emigrate from Italy. In spite of this immense exodus, the country witnesses its place in the family of civilized people growing smaller and smaller as it looks on with fear for its political and economic future. In fact, during the last eighty years, the English-speaking population throughout the world has risen from 22 to 90 million; the Russian-speaking population from 50 to 70; and so forth, down to the Spanish-speaking population, who were 18 million and are now 39. On the other hand, the Italian-speaking population has only increased from 20 to 31 million, and most of this growth has taken place within Italy's own geographical borders. This is not very surprising. At first, our emigrants were spreading Italy's name, language, and prestige in foreign countries, but since all, or nearly all, of them went to highly developed areas, their sons and grandsons were surrounded and attracted to the life of the vigorous people of the nations giving them hospitality, and ended up by forgetting the language of their fathers and forefathers. Now they merely increase the population of other nations, like branches that are grafted on a plant of a different species. . . .

Realizing that our stubbornness and our mistakes have cost us so much in the past and continue to cost us today, I believe that, even leaving aside all other considerations and taking into account only expenditures and the chances of success, it is less secure and more expensive to endeavor to cultivate three million hectares of barren land in Italy than to insure the prosperity of a large agricultural colony in Eritrea. . . .

Source 6 from G. W. Steevens, With Kitchener to Khartum, *first published 1898 (London: Greenhill Books photocopy of 1898 original, 1990), pp. 317–322.*

6. G. W. Steevens on the Sudan, 1898

The curtain comes down; the tragedy of the Sudan is played out. Sixteen years of toilsome failure, of toilsome, slow success, and at the end we have fought our way triumphantly to the point where we began.

It has cost us much, and it has profited us—how little? It would be hard to count the money, impossible to measure the blood. Blood goes by quality as well as quantity; who can tell what future deeds we lost when we lost Gordon . . . ? By shot and steel, by sunstroke and pestilence, by sheer wear of work, the Sudan has eaten up our best by hundreds. Of the men who escaped with their lives, hundreds more will bear the mark of its fangs till they die; hardly one of them but will die the sooner for the Sudan. And what have we to show in return?

At first you think we have nothing; then you think again, and see we have very much. We have gained precious national self-respect. We wished to keep our hands clear of the Sudan; we were drawn unwillingly to meddle with it; we blundered when we suffered Gordon to go out; we fiddled and failed when we tried to bring him back. We were humiliated and we were out of pocket; we had embarked in a foolish venture, and it had turned out even worse than anybody had foreseen. Now this was surely the very point where a nation of shopkeepers should have cut its losses and turned to better business elsewhere. If we were the sordid counter-jumpers that Frenchmen try to think us, we should have ruled a red line, and thought no more of a worthless land, bottomless for our gold, thirsty for our blood. We did nothing such. We tried to; but our dogged fighting dander would not let us. We could not sit down till the defeat was redeemed. We gave more money; we gave the lives of men we loved—and we conquered the Sudan again. Now we can permit ourselves to think of it in peace.

Chapter 9

Expansion

and Public

Opinion:

Advocates of

the "New

Imperialism"

The vindication of our self-respect was the great treasure we won at Khartum, and it was worth the price we paid for it. Most people will hardly persuade themselves there is not something else thrown in. The trade of the Sudan? For now and for many years you may leave that out of the account. The Sudan is a desert, and a depopulated desert. Northward of Khartum it is a wilderness; southward it is a devastation. It was always a poor country, and it always must be. Slaves and ivory were its wealth in the old time, but now ivory is all but exterminated, and slaves must be sold no more. Gum-arabic and ostrich feathers and Dongola dates will hardly buy cotton stuffs enough for Lancashire to feel the difference. . . .

It will recover—with time, no doubt, but it will recover. Only, meanwhile, it will want some tending. There is not likely to be much trouble in the way of fighting: in the present weariness of slaughter the people will be but too glad to sit down under any decent Government. There is no reason—unless it be complications with outside Powers, like France or Abyssinia—why the old Egyptian empire should not be reoccupied up to the Albert Nyanza and Western Darfur. But if this is done—and done it surely should be—two things must be remembered. First, it must be militarily administered for many years to come, and that by British men. Take the native Egyptian official even today. No words can express his ineptitude, his laziness, his helplessness, his dread of responsibility, his maddening red-tape formalism. His panacea in every unexpected case is the same. "It must be put in writing; I must ask for instructions." He is no longer corrupt—at least, no longer so corrupt as he was—but he would be if he dared. The native officer is better than the civilian official; but even with him it is the exception to find a man both capable and incorruptible. To put Egyptians, corrupt, lazy, timid, often rank cowards, to rule the Sudan, would be to invite another Mahdi as soon as the country had grown up enough to make him formidable.

The Sudan must be ruled by military law strong enough to be feared, administered by British officers just enough to be respected. For the second point, it must not be expected that it will pay until many years have passed. The cost of a military administration would not be very great, but it must be considered money out of pocket. . . .

Well, then, if Egypt is not to get good places for her people, and is to be out of pocket for administration—how much does Egypt profit by the fall of Abdullahi and the reconquest of the Sudan? Much. Inestimably. For as the master-gain of England is the vindication of her self-respect, so the master-gain of Egypt is the assurance of her security. As long as dervish raiders loomed on the horizon of her frontier, Egypt was only half a State. She lived on a perpetual war-footing. . . . Without us there would have been no Egypt to-day; what we made we shall keep.

That is our double gain—the vindication of our own honour and the vindication of our right to go on making Egypt a country fit to live in. Egypt's gain is her existence to-day. The world's gain is the downfall of the worst tyranny in the world, and the acquisition of a limited opportunity for open trade. The Sudan's gain is immunity from rape and torture and every extreme of misery.

The poor Sudan! The wretched, dry Sudan! Count up all the gains you will, yet what a hideous irony it remains, this fight of half a generation for such an emptiness. People talk of the Sudan as the East; it is not the East. The East has age and colour; the Sudan has no colour and no age—just a monotone of squalid barbarism. It is not a country; it has nothing that makes a country. Some brutish institutions it has, and some bloodthirsty chivalry. But it is not a country: it has neither nationality, nor history, nor arts, nor even natural features. Just the Nile—the niggard Nile refusing himself to the desert—and for the rest there is absolutely nothing to look at in the Sudan. Nothing grows green. . . .

QUESTIONS TO CONSIDER

Begin by examining each piece of evidence separately. Your task is to identify the principal arguments each speaker used to support imperialist ventures by his nation. To help you complete that task, recall the questions in Sources and Method: (1) What problem or problems does the speaker identify that he claims imperialism will solve? (2) How does the speaker regard the "host populations" of the regions to be colonized? (3) How does the speaker treat (if at all) the opponents of imperialism? How does he characterize them? (4) Does the speaker connect imperialism with other important and simultaneous trends and events? If so, how?

Friedrich Fabri offered many reasons for Germany's getting into the imperialist "scramble." And yet, in essence he put forth three principal reasons. What does he mean when he refers to the "unproductive political quarreling" that is going on within the new German state? How does he propose that colonialism can solve that problem? Second, recall that Germany was a very new nation in 1879 (when Fabri's work first appeared). What material gains might this new nation realize through imperialism? What nonmaterial gains might be made? Finally, Fabri spends a good deal of time analyzing the British. What does he want his readers to conclude? Was his work likely to produce some sort of rivalry between Germany and Great Britain? In your view, what is Fabri's strongest argument?

In his letter to the governor-general of Australia, missionary John G. Paton listed nine reasons why the British government should "take possession of the New Hebrides group of the South Sea islands." In your opinion, which of Paton's nine reasons were intended to impress the governor-general? Of the nine reasons, which ones do you think Paton cared about the most? How does Paton characterize the "host population" in the New Hebrides? What does that characterization reveal about Paton's thinking?

Many Westerners would have agreed with Jules Ferry when he wrote that

Chapter 9

Expansion

and Public

Opinion:

Advocates of

the "New

Imperialism"

"Colonial policy is the child of the industrial revolution." And yet Ferry went on to explain precisely how, in his view, this "child" was born. In his opinion, what might the industrialized nations of the West have done in order to avoid colonization? What, therefore, made that colonization inevitable? What role was played by high tariffs? According to Ferry, what would have happened to Tunisia, Indochina (Vietnam), Madagascar, and the Congo had the French not enveloped them? Why would that have been undesirable?

Historian Henri Brunschwig claims that Britain's was the most commercially motivated imperialism of all European nations. Does Joseph Chamberlain's speech support Brunschwig's hypothesis? How does Chamberlain attempt to convince the British working classes that imperialism will help them? Is the argument convincing?

Chamberlain barely refers to the "host populations." When he does, however, how does he portray them? On another note, how does Chamberlain characterize British anti-imperialists?

Chamberlain strikes a responsive chord (as evidenced by the applause he receives) when he refers to "those self-denying missionaries who have gone through all these wild and savage lands." What is the nature of that appeal to the working people of Birmingham? Finally, what principal trends and events does Chamberlain link to imperialism? In what way does he make those connections?

In contrast, in what ways does Ferdinando Martini see Italy's situation as unique among European nations? How does he see the power and prestige of Italy changing? What accounts for that change? More important, how might building an empire help to solve Italy's problems?

War correspondent Steevens admits that Britain's conquest of the Sudan would reap no economic gains for many years. How, then, does he justify what he admits was the enormous expenditure of blood and treasure? How would Great Britain benefit? How can Steevens's view of Britain's benefits be contrasted with those of Chamberlain? How would Egypt benefit? How does Steevens view the "host population"? Do you think he believes it capable of being "civilized"?

After reading all the selections and answering these questions, look at the six pieces of evidence collectively. What were the most important arguments imperialists used in trying to influence public opinion? How did they view the "host populations"? The anti-imperialists? Did the arguments in favor of imperialism differ significantly from nation to nation? If so, can you explain these differences?

EPILOGUE

The brief imperialistic surge of the late nineteenth and early twentieth centuries profoundly altered the history of the world. Because of it, most of the earth's lands fell under Western political and economic influence. In 1880 only about 10 percent of Africa was controlled by European nations; by 1900, however, only Ethiopia and Liberia had been able to resist the imperialist onslaught. In Asia, Western nations acquired some territory and effectively dominated the trade of most of the rest of the continent. And when Europe greedily eyed the vulnerable nations of Latin America, the United States—by 1900 itself a colonial power—announced that, in effect, that area fell within its national "sphere of influence." Indeed, by 1905 the nations of the West had come to believe that they were the center of the universe and that the rest of the earth existed to work for, produce profits for, and please the peoples of Europe and the United States. In their arrogance as the self-proclaimed "fittest" peoples in the world, most Westerners believed this dominance was only right and just.

This is not to say, however, that all Westerners approved of empire building. Though a minority, these critics of imperialism were extremely vocal and their criticisms could not be entirely ignored. Indeed, each of the justifications for colonial expansion in the Evidence section of this chapter was forcefully questioned and disputed by the foes of imperialism as they sought to attract attention and the support of the expanded electorate.

Attacks on imperialism can be divided into two general categories: "moral" and "practical." Popular French author Emile Zola asserted that imperialism was a "moral germ" that caused the West to lose its moral judgment. Zola and others charged that the West was being hypocritical when it claimed that imperialism was

for the good of the host populations. This claim was vigorously disputed by, among others, Irish nationalist Michael Davitt, who wrote (from prison) of the British actions in India as a series of "crimes, plunder, perjuries, and iniquities." As for the Western armies who, it was averred, brought civilization to the natives, one critic opined that the soldiers "were anything but a civilizing element and would require missionaries and civilizers themselves." On the oft-discussed subject of the "White Man's Burden," British anti-imperialist Wilfred Scawen Blunt dubbed it "the burden of cash." Finally, British citizens were shocked by the grisly Boer War, complete with its concentration camps, horrific death toll of children, and atrocities. As one historian has put it, the war caused "a loss of moral content, from which it [Britain] never completely recovered."[12]

As for the "practical" assaults on imperialism, perhaps the most telling were those of English economist John Atkinson Hobson (1858–1940), who attacked colonialism as economically unprofitable to all but a very few and ultimately as a losing proposition

12. On Zola see Richard Koebner and Helmut Dan Schmidt, *Imperialism: The Story and Significance of a Political Word, 1840–1960* (Cambridge: Cambridge University Press, 1964), p. 244. On the soldiers as civilizers see ibid., p. 238. For Davitt see his *Jottings in Solitary*, ed. Carla King (Dublin: University College of Dublin Press, 2003), p. 17. On the "White Man's Burden" see David Gilmour, *The Long Recessional: The Imperial Life of Rudyard Kipling* (New York: Farrar, Strauss & Giroux, 2002), p. 131. On Britain and the Boer War see A. P. Thornton, *The Imperial Idea and Its Enemies: A Study of British Power* (London: Macmillan & Co., 1959), pp. 109–113.

Chapter 9

Expansion

and Public

Opinion:

Advocates of

the "New

Imperialism"

because of the heavy government expenditures to maintain an empire. Expansion, Hobson maintained, did not help the working people of either nation, a direct challenge to the claims of Chamberlain and others. For his part, Vladimir Ilyich Lenin, soon to be the leader of the Bolshevik Revolution, saw imperialism as the last stage of capitalism, which ultimately would lead to war and revolution. Building on the work of Hobson, Lenin argued that investors actually were exporting investment capital from Europe to the developing colonies, to the detriment of the workers in the West. Other opponents of colonialism, however, disagreed with Lenin, maintaining (with considerable evidence), that capitalists did not invest in the colonies because they were too risky. However, while the "practical" anti-imperialists did not always agree with one another, together they loudly challenged the advocates of expansion.[13]

In France, the critics of imperialism were equally vocal. In 1904 French writer Anatole France warned that French imperialism was for the benefit of the military establishment, and that its ultimate result was a barbarism of both the military and civilian populations. For his part, socialist Jean Jaurès argued that the "host populations" would not remain a subjugated people for long, and that

France was opening a Pandora's box that it would be unable to close.

In the United States, anti-imperialists counted among their number industrialist Andrew Carnegie, author Mark Twain, philosopher William James, reformer Jane Addams, and political leader William Jennings Bryan. Yet these and other voices, though loud and articulate, for the most part went unheeded amid the almost frantic scramble for colonial possessions.

Armed with hindsight, we can see that these critics of colonialism had much stronger arguments than their contemporaries either realized or appreciated. For one thing, few of these colonies could provide the markets for European manufactured goods that Ferry and Chamberlain claimed. For example, between 1909 and 1913, tropical Africa represented only about 2 percent of Great Britain's total non-European trade. Statistics from France and Germany were roughly the same.[14]

Moreover, acquiring and administering an empire was an enormously expensive process, draining off funds that might have been used for economic and social reforms. Snuffing out resistance to colonial rule required the maintenance of a strong military presence that often responded to anti-Western upsurges with extreme brutality. Great Britain, for example, spent 53 percent of its total military budget on its troops in India. In China, resistance to imperialism was countered

13. On Hobson and Lenin see Lewis Feuer, *Imperialism and the Anti-Imperialist Mind* (Buffalo, N.Y.: Prometheus Books, 1986), pp. 10, 149; Koebner and Schmidt, *Imperialism*, pp. 221–222; and Bernard Porter, *Critics of Imperialism: British Radical Attitudes to Colonialism in Africa, 1895–1914* (London: Macmillan, 1968), p. 100.

14. William L. Langer, "A Critique of Imperialism," in Harrison M. Wright, ed., *The "New Imperialism": Analysis of Late Nineteenth Century Expansion* (Boston: D. C. Heath, 1961), p. 69.

with naval bombardments of cities and wholesale executions of resisters. In the Philippines, the United States used approximately 74,000 troops to crush the movement for independence, resorting to torture, repression, and other atrocities in order to "civilize" the Filipinos. In the Congo Free State, agents of Leopold II resorted to forced labor and incredibly brutal treatment, including mutilations of protestors, in order to extract ivory and rubber. In truth, colonialism could be both an exceedingly expensive and a morally reprehensible activity.[15]

Finally, the scramble for empire heightened the rivalry and conflict among Western nations and was one factor leading to World War I in 1914. In 1898 England and France very nearly came to blows at Fashoda (on the upper Nile River) until the French backed down. In 1905 Germany's attempts to intrude into Morocco almost brought it to war with France until the Algeciras Conference of 1906 awarded control of Morocco to the French. In 1904–1905, Russian imperialism in

15. For Britain's military expenditures see Thornton, *The Imperial Idea*, p. 122. As for the Congo Free State, Leopold's personal possession, it became so scandalous that the king was forced to turn over control to the Belgian government in 1908.

East Asia brought Russia into a war with Japan in which it suffered a humiliating defeat. As Western nations looked for power vacuums to exploit in Africa, China, and the Balkans, the threat of armed hostilities increased. Indeed, it was Russia's efforts to penetrate the Balkan tinderbox that led directly to war in 1914.

At the same time, the West's control of its newly acquired territories was never strong. Movements for national independence constantly had to be put down. Efforts to "westernize" Africans and Asians were never very successful, except among some of the elites of those regions. Though an increasing number of non-Westerners gradually came to embrace Western technology and political ideas in the twentieth century, they nevertheless insisted that the West should withdraw so that they could govern themselves. Thus, later movements for independence often tended to be "anti-Western" as well, to purge those societies of westernized elites, if not of Western technology. Within a half-century, all the empires built by the West in the late nineteenth century would be in shambles. For a time, the West lived in an imperialistic sunshine. Yet—to paraphrase Herman Melville—the brighter the sunshine, the greater the resulting shadows.

CHAPTER TEN

WOMEN IN RUSSIAN

REVOLUTIONARY MOVEMENTS

During the last half of the nineteenth century and the first decades of the twentieth, women throughout Europe became involved in a wide range of movements advocating political change. Inspired by liberal reform efforts to improve conditions in prisons and mental hospitals, expand educational opportunities, and broaden the suffrage, women in Europe and America began to call for the extension of women's legal rights, availability of higher education to women, and the right to vote. They formed national and international organizations to agitate for these changes. Gradually, married women were granted the right to own property, a scattering of colleges and universities allowed women to enroll in some courses, and a few countries, such as Norway, New Zealand, and Australia, allowed women the right to vote. Despite increasingly militant tactics by advocates of women's suffrage, most European countries did not grant women

the right to vote until after World War I (France did not extend this right until after World War II).

The nineteenth-century women's rights movement was largely made up of middle-class women, for whom changes such as greater access to education were extremely important, but working-class women also saw a need for reforms. Like working-class men, women laborers wanted the workday reduced from twelve hours to ten; safety conditions improved in mines, mills, and factories; an end to child labor; and the right to organize without losing their jobs. Working-class women also had specific concerns because they were women. They were often harassed sexually by their employers and fired when they became pregnant. Women's wages were always lower than men's, even when they performed the same tasks. Because their wages were low, women returned to work very soon after giving birth, a practice that was detrimental to their own health and that of their infants. Though both women and men worked the same long hours in mills and factories, the actual workday for women was even longer because they generally did most or all of the cooking, housework, and child care.

A number of working-class women sought to improve conditions for all workers, especially women, through organizing and political action. Some joined labor unions and socialist political parties; in Germany women formed a separate socialist women's organization. These actions were not always supported by the men who made up the vast majority of labor unions and socialist groups. Many working-class men viewed women workers with hostility because women were used as strikebreakers or to force wages down. Often these men did not want their own wives and daughters speaking out in public or acting as organizers. Their own low wages dictated that their wives and daughters worked, but many had internalized the middle-class notion that the woman's proper place was the home and so were unwilling to accept women joining them in the fight for workers' rights or better conditions.

In addition, some leaders of the socialist movement viewed separate women's organizations as harmful to working-class solidarity. Though Marx and Engels had both clearly advocated women's political equality and most socialist parties included votes for women as part of their platforms, working-class women were urged to work first for the overthrow of capitalism or for more gradual improvements in the status of the entire working class. Male socialist theorists argued that class solidarity should always take precedence over gender solidarity, and many prominent women socialists agreed with them.

The middle-class women's rights movement and the socialist movement began in western Europe, but both quickly found advocates in Russia, which boasted the most autocratic and repressive government in all of Europe. By the mid-nineteenth century, Russian women had already joined men in calling for the abolition of serfdom and the introduction of some representative institutions. A small middle-class women's movement advocated higher education for women and the right for women to leave home without their fathers' permission. Advocates of women's rights wrote articles about what was termed the "woman question," discussing the consequences of expanding women's educational and employment opportunities and legal rights. They viewed women's rights as an important part of any political reform, noting that the absolute power of the tsar was simply an extension of the absolute power of the father in Russian families.

A small number of women from all social classes felt the reformist aims of the women's rights movement were much too mild and gradual, and these women joined groups that advocated revolutionary change and the violent overthrow of the tsar. Because their actions often made political radicalism and women's emancipation seem like two sides of the same coin in the minds of many Russian officials, periods of general political repression also brought increasing restrictions on the rights of women.

Tsar Alexander II freed the serfs in 1861 and began a brief period of reform that also produced some alterations in the status of women. Women were allowed to attend selected classes at the universities, and local representative assemblies, called *zemstvos*, were established in the countryside. A woman who owned enough property could nominate a man of her choice as her proxy in a *zemstvo* or a municipal assembly in a city, though she could not attend herself. These reforms led to growing calls for more radical changes and an increasingly active terrorist movement. Alexander II reverted to a policy of repression that only increased the ardor of revolutionary groups; in 1881, one of them, the People's Will, succeeded in its attempts to assassinate him. The assassination was led by a woman, Sofia Perovskaia, who a month later became the first female in Russian history to be executed for a political crime: she was hung along with four male compatriots. Another female conspirator, Gesia Gelfman, was also sentenced, but her hanging was deferred because she was pregnant; she died in prison after childbirth. Perovskaia and Gelfman were not the only female revolutionaries; about 30 percent of the members of the People's Will were women, as were about 15 percent of all those arrested for political crimes in the 1870s, a much higher proportion of female membership than in any other contemporary European socialist or radical movement.

The assassination of Alexander II was followed by a period of repressive reaction under the tsar's successors. Women as well as men were arrested and exiled to Siberia, but this did not stop their activities. During the 1890s, Russia began to industrialize heavily and socialist organizers joined the work force of the new factories to convince workers of the need to organize for better working conditions, improved wages, and the right to form unions and political parties. Female organizers went to work in factories where large numbers of women were employed, spreading ideas about rights for both workers and women. Because workers' and socialist groups were illegal, joining one could lead to dismissal, imprisonment, or exile, but these groups still began to grow slowly. Women workers were more hesitant to join than men, probably because many worried more about the economic consequences of such an action for their families and less about abstract political rights. The low level of participation by women in workers' and socialist groups was also due in part to the low levels of literacy and skill among women workers, many of whom were peasants working only temporarily in factories. The organizers who were most successful in recruiting women were generally females themselves who addressed the specific concerns of working women such as sexual harassment, maternity leave, and women's lower wages.

Dissatisfaction among both peasants and workers came to a head during Russia's disastrous war with Japan. In January of 1905, soldiers fired on a crowd of workers who were marching peacefully to the tsar's palace to petition for reforms, an incident that sparked a series of riots, strikes, assassinations, naval mutinies, and peasant revolts. Workers in St. Petersburg and elsewhere spontaneously organized bodies advocating various reforms and set up their own councils, called *soviets*. The tsar was forced to allow the establishment of a national representative assembly, the *Duma*, to be elected by almost universal male suffrage.

The 1905 revolution was followed by a period of reaction. Under the Fundamental Law establishing the Duma, the tsar retained considerable power, including the right to dismiss this body and call for new elections. In 1907 voting rights were increasingly restricted so that landowners and wealthier urban voters had the most seats; the last two Dumas put up little objection to the tsar's policies before World War I.

None of the underlying political and economic problems had been solved, however, and they reemerged dramatically when Russia entered the war against Germany in 1914. Huge numbers of ill-equipped soldiers were killed in the first year of the war, and Nicholas II provided no leadership in solving problems of how to mobilize the country for an all-out war effort. The tsar decided to act as his ancestors always had, by assuming personal command at the front, leaving the government largely in the hands of his wife. As a firm believer in absolutism and autocracy, the tsarina, Alexandra, refused to yield to the Duma's and other groups' demands for change.

During the winter of 1916–1917, food supplies became increasingly scarce and women were desperate to feed their families. In February 1917, as part of an observance of International Women's Day, women in Petrograd (formerly St. Petersburg) organized a strike for food and better working conditions. Male union leaders tried to prevent the strike, asserting that a separate action by women was harmful to the solidarity of the workers' movement, but the women were not to be dissuaded. The strike proved extremely effective because the soldiers in the city refused to fire on the women, leading male union leaders finally to show their support. This strike led to sympathy strikes in the factories and public demonstrations of over 300,000 people. Soldiers joined the demonstrators, the Duma declared a Provisional Government, and Nicholas II was forced to abdicate.

The February Revolution was welcomed throughout the country, and the new government quickly advocated a program of liberal and democratic reforms, meanwhile deferring many actual reforms to concentrate on the war effort. Exiled radicals, among them V. I. Lenin, returned to the country and urged the Petrograd Soviet to push for more dramatic changes, including Russia's withdrawal from the war and the takeover of farms and factories by peasants and workers. Lenin hoped the war could be transformed into a socialist revolution in each of the belligerent countries. In October 1917, Lenin's political party, the Bolsheviks, led the Petrograd Soviet in a revolution against the Provisional Government and succeeded in taking over the city. Four months later, they signed a treaty with the Germans that ended Russian involvement in the war, though civil war would persist for another three years.

Continuing the radical movement tradition of the nineteenth century, women were involved and active in both the 1905 and 1917 revolutions. Your task in this chapter will be to analyze that involvement, using memoirs, political pamphlets, and histories to answer the following questions: What changes did those women involved in Russian revolutionary movements want to bring about, and what actions did they take to implement these changes? Did women's concerns, strategies, and objections differ from those of men, and if so, how?

SOURCES AND METHOD

The questions posed in this chapter, particularly the second one, ask you to make distinctions between the historical experience of women and men—in other words, to assess how gender affected people's experiences. Though it seems quite obvious that gender shapes an individual life to a great degree, only recently have historians begun to differentiate the historical past of females from that of males.

This awareness of gender is a result of the relatively new field of women's history, which arose in conjunction with the feminist movement of the 1960s. As historians studied the social history of women, they discovered that periods of advance for men, such as the Renaissance or the Enlightenment, did not bring corresponding advances for women. A timeline of great events in women's history would be very different from a timeline of great events in men's history (or what had until that point been called "human" history).

Once historians began exploring the history of women, they realized that because the male experience alone had most often been identified as the human experience, only rarely had men in the past been studied as men. Historians familiar with studying women increasingly began to discuss the ways in which systems of sexual differentiation affected both women and men, and by the early 1980s to use the word "gender" to describe these systems. At that point, they differentiated primarily between "sex," by which they meant physical and anatomical differences (what are often called "biological differences") and "gender," by which they meant a culturally constructed system that has changed over time. Historians interested in this new perspective asserted that gender is an appropriate category of analysis when looking at *all* historical developments, not simply those involving women or the family. *Every* political, intellectual, religious, economic, social, and even military change has had an impact on the actions and roles of men and women, and, conversely, a culture's gender structures have influenced every other structure or development.

Since the 1980s, "gender" has become a common term. Sometimes it is used simply as a substitute for "sex"—as on forms that ask us to specify our gender as M or F—but scholars use it to emphasize the cultural and social nature of this system of differences. Historians and others studying gender now explore such topics as changes in ideals of masculinity, ways in which the mass media have shaped notions of what it means to be a good mother or father, or differences in the understanding of what types of work are "masculine" or "feminine."

At the same time that "gender" was becoming a widely used word and gender analysis a familiar method of studying the past and the present, scholars in many fields and activists in various social movements also asserted that the boundaries between sex and gender are not as clear as we once thought. Where should the lines should be drawn? Were women "biologically" more peaceful and men "biologically" more skillful at math, or were such tendencies the result solely of their upbringing? What about individuals whose bodies did not fit with their own self-understanding, in other words, who were "physically" male but "psychologically" female? How are sex and gender related for such people? What about cultures in which there are more than two genders, with some individuals combining the clothing, tasks, and behavior of men and women and understood to belong to a completely different category? What about individuals who are anatomically ambiguous? In some of these cases, physicians and parents decide to alter the child's body surgically so that it better matches a "normal" male or female body. Doesn't that mean that in those cases ideas about gender—that everyone should be either clearly male or female—are

determining an individual's sex, rather than the other way around? Questions such as these, many of which are being highlighted in movies and television programs as well as scholarly books, have made the boundaries between sex and gender increasingly blurred and murky. At the same time, they have strengthened the recognition that gender is a central component of the human experience and intensified interest in studying gender in the past.

Studying the history of women has led historians not only to add gender as an essential category of historical analysis and to ask new questions of all historical events but also to look for new types of sources. Both intentionally and unintentionally, traditional sources often exclude the experience and activities of women. Most written records have come from the hands of men, who have either ignored women's experiences or viewed them as less important than those of men. Even newspapers and journals that purport to offer objective accounts were until very recently owned and run exclusively by men, which means that they, too, are gender biased. Discovering the history of women in any period thus involves creative sleuthing and the use of less traditional sources, such as private letters and diaries.

Studying the history of women in Russian revolutionary movements poses additional problems. After the Soviet state was established, "official" histories of the revolution played up the ideas and activities of leaders such as Lenin, excluding the activities of lesser figures, both male and female. Especially under the rule of

[271]

Stalin, individuals and groups whose ideas this leader disagreed with were totally excluded from Russian and Soviet history, and many of these same individuals were executed or exiled for life. Western historians' exclusion of women has been generally less intentional, emerging as it did from their emphasis on the theorists behind the movements, who were usually men, rather than on the organizers attempting to put theory into practice, who were often women as well as men.

For a balanced view of the actions of both men and women, we need to turn from official sources to the writings of women themselves. All the sources for this chapter either were written by women or directly report women's words. Simply locating women's writings is not always easy. Many of the women revolutionaries took very little time to write, and much of what revolutionaries of both sexes did write was destroyed by authorities. Before 1917, tsarist officials confiscated and destroyed not only many political pamphlets and propaganda but also private letters and journals. After 1917, Bolshevik officials destroyed documents written by those who did not agree with them— moderates, anarchists, Mensheviks, Socialist Revolutionaries, or Bolsheviks who had fallen out of favor with the party leadership. As noted women's writings that actually reached print were often forgotten or ignored in later histories of these movements. Many of the sources here have been rediscovered and translated only in the past ten or fifteen years by scholars interested in the history of women

who have combed archives and libraries for neglected material.

To realize how discovering and integrating material on women and adding gender as a category of analysis can change your understanding of events, first read (or reread) the section in your text that deals with nineteenth-century Russia and the Bolshevik Revolution. Which women are mentioned by name? What actions by women are described, and how are these integrated into the general narrative of events? Do the descriptions of various revolutionary movements make it clear that both men and women were involved? Are their experiences ever compared or differentiated by gender? Now read the sources in this chapter; when you have finished, you may discover that your text is in need of some revision.

The first three sources are excerpts from the memoirs of Russian women who were revolutionaries in the late nineteenth century. As you read these, make a list of the changes each author wished to bring about in Russian society and the actions she took to bring about these changes. (As you read the selections, keep your text handy as a reference to political developments and to well-known radicals whose ideas influenced the authors.)

Elizaveta Kovalskaia, the author of the first selection, was born to a serf mother and nobleman father, though her father later used his influence to have both Kovalskaia and her mother declared free citizens. The actions she describes here led to her arrest in 1880; she was sent to Siberia for twenty-three years. Source 2 is by

Olga Liubatovich, the daughter of an engineer, who grew up in Moscow and first came into contact with radical ideas in Zurich, where she had gone to study medicine. In 1875 she began organizing factory workers as a member of the Pan-Russian Social Revolutionary Organization, an activity for which she was imprisoned in Siberia. Liubatovich escaped three years later, resumed her revolutionary activities, and began to write her memoirs, from which these selections are taken. Source 3, by Praskovia Ivanovskaia, the daughter of a poor provincial village priest, describes her political activities in 1876. Later she became a member of the People's Will, the group that assassinated Alexander II, and was exiled to Siberia for twenty years for her involvement in the plot. Ivanovskaia escaped and played a very active role in the revolution of 1905.

What activities did these three women see as most important in bringing about fundamental social changes? What tactics did they recommend? How did their tactics change as the political circumstances changed? How did their tactics change as their own ideas matured and developed? What specific concerns of women did the authors address? In Source 2, what special problems did Gesia Gelfman face because she was female? How was she treated differently because of her sex? How were the problems facing working-class Russian women different from those facing middle-class women?

Source 4 is an excerpt from the memoirs of Eva Broido, who grew up in a moderately prosperous Jewish family and entered the revolutionary movement by organizing workers in St. Petersburg in 1899. Exiled to Siberia for running a secret printing press, she escaped and continued organizing. After the 1905 revolution, she became a Menshevik and carried out the activities she describes here. After the Bolshevik Revolution she was forced to leave Russia, but she returned in 1927 and probably died in the Stalinist purges of the 1930s. What role did Broido ascribe to workers' clubs? Why were these clubs especially important to women?

The fifth and sixth selections describe the actions of women during the 1905 revolution. Source 5 is taken from a history of the working women's movement in Russia written in 1920 by Alexandra Kollontai. Kollontai, the daughter of a prominent army officer, was the most important woman within the leadership of the Bolshevik party; after the October Revolution she became the commissar of social welfare and head of the women's department within the party, called the *Zhenotdel*. She wrote on a wide range of subjects, including many of special interest to women, such as marriage and the family. As you read this selection, add Kollontai's aims and actions to your list and also pay attention to the general tone of the piece. How does she portray women workers and peasants? How does she portray middle-class women? Source 6 is a petition brought by peasant women to the Duma established after the 1905 revolution. How had the changes brought about by this first revolution affected them differently from peasant men? Does this petition fit with the actions Kollontai describes in her history?

Source 7 is also a petition by women, this one brought to the Provisional Government after the February Revolution of 1917. Again, notice both content and tone. How had the February Revolution affected women's political status? How would you compare this petition with the 1905 petition?

The last two selections were also written by Alexandra Kollontai. Source 8 is an article from *Pravda*, the Bolshevik party newspaper, which appeared in May 1917, months before the Bolshevik Revolution, under the headline "In the Front Line of Fire." What actions does Kollontai suggest to the reader? Source 9 is taken from a pamphlet titled "Working Woman and Mother," written in 1914, which contains ideas Kollontai later tried to put into practice when she became the commissar of public welfare. What special problems of working women does she identify, and how does she propose to solve them?

Look over your list of each author's aims and actions. What aims did all share? Did any of their aims and tactics appear to contradict each other? Which authors make clear distinctions between the problems facing middle-class women and those facing women peasants and workers? Which authors believe the concerns of workers in general take precedence over those of women?

You should not let contradictions in the goals and beliefs of these women revolutionaries surprise you. It is as misleading to generalize about all women as it is to generalize about all men, though the first investigators of the history of women tended to do just this. Generalizations overlook the fact that because women make up half of every social class and economic category, their experiences are often much more similar to those of the men of their class than to women of other classes. Generalizations along class lines (e.g., "middle-class women think . . . ") can also be misleading, because class background alone is not enough to explain the diversity of opinion among women, just as it is not enough to explain the diversity of opinion among men. Viewing "middle-class women" or "working-class women" as an undifferentiated group ignores the fact that women develop their own ideas individually, just as men do.

Sources 1 through 3 from Barbara Alpern Engel and Clifford N. Rosenthal, editors and translators,
Five Sisters: Women Against the Tsar, *1987, pp. 210–212, 217–218, 226, 233–234; pp. 185–187,*
194; pp. 103–105. Reprinted by Permission of Unwin Hyman Inc., and the editors.

1. From the *Memoirs* of Elizaveta Kovalskaia, Moscow, 1926

The emancipation of the serfs in 1861 had given rise to the women's movement. Like a huge wave, the movement to liberate women swept over all the
urban centers of Russia. I, too, was caught up in it. My father had died soon
after I finished school, leaving me a large inheritance. In one of the houses he
left me, I organized free courses for women seeking higher education. Iakov
Kovalskii, whom I later married, worked with me on this. There were so
many auditors for the courses that we had trouble squeezing them all into the
house. Kovalskii gave lectures on physics, chemistry, and cosmography; de la
Rue, an assistant professor, taught the natural sciences; and we used university students for political economy, history, and higher mathematics.

At the same time, I belonged to the Kharkov Society for the Promotion of Literacy. At the Sunday schools where I worked, I picked out the most capable of
the women laborers and invited them to my house on holidays. Gradually, a
school for women workers was formed. I read them fragments of Russian fiction and recounted episodes from Russian history; I told them about the French
Revolution; but mainly, I conducted propaganda on the woman question.

A men's study circle devoted to social questions met in my house; its orientation was radical, although not revolutionary. Parallel to this group, I organized one exclusively for women who were interested in socialism. A male
comrade who had a good grasp of French, as well as access to the university
library, made excerpts from source works to help me in compiling papers on
Fourier, Saint-Simon, Owen, and other utopian socialists.

On holidays, some village schoolteachers who were friends of Kovalskii
came to visit us. We provided them with books and organized small conferences on pedagogy, in the course of which we also dealt with political topics.
During one of these conferences, a police officer and his entourage appeared in
our house. When he saw the maps and visual displays spread out on the desks,
he was taken aback. "All this is fine," he declared; "you're doing useful work
and I see nothing illegal in it. But according to the orders from my superiors,
all your meetings must cease, and if they don't, I'll have to arrest you all."

We had to stop everything.

Dmitrii Tolstoi, the minister of education, was supposed to visit Kharkov
around that time, and we agitated for the right to present a petition to him: we

wanted permission for women to enroll in the universities. Meetings were held constantly; I was chosen to the committee that drew up the petition, and also as a delegate to present it. But as it turned out, Tolstoi was very hostile to us: he declared that he would never allow women into the universities. . . .

[*Kovalskaia then went to St. Petersburg,
where she organized discussion circles for
women, but was ordered by her doctor to
go south for health reasons.*]

I soon went south, as I had been ordered. When I got there, I started to revive the circles I had organized earlier, but my doctors quickly packed me off to Zurich.

In Zurich I came into contact with various revolutionary currents, especially Lavrism and Bakuninism. I was attracted to Bakuninism,[1] and when my health had improved somewhat, I returned to Russia in order to "go to the people."

Because of my physical weakness, I was absolutely unsuited for the role of a manual laborer. Instead, I took a position as a schoolteacher in the district of Tsarskoe Selo, close to the Kolpino factory, where the young people of the village worked. I quickly came under surveillance for conducting propaganda and illegally distributing revolutionary pamphlets among the factory workers. One day, the *zemstvo* school inspector came to warn me that I was about to be arrested.

I escaped to St. Petersburg, where I got to know some workers and began providing them with illegal literature. My status was semi-illegal, but I managed to avoid arrest by dividing my time between St. Petersburg and Kharkov. Then, during the demonstration that followed Vera Zasulich's acquittal[2] [March 31, 1878, in St. Petersburg], I was severely beaten by the police. I had to spend almost a year in bed back in Kharkov.

After I recovered, I organized several groups—two circles of metalworkers from the factories and a third one composed of young people. . . .

I presented the program Shchedrin[3] and I had developed, which later served as the basis for the Union of Russian Workers of the South. It was

1. **Bakuninism:** the anarchist philosophy of the Russian nobleman Mikhail Bakunin, who believed that revolution should rise from locally controlled, grassroots movements of many social classes, but in particular from the peasantry, in contrast to Marx's emphasis on the industrial proletariat.

2. Vera Zasulich had shot General Trepov, the governor of St. Petersburg, because he had ordered the whipping of a political prisoner who had refused to remove his cap in Trepov's presence. The jury acquitted her, but the tsar refused to accept the acquittal and ordered her arrested again. Friends smuggled her out of Russia to Switzerland, where she spent most of the next twenty-five years. She returned to Russia after the 1905 revolution, and was viewed by many groups as a great hero.

3. **Shchedrin:** Nicolai Shchedrin, Kolvalskaia's comrade and friend.

essentially this: the goal was to transform the existing order into a socialist system. This was possible only by means of a *popular revolution.* The preconditions for such a revolution existed in Russia: the *obshchina,* or peasant land commune, and the propensity of the Russian people for workers' cooperatives and self-government. If there was to be a revolution in Russia, it could only be a socialist one, because the people would rise in rebellion only for the land; political demands made little sense to them. Any revolution that did not involve the participation of the people—even one carried out by a socialist party—would inevitably be *merely political:* that is, it would bring the country freedom similar to that enjoyed in Western Europe without changing the economic situation of the working people at all. It would simply make it easier for the bourgeoisie to organize itself and thus become a more formidable enemy of the workers.

Now, the peasants and workers of Russia were dissatisfied with their situation, but they lacked faith in their own ability to overthrow the established order, and this prevented them from rebelling. The people had to be instilled with the necessary confidence. Political terror directed at the center of the system was too remote for them to comprehend. *Economic terror* (we called it "democratic terror" then) defended their immediate interests. It involved the murder of the police officials and administrators of all sorts who were in closest contact with the people; its meaning would be clear to the people, and it would involve fewer sacrifices than the strike or local popular uprising. Only this kind of terror could increase the people's faith in *their own* ability to struggle, to organize and overthrow the existing structure themselves. It was virtually impossible for the intelligentsia to do political work in the countryside. It was easier among city workers. As these workers returned to their villages, they would be able to implement a program of action among the peasantry. . . .

We succeeded in organizing about seven hundred workers. We divided them into groups and met with a different one every night, seeing each only once a week. There were rarely fewer than a hundred people at a meeting—an enormous number for those times. We had no specific agenda for the discussions; our theoretical positions simply emerged as we talked about one or another current social ill. There was no need to dwell on how terrible things were in general for workers and peasants; people were already well aware of this. All we had to do was make the connections between this misery and the workings of the established order as a whole, then go back and integrate each specific instance of discontent.

Despite the organization's success, the struggle against the passivity instilled over the centuries was a difficult one. Often workers would listen attentively and then proceed to tell us that things would somehow get done without them. Everyone had his own version of this, depending on his degree of political development. The most sophisticated believed that some revolutionary committee would take the land away from the landlords for the peasants. Others said that the tsar had abolished serfdom and was now fighting the gentry in order to take away their lands and distribute them among the people. Those who had heard about the Chigirin affair[4] believed that the "tsar's commissars" were genuine, and that the nobles had captured and murdered them. There were some, too, who "knew for a fact" that foreign powers (they didn't know which ones in particular) were doing things to better the situation of the Russian common folk. The least sophisticated workers—even the young people—spoke with profound conviction of how "visions had begun," how the Virgin had appeared to their priest, saying; "Pray, for the day of rejoicing will soon be upon you." They believed in the elders who indicated definite dates on which "everything will be turned upside down and all the poor will be exalted."

Our main task, then, in organizing the workers was to stimulate their initiative so that they would take up their cause themselves.

2. From the *Memoirs* of Olga Liubatovich, Moscow, 1906

[*Liubatovich describes her first meeting with Gesia Gelfman, one of those arrested for assassinating Tsar Alexander II.*]

She told me her whole life story. She had grown up in Mozyr (Minsk province). Her father, a prosperous but fanatical Jew, gave her no education whatsoever; Gesia owed everything she had become to her own energy. When she reached the age of seventeen, her father decided—without consulting her—to marry her off. A dowry was prepared. The eve of her wedding came—time for the older women to perform on Gesia the repulsive rituals dictated by ancient Jewish custom. But Gesia's sense of modesty made her rebel, and she resolved to leave home. She grabbed her jewelry and escaped by night to the home of a Russian girlfriend who had promised to help her. Gesia moved to Kiev, where she enrolled in the courses in midwifery[5] so as to be able to make an honest living. She made friends among the progressive youth of Kiev, getting to know Alexandra Khorzhevskaia, one of the Fritsche,[6] in 1875. It was at this time that I met her.

---

4. **Chigirin affair:** during 1876–1877, radicals circulated fictitious tsarist orders, calling on the peasants of the Chigirin area to form armies to seize the nobility's land and redistribute it to people. Tsarist officials discovered this conspiracy and arrested all involved.

5. These were the only courses available to women in Kiev at the time.

6. **Fritsche:** a study group formed in 1872 by thirteen female emigré Russian students who had gone to Zurich to study because women were excluded from Russian universities. The group read the works of socialists and revolutionaries and resolved to return to Russia to carry out revolutionary activities.

Gesia was arrested in September 1875. Two years later, at the Trial of the Fifty,[7] she was convicted of serving as an intermediary for our organization, which had been engaged in propagandizing and organizing among the youth and workers of various cities of the Russian Empire. She could claim no legal privileges by virtue of her social status,[8] and so she was incarcerated in a St. Petersburg workhouse. In August 1878, when I reached St. Petersburg after escaping from Siberia, Gesia was still languishing in the workhouse. I corresponded with her, and once, after she was transferred to the Litovskii fortress, walked down the street beneath her window. It made her happy to see me free.

In the summer of 1879, Gesia was sent off under police guard to finish out her sentence at Staraia Russa (Novgorod province). Later that year she escaped, and we saw each other for the first time since our sentencing. She told me that she felt extremely weary after her prolonged confinement, that she wanted to rest. But those were times of feverish activity, and Gesia, like the rest of us, got swept up in the intense struggle. She was a very sensitive person, and her life was one of continuous sacrifice; she had the ability to love.

Now, at what proved to be my last meeting with Gesia, she was sad and looked rather ill, but she buried her personal grief amid the endless concerns imposed by her life as a revolutionary. For that matter, there were few cheerful people in revolutionary circles at the time: every day someone else was snatched away by the police, and the survivors, depressed by these losses, were straining every nerve for a final assault on the regime. Gesia seemed to have a foreboding that she was living out the last days of her freedom, the freedom she had enjoyed so briefly.

The apartment Gesia shared with Nikolai Sablin was used for briefings by the people who participated in the assassination of the tsar on March 1. On March 3 the place was raided by the police: Sablin killed himself, and Gelfman was arrested. A few weeks later, she was sentenced to death. Her pregnancy delayed the execution—dooming her instead to another, more horrible fate. She languished under the threat of execution for five months; finally her sentence was commuted, just before she was to deliver. At the hands of the authorities, the terrible act of childbirth became a case of torture unprecedented in human history. For the delivery, they transferred her to the House of Detention. They gave her a fairly large cell, but in it they posted round-the-clock sentries—a device that had driven other women, women who weren't pregnant, insane. The torments suffered by poor Gesia

---

7. **Trial of the Fifty:** a mass trial conducted in Moscow in March 1877. The government arrested fifty members of a revolutionary group, the Pan-Russian Social Revolutionary Organization, who had been organizing among workers. It hoped to brand them as criminals; instead, people viewed the radicals as idealists.

8. Russian criminal law exempted certain social categories of people (especially the nobility) from various forms of punishment.

Gelfman exceeded those dreamed up by the executioners of the Middle Ages; but Gesia didn't go mad—her constitution was too strong. The child was born live, and she was even able to nurse it. Under Russian law, Gesia's rights as a mother were protected, even though she was a convict; no one could take her baby away. But at that time, who would have considered being guided by the law? One night shortly after the child was born, the authorities came in and took her away from Gesia. In the morning, they brought her to a foundling home, where they abandoned her without taking a receipt or having her tagged—this despite the fact that many people (myself included) had offered to raise the child. The mother could not endure this final blow, and she soon died.

Thus ended the life of Gesia Gelfman, who fled from her father's house, filled with indignation at ancient custom, filled with indignation at the tramping of women's rights—only to perish as the victim of unprecedented violence against her sensibilities as a woman, a human being, and a mother.

> [*Liubatovich then returns to
> her own story.*]

The next day, as I was getting ready to leave for St. Petersburg, a comrade from the Executive Committee (Vera Figner, as I recall) came over to tell me that Sofia Bardina's husband, Shakhov, was in Moscow and wanted to see me.

How my heart started to beat when I heard that! Sofia and I might be able to reinvigorate the revolutionary movement. We had been comrades in the Pan-Russian Social Revolutionary Organization, a group that had developed considerable strength through its great ideological and moral unity. Back in 1875, we had laid the foundations for revolutionary workers' associations in Moscow and other cities. Our program reflected in embryo the course of the revolutionary movement in the seventies: from peaceful propaganda to armed resistance and disorganization of the government by means of terror. Many people subsequently told me that the solidarity we had achieved served as a model for the revolutionary organizations that came after us, particularly Land and Liberty. Our group didn't produce a single traitor, thanks to the principle on which it was based: the complete freedom and equality of all its members. Everyone—worker or member of the intelligentsia, man or woman—took a turn at carrying out administrative duties, which were both an obligation and a right. There were no elections. No one was anxious to enter the administration. The administrators had no power; they were intermediaries, and nothing more. But even apart from that, all of us placed a very high value on working directly among the people and doing ordinary manual labor. Although our period of activity was brief—less than a year—our propaganda left very perceptible traces among the people, and our legacy was put to use by those who came after us.

3. From the *Memoirs* of Praskovia Ivanovskaia, Moscow, 1925

I decided to spend the time in Odessa, where I could find factory work without showing my identity papers, which marked me as a member of the intelligentsia. . . .

I got up very early that first Monday morning, so early that the street was still deserted by the time I reached the factory gates. The factory buildings themselves were invisible from the street, blocked by the long, high stone walls—gray, ugly, mottled with obscene graffiti. The factory hadn't come to life yet: I found no one at the gate, which resembled that of a prison. Then the workingmen began to approach, sleepy and sullen, singly and in groups. The wicket gate opened to swallow them up and then slammed shut again, as if of its own volition. Finally, the women workers arrived—late, hurrying, adjusting their clothing on the run. They dived behind the gate, and once more the street was utterly deserted.

I knocked timidly. An eye appeared at a small window in the gate, and a voice shouted: "What do you want? A job? Come in." With no formalities whatsoever, I was led to the lower level of the factory, which reminded me of an enormous shed. It was crammed full of coils of rope, old and new, around which clusters of young girls and old women were bustling. Some insignificant character took my name, and I was led to a group of workers sitting cross-legged on the floor, surrounded on all sides by old rope.

The air was dense throughout the lower level, where old ropes were untwisted and pulled apart and new ropes were covered with canvas. Sometimes we were sent up to the second floor, where wagons carried us swiftly around outstretched ropes, which we lubricated with soap and resin. There was no dawdling here—the slightest carelessness could end in tragedy: I myself saw a youth lose three fingers in an instant. We workers ate and drank our tea sitting on dirty coils of rope; after dinner, we curled up on them like kittens and slept. No one brought dinner to the factory: we simply bought hunks of lard or olives and white bread at factory gate for five kopecks and took turns bringing boiling water from the tavern.

The air in the building was thick with resin and soap, and the resin quickly saturated all your clothing: within two or three days, every new worker had acquired the factory's distinctive odor, and within a week, there was no way you could get rid of it. The local landladies didn't like to rent rooms to rope workers—they spread their stench through the whole house.

The women were paid twenty-five kopecks a day; the men, as I recall, got thirty or forty. Most of the women workers were totally rootless: as many of them told me, they had nowhere else to go but the streets. Some had come to work there so as not to burden their families. In short, women were driven to the rope factory by the most pressing need, by the cruelest misfortune. Only women in this situation would put up with the ubiquitous rudeness, the men's disrespectful treatment of them, the pinches and searches as they entered or left the factory.

All the women workers were illiterate. They would have been eager to learn, but when was there time to teach them? After a brief dinner, they caught up on the hours of sleep they'd missed in the morning by curling up on the filthy ropes. By the time we went home, the sun was the thinnest of crescents, sinking into the sea. On holidays, the women couldn't study in their quarters even if they'd wanted to. How, then, could I conduct propaganda among these women, who were so cut off from everyone and everything? Perhaps if I'd remained at the factory longer than two or three months, I might have been able to get something going: a few girls were becoming interested in reading and had begun to drop in at my apartment, and in time I might have been able to propagandize and organize them. But I found conditions at the factory too difficult and depressing to continue working there.

Source 4 from Eva Broido, Memoirs of a Revolutionary, *edited and translated by Vera Broido, pp. 133–135. Copyright © 1967. Reprinted by permission of Oxford University Press.*

4. From the *Memoirs* of Eva Broido, Berlin, 1926

The most important centres of party work were our clubs. In them we concentrated all our propaganda activities: our propaganda was distributed from them, and there the workers came to hear lectures on current affairs. There, too, our members in the Duma came to report to us on their work. Virtually all the organizational work was centred on these clubs—general and special party meetings were held there, party publications were distributed from there, these were the "addresses" of the local district and sub-district branches, there all local news was collected, from there speakers were sent to factory meetings. And these were also the places where enlightened workers—men and women—could meet for friendly exchange of ideas and to read books and newspapers. All clubs aimed above all at having good libraries. And eventually they also encouraged art, there were music and song groups and the like.

At first clubs were exclusively political, but soon their character changed. Propaganda meetings gave place to lectures and discussions of a more general nature, the clubs became "colleges" of Marxism. Representatives of all club committees combined to work out systematic courses of lectures, to provide and distribute the necessary books and to supply book catalogues. Soon, groups of workers asked for courses on scientific subjects. And already in the winter of 1906–7 the programmes included physics, mathematics and technology alongside economics, historical materialism and the history of socialism and the labour movement.

In addition to the clubs there were many "evening schools"; they grew in number as the clubs attracted the attention of the police and were often closed down. These evening schools included some courses for the illiterate, and these were often attended by working-class men and women who were already playing influential roles in the movement.

Apart from their educational functions—varied and important as these were—the clubs provided the workers with their first training grounds in practical politics. This was their main value for the future and for the historical development of the Russian proletariat. But from the very start on democratic principles, the clubs taught the workers the techniques of elections—how to elect and be elected, to accept and exercise responsibility, to organize and lead the movement. It was in the clubs and in the trade unions that the elite of the Russian proletariat was trained. But the trade unions, which sprang up at the same time as the clubs, were more exposed to attacks by the Government and to harassment from the police. They dragged out a precarious, semi-legal existence right up to the outbreak of the World War, when they were practically wiped out.

All in all, the clubs can fairly be described as the pioneers of the new proletarian culture. In the past, after a century under the yoke of absolutism, workers had no place to meet in their leisure hours except the tavern. But now new and better ways of life were being created in the clubs, and this explains the devotion that the workers brought to them.

For the working woman the clubs were of the greatest importance. In earlier days they had even less opportunity than the men to meet outside the home or the factory. Now they loved to come to the clubs; and many of them, too, went on from there to play an important part in the movement. Characteristic of the times is the history of the first "women's club" in St. Petersburg. It was the brain-child of a group of intellectual women and was intended to give the working women a place of their own, where they could discuss their problems unhampered by the presence of men. But the idea of a separate club for women did not go down well with either men or women. It was considered utterly unfair: "Why should women exclude men from their clubs, when they have been enjoying equal rights in the other clubs? We have fought together for equality—now they talk of special rights for women, double rights!"—"If you want equal rights with us, give us equal rights in your women's club!" The indignation was so strong and the opposition so energetic that within a month men were allowed into the "women's club" and soon outnumbered the women—both as members and on the committee—until the club was discovered by the police and closed down. I had no part in the original creation of this club, but in due course I organized several debates there, which were attended by women workers from various factories. I wanted to find out the characteristic traits of life and work of the St. Petersburg working woman and I succeeded in learning a great deal during our informal talks. I assembled much of this material in a booklet, "The Russian Working Woman," which was later published by the party.

Source 5 from Alix Holt, editor and translator, Selected Writings of Alexandra Kollontai, *1977, pp. 42–48, 123–124, 132–139. Reprinted by permission of Lawrence Hill & Co. Publishers, Inc.*

5. From Alexandra Kollontai, *Towards a History of the Working Women's Movement in Russia,* 1920

The revolutionary year of 1905 had a profound effect on the working masses. For the first time the Russian worker sensed his strength and understood that the well-being of the nation rested on his shoulders. In the revolutionary years of 1905 and 1906 the woman worker also became aware of the world around her. She was everywhere. If we wanted to give a record of how women participated in that movement, to list the instances of their active protest and struggle, to give full justice to the self-sacrifice of the proletarian women and their loyalty to the ideals of socialism, we would have to describe the events of the revolution scene by scene. . . .

During the October days, exhausted by their working conditions and their harsh hungry existence, women would leave their machines and bravely deprive their children of the last crust of bread in the name of the common cause. The working woman would call on her male comrades to stop work. Her words were simple, compelling and straight from the heart. She kept up morale and imparted a renewed vigour to the demoralised. The working woman fought on tirelessly and selflessly; the more involved she became in action, the quicker the process of her mental awakening. The working woman gradually came to understand the world she was living in and the injustice of the capitalist system, she began to feel more bitter at all the suffering and all the difficulties women experienced. The voices of the working class began to ring out more clearly and forcefully for the recognition not only of general class demands but of the specific needs and demands of working women. In March 1905 the exclusion of women from the elections of workers' delegates to the Shidlovskii commission[9] aroused deep dissatisfaction; the hardships the men and women had been through together had brought them closer to each other, and it seemed particularly unjust to emphasize woman's inferior status at a time when she had shown herself an able fighter and a worthy citizen. When the woman chosen by the Sarnpsonevskaya factory as one of their seven delegates was ruled by the Shidlovskii commission to be ineligible for such office, indignant women workers from several different factories got together to present the commission with the following protest:

9. **Shidlovskii commission:** a commission, with elected workers' representatives, which the government instituted during the first weeks of the 1905 revolution to deal with the demands of the movement.

The working women deputies are not being allowed to take part in the commission of which you are chairman. This decision is unjust. At the factories and places of manufacture in St. Petersburg there are more women workers than men. In the textile industry the number of women workers increases every year. The men transfer to factories where the wages are higher. The workload of women workers is heavier. The employers take advantage of our helplessness and lack of rights; we get worse treatment than our comrades and we get less pay. When the commission was announced our hearts beat with hope: at last the rime has come, we thought, when the women workers of St. Petersburg can speak out to all Russia, and make known in the name of their sister workers the oppression, insults and humiliations we suffer, about which the male workers know nothing. Then, when we had already chosen our representatives, we were told that only men could be deputies. But we hope that this decision is not final. The government ukase,[10] at any rate, does not distinguish between women workers and the working class as a whole.

Deprived of representation, women workers were shut off from political life at the moment when through the first state Duma the population had its first opportunity to direct the affairs of the country. This seemed a glaringly unjust move against the women who had borne the brunt of the struggle for freedom. Working women frequently attended the meetings held in connection with the elections to the first and second Dumas, noisily expressing their dissatisfaction with a law that prevented their voting over such an important matter as the selection of delegates to the Russian parliament. There were instances in Moscow, for example, where working women broke up meetings with their demonstrations of protest.

The majority of the forty thousand persons who signed the petitions sent to the first and second Dumas demanding that the franchise be extended to women were working women. . . . Women's meetings were especially numerous during 1905 and 1906. Working women attended them willingly; they listened attentively to the bourgeois feminists but did not respond with much enthusiasm, since the speakers gave no suggestion as to how the urgent problems of those enslaved by capital might be solved. The women of the working class suffered from the harsh conditions at work, from hunger and insecurity. Their most urgent demands were: a shorter working day, higher wages, more human treatment from the factory authorities, less police supervision and more scope for "independent action." Such needs were foreign to the bourgeois feminists, who came to the working women with their narrow concerns and exclusively "women's demands."

The political awakening of women was not limited to the urban poor alone. For the first time the Russian peasant woman began to think in a stubborn and resolute way about herself. During the closing months of 1904 and all through 1905 there were continual "women's riots" in the countryside. The Japanese

10. **ukase:** a decree issued by the tsar.

war gave impetus to this movement. The peasant woman, as wife and mother, felt all the horror and hardship, all the social and economic consequences of this ill-fated war. Though her shoulders were already weighed down by a double workload and a double anxiety, she had to answer the call for more food supplies. She, who had always been incapable of standing alone and afraid of everything outside her immediate family circle, was suddenly forced to come face to face with the hostile world of which she had been ignorant. She was made to feel all the humiliation of her inferior status; she experienced all the bitterness of undeserved insults. For the first time the peasant women left their homes and their passivity and ignorance behind, and hurried to the towns to tread the corridors of government institutions in the hope of news of a husband, a son or a father, to make a fuss about allowances or to fight for various other rights. The women saw clearly and with their own eyes the ugliness of reality: they had no rights, and the existing social system was based on falsehood and injustice. They returned to their villages in a sober and hardened mood, their hearts full of bitterness, hatred and anger. In the south, during the summer of 1905, there was a series of "peasant women's riots." With an anger and boldness not usually expected from women the peasant women threatened the troops and the police and frequently gave the requisitioners a beating. Armed with rakes, forks and brooms, the peasant women drove the soldiers out of the villages. This was how they protested against the war. They were, of course, arrested, taken to court and harshly sentenced, but the unrest did not abate. These disturbances were in defence of general peasant interests and of specific women's interests—the two were so closely intertwined that it is impossible to separate them or to see the unrest as part of the "feminist" movement.

Besides the political protests there were others motivated by economic necessity. It was a time of general peasant unrest and strike activity over agricultural matters. The peasant women often took part, urging on their men or sometimes initiating activity: On occasion, when the men were reluctant to make a move, the women would go alone to the landlord's estate with their demands. And armed with what they could lay their hands on, they went out ahead of the village men to face the expeditionary forces. The peasant women, downtrodden by centuries of oppression, found themselves unexpectedly active and indispensable participants in the political drama. Over the period of the revolution they fought, in close unity with their men, in defence of the common peasant interests, and with amazing tact they brought up their own women's needs only when this did not threaten to harm the peasant cause as a whole.

This did not mean that the peasant women remained indifferent to or ignored their own needs as women. On the contrary, the mass entry of peasant women into the general political arena and their participation in the general struggle strengthened and developed their awareness of their position. In 1905 peasant women from Voronezh province sent two delegates to a peasant conference to demand "political rights" and "freedom" for men as well as women. Then there is the historic letter sent by peasant women from the

Voronezh and Tver' provinces to the first Duma. And the telegram from Nogatkino to the deputy Alad'in:

> In this great moment of struggle for rights we, the peasant women of the village of Nogatkino, greet those elected representatives who express their distrust of the government by demanding that the ministry resign. We hope that the representatives will support the people, give them land and freedom, open the doors of the prisons to liberate the fighters for the people's freedom and the people's happiness. We hope that the representatives obtain civil and political rights for themselves and for us Russian women, who are unfairly treated and without rights even within our families. Remember that a slave cannot be the mother of a free citizen. (Authorised by the seventy-five women of Nogatkino.)

The peasant women of the Caucasus were particularly militant in the fight for their rights. In Kutaisi province they brought forward resolutions at peasant meetings demanding that they be given equal political rights with men. There were women among the deputies to a meeting held in Tiflis province, where representatives from both the urban and the rural areas gathered to discuss the question of introducing the *zemstvo* system into the Caucasus, and these women were insistent on the need for women's rights.

Alongside the demands for political equality, peasant women everywhere were naturally vocal in defence of their economic interests; the question of the allocation of land was as much a cause of concern for the peasant women as for their men. In some areas the peasant women warmly supported the idea of confiscating privately-owned land, but lost their enthusiasm when it seemed that women might not benefit directly from the redistribution. "If they take the land from the landowners and give it only to the men, that will mean absolute enslavement for us women," was their reaction. "At the moment we at least earn our own kopeks, but if they divide up the land like that we would be simply working for the men instead of the landowner." However, the fears of the peasant women were completely unfounded, because out of purely economic considerations the peasants were forced to demand land for the "female souls" too. The agrarian interests of the peasant men and peasant women are so closely entwined that in struggling for the abolition of the existing oppressive land relations the peasants were fighting for the economic interests of their women. And at the same time the peasant women, while fighting for the economic and political interests of the peasantry as a whole, learned to fight for the special needs and demands of women. This was also true of the working women who fought unflaggingly in the general liberation movement, and who did even more than their country sisters to prepare public opinion to accept the principle of the equality of women. The realisation of civil equality for women in Soviet Russia was made possible by the spontaneous struggle of the masses of working and peasant women that came with the first Russian revolution in 1905.

[287]

Source 6 from Gail Warshofsky Lapidus, Women in Soviet Society: Equality, Development and Social Change *(Berkeley: University of California Press, 1978), p. 33.*

6. Petition to the Duma, 1906

We, peasant women of Tver gubernia, address ourselves to the honourable members of the State Duma elected from our gubernia. We are dissatisfied with our status. Our husbands and lads are glad to go out with us, but as far as the talk that is going on just now about the land and new laws is concerned, they simply will not talk sense to us. There was a time when, although our men might beat us now and then, we nevertheless decided our affairs together. Now they tell us: "You are not fit company for us. We shall go to the State Duma and take part in the government, perhaps not ourselves, but we will elect members. If the law had made us equal with you, then we would have asked your opinion." So now it happens that women and girls are pushed aside as people of no consequence, and are unable to decide anything about their own lives. This law is wrong; it leads to discord between women and men, and even enmity. . . . We lived in misery together, but when it got so far that everyone may live according to the law, we found we are not needed. . . . And they, the men, do not understand our women's needs. We are able to discuss things no worse than they. We have a common interest in all our affairs, so allow the women to take a hand in deciding them.

Source 7 from Linda Harriet Edmondson, Feminism in Russia, 1900–1917 *(London: Heinemann, 1984), p. 166.*

7. Petition to the Provisional
Government, 1917

We have come here to remind you that women were your faithful comrades in the gigantic struggle for the freedom of the Russian people; that they also have been filling up the prisons, and boldly marched to the galleys. The best of us looked into the eyes of death without fear. Here at my side stands V. N. Figner,[11] who has been struggling all her life for what has now been obtained.

11. **V. N. Figner:** Vera Figner was one of the members of the People's Will, the group that assassinated the szar in 1881. She was arrested in 1883 and spent the next twenty years in prison.

We declare that the Constituent Assembly[12] in which only one half of the population will be represented can in no wise be regarded as expressing the will of the whole people, but only half of it.

We want no more promises of good will. We have had enough of them! We demand an official and clear answer—that the women will have votes in the Constituent Assembly.

Sources 8 and 9 from Alix Holt, editor and translator, Selected Writings of Alexandra Kollontai, *1977, pp. 42–48; pp. 123–124; pp. 132–139. Reprinted by permisision of Lawrence Hill & Co. Publishers, Inc.*

8. Alexandra Kollontai, "In the Front Line of Fire," *Pravda*, May 7, 1917

"If we close down, you'll suffer—you'll be walking the streets without work." That's how the owners of the laundries try to frighten their women workers. This is the usual method used by the employers to scare their hired slaves. But the laundresses have no need to fear such threats. Just because the owners shut down, seeking more profitable investment for their capital, this does not mean that the demand for laundries disappears. Laundry workers are still needed and that means there is a way out of the situation, particularly now that the "New Russia" is being built.

The town itself must shoulder the responsibility of organising municipal laundries in all areas, and of organising them in such a way that the work is made easier by machines and technology, the working day does not exceed eight hours, wages are established by agreement between the municipality and the laundresses' union, a special cloakroom is provided where the working women can change into dry clothes after work, and much else besides is done to lighten the hard labour of the laundry workers.

During the elections to the regional and central town dumas the laundresses and all class-conscious, organised workers must express their support for these demands. This would be a clear and practical reply to the threat of redundancy and unemployment with which the employers attempt to intimidate the women on strike. It would then be the employers and [not] the laundresses who would be forced to swallow their pride and make concessions.

At the present moment the strike continues, but the employers are using all means at their disposal to break the firm stand of the three thousand women

12. **Constituent Assembly:** the Provisional Government promised that it would soon call for elections to a Constituent Assembly, which would write a constitution for Russia. The Constituent Assembly met for only one day in January 1918 before it was dispersed by Bolshevik troops.

workers organised in the union. The employers are acting in the most outrageous and insolent manner. They are trying to set up their own employers' union of strike-breakers, and when the organised women come to call out these women, who through their lack of understanding of their class interests are jeopardising the common cause, they are not only met with threats and foul language; there was one instance where a woman agitator had boiling water thrown at her, and in one enterprise the proprietress tried to use a revolver.

The employers do not let slip any opportunity to use violence and slander. The working women have only one method of self-defence—*organisation and unity.* By fighting for better working conditions in the laundries, for an eight-hour day and for a minimum wage of four rubles a day, the women are fighting not only for themselves but for all working people. The men and women working in other sections of the economy must understand this. The victory of the laundresses will be a fresh victory for the whole proletariat. But in order to guarantee victory a flow of aid is necessary; money is needed. We cannot, we must not deny our material and moral support to those who are fighting for the workers' cause and are bearing the hardships of strike-action.

Every gathering or meeting of working men and women should express its solidarity with the firm struggle waged by the laundry women and should make a collection for these women strikers. The Soviet of Workers' and Soldiers' Deputies[13] should declare their solidarity with the working women, for the women are fighting to force the employers to accede to demands passed by the Soviet. The refusal of the employers to fulfil these demands is thus a *direct challenge to Soviet.* Comrades, let us hasten to the aid of those who now stand in the trenches, defending the workers' cause; let us support those who are now in the "line of fire," facing the attacks of the capitalist employers.

9. Alexandra Kollontai, from the Pamphlet "Working Woman and Mother," 1914

Children are drying. The children of working men and women die like files. One million graves. One million sorrowing mothers. But whose children die? When death goes harvesting spring flowers, whose children fall to the scythe? As one would imagine, death gathers the poorest harvest amongst the wealthy families where the children live in warmth and comfort and are suckled on the milk of their mother or wet-nurse. In the families of royalty, only six or seven of every hundred new-born children die. In the workers' families, from thirty to forty-five die. . . . Death makes a firm place for itself in the homes of working-class families because such families are poor, their homes are overcrowded and damp, and the sunlight does not reach the

13. **Soviet of Workers' and Soldiers' Deputies:** the council formed in Petrograd to demand rights for workers.

basement; because where there are too many people, it is usually dirty; and because the working-class mother does not have the opportunity to care for her children properly. Science has established that artificial feeding is the worst enemy of the child: five times more children fed on cow's milk and fifteen times more children fed with other foods die than those who are breast fed. But how is the woman who works outside the home, at the factory or in a workshop to breast-feed her child? She is lucky if the money stretches to buying cow's milk; that does not happen all the time. And what sort of milk do the tradesmen sell to working mothers anyway? Chalk mixed with water. Consequently, 60% of the babies that die, die from diseases of the stomach. Many others die from what the doctors like to call "the inability to live": the mother worn out by her hard physical labour gives birth prematurely, or the child is poisoned by the factory fumes while still in the womb. How can the woman of the working class possibly fulfil her maternal obligations? . . .

Is there a solution to the problem?

If children are to be stillborn, born crippled or born to die like flies, is there any point in the working woman becoming pregnant? Are all the trials of childbirth worthwhile if the working woman has to abandon her children to the winds of chance when they are still so tiny? However much she wants to bring her child up properly, she does not have the time to look after it and care for it. Since this is the case, is it not better simply to avoid maternity?

Many working women are beginning to think twice about having children. They have not got the strength to bear the cross. Is there a solution to the problem? Do working women have to deprive themselves of the last joy that is left them in life? Life has hurt her, poverty gives her no peace, and the factory drains her strength; does this mean that the working woman must give up the right to the joys of having children? Give up without a fight? Without trying to win the right which nature has given every living creature and every dumb animal? Is there an alternative? Of course there is, but not every working woman is yet aware of it. . . .

How can the law help?

The first thing that can be done and the first thing that working men and women are doing in every country is to see that the law defends the working mother. Since poverty and insecurity are forcing women to take up work, and since the number of women out working is increasing every year, the very least that can be done is to make sure that hired labour does not become the "grave of maternity." The law must intervene to help women to combine work and maternity.

Men and women workers everywhere are demanding a complete ban on night work for women and young people, an eight-hour day for all workers, and a ban on the employment of children under sixteen years of age. They are demanding that young girls and boys over sixteen years of age be allowed to work only half the day. This is important, especially from the point of view of the future mother, since between the years of sixteen and eighteen the girl is growing and developing into a woman. If her strength is undermined during these years her chances of healthy motherhood are lost forever.

The law should state categorically that working conditions and the whole work situation must not threaten a woman's health; harmful methods of production should be replaced by safe methods or completely done away with; heavy work with weights or foot-propelled machines etc. should be mechanised; workrooms should be kept clean and there should be no extremes of temperature; toilets, washrooms and dining rooms should be provided, etc. These demands can be won—they have already been encountered in the model factories—but the factory-owners do not usually like to fork out the money. All adjustments and improvements are expensive, and human life is so cheap.

A law to the effect that women should sit wherever possible is very important. It is also vital that substantial and not merely nominal fines are levied against factory owners who infringe the law. The job of seeing that the law is carried out should be entrusted not only to the factory inspectors but also to representatives elected by the workers.

The workers' party in every country demands that there should be maternity insurance schemes that cover all women irrespective of the nature of their job, no matter whether a woman is a servant, a factory worker, a craftswoman or a poor peasant woman. Benefits must be provided before and after birth, for a period of sixteen weeks. A woman should continue receiving benefits if the doctor finds that she has not sufficiently recovered or that the child is not sufficiently strong. . . .

Responsibility for ensuring that the law is observed and that the woman in childbirth receives everything to which she is entitled must lie with delegates elected from among the working women. Pregnant and nursing mothers must have the legal right to receive free milk and, where necessary, clothes for the new baby at the expense of the town or village. The workers' party also demands that the town, *zemstvo* or insurance bureau build creches for young children at each factory. The money for this should be supplied by the factory owner, the town or the *zemstvo*. These creches must be organised so that each nursing mother can easily visit and feed her baby in the breaks from work that the law allows. The creche must be run not by philanthropic ladies but by the working mothers themselves.

These measures must not be stamped with the bitter label of "philanthropy." Every member of society—and that means every working woman and every citizen, male and female—has the right to demand that the state and community concern itself with the welfare of all. Why do people form a state, if not for this purpose? At the moment there is no government anywhere in the world that cares for its children. Working men and women in all countries are fighting for a society and government that will really become a big happy family, where all children will be equal and the family will care equally for all.

Then maternity will be a different experience, and death will cease to gather such an abundant harvest among the new-born.

What must every working woman do?

How are all these demands to be won? What action must be taken? Every working-class woman, every woman who reads this pamphlet must throw off her indifference and begin to support the working-class movement, which is fighting for these demands and is shaping the old world into a better future where mothers will no longer weep bitter tears and where the cross of maternity will become a great joy and a great pride. We must say to ourselves, "There is strength in unity"; the more of us working women join the working-class movement, the greater will be our strength and the quicker we will get what we want. Our happiness and the life and future of our children are at stake.

QUESTIONS TO CONSIDER

As with any historical source, in evaluating the material in this chapter you must consider why a specific piece was written. Sources 1 through 4 are memoirs, written after the fact by authors describing their personal experiences. Recall your study in Chapter 2 of the memoirist St.-Simon. Why might a person choose to write memoirs? How might the fact that the author was looking back at the events alter his or her perspective? Eva Broido wrote her memoirs after the Bolshevik Revolution, when she was in exile in England. How might this have affected what she wrote? Alexandra Kollontai's description of women's actions in the 1905 revolution (Source 5) was written in the early 1920s, also after the fact and after the Bolshevik Revolution, though she was a prominent member of the party leadership rather than an exile when it was published. How might these circumstances have affected the way her history was written?

Sources 6 and 7 simply quote petitions brought by women, but the last two pieces by Kollontai were again written with very specific purposes in mind. What does the author hope these writings will do? Alexandra Kollontai was the only prominent woman among the Bolshevik leadership other than Lenin's wife, Nadezhda Krupskaya, and she was largely responsible for persuading the party to address women's issues. How might Kollontai's unique position have affected what or the way she wrote? Would you expect the new Soviet government to accept the changes she proposes?

The aims of the women revolutionaries were not static but changed over time as the political situation changed. Do you see any changes in aims or tactics within Sources 1 through 4? How would you compare the aims of the authors of Sources 1 through 4 with those of Kollontai?

Though class background alone is not enough to explain an author's ideas, her family background, level of education, and occupation certainly shape her ideas and interpretation of events to some degree. Look again at the short description of each author. How might her family background have affected her ideas and actions? Why do you think so many women revolutionaries and advocates of workers' rights came from the middle rather than working classes?

Our primary task in this chapter is to assess the role of gender rather than class or education in shaping women's lives. Looking at your list and considering what you have read, what aims did women revolutionaries share with their male comrades? What objectives did some of them have that might have differed from those of the men in their movements?

What special problems did women revolutionaries face and how might these have affected their ideas?

You are now ready not only to answer the questions posed in this chapter but also to rewrite the narrative of the Russian revolutionary movements presented in your text. Are there any names or groups or issues that should be added? How might the language of the text be changed to incorporate what you have learned here? Think about other sections of the text—for example, descriptions of the socialist movements of western Europe. Would you expect that similar revisions might be necessary?

EPILOGUE

The women involved in the revolutionary movements of the 1870s— Elizaveta Kovalskaia, Olga Liubatovich, Praskovia Ivanovskaia, and others—were all arrested around the time of the tsar's assassination and spent long years in prison or in exile in Siberia. The groups to which they belonged, such as the People's Will, were destroyed by the police, and later revolutionary movements in Russia generally did not involve so large a proportion of women. Though their actions did not accomplish their aims, women revolutionaries were highly praised by their male comrades and survived Siberian exile more successfully than male revolutionaries because they took better care of each other. Many of them lived to see the revolutions of

1917, returning from Siberia once the tsarist government had been abolished. Many women revolutionaries who had been in voluntary exile abroad also returned to Russia in 1917, just as Lenin did.

The 1905 revolution did bring about some political changes, but none that proved especially beneficial to women. In fact, women's political status declined compared to that of men: before the 1905 revolution only a small group—the tsar and his advisers—held any real political power, whereas after the revolution some groups of men did. Gender became an important determinant in dividing those with a political voice from those without one, in the same way that it had after the American and French revolutions.

Women received the right to vote after the February Revolution of 1917, largely because of petitions like the one you read here, and they supported some of the moves of the new Provisional Government. Other policies of the new government, such as continuing the war effort and not carrying out land reforms, were opposed by large numbers of women and men, who lent their support to the Bolsheviks in their efforts to abolish the Provisional Government.

When the Bolsheviks took over after the October Revolution, they made sweeping changes in women's legal and economic status. Marriage became a civil ceremony; women workers were to receive equal pay for equal work, maternity leave, and breaks during the workday to nurse their infants. In 1918 a new Family Code was passed that tried to equalize relations between spouses. Wives could keep their own earnings and their own names as well as retain greater control over their children; divorce by either spouse was made much easier. Arguing that women workers could never achieve equality so long as they had the extra burden of housework and child care, Alexandra Kollontai and a few others pushed for the opening of communal kitchens, laundries, nurseries, and day-care centers.

Some of the Bolshevik leadership (all of whom were male) accepted Kollontai's ideas in principle, but their primary concern was fighting the civil war, modernizing the economy, and establishing a socialist system. Money and resources were scarce, so day-care centers and similar programs never received much funding; there was considerable resistance or indifference to such programs anyway. The dislocation caused by the war meant many women and children were homeless, and their wages never rose enough to allow women to provide for themselves easily. Simplified divorce led many men to abandon their wives and children, and a large number of women turned to prostitution to support themselves. In 1926 the Family Code was revised, making men again financially responsible for their children and declaring that any couple living together was to be considered legally married. In the short run, this alteration in the law served to benefit women because it eased the worst problems; in the long run, however, it harmed the women's movement by making the support of women and children an individual, rather than a collective, matter. Because of war deaths, women greatly outnumbered men. The many women who consequently never married needed to support themselves, a fact often overlooked by Soviet leadership, who chose to view the new Family Code as the solution to all women's problems. Women's rights lost their most powerful proponent when Lenin removed Kollontai from her position as head of the women's bureau. She was later appointed ambassador to Norway, which further lessened her influence.

Passing laws, in fact, proved easier than implementing them and changing attitudes. The equality between men and women envisioned by Kollontai was never achieved, and the Stalinist period brought further restrictions. Interested in women as workers and mothers of future workers, the Soviet leadership worried about the falling birth rate; it consequently restricted divorce, outlawed abortion (the only form of birth control available to most women), and championed motherhood as of supreme importance to the state. These changes were not accompanied by adequate practical assistance for working mothers, who continued to do double duty in the factory and at home. As a consequence, a smaller percentage of women continued in school or received promotions. In addition, the Stalinist emphasis on heavy industry meant crowded housing, few consumer goods, and a hard life for most people, especially working women, who carried the burden of household tasks and shopping.

After Stalin's death social restrictions eased somewhat. Divorce was made easier, and abortion was legalized again in 1955. Women were guaranteed paid maternity leave and, in theory, the opportunity to resume their previous jobs (in this the Soviet Union was ahead of the United States). A large share of the professional class consisted of women. Soviet women were still not politically or economically equal to men, however. Very few women attained the upper levels of the political hierarchy (about the same percentage as in the United States), and women still did almost all domestic work.

The end of the Soviet Union in 1991 brought dramatic changes to everyone in Russia. The economy was restructured from vast state-run enterprises to private businesses, which led to large-scale unemployment and widespread poverty. A few people became extremely wealthy, but most people suffered from the disappearance of government-subsidized food,

housing, and medical care; prices soared, and the elderly and those on fixed incomes were particularly affected. Rising oil prices in the 2000s have led to somewhat better conditions, but life expectancies remain lower than they were in 1990, with alcoholism and drug use contributing to high death rates. The Communist party is no longer the only political party allowed, but many people yearn for the stability of the Soviet era. Vladimir Putin, the president of Russia since 2000, has initiated reforms that bring energy companies and the media back under state control. Putin has strong support from a majority of the Russian people, though others worry that his centralization of power limits democracy.

Women have shared the difficulties of the post-Soviet era with men. Alcoholism and the resultant lower life expectancy are more common among men than women, but women outnumber men among the poor. Few women have been able to take advantage of opportunities offered in the new capitalist enterprises, and the closing of child-care facilities has made the lives of many working women harder. Consumer goods are more available, but many people do not have the money to purchase them. As in the Soviet era, very few women have high political positions, and women continue to do the majority of work in the household.

The protests that contributed to the end of the Soviet Union included a significant number of women, however, and younger women are demanding improvements in their lives at a faster pace. Putin's control of newspapers and television stations makes it more difficult to express opinions that differ from those of the government than it was during the 1990s, but criticisms still emerge. Thus at least a portion of Russian women are following in the long tradition of protest and action begun by their great-grandmothers over one hundred years ago.

CHAPTER ELEVEN

WORLD WAR I:

TOTAL WAR

In the first days of August 1914, every major capital city in Europe was the scene of enthusiastic patriotic demonstrations in favor of the declarations of war that began World War I. All confidently predicted victory for their own nation, and all expected a short war. Emperor William II (Kaiser Wilhelm II) told German troops departing for the front, "You will be home before the leaves have fallen from the trees." The war indeed ended in autumn, but it was the autumn of 1918, not 1914. Previous military history did not prepare Europeans in any way for the war they were to undertake in 1914.

Europe's last general war had ended in 1815 with Napoleon's defeat at Waterloo. Subsequent nineteenth-century conflicts never involved all the great powers, and they were invariably short wars. The Prussians, for example, had defeated Austria in six weeks during the Austro-Prussian War of 1866. In the last nineteenth-century conflict involving major powers, the Franco-Prussian War of 1870–1871, France and Prussia had signed an armistice after a little over twenty-seven weeks of combat.

These nineteenth-century wars after Waterloo were also highly limited conflicts, involving relatively small professional armies whose weapons and tactics differed little from those of the Napoleonic era. Civilian populations seldom felt much impact from such conflicts, although Paris endured a siege of eighteen weeks in the Franco-Prussian War.

The war on which Europeans so enthusiastically embarked in 1914 proved far different from the 1870–1871 conflict. The prewar alliance system meant that, for the first time in a century, all the great powers were at war, making the scope of the hostilities greater than in any recent fighting. Moreover, the conflict quickly became a world war as the belligerents fought one another outside Europe and as non-European powers such as Japan and the United States joined the ranks of warring nations.

Even more significant than the number of nations engaged in the conflict, however, was the nature of the war they fought. The Industrial Revolution of the nineteenth century had brought technical changes to warfare that were to transform the 1914 conflict into the Western world's first modern, total war. This would be a war of tremendous cost to both soldiers and civilians, a struggle requiring effort and sacrifice by every citizen of the warring countries.

Modern railroads and motorized transport permitted belligerent nations to bring the full weight of their new industrial strengths to the battlefields of World War I. Both sides for the first time made extensive use of the machine gun as well as new, longer-range heavy artillery. Whole new weapons systems included flame throwers, poison gas, the tank, the airplane, the lighter-than-air dirigible, and the submarine.

Generals trained in an earlier era of warfare failed at first to understand the increased destructive capacity of these new weapons and practiced military tactics of 1870 in fighting the war's first battles. As before, they attacked the enemy with massed infantrymen armed with bayonets fixed, flags flying, drums sounding, and led by officers in dress uniforms complete with white gloves. This was the kind of war Europeans had enthusiastically anticipated in 1914, but because of modern firepower, casualties in such attacks were extremely heavy—indeed, completely unprecedented.

Especially in western Europe, such losses resulted in increased reliance on what has been called the "infantryman's best friend," the shovel. To avoid the firepower of the new modern weaponry, opposing armies dug into the earth, and by Christmas 1914 they opposed each other in 466 miles of trenches stretching through France from the English Channel to the border of Switzerland. These trenches represented stalemate. They were separated by "No Man's Land," the open space an attacker had to cross to reach the enemy. Swept with machine gun and artillery fire and blocked by barbed wire and other obstacles, "No Man's Land" was an area that an attacking force could cross only with great losses. In such circumstances, neither side could achieve the traditional decisive breakthrough into the enemy's lines. Field Marshal Horatio Kitchener, an experienced commander of the old school of warfare and British secretary for war until 1916, expressed the frustration of many about such combat: "I don't know what is to be done—this isn't war."

In their efforts to achieve victory, generals and statesmen sought to break the stalemate in a number of ways that extended the impact of World War I. The warring nations mobilized unprecedented numbers of men; over 70 million were called to military service. Never before had so large a part of Europe's population been put in uniform: England mobilized 53 percent of its male population of military age in 1914 to 1918, and France and Germany called on the service of some 80 percent of their males of draft age.

Each warring government took unprecedented steps to meet its forces' needs for food, material, and ammunition. Governments rationed consumer goods to provide for their armies. England and Germany asserted extraordinary government control over raw materials, privately owned production facilities, and civilian labor in the name of war production.

Civilians felt the war in other ways, too. The stalemate meant a long war, and governments soon recognized that they could not maintain their war efforts during a long conflict if civilian morale broke. They therefore attempted to exert total control over news and public opinion, often at the expense of their citizens' rights. They censored the press, used propaganda to maintain civilian morale, and placed critics under surveillance or arrest.

The warring nations also recognized the equal importance of the home front to their enemies in achieving victory. As a result, civilians experienced the war in unprecedented ways. Blockades by surface fleets and submarine attacks on shipping aimed at slowing war production and destroying civilian morale by cutting off vital shipments of raw materials and food to enemy countries. New weapons systems also placed civilians in actual physical danger. Warring nations dropped bombs on their enemies' cities from dirigibles and primitive bomber aircraft, and long-range artillery rained shells on population centers miles from battlefronts.

This was the world's first total war; until the outbreak of another such war in 1939, participants remembered it as the "Great War." Your task in this chapter is to assess the all-encompassing nature of modern warfare through several different kinds of sources. Why was World War I different from previous wars? What impact did it have on the soldiers at the front? How did it affect civilians at home?

SOURCES AND METHOD

In this chapter we have assembled a variety of evidence, and we have arranged it to illustrate three aspects of World War I. We open with sources illustrating Europe's rush to war in 1914 amid an almost universal burst of enthusiasm and nationalist sentiment. A second group of sources presents the front-line experiences of the millions of men mobilized by their governments for military service. Finally, a third group of sources demonstrates the war's impact on European civilians on the home front.

A large portion of this chapter's evidence consists of literary sources, the work of young intellectuals who often welcomed the war as a conflict that would sweep away a decadent cultural life and replace it with one more vital.

Many talented and well-educated men sought to hasten this cultural transformation by volunteering for military service. Front-line combat, however, soon showed these young men that they were caught up in a war unlike any previous struggle.

Conscious of the uniqueness of their battlefield experience and aware that their front-line service would leave them forever changed, many made an effort to record their experiences. Letters, diaries, autobiographical works, paintings, and sketches by individual soldiers all supplement the dry official records kept by war ministries of the participating countries and give the historian an excellent sense of battlefield realities and their impact. Your main sources in this chapter comprise creative works, in the form of poetry and fiction, in which a number of talented soldiers sought to convey the experience of modern war and its effect on them.

Literature can be a valuable source for the student of history in understanding the past. We must, however, stay fully aware of its limits as well as its value. The utility of literature as a historical source is somewhat limited by its very nature: As the product of an individual, it reflects personal and social perspectives that must be identified. Most of the authors represented here, for example, came from the middle or upper classes because such individuals, not the sons of the working classes, had the education to write works of enduring significance. With such a social background, many served as officers, and the conditions they endured were in some ways better than those of the enlisted men: The war was often significantly worse for a private than for a captain.

Individuals have opinions, too, and opinions often invade war literature. The soldier often portrayed himself as a victim of forces beyond his control: a powerful government, modern technology, or the military authorities. As historians, we must note these opinions because they convey to us the individual's reaction to the war, but we must look beyond them as well to discern the objective wartime conditions the author was recording.

Not all chroniclers of the war were equally well placed to understand the war. We must ask if each work was based on actual front-line experience. If not, we should discount it as historical evidence. We must also ask if an author's work was written in the midst of war, in which case it may reflect the passions of the moment. If the work was written after the war, the author's selective memory for certain facts may have influenced his or her work. The evidence in this chapter presents works by front-line authors written at the outbreak of the war, at the time of their combat experiences, and after the war. Indeed, the great majority of literary works on the war appeared, like the literature on Vietnam, about a decade after the cessation of hostilities. Perhaps a gestation period is necessary for the minds of many to analyze the combat experience. If that is the case, we must recognize the frailty of the human memory and measure the message of postwar literature against those writings composed in the heat of battle.

Once the various viewpoints and perspectives are identified, however, a student of history can obtain an excellent sense of World War I through works of poetry and fiction. These works present the war in human terms far more vividly than do government reports and statistics. To assist your reading, some information on each of the writers presented here is in order. We turn first to the rush to war.

Rupert Brooke (1887–1915), the author of Source 1, was a graduate of Cambridge University and one of England's most promising young poets when he enlisted in September 1914 as a sublieutenant in the Royal Naval Division, a land force attached to the British navy. After brief service in Belgium in 1914, his unit was dispatched to the Middle East in 1915 as part of the British and French attack on the Turks at Gallipoli—a strategy designed to open the straits to the Black Sea so that Western supplies could reach Russia. (The attack itself, in which many Australian and New Zealand troops perished, was generally deemed a disaster.) Not quite twenty-eight years of age, Brooke died of blood poisoning en route to Gallipoli and was buried on the island of Skyros, Greece, home of Achilles of the ancient Homeric myths. The selection by Brooke presented here, the poem "Peace," reflects the romanticism characteristic of much prewar English poetry but also expresses Brooke's response to the war. What were his sensations as he watched the war engulf Europe? How does he characterize the spirit of pre–World War I Europe? What will awaken that spirit? Why do you think his poem suggests that Brooke would welcome death?

A remarkable Frenchman, Charles Péguy (1873–1914), wrote Source 2, "Blessed Are." Péguy was a talented poet and essayist, much of whose work expresses his nationalism as well as his concern for the poor and the cause of social justice. His writings also reflect a remarkable spiritual journey. Raised a Catholic, his dislike for the authoritarian character of the Church grew by the time he reached adulthood, and he declared himself an atheist about 1893. In 1908, however, he rediscovered a deep religious faith, though he kept his distance from the institutional Church and probably never participated in its sacramental life. Péguy's later writings bear witness to this religiosity as well as to his continued concern for his fellow man and his French nationalism.

Péguy was forty-one when war broke out in 1914, and he therefore qualified for the army reserve, not front-line duty. Always a man of action, however, he volunteered for active service. Commissioned a lieutenant of infantry, he died leading his men in an attack on September 5, 1914. Remember the details of his life as you read "Blessed Are." What elements of Péguy's thought does the poem combine? What was his view of war? Although Péguy's national and religious background was different from that of the English Protestant Brooke, what ideas did he share with Brooke? Why do you think other intellectuals also drew on the romanticism and nationalism of the late nineteenth and early twentieth centuries to welcome war?

Source 3, the "Hymn of Hate," is the work of the German poet Ernst Lissauer (1882–1937), who served as a private in the German army. Composed as the war broke out, the poem was soon set to music and became very popular in Germany. To appreciate its significance fully, you may wish to review in your textbook the sections on nineteenth-century nationalism and on the international rivalries that contributed to World War I. Which nation do the Germans see as their archenemy? Why, after consulting your textbook, do you think this country was so hated in Germany? What do these three sources reveal about Europeans' attitudes as they went to war in 1914?

With Source 4, we turn to the grim realities of the front-line experience. Sources 4 and 5 are actual combat photographs that offer exceptional evidence of wartime conditions. By 1914, technical advances in photography had made the camera portable enough so that it could be carried into combat zones to record the realities of war. The camera could thus show the combatants of World War I in action, and not in the posed scenes generally photographed behind the firing lines in late-nineteenth-century wars.

Source 4 is a photograph of a German infantry unit advancing in their autumn 1912 maneuvers. The German army, like many European armies, held elaborate annual maneuvers, also sometimes called war games, prior to the outbreak of World War I in 1914. In maneuvers, large portions of the nation's army practiced the tactics that they planned to employ in the next war, and military analysts carefully observed such war games for what they revealed of an army's techniques of warfare. Those analysts observed that in 1914 all large armies retained

traditional tactics based on the advance of massed infantry units that sought ultimate engagement with the enemy in bayonet fighting. Thus, French tacticians wrote of the *attaque à outrance* ("attack at the point of a knife"), Russian regulations required infantrymen to keep bayonets fixed to their rifles in permanent readiness for such attack, and the authors of the German army's infantry manual asserted their commitment to the traditional infantry offensive "cost what it may."

Examine Source 4 for what it reveals about the tactics that the German army, like most other European forces, brought to the early days of World War I. Notice that the soldiers advance in tight formation and in straight ranks commanded by mounted officers and that they employ infantry tactics that had changed little in over two centuries. Nevertheless, the weapons of war had changed dramatically by 1914. In a real battle, these soldiers' objective would have been defended by modern artillery and machine guns capable of firing 400 or 500 rounds per minute. What effect do you think such modern firepower would have had on this attack force? Why might you conclude that such tactics revealed the lack of preparation of all armies for the realities of modern warfare in 1914? Why would you not be surprised to learn that the French army, which also used such tactics, suffered staggering losses in the war's first four months (August to December, 1914) totaling an estimated 754,000 casualties (dead, wounded, missing in action, and captured)? What tactics might seem more appropriate than those employed in the war's first months?

Source 5 is a photo of British infantry going "over the top," that is, exiting a trench and moving out into "No Man's Land," the open area between their own trenches and those of their opponents swept by artillery and machine gun fire. The specific object of this attack in April 1918 was Kemmel Hill, a high point in the Flanders region of Belgium. How have infantry tactics changed since 1914? What was the purpose of the position from which the soldiers are shown attacking? How have infantry tactics remained the same? What evidence do you find of modern military technology in this photograph? Note especially the helmets and gas masks that the soldiers wear and the barbed wire strung in front of their trench.

With Source 6, we return to the analysis of literary evidence. Novelists also drew on their wartime experiences. Henri Barbusse (1873–1935), the author of *Under Fire,* worked as a French government employee and a journalist before World War I. Politically a socialist, he was swept up by the general surge of patriotism in 1914 and volunteered for military service. He served in the French army from 1914 through the early days of the great Battle of Verdun in 1916, when he was wounded and left the service. In *Under Fire,* which was written in the trenches, he attempted to portray realistically the physical and psychological impact of modern war. The novel was recognized early as an important work and received France's most prestigious literary award, the Goncourt Prize, in 1916.

The excerpt presented as Source 6 describes an attack on the Germans by veteran French infantrymen led by their trusted Corporal Bertrand. How does Barbusse describe modern warfare?

Excerpts from a second novel, *All Quiet on the Western Front* (Source 7), offer us the view of the losing side in the war. Its author, Erich Maria Remarque (1898–1970), grew up the son of a German bookbinder. Drafted at the age of eighteen, he served in the German army from 1916 to the war's end. Remarque had already begun to write before his military service, and his *All Quiet on the Western Front* represented such a realistic picture of the war that many perceived it as an attack on German patriotism. As a consequence, the novel was among the first batch of books burned by the Nazis in 1933. How does Remarque describe the experience of modern warfare? What effect did it have on the many youthful front-line soldiers like the main character, Paul Baumer? What impact did that war have on German civilians?

Two poems conclude our literary evidence on World War I. Source 8, "Dulce et Decorum Est" ("It is sweet and fitting"), is the work of Wilfred Owen (1893–1918). Owen studied briefly at the University of London before the war, intending a career in the clergy. He enlisted in the British army in 1915, aged twenty-two, and as an infantry lieutenant served in France in the great Battle of the Somme. Owen was wounded three times in 1917 and recuperated in England, where he met Siegfried Sassoon, author of the next selection, who encouraged Owen in his writing. After recovering from his wounds, Owen again served on the western front. He received the Military Cross for bravery in October 1918 and died leading his men in an attack on November 4, 1918, one week before the war's end.

Owen's battlefield experiences shaped his poetry. "Dulce et Decorum Est" is titled with a phrase from the Roman poet Horace, whose work would have been familiar to all upper-class English schoolboys of Owen's day. How would you summarize Owen's view of the war, especially his opinion of those on the home front who blindly supported it?

Siegfried Sassoon (1886–1967), author of "The General" (Source 9), was seven years older than his friend Owen, and his poetic response to the war is the reaction of one with greater experience of life and its problems. A Cambridge graduate like Rupert Brooke, he had written poetry since his boyhood. The war transformed Sassoon from an upper-class young man who enjoyed the hunt to a postwar social activist and socialist. Although he served with great bravery as a front-line officer, he experienced an increasingly bitter sense of the war's futility. Wounded in 1917, he had a long convalescence in England and went through an emotional crisis as he attempted to balance his growing pacifism with his enduring sense of duty and the comradeship he felt with those still on the front line. Sassoon's response was to throw away his Military Cross awarded for bravery and to draft a letter of protest of the war to his commanding officer. Stating that a war undertaken as one of defense had become a war of conquest, he declared, "I can no longer be a party to prolong those sufferings for ends which I believe to be evil and unjust." Such a letter from an officer in wartime would normally have resulted in court-martial. Intervention of friends on his behalf led instead to Sassoon's treatment for shell shock, a common psychological problem among front-line troops. It was during his hospitalization for this treatment that Sassoon met Owen. Returning to service in 1918, Sassoon was wounded again but lived to survive the war. His poem, "The General," is very brief, but it reflects Sassoon's attitude toward the war. How does Sassoon view the general?

Participants in the war left other personal records of the conflict in the form of letters and autobiographical works. The letter in Source 10 records such a remarkable event in the midst of total war that people then, as now, tended to doubt that it ever occurred. Nevertheless, the story of this anonymous German soldier can be verified in the writings of his battlefield opponents. How had initial enthusiasm for the war and hatred of the enemy fared at the front? Why?

With Source 11, we turn to the war's impact on civilians. World War I was the first conflict to demand great participation in the war effort from women. Yet, oddly, few left extensive written records of the war's effect on them. Source 11, drawn from the Englishwoman Vera Brittain's (1893–1970) *The Testament of Youth,* is one of the few works we have by a woman. A student at Oxford when England declared war, Brittain left her studies shortly after for service as a nurse, and her book in part records the war from that vantage point. It also gives us a sense of the war's impact on those at the home front. What kind of warfare does Brittain describe the Germans as practicing? What was their objective in such warfare? What effect did the war have on Brittain?

Sources 12 through 15 are evidence of a nonpersonal nature, reports and statistics amassed by modern governments of the kind we have examined in earlier chapters. Nevertheless, such material will allow you to amplify your understanding of the impact of total warfare. Source 12, taken from the official record compiled by the U.S. army's forces occupying the Rhineland area of Germany at the war's end, describes the rations for Germany's civilian population during the last days of the war in 1918. These rations reflect the effects of a British naval blockade of the ports of Germany, established to cut the country off from imported food and strategic raw materials. Because prewar Germany was not self-sufficient in food production, the effect of such a blockade was great.

In analyzing this ration information, we must, as students of history, recognize that the supplies shown here may not completely reflect the German dietary situation. Rationing presumes that producers placed all foodstuffs at their government's disposal. In practice they did not, because rationing was based on government-regulated prices that were invariably lower than free market prices in a period of shortage. The result was a lively black market trade in foodstuffs for those who could pay higher prices.

Still, the evidence here does indicate the basic ration for many Germans. Analyze this record. What dietary basics do you find lacking or in short supply? What did German civilians eat a great deal of during the war? What cumulative effect do you think such a diet, imposed by total war, had on German civilians?

The strain of warfare was not only a matter of food and other material restrictions, however. As we noted earlier, warring governments tried to gauge and influence public opinion because they knew that total warfare would become untenable if civilian spirit broke. In Source 13 you will read a report to French police officials from the area of Grenoble in southeastern France in 1917. What does that report show about public opinion? In calling millions of men for military service, total war created tremendous labor shortages and yet another strain on civilians in all countries. Who filled the jobs vacated by men in England, according to Source 14?

The ultimate cost of the war can be measured in human lives lost. Official casualty figures, however, present considerable problems of analysis. We must first understand that all such figures are approximate. Deficiencies in wartime record keeping are part of the problem, but governments manipulated figures, too. During the war, security considerations led to consistent understatements of losses by each warring nation to prevent the enemy from knowing its manpower resources. At the war's end, some victorious governments allegedly inflated figures as a basis for postwar claims on their defeated enemies.

The figures for military deaths in Source 15 are taken from a recent study attempting to determine the best estimates of war losses from several sources, not just governmental records. Though we still must accept those figures as only approximations, they do allow a good sense of the relative losses of each country. Which suffered the greatest numerical losses? In which armies did a man mobilized for military service have the greatest chance of being killed? What do the high casualty rates of certain eastern European countries tell you about those nations' capacities to wage modern warfare? Among the great powers, which nation lost the greatest portion of its population?

As you now read the evidence for this chapter, keep all these questions in mind. They should aid you in answering the central questions posed: Why was World War I different from previous wars? What impact did it have on soldiers at the front? How did it affect civilians at home?

THE EVIDENCE

THE RUSH TO WAR

Source 1 from Geoffrey Keynes, editor, The Poetical Works of Rupert Brooke *(London: Faber and Faber, 1960), p. 19.*

1. Rupert Brooke, "1914 Sonnet: I. Peace," 1914

Now, God be thanked Who has matched us with His hour,
  And caught our youth, and wakened us from sleeping,
With hand made sure, clear eye, and sharpened power,
  To turn, as swimmers into cleanness leaping,
Glad from a world grown old and cold and weary,
  Leave the sick hearts that honour could not move,
And half-men, and their dirty songs and dreary,
  And all the little emptiness of love!

Oh! we, who have known shame, we have found release there,
  Where there's no ill, no grief, but sleep has mending,
    Naught broken save this body, lost but breath;

Nothing to shake the laughing heart's long peace there
   But only agony, and that has ending;
      And the worst friend and enemy is but Death.

Source 2 from Charles Péguy, Basic Verities: Prose and Poetry, *translated by Ann and Julian Green (New York: Pantheon, 1943), pp. 275–277.*

2. Charles Péguy, "Blessed Are," 1914

Blessed are those who died for carnal earth
Provided it was in a just war.
Blessed are those who died for a plot of ground.
Blessed are those who died a solemn death.

Blessed are those who died in great battles,
Stretched out on the ground in the face of God.
Blessed are those who died on a final high place,
Amid all the pomp of grandiose funerals.

Blessed are those who died for carnal cities.
For they are the body of the city of God.
Blessed are those who died for their hearth and their fire,
And the lowly honors of their father's house. . . .

Blessed are those who died, for they have returned
Into primeval clay and primeval earth.
Blessed are those who died in a just war.
Blessed is the wheat that is ripe and the wheat that is gathered in sheaves.

Source 3 from Ernst Lissauer, Jugend *(1914). Translated by Barbara Henderson,* New York Times, *October 15, 1914.*

3. Ernst Lissauer, "Hymn of Hate," 1914

French and Russian they matter not,
A blow for a blow and a shot for a shot;
We love them not, we hate them not,
We hold the Weichsel and Vosges-gate,[1]

---

1. The Germans possessed defensible boundaries against the Russians and the French. In the east, they held the Vistula (Weichsel) River in Poland as a barrier to Russian attack. In the west, they blocked the French attack with their possession of the Vosges Mountains.

We have but one—and only hate,
We love as one, we hate as one,
We have one foe and one alone.

He is known to you all, he is known to you all,
He crouches behind the dark grey flood,
Full of envy, of rage, of craft, of gall,
Cut off by waves that are thicker than blood.
Come, let us stand at the Judgment place,
An oath to swear to, face to face,
An oath of bronze no wind can shake,

An oath for our sons and their sons to take.
Come, hear the word, repeat the word,
Throughout the Fatherland make it heard.
We will never forgo our hate,
We have all but a single hate,
We love as one, we hate as one,
We have one foe, and one alone—

ENGLAND!

In the Captain's mess, in the banquet hall,
Sat feasting the officers, one and all,
Like a sabre-blow, like the swing of a sail,
One seized his glass held high to hail;
Sharp-snapped like the stroke of a rudder's play,
Spoke three words only: "To the Day!"[2]
Whose glass this fate?
They had all but a single hate.
Who was thus known?
They had one foe, and one alone—

ENGLAND!

Take you the folk of the Earth in pay,
With bars of gold your ramparts lay,
Bedeck the ocean with bow on bow,
Ye reckon well, but not well enough now.
French and Russian they matter not,
A blow for a blow, a shot for a shot,
We fight the battle with bronze and steel,
And the time that is coming Peace will seal.

---

2. **To the Day!:** In German naval officers' messes before World War I, it was customary to offer a
toast to "the Day," that is, the day England would be defeated.

You will hate with a lasting hate,
We will never forgo our hate,
Hate by water and hate by land,
Hate of the head and hate of the hand,
Hate of the hammer and hate of the crown,
Hate of seventy millions, choking down.
We love as one, we hate as one,
We have one foe, and one alone—

ENGLAND!

THE FRONT LINES

Source 4 from Julius Hoppenstedt, Das Volk in Waffen, *vol. 1:* Das Heer *(Dachau, 1913). Reprinted in Eric Dorn Brose,* The Kaiser's Army: The Politics of Military Technology in Germany During the Machine Age, 1870–1918 *(Oxford: Oxford University Press, 2001), p. 157. Photograph: Hoppenstedt, Das Heer.*

4. German Infantrymen Attack in Close Order in the Autumn 1912 Maneuvers

Source 5 from John Ellis, Eye-Deep in Hell: Trench Warfare in World War I *(Baltimore: Johns Hopkins University Press, 1976), p. 90. Photo source cited: John MacClancy.*

5. British Infantry Going "Over the Top" in Attack on Kemmel Hill, April 1918

Source 6 from Henri Barbusse, Under Fire: The Story of a Squad, *translated by Fitzwater Wray (New York: E. P. Dutton, 1917), pp. 250–259.*

6. From Henri Barbusse, *Under Fire: The Story of a Squad,* 1916

We are ready. The men marshal themselves, still silently, their blankets cross-wise, the helmet-strap on the chin, leaning on their rifles. I look at their pale, contracted, and reflective faces. They are not soldiers, they are men. They are not adventurers, or warriors, or made for human slaughter, neither butchers nor cattle. They are laborers and artisans whom one recognizes in their uniforms. They are civilians uprooted, and they are ready. They await the signal for death or murder; but you may see, looking at their faces between the vertical gleams of their bayonets, that they are simply men.

Each one knows that he is going to take his head, his chest, his belly, his whole body, and all naked, up to the rifles pointed forward, to the shells, to the bombs piled and ready, and above all to the methodical and almost infallible machine-guns—to all that is waiting for him yonder and is now so frightfully silent—before he reaches the other soldiers that he must kill. They are not careless of their lives, like brigands, nor blinded by passion like savages. In spite of the doctrines with which they have been cultivated they are not inflamed. They are above instinctive excesses. They are not drunk, either physically or morally. It is in full consciousness, as in full health and full strength, that they are massed there to hurl themselves once more into that sort of madman's part imposed on all men by the madness of the human race. One sees the thought and the fear and the farewell that there is in their silence, their stillness, in the mask of tranquillity which unnaturally grips their faces. They are not the kind of hero one thinks of, but their sacrifice has greater worth than they who have not seen them will ever be able to understand.

They are waiting; a waiting that extends and seems eternal. Now and then one or another starts a little when a bullet, fired from the other side, skims the forward embankment that shields us and plunges into the flabby flesh of the rear wall. . . .

A man arrives running, and speaks to Bertrand, and then Bertrand turns to us—

"Up you go," he says, "it's our turn."

All move at once. We put our feet on the steps made by the sappers, raise ourselves, elbow to elbow, beyond the shelter of the trench, and climb on to the parapet.

Bertrand is out on the sloping ground. He covers us with a quick glance, and when we are all there he says, *"Allons,* forward!"[3]

Our voices have a curious resonance. The start has been made very quickly, unexpectedly almost, as in a dream. There is no whistling sound in the air. Among the vast uproar of the guns we discern very clearly this surprising silence of bullets around us—

We descend over the rough and slippery ground with involuntary gestures, helping ourselves sometimes with the rifle. . . . On all sides the slope is covered by men who, like us, are bent on the descent. On the right the outline is defined of a company that is reaching the ravine by Trench 97—an old German work in ruins. We cross our wire by openings. Still no one fires on us. Some awkward ones who have made false steps are getting up again. We form up on the farther side of the entanglements and then set ourselves to topple down the slope rather faster—there is an instinctive acceleration in the movement. Several bullets arrive at last among us. Bertrand shouts to us to reserve our bombs and wait till the last moment.

But the sound of his voice is carried away. Abruptly, across all the width of the opposite slope, lurid flames burst forth that strike the air with terrible detonations. In line from left to right fires emerge from the sky and explosions from the ground. It is a frightful curtain which divides us from the world, which divides us from the past and from the future. We stop, fixed to the ground, stupefied by the sudden host that thunders from every side; then a simultaneous effort uplifts our mass again and throws it swiftly forward. We stumble and impede each other in the great waves of smoke. With harsh crashes and whirlwinds of pulverized earth, towards the profundity into which we hurl ourselves pell-mell, we see craters opened here and there, side by side, and merging in each other. Then one knows no longer where the discharges fall. Volleys are let loose so monstrously resounding that one feels himself annihilated by the mere sound of the downpoured thunder of these great constellations of destruction that form in the sky. One sees and one feels the fragments passing close to one's head with their hiss of red-hot iron plunged in water. The blast of one explosion so burns my hands, that I let my rifle fall. I pick it up again, reeling, and set off in the tawny-gleaming tempest with lowered head, lashed by spirits of dust and soot in a crushing downpour like volcanic lava. The stridor of the bursting shells hurts your ears, beats you on the neck, goes through your temples, and you cannot endure it without a cry. The gusts of death drive us on, lift us up, rock us to and fro. We leap, and do not know whither we go. Our eyes are blinking and weeping and obscured. The view before us is blocked by a flashing avalanche that fills space.

3. *Allons:* "Let's go!"

It is the barrage fire. We have to go through that whirlwind of fire and those fearful showers that vertically fall. We are passing through. We are through it, by chance. Here and there I have seen forms that spun round and were lifted up and laid down, illumined by a brief reflection from over yonder. I have glimpsed strange faces that uttered some sort of cry—you could see them without hearing them in the roar of annihilation. A brasier full of red and black masses huge and furious fell about me, excavating the ground, tearing it from under my feet, throwing me aside like a bouncing toy. I remember that I strode over a smoldering corpse, quite black, with a tissue of rosy blood shriveling on him; and I remember, too, that the skirts of the great-coat flying next to me had caught fire, and left a trail of smoke behind. On our right, all along Trench 97, our glances were drawn and dazzled by a rank of frightful flames, closely crowded against each other like men.

Forward!

Now, we are nearly running. I see some who fall solidly flat, face forward, and others who founder meekly, as though they would sit down on the ground. We step aside abruptly to avoid the prostrate dead, quiet and rigid, or else offensive, and also—more perilous snares!—the wounded that hook on to you, struggling.

The International Trench! We are there. The wire entanglements have been torn up into long roots and creepers, thrown afar and coiled up, swept away and piled in great drifts by the guns. Between these big bushes of rain-damped steel the ground is open and free.

The trench is not defended. The Germans have abandoned it, or else a first wave has already passed over it. Its interior bristles with rifles placed against the bank. In the bottom are scattered corpses. From the jumbled litter of the long trench, hands emerge that protrude from gray sleeves with red facings, and booted legs. In places the embankment is destroyed and its woodwork splintered—all the flank of the trench collapsed and fallen into an indescribable mixture. In other places, round pits are yawning. . . .

We have spread out in the trench. The lieutenant, who has jumped to the other side, is stooping and summoning us with signs and shouts—"Don't stay there; forward, forward!"

We climb the wall of the trench with the help of the sacks, of weapons, and of the backs that are piled up there. In the bottom of the ravine the soil is shot-churned, crowded with jetsam, swarming with prostrate bodies. Some are motionless as blocks of wood; others move slowly or convulsively. The barrage fire continues to increase its infernal discharge behind us on the ground that we have crossed. But where we are at the foot of the rise it is a dead point for the artillery.

A short and uncertain calm follows. We are less deafened and look at each other. There is fever in the eyes, and the cheek-bones are blood-red. Our breathing snores and our hearts drum in our bodies.

In haste and confusion we recognize each other, as if we had met again face to face in a nightmare on the uttermost shores of death. Some hurried words are cast upon this glade in hell—"It's you!"—"Where's Cocon?"—"Don't know."—"Have you seen the captain?"—"No."—"Going strong?"—"Yes."

The bottom of the ravine is crossed and the other slope rises opposite. We climb in Indian file by a stairway rough-hewn in the ground: "Look out!" The shout means that a soldier half-way up the steps has been struck in the loins by a shell-fragment; he falls with his arms forward, bareheaded, like the diving swimmer. We can see the shapeless silhouette of the mass as it plunges into the gulf. I can almost see the detail of his blown hair over the black profile of his face.

We debouch upon the height. A great colorless emptiness is outspread before us. At first one can see nothing but a chalky and stony plain, yellow and gray to the limit of sight. No human wave is preceding ours; in front of us there is no living soul, but the ground is peopled with dead—recent corpses that still mimic agony or sleep, and old remains already bleached and scattered to the wind, half assimilated by the earth.

As soon as our pushing and jolted file emerges, two men close to me are hit, two shadows are hurled to the ground and roll under our feet, one with a sharp cry, and the other silently, as a felled ox. Another disappears with the caper of a lunatic, as if he had been snatched away. Instinctively we close up as we hustle forward—always forward—and the wound in our line closes of its own accord. The adjutant stops, raises his sword, lets it fall, and drops to his knees. His kneeling body slopes backward in jerks, his helmet drops on his heels, and he remains there, bareheaded, face to the sky. Hurriedly the rush of the rank has split open to respect his immobility.

But we cannot see the lieutenant. No more leaders, then—— Hesitation checks the wave of humanity that begins to beat on the plateau. Above the trampling one hears the hoarse effort of our lungs. "Forward!" cries some soldier, and then all resume the onward race to perdition with increasing speed.

"Where's Bertrand?" comes the laborious complaint of one of the foremost runners. "There! Here!" He had stooped in passing over a wounded man, but he leaves him quickly, and the man extends his arms toward him and seems to sob.

It is just at the moment when he rejoins us that we hear in front of us, coming from a sort of ground swelling, the crackle of a machine-gun. It is a moment of agony—more serious even than when we were passing through the flaming earthquake of the barrage. That familiar voice speaks to us across the plain, sharp and horrible. But we no longer stop. "Go on, go on!"

Our panting becomes hoarse groaning, yet still we hurl ourselves toward the horizon.

"The Boches!⁴ I see them!" a man says suddenly.

"Yes—their heads, there—above the trench—it's there, the trench that line. It's close. Ah, the hogs!"

We can indeed make out little round gray caps which rise and then drop on the ground level, fifty yards away, beyond a belt of dark earth, furrowed and humped. Encouraged they spring forward, they who now form the group where I am. So near the goal, so far unscathed, shall we not reach it? Yes, we will reach it! We make great strides and no longer hear anything. Each man plunges straight ahead, fascinated by the terrible trench, bent rigidly forward, almost incapable of turning his head to right or to left. I have a notion that many of us missed their footing and fell to the ground. I jump sideways to miss the suddenly erect bayonet of a toppling rifle. Quite close to me, Farfadet jostles me with his face bleeding, throws himself on Volpatte who is beside me and clings to him. Volpatte doubles up without slackening his rush and drags him along some paces, then shakes him off without looking at him and without knowing who he is, and shouts at him in a breaking voice almost choked with exertion: "Let me go, let me go, *nom de Dieu!*⁵ They'll pick you up directly—don't worry."

The other man sinks to the ground, and his face, plastered with a scarlet mask and void of all expression, turns in every direction; while Volpatte, already in the distance, automatically repeats between his teeth, "Don't worry," with a steady forward gaze on the line.

A shower of bullets spurts around me, increasing the number of those who suddenly halt, who collapse slowly, defiant and gesticulating, of those who dive forward solidly with all the body's burden, of the shouts, deep, furious, and desperate, and even of that hollow and terrible gasp when a man's life goes bodily forth in a breath. And we who are not yet stricken, we look ahead, we walk and we run, among the frolics of the death that strikes at random into our flesh.

The wire entanglements—and there is one stretch of them intact. We go along to where it has been gutted into a wide and deep opening. This is a colossal funnel-hole, formed of smaller funnels placed together, a fantastic volcanic crater, scooped there by the guns.

The sight of this convulsion is stupefying; truly it seems that it must have come from the center of the earth. Such a rending of virgin strata puts new edge on our attacking fury, and none of us can keep from shouting with a solemn shake of the head—even just now when words are but painfully torn from our throats—"Ah, Christ! Look what hell we've given 'em there! Ah, look!"

Driven as if by the wind, we mount or descend at the will of the hollows and the earthy mounds in the gigantic fissure dug and blackened and burned

4. **Boches:** a derogatory term applied by the French to German soldiers, originating from the French *caboche*, or blockhead.

5. *nom de Dieu:* "Name of God!"

by furious flames. The soil clings to the feet and we tear them out angrily. The accouterments and stuffs that cover the soft soil, the linen that is scattered about from sundered knapsacks, prevent us from sticking fast in it, and we are careful to plant our feet in this débris when we jump into the holes or climb the hillocks.

Behind us voices urge us—"Forward, boys, forward, *nom de Dieu!*"

"All the regiment is behind us!" they cry. We do not turn round to see, but the assurance electrifies our rush once more.

No more caps are visible behind the embankment of the trench we are nearing. Some German dead are crumbling in front of it, in pinnacled heaps or extended lines. We are there. The parapet takes definite and sinister shape and detail; the loopholes—we are prodigiously, incredibly close!

Something falls in front of us. It is a bomb. With a kick Corporal Bertrand returns it so well that it rises and bursts just over the trench.

With that fortunate deed the squad reaches the trench.

Pépin has hurled himself flat on the ground and is involved with a corpse. He reaches the edge and plunges in—the first to enter. Fouillade, with great gestures and shouts, jumps into the pit almost at the same moment that Pépin rolls down it. Indistinctly I see—in the time of the lightning's flash—a whole row of black demons stooping and squatting for the descent, on the ridge of the embankment, on the edge of the dark ambush.

A terrible volley bursts point-blank in our faces, flinging in front of us a sudden row of flames the whole length of the earthen verge. After the stunning shock we shake ourselves and burst into devilish laughter—the discharge has passed too high. And at once, with shouts and roars of salvation, we slide and roll and fall alive into the belly of the trench!

Source 7 from Erich Maria Remarque, All Quiet on the Western Front *(New York: Fawcett Crest, 1969), pp. 167–171, 174–175. "Im Westen Nichts Neues" copyright 1928 by Ullstein A.G.; copyright renewed 1956 by Erich Maria Remarque. "All Quiet on the Western Front" copyright 1929, 1930 by Little, Brown and Company; copyright renewed 1957, 1958 by Erich Maria Remarque.*

7. From Erich Maria Remarque, *All Quiet on the Western Front,* 1928

We have been able to bury Müller, but he is not likely to remain long undisturbed. Our lines are falling back. There are too many fresh English and American regiments over there. There's too much corned beef and white wheaten bread. Too many new guns. Too many aeroplanes.

But we are emaciated and starved. Our food is so bad and mixed up with so much substitute stuff that it makes us ill. The factory owners in Germany have grown wealthy;—dysentery dissolves our bowels. The latrine poles are always densely crowded; the people at home ought to be shown these grey, yellow, miserable, wasted faces here, these bent figures from whose bodies the colic wrings out the blood, and who with lips trembling and distorted with pain, grin at one another and say: "It is not much sense pulling up one's trousers again—"

Our artillery is fired out, it has too few shells and the barrels are so worn that they shoot uncertainly, and scatter so widely as even to fall on ourselves. We have too few horses. Our fresh troops are anæmic boys in need of rest, who cannot carry a pack, but merely know how to die. By thousands. They understand nothing about warfare, they simply go on and let themselves be shot down. A single flyer routed two companies of them for a joke, just as they came fresh from the train—before they had ever heard of such a thing as cover.

"Germany ought to be empty soon," says Kat.

We have given up hope that some day an end may come. We never think so far. A man can stop a bullet and be killed; he can get wounded, and then the hospital is his next stop. There, if they do not amputate him, he sooner or later falls into the hands of one of those staff surgeons who, with the War Service Cross in his buttonhole, says to him: "What, one leg a bit short? If you have any pluck you don't need to run at the front. The man is A1.[6] Dismiss!"

Kat tells a story that has travelled the whole length of the front from the Vosges to Flanders;—of the staff surgeon who reads the names on the list, and when a man comes before him, without looking up says: "A1. We need soldiers up there." A fellow with a wooden leg comes up before him, the staff surgeon again says A1—"And then," Kat raises his voice, "the fellow says to him: 'I already have a wooden leg, but when I go back again and they shoot off my head, then I will get a wooden head made and become a staff surgeon.' " This answer tickles us all immensely.

There may be good doctors, and there are, lots of them; all the same, every soldier some time during his hundreds of inspections falls into the clutches of one of these countless hero-grabbers who pride themselves on changing as many C3's and B3's as possible into A1's.

There are many such stories, they are mostly far more bitter. All the same, they have nothing to do with mutiny or lead-swinging. They are merely honest and call a thing by its name; for there is a very great deal of fraud, injustice, and baseness in the army.—Is it nothing that regiment after regiment returns again and again to the ever more hopeless struggle, that attack follows attack along the weakening, retreating, crumbling line?

From a mockery the tanks have become a terrible weapon. Armoured they come rolling on in long lines, and more than anything else embody for us war's horror.

We do not see the guns that bombard us; the attacking lines of the enemy infantry are men like ourselves; but these tanks are machines, their caterpillars

---

6. **A1:** the highest category of physical fitness, that is, qualified for front-line duty.

run on as endless as the war, they are annihilation, they roll without feeling into the craters, and climb up again without stopping, a fleet of roaring, smoke-belching armour-clads, invulnerable steel beasts squashing the dead and the wounded—we shrivel up in our thin skin before them, against their colossal weight our arms are sticks of straw, and our hand-grenades matches.

Shells, gas clouds, and flotillas of tanks—shattering, starvation, death.

Dysentery, influenza, typhus—murder, burning, death.

Trenches, hospitals, the common grave—there are no other possibilities.

In one attack our company commander, Bertinck, falls. He was one of those superb front-line officers who are foremost in every hot place. He was with us for two years without being wounded, so that something had to happen in the end.

We occupy a crater and get surrounded. The stink of petroleum or oil blows across with the fumes of powder. Two fellows with a flame-thrower are seen, one carries the tin on his back, the other has the hose in his hands from which the fire spouts. If they get so near that they can reach us we are done for, we cannot retreat at the moment.

We open fire on them. But they work nearer and things begin to look bad. Bertinck is lying in the hole with us. When he sees that we cannot escape because under the sharp fire we must make the most of this cover, he takes a rifle, crawls out of the hole, and lying down propped on his elbows, he takes aim. He fires—the same moment a bullet smacks into him, they have got him. Still he lies and aims again;—once he shifts and again takes his aim; at last the rifle cracks. Bertinck lets the gun drop and says: "Good," and slips back into the hole. The hindermost of the two flame-throwers is hit, he falls, the hose slips away from the other fellow, the fires squirts about on all sides and the man burns.

Bertinck has a chest wound. After a while a fragment smashes away his chin, and the same fragment has sufficient force to tear open Leer's hip. Leer groans as he supports himself on his arm, he bleeds quickly, no one can help him. Like an emptying tube, after a couple of minutes he collapses.

What use is it to him now that he was such a good mathematician at school?

The months pass by. The summer of 1918 is the most bloody and the most terrible. The days stand like angels in gold and blue, incomprehensible, above the ring of annihilation. Every man here knows that we are losing the war. Not much is said about it, we are falling back, we will not be able to attack again after this big offensive, we have no more men and no more ammunition. . . .

There are so many airmen here, and they are so sure of themselves that they give chase to single individuals, just as though they were hares. For every one German plane there come at least five English and American. For one hungry, wretched German soldier come five of the enemy, fresh and fit. For one German army loaf there are fifty tins of canned beef over there. We are not beaten, for as soldiers we are better and more experienced; we are simply crushed and driven back by overwhelmingly superior forces.

[319]

Behind us lie rainy weeks—grey sky, grey fluid earth, grey dying. If we go out, the rain at once soaks through our overcoat and clothing;—and we remain wet all the time we are in the line. We never get dry. Those who still wear high boots tie sand bags round the top so that the mud does not pour in so fast. The rifles are caked, the uniforms caked, everything is fluid and dissolved, the earth one dripping, soaked, oily mass in which lie the yellow pools with red spiral streams of blood and into which the dead, wounded, and survivors slowly sink down.

The storm lashes us, out of the confusion of grey and yellow the hail of splinters whips forth the childlike cries of the wounded, and in the night shattered life groans wearily to the silence.

Our hands are earth, our bodies clay and our eyes pools of rain. We do not know whether we still live. . . .

It is autumn. There are not many of the old hands left. I am the last of the seven fellows from our class.

Everyone talks of peace and armistice. All wait. If it again proves an illusion, then they will break up; hope is high, it cannot be taken away again without an upheaval. If there is not peace, then there will be revolution.

I have fourteen days' rest, because I have swallowed a bit of gas; in a little garden I sit the whole day long in the sun. The armistice is coming soon, I believe it now too. Then we will go home.

Here my thoughts stop and will not go any farther. All that meets me, all that floods over me are but feelings—greed of life, love of home, yearning of the blood, intoxication of deliverance. But no aims.

Had we returned home in 1916, out of the suffering and the strength of our experiences we might have unleashed a storm. Now if we go back we will be weary, broken, burnt out, rootless, and without hope. We will not be able to find our way any more.

And men will not understand us—for the generation that grew up before us, though it has passed these years with us here, already had a home and a calling; now it will return to its old occupations, and the war will be forgotten—and the generation that has grown up after us will be strange to us and push us aside. We will be superfluous even to ourselves, we will grow older, a few will adapt themselves, some others will merely submit, and most will be bewildered;—the years will pass by and in the end we shall fall into ruin.

But perhaps all this that I think is mere melancholy and dismay, which will fly away as the dust, when I stand once again beneath the poplars and listen to the rustling of their leaves. It cannot be that it has gone, the yearning that made our blood unquiet, the unknown, the perplexing, the oncoming things, the thousand faces of the future, the melodies from dreams and from books, the whispers and divinations of women, it cannot be that this has vanished in bombardment, in despair, in brothels.

Here the trees show gay and golden, the berries of the rowan stand red among the leaves, country roads run white out to the sky-line, and the canteens hum like beehives with rumours of peace.

I stand up.

I am very quiet. Let the months and years come, they bring me nothing more, they can bring me nothing more. I am so alone, and so without hope that I can confront them without fear. The life that has borne me through these years is still in my hands and my eyes. Whether I have subdued it, I know not. But so long as it is there it will seek its own way out, heedless of the will that is within me. . . .

He fell in October 1918, on a day that was so quiet and still on the whole front, that the army report confined itself to the single sentence: All quiet on the Western Front.

He had fallen forward and lay on the earth as though sleeping. Turning him over one saw that he could not have suffered long; his face had an expression of calm, as though almost glad the end had come.

Source 8 from C. Day Lewis, editor, The Collected Poems of Wilfred Owen *(New York: New Directions, 1964), p. 55.*

8. Wilfred Owen,
"Dulce et Decorum Est,"
ca 1917

Bent double, like old beggars under sacks,
Knock-kneed, coughing like hags, we cursed through sludge,
Till on the haunting flares we turned our backs
And towards our distant rest began to trudge.
Men marched asleep. Many had lost their boots
But limped on, blood-shod. All went lame; all blind;
Drunk with fatigue; deaf even to the hoots
Of tired, outstripped Five-Nines[7] that dropped behind.

Gas! Gas! Quick, boys!—An ecstasy of fumbling,
Fitting the clumsy helmets just in time;
But someone still was yelling out and stumbling
And flound'ring like a man in fire or lime . . .
Dim, through the misty panes and thick green light,
As under a green sea, I saw him drowning.

7. **Five-Nines:** one of the types of artillery used by the Germans was the 5.9-inch howitzer, which projected a very large shell in a high arc. As the barrels of such guns became worn, their accuracy was impaired.

In all my dreams, before my helpless sight,
He lunges at me, guttering, choking, drowning.

If in some smothering dreams you too could pace
Behind the wagon that we flung him in,
And watch the white eyes writhing in his face,
His hanging face, like a devil's sick of sin;
If you could hear, at every jolt, the blood
Come gargling from the froth-corrupted lungs,
Obscene as cancer, bitter as the cud
Of vile, incurable sores on innocent tongues,—
My friend, you would not tell with such high zest
To children ardent for some desperate glory,
The old Lie: Dulce et decorum est
Pro patria mori.[8]

Source 9 from Siegfried Sassoon, Collected Poems, 1908–1956 *(London: Faber and Faber, 1961), p. 75.*

9. Siegfried Sassoon, "The General," ca 1917

'Good-morning; good-morning!' the General said
When we met him last week on our way to the line.
Now the soldiers he smiled at are most of 'em dead,
And we're cursing his staff for incompetent swine.
'He's a cheery old card,' grunted Harry to Jack
As they slogged up to Arras[9] with rifle and pack.

But he did for them both by his plan of attack.

---

8. From Horace, *Odes,* III, 2, 3: "It is sweet and fitting to die for one's country."

9. **Arras:** city of northeastern France that was the site of a major British attack in April 1917. With heavy artillery bombardment and the element of surprise, the British were able to break through German lines. Unfortunately, excessive caution on the part of British commanders in exploiting their costly initial successes permitted the Germans time to regroup and deprived the British of a sweeping victory.

Source 10 from Rudolf Hoffman, editor, Der deutscher Soldat: Briefe aus dem Weltkrieg *(Munich: 1937), pp. 297–298. Translated and quoted in Hanna Hafkesbrink,* Unknown Germany: An Inner Chronicle of the First World War Based on Letters and Diaries *(New Haven, Conn.: Yale University Press, 1948), p. 141.*

10. New Year's Eve, 1914: Letter from a Former German Student Serving in France

On New Year's Eve we called across to tell each other the time and agreed to fire a salvo at 12. It was a cold night. We sang songs, and they clapped (we were only 60–70 yards apart); we played the mouth-organ and they sang and we clapped. Then I asked if they haven't got any musical instruments, and they produced some bagpipes (they are the Scots guards, with the short petticoats and bare legs) and they played some of their beautiful elegies on them, and sang, too. Then at 12 we all fired salvos into the air! . . . It was a real good "Sylvester,"[10] just like in peace-time!

THE HOME FRONT

Source 11 from Vera Brittain, The Testament of Youth: An Autobiographical Study of the Years 1900–1925 *(London: Gollancz, 1981), pp. 365–366.*

11. Vera Brittain: A London Air Raid, June 13, 1917

Although three out of the four persons were gone who had made all the world that I knew,[11] the War seemed no nearer a conclusion than it had been in 1914. It was everywhere now; even before Victor was buried, the daylight air-raid of June 13th "brought it home," as the newspapers remarked, with such force that I perceived danger to be infinitely preferable when I went after it, instead of waiting for it to come after me.

I was just reaching home after a morning's shopping in Kensington High Street when the uproar began, and, looking immediately at the sky, I saw the sinister group of giant mosquitoes sweeping in close formation over London. My mother, whose temperamental fatalism had always enabled her to sleep

10. **Sylvester:** Roman Catholics observe December 31 as the feast of Saint Sylvester.

11. Vera Brittain lost her fiancé and two other male friends in World War I. The fourth person, her brother Edward, was still alive in June 1917, but perished while serving with the British army in Italy later in 1917.

peacefully through the usual night-time raids, was anxious to watch the show from the roof of the flats, but when I reached the doorway my father had just succeeded in hurrying her down to the basement; he did not share her belief that destiny remained unaffected by caution, and himself derived moral support in air-raids from putting on his collar and patrolling the passages.

The three of us listened glumly to the shrapnel raining down like a thunder-shower upon the park—those quiet trees which on the night of my return from Malta[12] had made death and horror seem so unbelievably remote. As soon as the banging and crashing had given way to the breathless, apprehensive silence which always followed a big raid, I made a complicated journey to the City[13] to see if my uncle had been added to the family's growing collection of casualties.

When at last, after much negociation [sic] of the crowds in Cornhill and Bishopsgate, I succeeded in getting to the National Provincial Bank, I found him safe and quite composed, but as pale as a corpse; indeed, the whole staff of men and women resembled a morose consignment of dumb spectres newly transported across the Styx.[14] The streets round the bank were terrifyingly quiet, and in some places so thickly covered with broken glass that I seemed to be wading ankle-deep in huge unmelted hailstones. I saw no dead nor wounded, though numerous police-supervised barricades concealed a variety of gruesome probabilities. Others were only too clearly suggested by a crimson-splashed horse lying indifferently on its side, and by several derelict tradesman's carts bloodily denuded of their drivers.

These things, I concluded, seemed less inappropriate when they happened in France, though no doubt the French thought otherwise.

Source 12 from the American Military Government of Occupied Germany, 1918–1920, Report of the Officer in Charge of Civil Affairs, Third Army and American Forces in Germany (Washington, D.C.: U.S. Government Printing Office, 1943), pp. 155–156.

12. German Wartime Civilian Rations, 1918

Conditions on arrival of Third Army.—When the Third Army entered its area of occupation, it found the principal foodstuffs rationed, as had been the case for several years. In brief, the situation may be outlined thus, [:] prior to the war, the average food consumption for the German population, expressed in calories, was about 3500 calories per person per day. According to German

12. Brittain had served as a military nurse on the British island of Malta in the Mediterranean.
13. **the City:** the financial district of London.
14. **Styx:** in Greek mythology, the river that the souls of the dead must cross as they leave the world of the living.

figures, this had shrunk to 3000 calories in 1914, 2000 in 1915, 1500 in 1916, and to 1200 in the winter of 1917–1918.

All the principal foodstuffs had been rationed during the war, and, on paper at least, every resource of the Empire in the way of food was entirely under control and carefully distributed.

The ration at the beginning of the occupation was essentially as follows:

Bread	260 grams per head per day[15]
Potatoes	500 grams per head per day

The main reliance for sustenance was placed on the above two foods and, except in the large cities, where the supply was subject to much fluctuation, the amounts indicated, or more, were fairly consistently provided during the whole of the year 1919.

In addition, the following substances constituted a part of the ration in the amounts indicated:

Meat	200 grams per head per week. Frequently reduced in amount, and often not issued at all.
Fat	150–200 grams per head per week. Later became very scarce.
Butter	20 grams per head per week. Practically never issued in the ration.
Sugar	600–750 grams per head per month.
Marmalade	200 grams per head per week. Often unavailable.
Milk	Not issued at all to the population in general, on account of its scarcity. Issued only to children under 6 years of age and, on physicians' certificates, to the sick, nursing mothers, pregnant women and the aged. One half to one litre per day.

Fresh vegetables, in general, were not rationed and were fairly plentiful. Additional substances, such as rice, oats, grits, margarine, sausage, "Ersatz" (substitute) coffee, eggs, and additional flour, were added to the ration from time to time when available.

15. To convert grams to ounces, multiply grams by 0.035. Thus the German bread ration was a little over 9 ounces per day per person, and the potato ration was 17.5 ounces per person per day.

Source 13 from Jean-Jacques Becker, The Great War and the French People, *translated by Arnold Pomerans (New York: St. Martin's, 1986), pp. 232–234. Reprinted by permission of Berg Publishers.*

13. Report on French Public Opinion in the Department of the Isère

Grenoble, 17 June 1917

The Prefect[16] *of the Department of Isère to the Minister of the Interior*[17]

Office of the Sûreté Générale[18]

I have the honour to reply herewith to the questions contained in your confidential telegram circulated on *10 June inst.*:[19]

The inquiry I have myself conducted, or with the help of colleagues, to test the opinion of certain leading personages has shown that the morale of the people of Isère is far from satisfactory and that their exemplary spirit has suffered a general decline during the past two months. Today there is weariness bordering on dejection, a result less of the curtailment of the public diet and supply difficulties than of the disappointment caused by the failure of our armies in April,[20] the feeling that military blunders have been made, that heavy losses have been sustained without any appreciable gains, that all further offensives will be both bloody and in vain. The inactivity of Russia, whose contribution now seems highly doubtful, has accentuated the decline in morale.[21] The remarks of

16. **prefect:** since the Revolution of 1789, France has been divided into departments. The chief administrative officer in each department, since the time of Napoleon, has been the prefect. The prefect historically has been an appointee of the central government and thus responsible to it and not to local interests.

17. **minister of the Interior:** most police services in France are under the control of the central government's Ministry of the Interior.

18. **Sûreté Général:** the central police command charged with criminal investigations.

19. **inst.:** An archaic use of "instant" to mean "current." Here it is used to express "June 10th of the current year."

20. In April 1917, the French army had received a new commander, General Nivelle, who launched a massive and costly offensive to break through German lines and end the war. The offensive failed and, coming after great French losses at Verdun in 1916, provoked a mutiny in the army in which soldiers refused orders to attack until August 1917. The mutinies placed the entire French war effort at risk. Order was restored only by a new commander, General Pétain, and a new and authoritarian prime minister, Georges Clemenceau.

21. Russia had experienced a revolution in February 1917 that toppled Tsar Nicholas II from power and replaced him with a republic under a Provisional Government. Although the leaders of this government were committed to Russia's war against Germany, disorganization of Russian armies by the revolution prevented effective Russian action. Because the Russian collapse accompanied Germany's unrestricted submarine warfare against all shipping around England and the disastrous defeat of the Italian armies at Caporetto in October, 1917 was the great year of crisis for France and its allies.

soldiers coming back from the front are the major cause of this decline: these re-marks, made in the trains, in the railway stations, in the cafés on the way home, and then in the villages, convey a deplorable picture of the mentality of a great number of servicemen. Each one tells of and amplifies this or that unpleasant incident, this or that error committed by his commander, this or that useless battle, this or that act of insubordination presented as so many acts of courage and determination. These remarks, listened to with a ready ear by those who are already nervous or depressed enough as it is, are then peddled about and exaggerated with the result that discontent and anxiety are increased fur-ther. Each day, incidents in public places, particularly in the large railway stations and on the trains, reflect the most deplorable attitude in the minds of servicemen.

In the countryside, the restive mood is less obvious than it is in the towns; the peasants work, but they do not hide the fact that 'it's been going on too long'; they are tired of their continuous over-exertion in the fields, of the lack of hands and of the very heavy burden of the requisitions. They are growing more and more suspicious and indifferent to the idea of collective effort and mutual solidarity, and to patriotic appeals, and can think only of their imme-diate interests and their own safety.

Growers increasingly complain about price rises, even though they probably suffer less than others from the cost of living and even though their produce is sold at ever higher prices.

Nevertheless, it is among the rural populations that one finds the greatest composure and resignation.

In the towns, and particularly in the industrial centres, the more impres-sionable and hence more excitable population—the workers, the ordinary people—are upset about the duration of the struggle, impatient with the in-creasing cost of living, irritated by the considerable profits being made out of the war by the big industrialists in their neighbourhood, and increasingly taken in by the propagandists of the united Socialist Party and their interna-tionalist ideas. Under the influence of the Russian Revolution they already dream of workers' and soldiers' committees and of social revolution. These sentiments are aired frequently at workers' meetings, called ostensibly to dis-cuss economic or union matters, and in their paper, *Le Droit du Peuple*,[22] which is waging a very skillful anti-war and internationalist campaign.

This attitude, together with the constant rise in the cost of living, has fuelled a widespread demand for wage increases which the employers have quietly met to a large degree. Unfortunately, the calm following these in-creases has been momentary only. The cost of living keeps rising further and it is painful to watch each wage increase being followed directly by a corre-sponding increase in the price of food and the cost of board and lodging. Al-ready those workers engaged on national defence contracts are finding that

---

22. *Le Droit du Peuple: The Right of the People.*

the new wage scales agreed less than two months ago for Grenoble and district have become inadequate; they are presently asking for a cost-of-living allowance of 2 francs a day and have made it quite clear that if their demand is not met there will be trouble in the streets; some of them have even gone so far as to declare that they know where to find the necessary arms, alluding to the shell and explosives factories in the suburbs of Grenoble. I know perfectly well that these remarks were presumably made in order to intimidate the citizens, but it is nevertheless symptomatic that they should have been made in the first place. When they lack the courage to speak out themselves, the factory propagandists use the women working beside them who, running smaller risks, are less restrained in their threats. The demands of the reservists in the munitions factories have been forwarded to the ministry of supply and a number of agitators have been sent away—not to the front, which would have been dangerous, but to other factories in various parts of the area. Calm has therefore been restored, but there are fears that the present lull may be temporary.

If working-class militancy were to make itself felt in the munitions factories in Grenoble and in the industrial centres of the department, it would be very difficult and extremely risky to try to control it by force: the local police force would prove inadequate, even if it were reinforced by gendarmes. It is clearly necessary to strengthen the police contingent, but this can only be done through the deferment of professional policemen serving in the territorial army or the reserve. The auxiliary policemen drawn from the ranks of the retired are admittedly men of goodwill, but they are physically and mentally worn out, and their contribution and energy are inadequate. The relocation, or rather the transfer, of some gendarmerie brigades would be very useful, but the consequent changes in domicile would involve cumbersome formalities. . . . It would not be unhelpful if an intelligent, serving special commissioner were put in charge, with particular emphasis on the surveillance of aliens who continue to move about freely in the department and can undermine the morale of our people even as these aliens go about the business of gathering information useful to the enemy.

In conclusion, I believe that the present situation, both in respect of morale and also of social stability, while not giving cause for alarm, is far from satisfactory and that it ought to be considered serious enough to call for precautionary measures, and if necessary for energetic intervention.

What is really needed to lift flagging courage and to restore confidence in the future is a military success by our armies, a major Russian offensive, or just a German retreat.

Source 14 from Report of the War Cabinet Committee on Women in British Industry *(London: His Majesty's Stationery Office, 1919).*

14. Employment of Women in Wartime British Industry

Trades	Est. Number Females Employed in July 1914	Est. Number Females Employed in July 1918	Difference Between Numbers of Females Employed in July 1914 and July 1918	Percentage of Females to Total Number Workpeople Employed		Est. Number Females Directly Replacing Males in Jan. 1918
				July 1914	July 1918	
Metal	170,000	594,000	+424,000	9	25	195,000
Chemical	40,000	104,000	+ 64,000	20	39	35,000
Textile	863,000	827,000	− 36,000	58	67	64,000
Clothing	612,000	568,000	− 44,000	68	76	43,000
Food, drink, and tobacco	196,000	235,000	+ 39,000	35	49	60,000
Paper and printing	147,500	141,500	− 6,000	36	48	21,000
Wood	44,000	79,000	+ 35,000	15	32	23,000
China and earthenware	32,000 }					
Leather	23,100	197,100	+ 93,000	4	10	62,000
Other	49,000					
Government establishments	2,000	225,000	+223,000	3	47	197,000
Total	2,178,600	2,970,600	+792,000	26	37	704,000

Source 15 from J. M. Winter, The Great War and the British People (Cambridge, Mass.: Harvard University Press, 1986), p. 75. Reprinted by permission.

15. Estimated Military Casualties, by Nation

Country	Total Killed or Died	Total Mobilized (in thousands)	Prewar Male Pop. 15–49	Total Prewar Pop.	Total Killed		
					Per 1,000 Mobilized	Per 1,000 Males 15–49	Per 1,000 People
Britain, Ireland	723	6,147	11,540	45,221	118	63	16
Canada	61	629	2,320	8,100	97	26	8
Australia	60	413	1,370	4,900	145	44	12
New Zealand	16	129	320	1,100	124	50	15
South Africa	7	136	1,700	6,300	51	4	1
India	54	953	82,600	321,800	57	1	0
France	1,327	7,891	9,981	39,600	168	133	34
French colonies	71	449	13,200	52,700	158	5	1
Belgium	38	365	1,924	7,600	104	20	5
Italy	578	5,615	7,767	35,900	103	75	16
Portugal	7	100	1,315	6,100	70	5	1
Greece	26	353	1,235	4,900	73	21	5
Serbia	278	750	1,225	4,900	371	227	57
Rumania	250	1,000	1,900	7,600	250	132	33
Russia	1,811	15,798	40,080	167,000	115	45	11
United States	114	4,273	25,541	98,800	27	4	1
Allied Total	5,421	45,001	204,018	812,521	120	27	7
Germany	2,037	13,200	16,316	67,800	154	125	30
Austria-Hungary	1,100	9,000	12,176	58,600	122	90	19
Turkey	804	2,998	5,425	21,700	268	148	37
Bulgaria	88	400	1,100	4,700	220	80	19
Central Powers' Total	4,029	25,598	35,017	152,800	157	115	26
Total Overall	9,450	70,599	239,035	965,321	134	40	10

QUESTIONS TO CONSIDER

Now that you have read the selections, try to consider them collectively, drawing out the effects of war on the people of western Europe. First, consider the initial reaction to war. We saw in the Problem that war was universally greeted with patriotic enthusiasm. What forms did that enthusiasm assume in the poems of Brooke, Péguy, and Lissauer? What previous experience had these authors with modern warfare?

Next, assess the experience of front-line service as it is expressed in the literary and other sources. Why do you think the initial ardor for warfare wore off quickly? On whom or what did the writers lay the blame for the horrors of war? How radical was their discontent? Consider again the casualty figures in Source 15, the scenes of combat in Sources 4 and 5, and the descriptions of trench warfare in Sources 6 and 7. Remember that Barbusse wrote during the war and Remarque a decade later. Do their descriptions of modern warfare differ substantially? What do you think was uppermost in the minds of men subjected to such conditions?

The war inflicted unprecedented battle losses on every belligerent country, but societal groups within the warring countries did not suffer equally. In any combat situation, the highest casualty rate affects noncommissioned and junior officers—the sergeants, lieutenants, and captains who lead attacks at the front of their units. What social groups does Remarque's *All Quiet on the Western Front* suggest made up the officer corps of each warring nation? What postwar effect do you think the loss of such men might have?

The front-line experience had costs for those who survived, too. Why might you conclude from the German soldier's account of the holiday in 1914 that one of the war's first casualties was patriotic devotion to its cause? As the war wore on, other reactions to combat became widespread among soldiers. Barbusse said that the war created two separate Frances, front line and civilian. Does the character of Baumer in Remarque's novel reflect a similar division in Germany? Do you think a sense of alienation was a common reaction among veterans? How would it affect adjustment to postwar civilian life? Finally, assess the poems of Wilfred Owen and Siegfried Sassoon. How might you describe the sentiments expressed in those poems? What view of military authority does Sassoon's poem express? How old were Owen and Sassoon when they began military service? Are sentiments such as theirs usual in persons so young? What was the source for these views?

World War I affected civilian populations in ways no previous conflict had. Drawing on the German ration data, how do you think you would have found German wartime conditions? Why do you think Germans suffered nutritional deficiencies? Did such shortages also affect the German military, according to Source 7?

Every belligerent country recognized that the home front was essential to victory. The areas the Germans attacked in the London bombing described by Vera Brittain certainly lacked obvious military value. The Germans also launched long-range attacks on Paris, and one shell fell on a crowded church on Good Friday, 1918, killing or injuring 200 people. What was the goal of such attacks on targets of no military value? Recall the report to the French police on public opinion in the Grenoble area. What ideas were current among civilians? Why were French authorities so concerned about public opinion?

The war had a deep impact on women, too. Source 14 clearly shows a great spurt in the employment of Englishwomen in many industries. In which industries especially did they find employment? How were these jobs probably related to the war effort? Women left certain jobs, too. Which did they abandon? Many of the industries they left traditionally offered low-paying employment for unskilled or semiskilled workers. How did wartime conditions allow women to improve their economic positions in England and, indeed, in all the warring nations? Do you think women's wartime contributions (remember that the nursing efforts of Vera Brittain and other women are not reflected in Source 14) would argue for improved postwar status for women?

The effects of World War I would be felt long after the armistice that ended hostilities in 1918. Refer to the table in Source 15. Notice the total numbers of men mobilized, recalling that in countries like France and Germany 80 percent of the military-age male population was in uniform. What effect do you think the absence of so many young men from their homes had on the birth rate during the years 1914 to 1918? What enduring impact did the deaths of many of these men have on their countries' birth rates? What implications could all these factors have had for future defense considerations? Among the great powers, which country suffered the greatest proportional war losses? What do you predict the public attitudes in this country might be when war threatened again within twenty years of World War I's end? Do you think the costs of war would evoke the same response in all countries?

Your examination of these issues should now allow you to answer the main questions of this chapter: Why was World War I different from previous wars? What impact did it have on the soldiers at the front? How did it affect civilians at home?

EPILOGUE

World War I permanently changed Europe and the world. As this chapter demonstrated, the conflict introduced a new kind of warfare, a total

warfare that inflicted suffering on the civilian citizens of belligerent countries as well as on their men in military service. But World War I permanently changed much else, too.

The political old order of Europe expired in the trenches along with a generation of young men. The stress of modern warfare meant that no government survived politically when its war effort ended in defeat. At the war's end revolutions overthrew the old monarchies in Russia, Germany, Austria-Hungary, Bulgaria, and Turkey. The governmental change was most dramatic in Russia, where that country's wartime problems led to revolution and eventually to the world's first communist dictatorship, but everywhere defeat meant political collapse. That political collapse also contributed to numerous changes in national boundaries. The breakdown of governmental authority in many defeated countries permitted national minorities in these states to seek independence. Austria-Hungary and Turkey disappeared from the map as large, multinational empires as their subject peoples declared independence at war's end. And the Russian empire lost a large part of its western territory as Finns, Poles, Latvians, Lithuanians, Estonians, and Romanians used the moment of tsarist collapse to escape Russian rule.

World War I also facilitated the transformation of Western society. Women's labor in war industries, their work in nursing, and their participation in uniformed auxiliary services of the armed forces sustained the prewar demands of women for a political voice. In most Western countries, women gained the right to vote after World War I, a major step in attaining a status equal to that of males.

The war changed Europe economically, too. The financial needs of total warfare forced every government to borrow. The most obvious change was that the United States emerged from the war as the greatest creditor nation, but other economic changes occurred as well. As warring nations purchased raw materials and manufactured goods in the Americas and Asia during the conflict, the West's wealth began to shift out of Europe. In addition, western European nations, particularly France, faced tremendous war-related property damage whose repair would consume funds for years to come.

Another cost of the war in both economic and human terms was found among its victims. The injured and crippled had to be treated, rehabilitated, and paid pensions. The situation of England illustrates the extent of the problem. When the government finalized its pension rolls in 1929, 2,424,000 men were receiving some sort of disability pension, about 40 percent of all the soldiers who had served in the British army in the war.

The war's unhappiest result, however, was that it did not become what U.S. president Woodrow Wilson called "a war to end all wars." Rather, seeds for the next conflict were sown by the events and consequences of World War I. Total war created the desire for total victory, and the peace treaties reflected animosities produced by four years of bloody conflict. The Treaty of Versailles presented Germany with a settlement that would produce a desire for revision of the peace terms and even revenge. At the same time, the great losses of life in World War I engendered in many people in victorious nations a "never again" attitude that would lead them to seek to avoid another war at all costs. This attitude would in part result in efforts to appease a resurgent and vengeful Germany under Adolf Hitler (see Chapter 12) in the 1930s.

The alienation of former soldiers from civilian life led many to search out civilian opportunities for renewing the comradeship of the front, such as veterans' groups and paramilitary organizations. Especially in the defeated countries or in those victorious countries disappointed with their gains, this impulse had dangerous consequences. In Italy and Germany, veterans enlisted in great numbers in the ranks of uniformed right-wing organizations that became the power base for the brutal armed supporters of the dictators Mussolini and Hitler (see Chapter 12). Pledged to winning back the losses in their nations' defeats in World War I, such leaders as Hitler and Mussolini seized political power by exploiting postwar problems and resentments. Their policies were to breed a second global conflict.

CHAPTER TWELVE

SELLING A

TOTALITARIAN SYSTEM

Hitler's dictatorship differed in one fundamental point from all its predecessors in history. His was the first dictatorship in the present period of modern technical development, a dictatorship which made complete use of all technical means for the domination of its own country.

Through technical devices like the radio and the loudspeaker, eighty million people were deprived of independent thought. It was thereby possible to subject them to the will of one man. . . .

Earlier dictators needed highly qualified assistants, even at the lowest level, men who could think and act independently. The totalitarian system in the period of modern technical development can dispense with them; the means of communication alone make it possible to mechanize the lower leadership. As a result of this there arises the new type of the uncritical recipient of orders. . . . Another result was the far-reaching supervision of the citizens of the State and the maintenance of a high degree of secrecy for criminal acts.

The nightmare of many a man that one day nations could be dominated by technical means was all but realized in Hitler's totalitarian system.[1]

This was how Albert Speer, once one of Hitler's most trusted subordinates, sought to answer the question that every student of the Nazi phenomenon must ultimately ask: "How could it have happened?"[2] Because your

1. Final statement by Albert Speer to the International Military Tribunal for major war criminals at Nuremberg, 1946. Quoted in Alan Bullock, *Hitler: A Study in Tyranny,* rev. ed. (New York: Harper & Row, 1964), p. 380. An architect by training, Speer (1905–1981) first attracted Hitler's attention because of his expertise in that field and talent for orchestrating party rallies. He testified at Nuremberg, "If Hitler had had any friends, I would certainly have been one of his close friends." (*Inside the Third Reich: Memoirs by Albert Speer,* trans. Richard and Clara Winston [New York: Macmillan, 1970], p. 609.) Hitler promoted Speer to minister of armaments during World War II, and in that capacity, Speer's efforts maintained German war production despite Allied bombing. As it became clear, however, that the war was lost and that Hitler was determined to fight on regardless of the cost to Germany, Speer made an attempt to assassinate the dictator.

2. See, for example, Richard F. Hamilton, *Who Voted for Hitler?* (Princeton, N.J.: Princeton University Press, 1982), p. 3.

textbook examines the roots and development of Hitler's doctrines, we will not focus in this chapter on the horrific ideology of the Nazi movement. Rather, we will examine the question that Speer addressed, for in the political history of the West, the Nazi party was the first totalitarian movement to make full use of modern media to gain and maintain power.

In their use of modern media and campaign techniques to achieve power, Hitler and his followers built on a number of developments in Western politics, technology, and intellectual life. As we observed in Chapter 7, the nature of politics in the West had begun to change in the late nineteenth century. The right to vote in the more advanced European countries expanded to include all men and, after World War I, women as well. The increased electorate demanded new political techniques. No longer could gentleman politicians gain power by winning the support of a small, male, socially privileged electorate. A mass audience had to be addressed. Although many politicians at first refused to degrade themselves by appealing for support to such an audience, we can see emerging in late-nineteenth-century campaigns the modern political objective—and the requirement—of swaying large numbers of voters.

In 1879 and 1880, the British statesman William E. Gladstone (1809–1898) won election to Parliament from Midlothian County, Scotland, following a campaign that became the model for modern ones, especially after Gladstone built his victory into his second term as prime minister.

In Midlothian Gladstone delivered numerous public speeches. He presented many of these from the platform of his campaign train at a variety of locations, the first "whistle-stop campaign." Gladstone's campaign style found imitators in other democracies, although they did not always achieve his success. In the U.S. presidential campaign of 1896, the Democratic candidate, William Jennings Bryan (1860–1925), traveled about 18,000 miles and gave more than 600 speeches in an unsuccessful campaign against the Republican candidate, William McKinley (1843–1901). McKinley, who epitomized the old-style campaigner, simply received visitors from the press and public at the front porch of his Ohio home. Other candidates in many democracies would follow the example of Gladstone and Bryan.

Technological advances aided political leaders in their appeals for mass support. By the 1890s, developments like the Linotype machine, which mechanized typesetting, greatly reduced the price of newspapers and other printed materials for an increasingly literate public. Mass-circulation daily newspapers had tremendous potential for shaping public opinion. Political leaders also used other technological developments in delivering their messages. By 1920 the motion picture, photograph, radio, and microphone and public-address system all represented new media through which to influence the public.

At the same time that new media became available to political leaders, a greater understanding of how to influence public opinion was emerging in the early-twentieth-century West. During World War I, many belligerent countries employed increasingly sophisticated propaganda techniques to sustain the morale of their own citizens or to erode the will to fight among enemy populations. The lessons learned on influencing public opinion were not forgotten, as we will see.[3]

Industrial mass production required mass markets, and in the United States modern advertising techniques developed to stimulate the consumption necessary to sustain production. Advertising had political applications as well. One advertising strategy is to generate interest in a new product by creating suspense about it. When the Nazis launched a new Berlin newspaper, *Der Angriff* (*The Attack*), in 1927, a poster campaign was launched to heighten interest in it. The first posters issued simply stated, "The Attack?" The next group of posters proclaimed, "The Attack takes place on July 4!" The last set of posters was informational, alerting readers that the paper would appear on Mondays, that its motto was "For the Suppressed against the Exploiters," and that "Every German man and every German woman will read 'The Attack' and subscribe to it!"[4]

Even science, particularly psychology, contributed to the understanding of human thought essential to those who sought to shape opinion. The French social psychologist Gustave Le Bon (1841–1931), for example, affected Hitler's political technique. Le Bon's ideas, although doubted today, were highly influential in the early twentieth century. A student of mass psychology, Le Bon claimed that the mind of the crowd was most susceptible to sentiment and emotion, not reason.[5]

The rapid pace of technological development and the equally swift emergence of techniques for molding public opinion meant that, by the 1920s, there existed an incompletely understood, underused, but nonetheless formidable arsenal for the politically ambitious to employ in attaining power. Forces prepared to exploit these technological and methodological developments emerged in the politically unstable environment of much of the post–World War I West.

Rooted in defeat, frustration in World War I, or the economic debacle of the Great Depression beginning in 1929, totalitarian movements emerged in many European countries. None of these movements proved more dangerous to traditional Western values than a German party that began insignificantly in 1919 as one of a multitude of right-wing, nationalist parties founded in response to the German defeat in the Great War. The party came to be known as the National Socialist German Workers' Party (Nazi),

3. Hitler in *Mein Kampf* (trans. Ralph Manheim [Boston: Houghton Mifflin, 1943], pp. 176–186) wrote of the lessons he had drawn from Allied propaganda during World War I.

4. Described in Ernest K. Bramsted, *Goebbels and National Socialist Propaganda, 1925–1945* (East Lansing, Mich.: Michigan State University Press, 1965), p. 30.

5. Le Bon's great work was *The Crowd: A Study of the Popular Mind,* originally published in 1897 and available in German.

and Adolf Hitler quickly emerged not only as its leader but as a master of the new style of politics, including political propaganda.

The successful propagandist must correctly identify the fears and hopes of the people he or she wishes to influence. In Germany after World War I, Nazi propaganda had a great number of fears and hopes to exploit. Most Germans rejected the Treaty of Versailles that ended the war. Humiliated by the treaty's assignment of war guilt to Germany, they were also angered by the huge reparations their country was forced to pay the victorious allies. German nationalists especially rejected the unilateral disarmament the treaty sought to impose on Germany. All Germans hoped for some revision of the Treaty of Versailles.

Some Germans blamed the nation's defeat on internal enemies, not on battlefield disasters. These persons, mostly conservative, identified two chief groups on which to place responsibility for the internal dissent at the war's end that had brought the overthrow of Emperor William II (Kaiser Wilhelm II) and armistice. The first groups condemned for the defeat were the parties of the left, the socialists and communists, who had participated in the revolution of 1918 that created the Weimar Republic. To many, the communists seemed the greatest threat because that party had attempted to seize power and create a Marxist state by force in the Spartacist Revolt of 1919. The communist threat, moreover, persisted after 1919. The party's voting bloc grew as the economic problems of the Great Depression intensified, and many feared that

the communists might gain power through election.

The other group on whom some Germans sought to fix the blame of their defeat was the country's small Jewish minority. Such Germans drew on nineteenth-century nationalist prejudices to allege some Jewish involvement in Germany's defeat. Certain political leaders of the early German republic, the men whose government signed the Versailles Treaty, were Jews. One prominent Jewish official, Walter Rathenau (1867–1922), died at the hands of a nationalist fanatic.

The Great Depression also increased Germans' fears after 1929. The depression hit Germany particularly hard, threatening economic ruin to many. Many parties and movements identified those fears and hopes of postwar Germans and sought to address them by rejecting the Treaty of Versailles, by portraying themselves as anticommunist or anti-Semitic, and by proposing solutions to the depression. But, as we will see, it was the skill of Hitler and the Nazis in the new politics and propaganda that allowed them to exploit most effectively Germans' fears and hopes to gain power.

It was Hitler who transformed a party that essentially had been little more than a collection of malcontents in the back room of a Munich beer hall into a movement with a considerable following in the 1920s. It was Hitler who gave the party a visual identity by adopting its symbol, the swastika, and by creating its banners. It was also Hitler who exploited the alienation of many war veterans by drawing them into the S.A. (*Sturm Abteilung*), the Storm Troopers or uniformed, paramilitary branch of the party, which was prepared to use violence and intimidation against communists and socialists. And it was Hitler who launched an abortive attempt in 1923 to seize power forcibly for his party.

Hitler's failed revolution resulted in his brief imprisonment, during which he wrote *Mein Kampf* (*My Struggle*), the political statement of his movement. On his release Hitler resolved to seek power within the political system—that is, to win power through the electoral system of the German republic. To his quest for power Hitler brought the Nazi party apparatus and symbols, his excellent oratorical ability, and, most dangerously, a keen understanding of the uses of political propaganda and modern media to mold public opinion. Aiding him in presenting his party to German voters was Joseph Goebbels (1897–1945), a man whose speaking abilities, understanding of propaganda and modern media, and political unscrupulousness rivaled Hitler's own.

In his quest for power after 1923, Hitler led the Nazis through a number of electoral campaigns. The first results of Nazi appeals to German voters disappointed many of Hitler's followers. Indeed, in elections to the Reichstag, Germany's parliament, the party's vote actually declined during the 1920s. In the elections of May 1924, it captured 6.5 percent of the vote; that total declined to 3.0 percent in December 1924 and 2.6 percent in May 1928. The party's electoral breakthrough of 1930, however, reversed this trend as the Nazis increased their share of the Reichstag vote to 18.3 percent. Certainly, in achieving their victory, the Nazis' extreme nationalist message capitalized on the Young Plan of 1929, which had failed to reduce the war reparation payments to the allies so deeply resented by many Germans. The growing severity of the Great Depression after 1929 also encouraged many Germans to look to the strong leadership that Hitler claimed to offer. As party membership and dues grew, and as Hitler secured some limited financial aid from a few wealthy opponents of the Young Plan such as Alfred Hugenberg,[6] for the first time the Nazis had sufficient funds to exploit the modern media thoroughly.

The Nazi share of the vote increased rapidly after 1930. The party especially demonstrated its media skills in 1932, when Hitler ran for president of Germany against the incumbent, the octogenarian war hero Field Marshal Paul von Hindenburg. Although Hindenburg won the election with 53 percent of the vote to Hitler's 36.8 percent, the campaign built momentum for the Nazis and

---

6. **Alfred Hugenberg** (1865–1951): leader of the Nationalist party and a bigoted conservative ultranationalist with tremendous wealth based in industry and great influence founded on his control of a number of newspapers and Germany's largest film and newsreel firm. His newsreels, shown regularly in German theaters, and his newspapers gave the Nazis considerable coverage. Like other conservatives, Hugenberg made the mistake of classifying Hitler with other politicians. Hitler quickly excluded Hugenberg from the government once the Nazis had gained power.

helped them to perfect their campaign style. In the Reichstag elections held in July 1932, the Nazis won 37.4 percent of the vote to become the largest single party in parliament, a distinction they retained despite a diminished Nazi 33.1 percent of the vote in Reichstag elections in November 1932. On the basis of these victories, which gave the Nazis control of the largest single bloc of seats in the Reichstag, conservative associates of President von Hindenburg finally convinced him to name Hitler chancellor or prime minister on January 30, 1933. The Nazis had gained control of the government, and German democracy was their first victim: by the end of the year the country was a one-party, totalitarian state.

To achieve power, the Nazis had persuaded substantial numbers of German voters to support their candidates. Certainly in the aftermath of Germany's defeat in 1918, the party's extreme nationalism attracted support, as did its anti-Semitism, which blamed the country's economic and political woes on its tiny Jewish minority. This Nazi political rhetoric of hatred ultimately became government policy when Hitler gained power. Anti-Semitism took on brutal form in the Holocaust. Extreme nationalism manifested itself in the Nazi goal of settling Germans in eastern Europe by pushing out the area's Slavic natives. But other German parties in the 1920s and early 1930s also expressed anti-Semitic and nationalistic ideas. Your objective in this chapter is to determine how Nazi use of modern media and techniques, such as propaganda for molding public opinion, allowed Hitler's party to draw the German voter's attention. As you assess the evidence that follows, you should ask yourself what kind of image the Nazis projected. Why did it appeal to German voters? How did the Nazis use media to aid their rise to power? As a result of your analysis, you should be able to answer in some form that most disturbing question, "How could it have happened?"

SOURCES AND METHOD

This chapter presents a variety of evidence: theoretical writings on Nazi political strategy, visual propaganda used by Nazis to publicize their cause, and observations on the public reception of Hitler's media campaign. Through individual and comparative study of these sources, you should be able to determine the nature of the attraction of the Nazis for German voters.

The evidence opens with two selections by Hitler on the means for gaining power. Sources 1 and 2 are taken from Hitler's *Mein Kampf,* which he wrote during his imprisonment in 1923 to 1924. In this work, often ignored in his early days, Hitler stated much of his future program, including his rabidly anti-Jewish and anti-Marxist policies and his plans to expand Germany eastward. In the evidence presented in this chapter, you will read Hitler's ideas on the use of propaganda and other tactics for coming to power. How were the ideas for seizing power that he expressed in 1924 to be realized within a decade? How would you assess his understanding of human psychology?

When you finish the Hitler materials, you will find an assortment of evidence selected to further your analysis of how the Nazis sought to win support for their party. You will be examining, in effect, a thoroughly modern public relations effort, complete with slogans. In Source 3, assess the nature of the Nazi propaganda effort as defined by its director, Joseph Goebbels. Why do you think Goebbels so closely controlled the party's propaganda?

Consider next the S.A., remembering, of course, that orders like that in Source 4 are not always rigidly obeyed by subordinates in any organization. Examine the pictorial evidence on the S.A. in Sources 5 and 6. The banners express Nazi slogans; the Regensburg S.A. banner proclaims, "Everything for the Fatherland." Nazi meetings always opened with solemn processions of such banners. What impression did the marching men seek to convey to their audience on the streets of Spandau?

Next read Source 7, the report of the brawl in the Pharus Hall in 1927. You should understand that this brawl was no accident; Goebbels deliberately scheduled the meeting to take place in a hall used by the Nazis' enemies, the communist and socialist political and labor groups. The hall, moreover, was in the heart of a left-wing, working-class district of Berlin. What could Goebbels have hoped to gain from the fight that was bound to ensue from his provocative action in selecting such a meeting site?

The next evidence consists of posters produced by the Nazis. The poster, a traditional political medium, was used extensively by the Nazis. They relied especially on posters in their early days, before they secured the funds necessary to exploit more novel media. The poster in Source 8 was part of the propaganda campaign Nazi leaders organized for the spring 1924 German legislative elections. At the time of the elections, Hitler remained in prison as a result of his failed attempt to seize power in 1923, and his party nominally was outlawed. Thus party leaders entered the campaign as part of a right-wing, nationalist coalition, the "Völkischen Block" identified on the poster. The German word *Volk* is difficult to translate. Superficially, it may be translated as "people" or "nation," but for early-twentieth-century Germans the word had a much more complex meaning conveying the innate superiority of German culture, language, and people over non-German cultures and peoples. Thus its use to identify a right-wing, nationalistic political alliance was not accidental, and was entirely consistent with Nazi ideology. Indeed, the Nazi origins of this poster are evident in the party's insignia, the swastika, in the lower corners of the poster. Analyze the poster to ascertain what sentiments the Nazis appealed to in post–World War I Germany and to which classes they looked for support. What group did the "String-puller" represent (notice his watch chain)? What message did his identity convey to Germans?

[341]

The second poster, Source 9, conveys much about Germany in the 1920s. Why might the Nazis address females? Of what problems did this poster, issued in the midst of the depression, remind Germans? What did it promise them? The third poster, Source 10, was the work of a skilled propaganda artist, "Mjolnir" ("Hammer"), who drew cartoons extensively for the Berlin newspaper *Der Angriff*, edited by Goebbels. Analyze the artist's message by examining the faces of the Storm Troopers. What sentiment do you find there? What sort of message does this poster convey about the party and its solutions for Germany?

Another Nazi political device was the public mass meeting, designed to convey the impression of vast support for the party. It was a technique Hitler learned early while observing Social Democratic demonstrations as a youth in Vienna. He wrote in *Mein Kampf*:

> With what changed feeling I now gazed at the endless columns of a mass demonstration of Viennese workers that took place one day as they marched past four abreast! For nearly two hours I stood there watching with bated breath the gigantic human dragon slowly winding by.

As their resources increased, the Nazis perfected the mass meeting. Source 11 shows one such rally in Berlin's Sports Palace, a favored site because it seated a large audience of 12,000 persons. Events like this were always carefully staged: The aisles are lined with the party faithful, ready for the entry of the speakers, accompanied by a uniformed S.A. guard unit and party banners. Why would such an elaborate spectacle have been important to the party cause?

The Nazis also employed music as propaganda to win support. The person whose name the song bears in Source 12, Horst Wessel, was a young Nazi who wrote the words to the song as a poem. The words eventually were set to a traditional stirring tune, but Horst Wessel himself drifted away from the party in pursuit of a female prostitute. He took up residence with her and was fatally shot by her procurer, who coincidentally was a communist, in February 1930. In Goebbels's hands, Horst Wessel's misspent life was transformed into that of a hero martyred in the Nazis' cause by their communist enemies. His song became Germany's second national anthem after Deutschland über Alles (Germany Above All) in the Nazi era. In reading the song's words, identify the problems it identifies. What benefits does the song claim the party offered Germans?

Also part of Nazi political propaganda was the creation of what Goebbels himself called the "Führer (Leader) Myth." This myth, which Goebbels regarded as one of his great propaganda accomplishments, attempted to convince Germans that a strong, courageous, and brilliant Hitler personified a Germany restored from its defeat. In its more extreme manifestations, the myth almost deified Hitler, appealing

[342]

to many Germans accustomed to strong rulers during the monarchy and therefore unhappy with what they believed to be the weak government of the republic. Source 13 is drawn from an elementary school textbook published shortly after the Nazis gained power, but it describes Hitler's campaign for power. What qualities did the party's propaganda apparatus wish the young to believe that Hitler possessed?

The Nazis did not come to power solely through conveying a positive image for their party and leader, however. They also used propaganda to exploit fears, employed violence to intimidate voters, and used new technologies to sway the thinking of their fellow Germans. Source 14 is a pamphlet, issued, you must remember, in the midst of the economic collapse of the early 1930s. Recall the events of Germany's past as you read it, and analyze its appeal.

The violence of the Hitler movement can best be viewed on the local level. The graph in Source 15 presents the rhythm of political life in the German town of Northeim. The number of political meetings, to which the Nazis contributed more than their share, increased sharply at election times. What else increased?

Source 16 presents the political beliefs of Dr. Joseph Goebbels, a fervent Nazi and a master of political propaganda. Convinced of his own historical importance, Goebbels kept a diary from his earliest days in politics to give future generations a record of his thoughts and activities.

He was still making entries in 1945 as the war ended. When Russian armies closed in on Berlin, Goebbels committed suicide. His diary, like any diary, must be used with caution, because most writers tend to put their own behavior and motivations in the best light. Nonetheless, it does offer an important perspective on Goebbels's propaganda work. Assess his command of his job as you read the selection. What new technologies did he employ in winning popular support for the Nazis?

The evidence in this chapter concludes with two observations on the impact of Nazi efforts to win support among Germans. The first is a report by a German Protestant leader noting membership losses from the Protestant youth movement to the Nazis. The second is by the American correspondent William L. Shirer (1904–1993), who covered events in Germany from 1934 to 1941. A perceptive observer of the Hitler movement, Shirer was able to assess the kind of appeal it had been building in Germany during the years before he arrived. What appeal to Germans do these two very different persons note in the Nazi movement?

Now turn to the evidence. You should read it with the foregoing considerations in mind, seeking to answer the central questions of this chapter: What image did the Nazis convey to German voters? Why did they appeal to German voters? How did the Nazis use media to aid their rise to power?

FUNDAMENTAL POLITICAL STRATEGIES OF THE NAZI PARTY

Sources 1 and 2 from Adolf Hitler, Mein Kampf, *translated by Ralph Manheim. Copyright 1943 and renewed 1971 by Houghton Mifflin Company. Reprinted by permission of Houghton Mifflin Company. All rights reserved.*

1. Hitler on the Nature and Purpose of Propaganda

The goal of a political reform movement will never be reached by enlightenment work or by influencing ruling circles, but only by the achievement of political power. Every world-moving idea has not only the right, but also the duty, of securing, those means which make possible the execution of its ideas. Success is the one earthly judge concerning the right or wrong of such an effort, and under success we must not understand, as in the year 1918, the achievement of power in itself, but an exercise of that power that will benefit the nation. Thus, a coup d'état must not be regarded as successful if, as senseless state's attorneys in Germany think today, the revolutionaries have succeeded in possessing themselves of the state power, but only if, by the realization of the purposes and aims underlying such a revolutionary action, more benefit accrues to the nation than under the past régime. Something which cannot very well be claimed for the German revolution, as the gangster job of autumn, 1918, calls itself.[7] . . .

The victory of an idea will be possible the sooner, the more comprehensively propaganda has prepared people as a whole and the more exclusive, rigid, and firm the organization which carries out the fight in practice. . . .

To whom should propaganda be addressed? To the scientifically trained intelligentsia or to the less educated masses?

It must be addressed always and exclusively to the masses.

What the intelligentsia—or those who today unfortunately often go by that name—what they need is not propaganda but scientific instruction. The content of propaganda is not science any more than the object represented in a poster is art. The art of the poster lies in the designer's ability to attract the attention of the crowd by form and color. A poster advertising an art exhibit

---

7. **the gangster job of autumn 1918**: the revolution of October and November 1918 that overthrew Emperor William II and established the Weimar Republic. Hitler, like many of the German right, believed that revolution to have been the work of socialists, communists, and Jews, who, by toppling the old government, had "stabbed in the back" the German army at the front in World War I and made defeat in that conflict inevitable.

must direct the attention of the public to the art being exhibited; the better it succeeds in this, the greater is the art of the poster itself. The poster should give the masses an idea of the significance of the exhibition, it should not be a substitute for the art on display. Anyone who wants to concern himself with the art itself must do more than study the poster; and it will not be enough for him just to saunter through the exhibition. We may expect him to examine and immerse himself in the individual works, and thus little by little form a fair opinion.

A similar situation prevails with what we today call propaganda.

The function of propaganda does not lie in the scientific training of the individual, but in calling the masses' attention to certain facts, processes, necessities, etc., whose significance is thus for the first time placed within their field of vision.

The whole art consists in doing this so skillfully that everyone will be convinced that the fact is real, the process necessary, the necessity correct, etc. But since propaganda is not and cannot be the necessity in itself, since its function, like the poster, consists in attracting the attention of the crowd, and not in educating those who are already educated or who are striving after education and knowledge, its effect for the most part must be aimed at the emotions and only to a very limited degree at the so-called intellect.

All propaganda must be popular and its intellectual level must be adjusted to the most limited intelligence among those it is addressed to. Consequently, the greater the mass it is intended to reach, the lower its purely intellectual level will have to be. But if, as in propaganda for sticking out a war, the aim is to influence a whole people, we must avoid excessive intellectual demands on our public, and too much caution cannot be exerted in this direction.

The more modest its intellectual ballast, the more exclusively it takes into consideration the emotions of the masses, the more effective it will be. And this is the best proof of the soundness or unsoundness of a propaganda campaign, and not success in pleasing a few scholars or young aesthetes.

The art of propaganda lies in understanding the emotional ideas of the great masses and finding, through a psychologically correct form, the way to the attention and thence to the heart of the broad masses. The fact that our bright boys do not understand this merely shows how mentally lazy and conceited they are.

Once we understand how necessary it is for propaganda to be adjusted to the broad mass, the following rule results:

It is a mistake to make propaganda many-sided, like scientific instruction, for instance.

The receptivity of the great masses is very limited, their intelligence is small, but their power of forgetting is enormous. In consequence of these facts, all effective propaganda must be limited to a very few points and must harp on these in slogans until the last member of the public understands what you want him to understand by your slogan. As soon as you sacrifice this slogan and try to be many-sided, the effect will piddle away, for the crowd can neither digest nor retain the material offered. In this way the result is weakened and in the end entirely cancelled out.

Thus we see that propaganda must follow a simple line and correspondingly the basic tactics must be psychologically sound. . . .

But the most brilliant propagandist techniques will yield no success unless one fundamental principle is borne in mind constantly and with unflagging attention. It must confine itself to a few points and repeat them over and over. Here, as so often in this world, persistence is the first and most important requirement for success.

2. Hitler on Terror in Politics

Like the woman, whose psychic state is determined less by grounds of abstract reason than by an indefinable emotional longing for a force which will complement her nature, and who, consequently, would rather bow to a strong man than dominate a weakling, likewise the masses love a commander more than a petitioner and feel inwardly more satisfied by a doctrine, tolerating no other beside itself, than by the granting of liberalistic freedom with which, as a rule, they can do little, and are prone to feel that they have been abandoned. They are equally unaware of their shameless spiritual terrorization and the hideous abuse of their human freedom, for they absolutely fail to suspect the inner insanity of the whole doctrine. All they see is the ruthless force and brutality of its calculated manifestations, to which they always submit in the end. . . .

I achieved an equal understanding of the importance of physical terror toward the individual and the masses.

Here, too, the psychological effect can be calculated with precision.

Terror at the place of employment, in the factory, in the meeting hall, and on the occasion of mass demonstrations will always be successful unless opposed by equal terror.

NAZI TECHNIQUES FOR
PUBLICIZING THEIR CAUSE

Sources 3 and 4 from Jeremy Noakes and Geoffrey Pridham, editors, Documents on Nazism, *1919–1945, pp. 83–84, 106, 108. Reprinted by permission of Sterling Lord Literistic, Inc. Copyright 1974 by Jeremy Noakes.*

3. Joseph Goebbels,
Directives for the Presidential
Campaign of 1932

(1) Reich Propaganda Department to all *Gaue*[8] and all *Gau* Propaganda Departments.

8. **Gaue:** the administrative divisions of Germany set up by the Nazi party.

. . . A striking slogan:

> Those who want everything to stay as it is vote for Hindenburg. Those who want everything changed vote for Hitler. . . .

(2) Reich Propaganda Department to all *Gaue* and all *Gau* Propaganda Departments.

. . . Hitler Poster. The Hitler poster depicts a fascinating Hitler head on a completely black background. Subtitle: white on black—"Hitler." In accordance with the Führer's wish this poster is to be put up only during the final days [of the campaign]. Since experience shows that during the final days there is a variety of coloured posters, this poster with its completely black background will contrast with all the others and will produce a tremendous effect on the masses. . . .

(3) Reich Propaganda Department
Instructions for the National Socialist Press for the election of the Reich President

1. From Easter Tuesday 29 March until Sunday 10 April inclusive, all National Socialist papers, both daily and weekly, must appear in an enlarged edition with a tripled circulation. Two-thirds of this tripled circulation must be made available, without charge, to the *Gau* leadership responsible for its area of distribution for propaganda purposes. . . .

2. From Easter Tuesday 29 March until Sunday 3 April inclusive, a special topic must be dealt with every day on the first page of all our papers in a big spread. Tuesday 29 March: Hitler as a man. Wednesday 30 March: Hitler as a fighter (gigantic achievement through his willpower, etc.). Friday 1 April: Hitler as a statesman—plenty of photos. . . .

3. On Sunday 3 April, at noon (end of an Easter truce), the great propaganda journey of the Führer through Germany will start, through which about a million people are to be reached directly through our Führer's speeches. . . . The press organization is planned so that four press centres will be set up in Germany, which in turn will pass on immediately any telephone calls to the other papers of their area, whose names have been given them.

4. S.A. Order 111 of Adolf Hitler, 1926

1. The SA will appear in public only in closed formation. This is at the same time one of the most powerful forms of propaganda. The sight of a large number of men inwardly and outwardly uniform and disciplined, whose total

commitment to fighting is clearly visible or can be sensed, makes the deepest impression on every German and speaks a more convincing and inspiring language to his heart than speech, logic, or the written word is ever capable of doing.

Calm composure and natural behaviour underline the impression of strength—the strength of marching columns and the strength of the cause for which they are marching.

The inner strength of the cause makes the German conclude instinctively that it is right: "for only what is right, honest and good can release real strength." Where whole crowds purposefully risk life and limb and their livelihood for a cause (not in the upsurge of sudden mass suggestion), the cause must be great and true!

Here lies the task of the SA from the point of view of propaganda and recruiting. The SA leaders must gear the details and forms of their appearances to a common line.

2. This instinctive "proof of truth" is not underlined but disturbed and dissipated by the addition of logical arguments and propaganda. The following should be avoided: cheers and heckling, posters about day-to-day controversies, abuse, accompanying speeches, leaflets, festivals, public amusements.

3. It is inappropriate for the SA to work in one way one day and differently the next, according to circumstances. The SA must always and on principle refrain from all actual political propaganda and agitation. This should remain the task of the political leadership alone. However, each SA man is also a member of the Party and as such of course must cooperate as much as he can in the propaganda of the political leadership. But not the SA as such. Not the SA men on duty and in uniform.

The SA man is the holy freedom fighter. The member of the Party is the clever propagandist and skilled agitator. Political propaganda tries to enlighten the opponent, to argue with him, to understand his point of view, to enter into his thoughts, to agree with him to a certain extent. But when the SA arrives on the scene, this stops. It makes no concessions. It goes all out. It only recognizes the motto (metaphorically): Kill or be killed!

4. It is forbidden for an SA to appeal to the public (or its opponents) orally or in writing, either through proclamations, announcements, leaflets, press "corrections," letters, advertisements, invitations to festivals or meetings, or in any other way.

Public consecrations of the colours and sports competitions must take place within the framework of an event organized by a local branch, which alone issues the invitations or announcements for it.

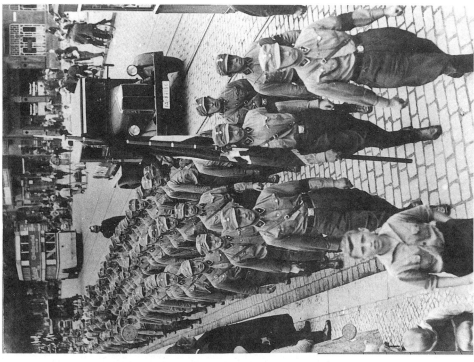

6. S.A. Propaganda Rally in Spandau, 1932

Sources 5 and 6 Bild 146/70/24/49/Bundesarchiv, Koblenz and Bild 146/27/148/214/Bundesarchiv, Koblenz.

5. Banners of the Regensburg
   S.A.: "Everything for the
   Fatherland, 1923"

Source 7 from Jeremy Noakes and Geoffrey Pridham, editors, Documents on Nazism, 1919– 1945, *pp. 83–84, 106, 108. Reprinted by permission of Sterling Lord Literistic, Inc. Copyright 1974 by Jeremy Noakes.*

7. Report of a Nazi Meeting Held in a Heavily Communist Quarter of Berlin, February 1927

On the 11th of this month the Party held a public mass meeting in the "Pharus [Beer] Halls" in Wedding, the real working-class quarter, with the subject: "The Collapse of the Bourgeois Class State." Comrade Dr Goebbels was the speaker. It was quite clear to us what that meant. It had to be visibly shown that National Socialism is determined to reach the workers. We succeeded once before in getting a foothold in Wedding. There were huge crowds at the meeting. More than 1,000 people filled the hall whose political composition was four-fifths SA to one-fifth KPD.[9] But the latter had gathered their main forces in the street. When the meeting was opened by Comrade Daluege, the SA leader, there were, as was expected, provocative shouts of "On a point of order!" After the KPD members had been told that *we,* not they, decided points of order, and that they would have the right to ask questions after the talk by Comrade Dr Goebbels, the first scuffling broke out. Peace seemed to be restored until there was renewed heckling. When the chairman announced that the hecklers would be sent out if the interruptions continued, the KPD worked themselves into a frenzy. Meanwhile, the SA had gradually surrounded the centre of the disturbance, and the Communists, sensing the danger, suddenly became aggressive. What followed all happened within three or four minutes. Within seconds both sides had picked up chairs, beer mugs, even tables, and a savage fight began. The Communists were gradually pushed under the gallery which we had taken care to occupy and soon chairs and glasses came hurtling down from there also. The fight was quickly decided: the KPD left with 85 wounded, more or less: that is to say, they could not get down the stairs as fast as they had calmly and "innocently" climbed them. On our side we counted 3 badly wounded and about 10–12 slightly. When the police appeared the fight was already over. Marxist terrorism had been bloodily suppressed.

9. **Kommunistische Partei Deutschlands:** the German Communist party.

Source 8 from Anshcläge: Ebenhausen: Langewiesche-Brandt Verlag.

8. Poster: "The String-Puller. White Collar and Manual Laborers: Vote for the Völkischen Block," 1924

10. Poster: "National Socialism: The Organized Will of the People," 1932

NATIONAL-SOZIALISMUS

DER ORGANISIERTE WILLE DER NATION

9. Poster: "Women! Millions of Men Are Without Work. Millions of Children Are Without a Future. Save the German Family! Vote for Adolf Hitler!," 1932

Frauen!

Adolf Hitler!

Source 11 from Bundesarchiv, Koblenz.

11. A National Socialist Rally in the Berlin Sports Palace, September 1930

Source 12 from Liederbuch der Nationalsozialistischen Deutschen Arbeiterpartei *(Munich: Zentralverlag der NSDAP, 1938). Selection translated by Julius R. Ruff.*

12. "The Horst Wessel Song," ca 1930

Raise high the banner! Close the serried ranks!
S.A. marches on with calm, firm stride.
Comrades killed by the Red Front and the Reaction[10]
March in spirit in our ranks.

Clear the streets for the brown battalions![11]
Clear the streets for the Storm Troopers!
The swastika gives hope to millions.
The day of freedom and bread is breaking.

10. **Red Front:** the *Rot Frontkämpfer Bund* or Red Fighters League, the communist opposition to the Storm Troopers. The more traditional right, the Nationalist party, which sought a restoration of a monarchy and is here called the **Reaction,** had an armed force, too, uniformed in green.

11. The S.A. uniform was brown.

[353]

The roll call is heard for the last time!
We all stand ready for the struggle!
Soon Hitler's banner will fly over every street
And Germany's bondage will soon end.

Source 13 from George L. Mosse, editor, Nazi Culture: Intellectual, Cultural, and Social Life in the Third Reich *(New York: Grosset and Dunlap, 1966), pp. 291–293. Selection translated by the editor. Used by permission of George L. Mosse.*

13. Otto Dietrich, Description of Hitler's Campaign by Airplane, 1932

On April 8, 1932, a severe storm, beyond all imagining, raged over Germany. Hail rattled down from dark clouds. Flash floods devastated fields and gardens. Muddy foam washed over streets and railroad tracks, and the hurricane uprooted even the oldest and biggest trees.

We are driving to the Mannheim Airport. Today no one would dare expose an airplane to the fury of the elements. The German Lufthansa has suspended all air traffic.

In the teeming rain stands the solid mass of the most undaunted of our followers. They want to be present, they want to see for themselves when the Führer entrusts himself to an airplane in this raging storm.

Without a moment's hesitation the Führer orders that we take off at once. We have an itinerary to keep, for in western Germany hundreds of thousands are waiting.

It is only with the greatest difficulty that the ground crew and the SA troopers, with long poles in their strong fists, manage to hold on to the wings of the plane, so that the gale does not hurl it into the air and wreck it. The giant motors begin to turn over. Impatient with its fetters, the plane begins to buck and shake, eager for the takeoff on the open runway.

One more short rearing up and our wild steed sweeps across the greensward. A few perilous jumps, one last short touch with earth, and presto we are riding through the air straight into the witches' broth.

This is no longer flying, this is a whirling dance which today we remember only as a faraway dream. Now we jump across the aerial downdrafts, now we whip our way through tattered clouds, again a whirlpool threatens to drag us down, and then it seems that a giant catapult hurls us into steep heights.

And yet, what a feeling of security is in us in the face of this fury of the elements! The Führer's absolute serenity transmits itself to all of us. In every hour of danger he is ruled by his granite-like faith in his world-historical mission, the unshakable certainty that Providence will keep him from danger for the accomplishment of his great task.

[354]

Even here he remained the pre-eminent man, who masters danger because in his innermost being he has risen far above it. In this ruthless contest between man and machine the Führer attentively follows the heroic battle of our Master Pilot Bauer as he steers straight through the gale, or quickly jumps across a whole storm field, and then again narrowly avoids a threatening cloud wall, while the radio operator on board zealously catches the signals sent by the airfields.

Source 14 from Jeremy Noakes and Geoffrey Pridham, editors, Documents on Nazism, *1919–1945, pp. 83–84, 106, 108. Reprinted by permission of Sterling Lord Literistic, Inc. Copyright 1974 by Jeremy Noakes.*

14. Nazi Pamphlet, ca 1932

Attention! Gravediggers at work!

Middle-class citizens![12] Retailers! Craftsmen! Tradesmen!

A new blow aimed at your ruin is being prepared and carried out in Hanover!

The present system enables the gigantic concern

WOOLWORTH (America)

supported by finance capital, to build a new vampire business in the centre of the city in the Georgstrasse to expose you to complete ruin. This is the wish and aim of the black-red[13] system as expressed in the following remarks of Marxist leaders.

The Marxist Engels declared in May 1890: "If capital destroys the small artisans and retailers it does a good thing. . . ."

That is the black-red system of today!

Put an end to this system and its abettors! Defend yourself, middle-class citizen! Join the mighty organization that alone is in a position to conquer your arch-enemies. Fight with us in the Section for Craftsmen and Retail Traders within the great freedom movement of Adolf Hitler!

Put an end to the system!

Mittelstand,[14] *vote for List 8!*

---

12. **middle-class citizens:** this is a rather imprecise translation of the original German *Mittelstand.* That word, which is difficult to translate, here describes a very specific segment of society to whom the Nazis made special appeal: small shopkeepers and craftsmen whose livelihoods increasingly were threatened by competition from large department stores and big industrial concerns.

13. Prussia was governed by a coalition of the Catholic Center party and the Social Democrats. Because of its association with the Church, the Center was labeled "Black"; the leftist socialists were labeled "Red."

14. *Mittelstand:* middle-class shopkeepers and craftsmen.

Source 15 adapted from William Sheridan Allen, The Nazi Seizure of Power: The Experience of a Single German Town, 1922–1945, revised ed. (New York: Franklin Watts,
1984), p. 321. Copyright © 1965, 1984 by William Sheridan Allen. Used with permission of
the publisher, Franklin Watts, Inc.

15. Political Violence in Northeim, Germany, 1930–1932

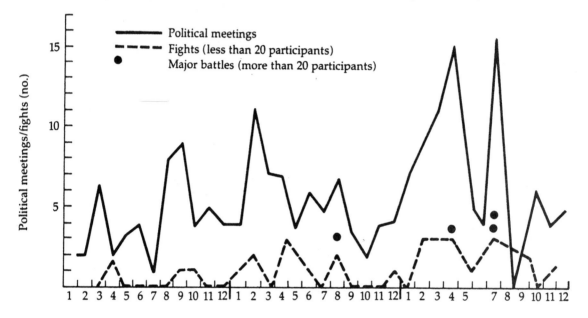

Source 16 from Joseph Goebbels, My Part in Germany's Fight, translated by Kurt Fielder
(New York: Howard Fertig, 1979), pp. 44, 47–48, 55, 66, 145–146, 214.

16. Joseph Goebbels, *My Part in Germany's Fight*, 1934

February 29th, 1932.

Our propaganda is working at high pressure.

The clerical work is finished. Now the technical side of the fight begins. What
enormous preparations are necessary to organize such a vast distribution!

Reported to the Leader (Hitler) at noon. I gave him details as to the measures we are taking. The election campaign is chiefly to be fought by means of
placards and addresses. We have not much capital, but as the Party is working
gratuitously a little money goes a long way.

Fifty thousand gramophone records have been made, which are so small they
can be slipped into an ordinary envelope. The supporters of the Government
will be astonished when they place these miniature records on the gramophone!

In Berlin everything is going well.

A film (of me) is being made and I speak a few words in it for about ten minutes. It is to be shown in all public gardens and squares of the larger cities. . . .

March 8th, 1932.

Dictate two articles and heaps of handbills. The placard war has reached its climax. Up till now we lead in the race.

Interview with the *Popolo d'Italia.*[15] I describe our methods and means of propaganda. The representative of this influential Italian paper is positively dumbfounded. "The vastest and most up-to-date propaganda of Europe." . . .

March 18th, 1932.

A critical innovation: the Leader will conduct this next campaign by plane. By this means he will be able to speak three or four times a day at various places as opportunity serves, and address about one and a half millions of people in spite of the time being so short.

April 14th, 1932.

The Leader is planning a new plane campaign for the Prussian elections. He intends to start on Sunday. His perseverance is admirable, and it is amazing how he stands the continual strain.

At work again organizing his great 'plane trips. Now we have quite a lot of experience in these matters.

An important problem is how to make use of the Leader's propaganda flights for the Press. Everything has to be minutely prepared and organized beforehand.

October 4th, 1932.

Monday: Berlin. Prepared for the Leader's meeting at Munich. Dashed off designs for seven huge placards. Things knocked off quickly and enthusiastically are always good.

It is difficult to adapt men used to editorial work to the necessities of electioneering. They are too accurate and slow. . . .

---

15. ***Popolo d'Italia:*** a newspaper founded by the Italian Fascist leader Mussolini in 1914 and edited by him until he gained political control of Italy in 1922, this journal was the official organ of the Fascist dictatorship in Italy by 1932. Indeed, until the newspaper ceased publication in 1943, Mussolini still set its general editorial direction and even contributed articles himself.

January 18th, 1933.

In the evening we go to see the film "Rebel," by Luis Trencker. A first-class production of an artistic film. Thus I could imagine the film of the future, revolutionary in character, with grand mass-scenes, composed with enormous vital energy. In one scene, in which a gigantic crucifix is carried out of a small church by the revolutionaries, the audience is deeply moved. Here you really see what can be done with the film as an artistic medium, when it is really understood. We are all much impressed.

February 10th, 1933.

The Sportpalast[16] is already packed by six o'clock in the evening. All the squares in the city swarm with people waiting to hear the Leader's speech. In the whole Reich twenty to thirty millions more are listening in to it.

Drag myself to the Sportpalast, still weak with the illness from which I have not yet fully recovered. On the platform first I address the Press, and then for twenty minutes at the microphone speak to the audience in the Sportpalast. It goes better than I had thought. It is a strange experience suddenly to be faced with an inanimate microphone when one is used to addressing a living crowd, to be uplifted by the atmosphere of it, and to read the effect of one's speech in the expression on the faces of one's hearers.

The Leader is greeted by frantic cheering. He delivers a fine address containing an outspoken declaration of war against Marxism. Towards the end he strikes a wonderful, incredibly solemn note, and closes with the word "Amen"! It is uttered so naturally that all are deeply moved and affected by it. It is filled with so much strength and belief, is so novel and courageous, that it is not to be compared to anything that has gone beforehand.

This address will be received with enthusiasm throughout Germany. The nation will be ours almost without a struggle.

The masses at the Sportpalast are beside themselves with delight. Now the German Revolution has truly begun.

'Phone calls from different parts of the country report on the fine effect the speech has made even over the Radio. As an instrument for propaganda on a large scale the efficacy of the Radio has not yet been sufficiently appreciated. In any case our adversaries did not recognize its value. All the better, we shall have to explore its possibilities.

16. **Sportpalast:** the Sports Palace, a large, indoor sports arena in Berlin.

[358]

THE IMPACT OF NAZI METHODS

Source 17 from Jeremy Noakes and Geoffrey Pridham, editors, Documents on Nazism, *1919–1945, pp. 83–84, 106, 108. Reprinted by permission of Sterling Lord Literistic, Inc. Copyright 1974 by Jeremy Noakes.*

17. Report on the Problem of Stemming the Spread of Nazi Ideas in the Protestant Youth Movement, 1931

The cause which at the moment is most closely associated with the name of National Socialism and with which, at a moderate estimate, certainly 70 per cent of our young people, often lacking knowledge of the facts, are in ardent sympathy, must be regarded, as far as our ranks are concerned, more as an ethical than a political matter. Our young people show little political interest. Secondary school students are not really much concerned with the study of Hitler's thoughts; it is simply something irrational, something infectious that makes the blood pulse through one's veins and conveys an impression that something great is under way, the roaring of a stream which one does not wish to escape: "If you can't feel it you will never grasp it. . . ."

All this must be taken into account when we see the ardour and fire of this movement reflected in our ranks. A pedantic and nagging approach seems to me useless, and so do all attempts, however well-intentioned, by the leader to refute the policy of National Socialism in detail. The majority of the young fight against this with a strange instinct. We must, in keeping with our responsibility, though it is difficult in individual cases, try first to influence the ethos, and in this we must maintain an attitude above parties. We must educate in such a way that this enthusiasm is duly tempered by deeper understanding and by disenchantment, that words like "national honour and dignity" do not become slogans but arouse individual responsibility so that no brash demagogues grow up among us.

Source 18 from William L. Shirer, Berlin Diary, The Journal of a Foreign Correspondent, *1934–1941 (New York: Knopf, 1941), pp. 18, 19, 21, 22, 23. Reprinted by permission of Don Congden Associates, Inc. Copyright © 1941, renewed 1969 by William L. Shirer.*

18. William L. Shirer, Reactions to the Nazi Party Rally at Nuremberg, 1934

NUREMBERG, *September 5*

I'm beginning to comprehend, I think, some of the reasons for Hitler's astounding success. Borrowing a chapter from the Roman church,[17] he is restoring pageantry and colour and mysticism to the drab lives of twentieth-century Germans. This morning's opening meeting in the Luitpold Hall on the outskirts of Nuremberg was more than a gorgeous show; it also had something of the mysticism and religious fervour of an Easter or Christmas Mass in a great Gothic cathedral. The hall was a sea of brightly coloured flags. Even Hitler's arrival was made dramatic. The band stopped playing. There was a hush over the thirty thousand people packed in the hall. Then the band struck up the *Badenweiler March,* a very catchy tune, and used only, I'm told, when Hitler makes his big entries. Hitler appeared in the back of the auditorium, and followed by his aides, Göring, Goebbels, Hess, Himmler, and the others, he strode slowly down the long centre aisle while thirty thousand hands were raised in salute. It is a ritual, the old-timers say, which is always followed. Then an immense symphony orchestra played Beethoven's *Egmont* Overture. Great Klieg lights played on the stage, where Hitler sat surrounded by a hundred party officials and officers of the army and navy. Behind them the "blood flag," the one carried down the streets of Munich in the ill-fated putsch. Behind this, four or five hundred S.A. standards. When the music was over, Rudolf Hess, Hitler's closest confidant, rose and slowly read the names of the Nazi "martyrs"—brown-shirts who had been killed in the struggle for power—a roll-call of the dead, and the thirty thousand seemed very moved.

In such an atmosphere no wonder, then, that every word dropped by Hitler seemed like an inspired Word from on high. Man's—or at least the German's—critical faculty is swept away at such moments, and every lie pronounced is accepted as high truth itself.

NUREMBERG, *September 7*

Another great pageant tonight. Two hundred thousand party officials packed in the Zeppelin Wiese with their twenty-one thousand flags unfurled in the searchlights like a forest of weird trees. "We are strong and will get

17. **Roman church:** the Roman Catholic Church.

stronger," Hitler shouted at them through the microphone, his words echoing across the hushed field from the loud-speakers. And there, in the floodlit night, jammed together like sardines, in one mass formation, the little men of Germany who have made Nazism possible achieved the highest state of being the Germanic man knows: the shedding of their individual souls and minds—with the personal responsibilities and doubts and problems—until under the mystic lights and at the sound of the magic words of the Austrian they were merged completely in the Germanic herd. Later they recovered enough—fifteen thousand of them—to stage a torchlight parade through Nuremberg's ancient streets, Hitler taking the salute in front of the station across from our hotel.

NUREMBERG, *September* 10

(Later)—After seven days of almost ceaseless goose-stepping, speech-making, and pageantry, the party rally came to an end tonight. And though dead tired and rapidly developing a bad case of crowd-phobia, I'm glad I came. You have to go through one of these to understand Hitler's hold on the people, to feel the dynamic in the movement he's unleashed and the sheer, disciplined strength the Germans possess. And now—as Hitler told the correspondents yesterday in explaining his technique—the half-million men who've been here during the week will go back to their towns and villages and preach the new gospel with new fanaticism. . . .

QUESTIONS TO CONSIDER

This chapter posed three basic questions: What image did the Nazis convey to German voters? Why did they appeal to German voters? How did the Nazis use media to aid their rise to power?

First examine the image the party conveyed to Germans in the 1920s and early 1930s. Start by considering the highly visible uniformed wing of the party, the S.A. Why did the S.A. Order 111 (Source 4) place such emphasis on how the S.A. appeared in public? What was the Storm Trooper supposed to epitomize? How was that visual effect designed to build a certain image for the party? How might

columns of marching men and political banners contribute to this image? Reflect, too, on the mass meetings so carefully mounted by the party. What impression might they have conveyed to the average man or woman on the street? How did the Leader myth contribute to a certain image for the party? Remember that Hitler was relatively young, forty-three years of age, when he gained power. How do you think many Germans viewed a young party leader whose use of airplanes made him seem omnipresent?

With your concept of the party's image now clearly in mind, assess the Nazi appeal to voters. You may wish to review the numerous problems facing Germany in the 1920s and early 1930s that we examined in the

[361]

introduction. What did the Nazis propose as solutions to the Versailles Treaty, the threat of communist takeover, and the ills of the depression? Did the Nazis convey an image that would lead Germans to believe the party could solve the country's problems? Consider the S.A. and the Leader myth. How did they reinforce a promise to restore German power?

What groups did the Nazis specifically appeal to in our evidence, and what were their specific problems? What were the alleged conditions of the workers in Source 8, the poster of "The String-Puller"? Who was threatened by the proposed Woolworth's store in Hanover (Source 14)? How did the Nazis win support in these groups?

Beyond its proposed answers to Germany's problems and its specific appeal to certain groups, the Nazi party also had a more general appeal by seemingly offering solutions to problems of modern life. In nineteenth- and twentieth-century urban, industrial society, individuals uprooted from traditional, rural societies often experienced a loss of identity and purpose in their new environments, a condition identified as *anomie* by the pioneering French sociologist Emile Durkheim (1858–1917). In what ways do you think participation in mass meetings might combat this feeling? What sorts of positive feelings might it seem to provide? The twentieth century also witnessed for many a weakening of both the ritual and authority of traditional religion. How do the photographs of the banners and rally (Sources 5 and 6) and Shirer's account (Source 18) indicate a conscious

attempt by the Nazis to exploit this development? Why would you not be surprised to find German religious youth movements losing members to the Nazis? Why are you shocked but not surprised at the conclusion of Hitler's speech of February 10, 1933 (Source 16)?

Finally, consider the Nazis' techniques, their use of media and propaganda in achieving their goal of power. In this regard, consider the theoretical bases for Nazi propaganda. What was Hitler's view of the masses? According to Hitler, why would the masses submit to terror? Recall the account of the brawl in the Pharus Hall in Source 7. What effect might this event have had on Hitler's opponents? Reexamine the graph of violence in Northeim. Why did Nazi violence break out when it did? How did it affect the party's image?

Examine the party's use of media technology for propaganda. What was the response of the Italian journalist to Nazi propaganda, according to Goebbels (Source 16)? What new electronic media did the Nazis employ? What do you think the Nazis' level of success would have been without such modern technology as the microphone? What features of Nazi campaign technology have become part of modern campaigning?

As you consider these questions, you should have a better understanding of the Nazi seizure of power in Germany. The Nazis used technology and methods of political manipulation that were new to the modern world. To understand fully the magnitude of their political revolution in winning the German masses, conclude your examination by referring to Chapter 2 of this volume. Which social groups was Louis XIV of France trying to influence? What was his message? How did Western political strategies change in the almost three centuries separating Louis XIV and Hitler?

EPILOGUE

Nazi media mastery and propaganda worked well enough by January 1933 for the party to secure the chancellorship for Hitler. In free elections, however, the Nazis never secured more than 44 percent of the vote.[18] Once Hitler became chancellor, the task for the party and Goebbels was to use modern media and propaganda either to win the support of the majority of Germans or at least to convince them that opposition to the new political order was futile. As had been the case with the Nazi drive for power, implicit in this effort was the threat that force would be used against the recalcitrant. But Hitler did seem to keep his promises. The Communist party was outlawed in 1933; building projects and eventually rearmament stimulated the economy and created jobs; and Germany restored its military power and defied the Treaty of Versailles. Ominously, Hitler's promises also pointed to the terrible tragedy of the Holocaust for European Jews, and to

World War II. But Goebbels's propaganda machine never let Germans forget the regime's successes.

The Hitler government centralized control of all information and media in a new Ministry of Public Enlightenment and Propaganda, headed by Goebbels, which closely regulated Germany's press, film, and radio after 1933. Especially significant was Goebbels's understanding of the role of radio as a propaganda device and his use of it once in power. He said, "With the radio we have destroyed the spirit of rebellion,"[19] because the radio could bring the Nazi message into every German home. The regime saw to it that cheap radios were made available to Germans, and the number of receivers increased from 5 million in 1932 to 9.5 million in 1938. A system of government wardens notified citizens to tune in important programs, and the Propaganda Ministry increased their impact still further by setting up loudspeakers in the streets and squares of Germany during key broadcasts.

Goebbels's ministry also sought to sway opinion via the medium of film. After some early crude and unpopular efforts, Goebbels's understanding of film as a propaganda device grew

18. In the last free Reichstag elections held in March 1933, the Nazis won only 43.9 percent of the vote, despite S.A. intimidation of voters and the great political advantage accruing to the party from Hitler's position as chancellor. The Nazis finally secured a Reichstag majority only when Hitler expelled the Communist members from the chamber.

19. Quoted in Roger Manvell and Heinrich Fraenkel, *Doctor Goebbels: His Life and Death* (London: Heinemann, 1960), pp. 127–128.

greatly. He wrote in 1942 of the subtle possibilities inherent in the medium:

> Even entertainment can be politically of special value, because the moment a person becomes conscious of propaganda, propaganda becomes ineffective. However, as soon as propaganda as a tendency, as a characteristic, as an attitude remains in the background and becomes apparent through human beings, then propaganda becomes effective in every respect.[20]

The propaganda machine of Goebbels faced its ultimate test, however, with the outbreak of World War II. Because Hitler was convinced that Germany's World War I defeat stemmed in large measure from the collapse of civilian morale, the Nazi regime sought to maintain that morale in this new war by using propaganda and minimizing the conflict's impact on citizens. The slogan "As much normality as possible, as much war as necessary" summed up the regime's goal, but convincing Germans that times were "normal" and that their country was doing well in the war became increasingly difficult with mounting manpower losses, Allied bombings, and growing shortages of essential commodities. Nevertheless, Goebbels toiled on, and a measure of the regime's faith in the power of propaganda was its dedication of increasingly scarce resources to it. As Germany's military situation grew more desperate in 1943 and 1944, the propaganda minister diverted thousands of troops from the battlefront to serve as extras in a motion picture historical epic, *Kolberg*, intended to inspire civilian morale by showing the heroism of German soldiers fighting Napoleon in 1806 and 1807. While civilian morale did erode, and there was opposition to the dictatorship, including a number of plots against Hitler himself, the regime managed to contain such active resistance within a minority of the population. Modern media and propaganda techniques and a message that attracted many, combined with the omnipresent threat of state police power, proved to be effective devices that aided the regime in maintaining its ascendancy. Such employment of modern media and propaganda techniques, supported by the police power of the state, would characterize many later twentieth-century totalitarian regimes.

20. Joseph Goebbels, *Tagebuch,* unpublished sections, in Institut für Zeitgeschichte, Munich, entry for March 1, 1942. Quoted in David Welch, *Propaganda and the German Cinema, 1933–1945* (Oxford: Clarendon Press, 1983), p. 45.

CHAPTER THIRTEEN

THE PERILS OF PROSPERITY:

THE UNREST OF

YOUTH IN THE 1960s

Commuters just emerging from subway exits in the university district of Paris on the evening of Friday, May 3, 1968, must have been bewildered. They stepped out into a neighborhood transformed since morning into a war zone in which police and students battled over the future of France's governmental and economic systems. These commuters witnessed a conflict in which French students, like students in many other countries in 1968, called into question a material prosperity purchased, in their view, with a loss of individual liberty in the face of the power of the modern state and giant industrial concerns.

The postwar Western world indeed was experiencing unprecedented prosperity by the late 1960s. The United States enjoyed the world's highest living standard. In Western Europe, the European Economic Community (or EEC), today part of the European Union, served as a key instrument for economic recovery and growth for war-ravaged France, West Germany, Italy, Belgium, the Netherlands, and Luxembourg. Non-EEC countries, including Great Britain and the Scandinavian nations, also shared in this economic success. Even in communist Eastern Europe, war damage was repaired and the socialist economies of the region produced standards of living for their peoples substantially improved over those of the early postwar years.

Behind the façade of material success, however, were a number of problems that led to widespread unrest, especially among the young, in the 1960s. Part of the basis for this discontent may be found in the very economic success of the postwar period. Several Western countries, including France and Great Britain, encouraged growth by government intervention in the economy or national ownership of industries. The economic life of communist Eastern Europe, of course, was entirely under

Chapter 13

The Perils of

Prosperity:

The Unrest of

Youth in

the 1960s

government control. The result was a growing state economic bureaucracy in which the individual had little voice. The nature of the economic growth was unsettling, too. The West was entering a new phase of industrialization. New and sophisticated industries, such as computers and electronics, flourished; the service sector of the economy grew while older heavy industries declined in importance. The result was deep concern among many workers, who found little demand for their traditional skills and who felt powerless to avoid unemployment or underemployment. These structural economic problems converged in the 1960s with shorter-term economic difficulties to create potentially explosive worker dissatisfaction. Historians long have noted that political unrest often ensues when an economic downturn suddenly interrupts a period of extended prosperity marked by rising human expectations. Such a downturn was under way in much of Europe in the 1960s. Western European nations, like France, were in a recession in 1967 and 1968 that added to unemployment and reduced the buying power of those fortunate enough to keep their jobs. In many communist countries, the rigid state economic planning, which had produced remarkable annual rates of economic growth in rebuilding wartime damage to heavy industry in the 1950s, faltered in the 1960s, revealing its inefficiencies as it turned to meeting more mundane consumer needs.

Many European students were dissatisfied with the system of higher education. A partial reason may be found in the West's great population growth after World War II. The postwar baby boom of 1946 to 1964, which affected both Europe and America, coincided with a prosperity that permitted Western democracies to provide their youth with greater educational opportunity than had been offered any earlier generation. In two decades student populations vastly increased. From 1950 to 1970, university enrollments increased from 38,900 to 105,600 in Czechoslovakia; from 140,000 to 651,000 in France; from 145,000 to 561,000 in Italy; from 117,000 to 410,000 in West Germany; and from 102,200 to 250,000 in Great Britain.[1] But often the quality of the educational experience declined as the system strained to cope with unprecedented enrollments. University faculty and facilities failed to grow as fast as their student bodies, resulting in crowded lecture halls and student-faculty ratios that went as high as 105 to 1 in Italy and rendered professors inaccessible to students.

Other problems also affected the student population. University curricula often provided a traditional education that did little to prepare a student to succeed in the new service-oriented economy. When European governments decreed halfhearted curriculum reforms to respond to economic change, they often, as in France, extended a student's course of study. The university also seemed divorced from the real problems of society, such as poverty

1. B. R. Mitchell, ed., *European Historical Statistics*, abridged ed. (New York: Columbia University Press, 1978), pp. 396–400.

and crime, a fact reflected in the rarity of sociology courses dealing with those problems.

These curricular problems and the impersonal nature of the modern university led to student demands for sweeping change in the educational establishment. The students wished a voice in the decisions that affected them. They increasingly demanded a say in what was taught, who taught, and how the universities were administered. As we will see, such demands also reflected the feelings of many nonstudents who bitterly felt their inability to affect the modern institutions that controlled their lives.

Students of the 1960s were disappointed and angered by educational shortcomings, but they were even more frustrated by their inability to effect political change. The student generation of the 1960s was physically more mature than any previous generation, thanks to improved nutrition. Their sense of adulthood was heightened by the spread of techniques of birth control that freed women from the fear of pregnancy outside of marriage and fostered a youthful revolt against traditional sexual mores. That revolt could have political ramifications; a slogan frequently heard among French students in 1968 was: "Every time I make love I want to make the revolution; every time I make the revolution I want to make love." But these self-consciously mature young people could change little around them. Everywhere, those under twenty-one were eligible for military service but had no right to vote. Nor had students even a voice in their universities' governance.

Typically, European governments controlled universities through centralized bureaucracies. In France, for example, such minor events as student dances had to be approved by the Ministry of Education.

Yet for all the dissatisfaction among students and workers, traditional twentieth-century political ideologies offered scant appeal. The cold war had polarized Europe for twenty years, and neither of the opposing doctrines—Russian communism or the democratic capitalism of the United States—offered real answers to student demands. Indeed, in a political sense both doctrines increasingly lost credibility for students. For some, the democratic ideals of the United States no longer seemed attractive because of that nation's increasingly unpopular war in Vietnam. Many saw that Southeast Asian conflict, which engaged about 500,000 American servicemen by 1968, as a war to uphold a favored minority in South Vietnam through military involvement. Those who looked toward a communist vision of a better world similarly were disappointed. The Soviet Union, with its regimented society, inefficient economy, and forceful crushing of dissent in its East German, Polish, and Hungarian satellites in the 1950s, was hardly the best advertisement for Marxian socialism.

Ideological disillusionment led a minority of students to radical doctrines rejecting orthodox Marxism as well as liberal democracy. The ideas of Leon Trotsky, a Marxist who rejected the need for a bureaucracy in a socialist state, attracted some. The example of Mao Zedong,

Chapter 13

The Perils of

Prosperity:

The Unrest of

Youth in

the 1960s

the Chinese revolutionary, stirred other students to reject all authority and to attempt to rally working people to the cause of revolutionary change. Still others were attracted by nineteenth-century anarchist thought that rejected any hierarchy of control over the individual. Some also found inspiration in the revolutionary activism of Cuba's Fidel Castro and Che Guevara. Common to all was the belief that the institutions of society favored the rich, manipulated the poor, and substituted materialism bred of postwar economic growth for individual liberty and any high-minded questioning of the established order. Everywhere student demands could be summed up as calls for participation by individuals in all the decisions that shaped their lives, a concept that French students labeled *autogestion*.

Whatever their ideology, student radicals sought confrontation with established governmental and educational authority in the hope of garnering a mass following for change among the nonrevolutionary majority of students, workers, and others. The radicals increasingly found student followers in many countries. Unrest due to the Vietnam War was widespread on campuses in the United States from the mid-1960s. In Europe, riots began in Italy in 1965 at the universities of Milan and Trento as students demanded a voice in academic policy. Italian unrest continued into the late 1960s, when student radicals combined ideas for a complete overthrow of traditional society with their demands for educational change. Incidents rooted in the desire

for political change were common to German and British universities, too. In most of these countries, however, youthful radicals generated little support beyond their campuses. Only in France and Czechoslovakia did youthful unrest spread beyond students and thus threaten the existence of established governments.

In 1968 France had been led for ten years by President Charles de Gaulle, the seventy-eight-year-old hero of World War II whose imperial style of government only increased the extreme state centralization traditional in that country. Significantly, too, France was suffering an economic recession that heightened the discontent of many workers. Problems began at the new Nanterre campus of the University of Paris. Placed amid slums housing immigrant workers, this modern university center seemed to radicals a dramatic illustration of the failings of modern consumer society. Led by the anarchist Daniel Cohn-Bendit in a protest of university regulations, Nanterre students forced the closing of their campus in the spring of 1968.

Nanterre radicals next focused their attention on the main campus of the University of Paris, at the Sorbonne, after university authorities had begun disciplinary action against Cohn-Bendit and others on May 3, 1968. As police removed protesting student radicals from the Sorbonne, antipolice violence erupted among crowds of students around the university. The very appearance of the police on university grounds provoked student anger. University confines were normally beyond the jurisdiction of the police, who had last entered the Sorbonne in 1791. The crowd threw rocks and, more dangerously, the heavy cobblestones of Paris streets. Police beat students brutally, and the broadcast of such scenes on the evening television news generated widespread support for the radicals, who now demanded a change in France's government.

For the next two weeks, the university district of Paris was the scene of street fighting between police and students that drew on the traditions of a Paris that had often defied government in the past.[2] Ominously for the government, the student unrest spread to other parts of society. On May 13, 1968, unions scheduled a twenty-four-hour general strike to protest police brutality, despite the opposition of the large French Communist party, which feared the unorthodoxy of the spreading revolt. On May 14 workers began to occupy factories and to refuse to work, the young among them demanding, like the students, a voice in decisions affecting them. For other workers, improved wages were a demand. Within a week, perhaps as many as 10 million workers nationwide had seized their factories and were on strike. Even professionals in broadcasting, sports, and other fields joined the strike. The country was paralyzed, and the government seemed on the brink of collapse as opposition leaders began to discuss alternative regimes.

As the government faltered, both sides in the confrontation clearly saw the significance of the growing revolt. Cohn-Bendit characterized it as "a whole generation rising against a certain sort of society—bourgeois society." A leader of the establishment, France's Prime Minister Georges Pompidou, defined the revolt as one against modern society itself. Even the authoritarian de Gaulle heard the message, conceding on May 19, "Reform yes, anarchy no."[3]

Prime Minister Pompidou began to defuse the crisis by offering wage increases to the striking unions. Faced with destroying the consumer society or enjoying more of its benefits, many striking workers quickly chose the latter option. Then, on May 29, de Gaulle flew to West Germany, assured himself of the support of French army units stationed there in case of the need of force, and returned to Paris to end the crisis. Addressing the nation on radio the next day, the president refused to resign as the protesters demanded and instead dissolved the National Assembly, calling for new elections to that body. The maneuver saved the government's cause. The protesters could

2. Students fought much as Parisians had in the eighteenth and nineteenth centuries, tearing up paving stones and piling them with overturned vehicles and fallen trees to create street barricades from behind which they fought police. When the student revolt ended, the government paved cobblestone streets with asphalt.

3. In the present context, *anarchy* is probably the best English word to convey briefly what de Gaulle meant. De Gaulle probably sought a certain effect by using an army colloquialism, *chien lit,* which even the French press had difficulty expressing adequately. It means making "a mess in one's own bed"—in other words, "fouling one's own nest."

Chapter 13

The Perils of

Prosperity:

The Unrest of

Youth in

the 1960s

not call repressive a government that was willing to risk its control of the legislature in elections called ahead of schedule. Although student radicals tried to continue the revolt, most workers accepted proffered pay increases and new elections and returned to work. De Gaulle's supporters won a majority of the seats in the National Assembly on June 23, 1968, and the president retained the power to govern.

As students and workers battled police in France, equally dramatic events were moving to a climax across Europe in Czechoslovakia. Although unrest in democratic France and one-party Czechoslovakia displayed differences, the revolts in both countries had common roots in a youthful rejection of highly centralized and unresponsive authority.

Czechoslovakia, an industrialized country with Western democratic traditions, experienced a coup in 1948 that established a communist government. The leaders of that regime, party first secretaries Klement Gottwald (1948–1953) and Antonín Novotný (1953–1968), were steadfast followers of authoritarian Stalinist communism, even though the Soviet Union itself began a process of "de-Stalinization" after 1956. But by 1967 Novotný's style of communism was becoming increasingly unacceptable to Czechoslovakians in two chief regards. The most basic problem concerned the nation's two largest ethnic groups: the Czechs and the Slovaks. For a long time the Slovaks had been unhappy with Czech domination of both the Communist party and the state apparatus. The Novotný regime

perpetuated this Czech domination as the Slovaks clamored for a stronger voice in national affairs.

Even more fundamental than the regime's ethnic difficulties, however, was its rigid and authoritarian Stalinist communism. Economically, this meant a managed economy, oriented toward heavy industrial goods rather than consumer items, that was hampered by centralized control, no profit motive, and low productivity. High annual rates of increase in the gross national product (or GNP, the total value of goods and services produced by an economy) in the 1950s masked these problems as Czechoslovakia rebuilt its heavy industry after World War II. Indeed, the GNP grew by a remarkable 11 percent in 1959. But by the 1960s, the problems of a rigid, planned economy were evident. Growth in the GNP dipped to 6.2 percent in 1962, and the economy's output actually diminished in 1963. Shortages of food and housing graphically demonstrated the regime's economic shortcomings. Politically, Novotný's government gave the country rigid control by a small party inner circle sustained by a secret police, press censorship, and extreme curbs on intellectual freedom.

A series of events led to change in Czechoslovakia through the efforts of the younger generation of party officials, intellectuals, and students. As in France, loss of support for the regime began among those who were being groomed in the educational system as future leaders, not with the materially deprived. Pressure for change in the country's highest leadership mounted as Novotný's authoritarian style of government resisted reform and economic problems persisted.

In 1963 the Slovak branch of the Communist party named a new first secretary, the reform-minded Alexander Dubček. In a country where literature long had been politicized, writers began to desert the regime; at the Congress of Czechoslovak Writers in June 1967, they demanded an end to censorship and freedom for their craft. Other intellectuals also grew restive with the regime. But, as in France, it was young people who brought matters to a crisis point. Cries of "We want freedom, we want democracy" and "A good communist is a dead communist" punctuated traditional student May Day observances in 1966 and resulted in arrests by policemen whom the students called "Gestapo," after the Nazi security police. The government responded forcefully, expelling from the universities and drafting into the army leaders of student organizations who had called for more freedom. Nonetheless, opposition to the Novotný regime not only continued but increased, especially after the events of October 31, 1967. On that night, as on numerous previous occasions, an electrical failure left the large complex of student dormitories in Prague, the capital, without light. Students took up candles and began a procession chanting "We want light," a phrase that could indicate far more than their need for electric power. The brutal acts of the police in confronting the students outraged public opinion, thus strengthening reform elements in the party's Central Committee sufficiently for them to gain a majority in that body. On January 5, 1968, the reformers replaced Novotný with the Slovak Alexander Dubček as first secretary of the national Communist party. On March 22, 1968, war hero Ludvik Svoboda replaced Novotný as president of the nation. A bloodless revolution had occurred in Prague.

The spring of 1968 was an exhilarating one for the people of Czechoslovakia. Dubček announced his intention to create "socialism with a human face," a socialism that would allow "a fuller assertion of the personality than any bourgeois democracy," a socialism that would be "profoundly democratic." Rigid press censorship ended, as did other controls on the individual. But Dubček soon found himself in a difficult position. Permitted freedom of expression for the first time in twenty years, Czechoslovaks demanded far more, including even a free political system with a role for noncommunist parties. Such developments, however, threatened neighboring communist dictatorships in East Germany and Poland and risked depriving the Soviet Union of strategically located Czechoslovakia in its Warsaw Pact alliance system.

On August 21, after having watched developments in Prague for months with growing alarm, the Soviet Union acted. Troops from the Soviet Union, East Germany, Hungary, Poland, and Bulgaria entered Czechoslovakia. In the largest movement of troops in Europe since 1945, they forcibly ended the "Prague Spring" experiment.

Chapter 13

The Perils of

Prosperity:

The Unrest of

Youth in

the 1960s

The Soviets were met with widespread passive nationalist resistance. The majority of the population seemed to wish continuation of reform, but earlier unrest in Eastern Europe, as in the failed Hungarian revolt of 1956, had demonstrated the futility of civilians' active opposition to Soviet arms. Students again took part in resistance, however, and two, Jan Palach and Jan Zajíc, burned themselves alive in early 1969 in protest. Force prevailed, however, and Soviet pressure ensured the gradual replacement of Dubček and his reform leadership with men more subservient to Moscow's wishes. Soviet party first secretary Leonid Brezhnev announced that events in Czechoslovakia represented an expression of what came to be called the "Brezhnev Doctrine"—that is, the Soviet Union's policy to act against any threat to the stability of an East European communist regime.

SOURCES AND METHOD

Modern political causes seek to mobilize support in various ways. Because posters, pamphlets, and other publications as well as simple slogans scrawled on walls all aim to energize support for a movement by publicizing its ideas, analyzing such materials provides a broad understanding of the goals and methods of any cause. In this chapter we have assembled two groups of evidence, one relating to the French disorders and the other to the Czechoslovakian reform movement of 1968.

Those supporting change in both France and Czechoslovakia were acutely aware of the need to sway public opinion in their favor. This task was made difficult by government controls of the media: In France, the radio and television systems were state controlled; in Czechoslovakia, the regime controlled not only electronic media but the press as well. Your problem in this chapter is to analyze events in France and Czechoslovakia in 1968 by examining the materials issued by those who sought to rally support for change. Deprived of media controlled by the political establishment, proponents of change issued leaflets, posters, and cartoons designed to win support. What aspects of the modern state and economy provoked the events of 1968? What vision of the future did the leaders of the French and Czechoslovakian movements embrace? How did they propose to achieve it?

Let us consider the French evidence first. Source 1 is a pamphlet distributed to striking workers by the March 22 Movement, a student group whose name commemorated the student upheaval at the Nanterre campus. It appeared on May 21, 1968. What were the students' goals for the future society and economy of France? What were the aims of workers in their strike? How did student leaders try to unify student and worker causes in this pamphlet? Source 2, a leaflet that appeared on May 22, 1968, was issued by a number of student and worker groups. Consider the views expressed here about President de Gaulle, the government, and the economy. Would the authors have been satisfied only with the departure of de Gaulle from the political scene? What do you deduce from their refusal of "summit negotiations" with government and management? To whom does the leaflet appeal? What vision of the future does it advocate?

You must analyze the language of Source 3 to understand the message it seeks to convey. This is a list of slogans that the student Sorbonne Occupation Committee suggested to its followers on May 16, 1968. Note the locations proposed for such slogans. The one advocating the end of bureaucrats was painted across a large mural in the Sorbonne administration building. How did this and some of the other suggested locations reflect student attitudes toward authority? Now turn to the words themselves. Slogans are important in politics; as we noted in Chapter 12, the simpler they are, the more easily they can be spread to influence large numbers of people. Each side of the 1968 confrontations sought to dismiss the validity of the other's ideas by extreme and often inaccurate name calling. In France as well as in the United States and other countries, students referred to policemen as "pigs" or "fascists." French students' chants of "CRS—SS!" likened the riot police, the CRS (*Compagnies Républicaines de Securité*), to the Nazi SS (*Schutz Staffeln* or security echelon, whose insignia resembled a sharp double *S*). The students' opponents responded in kind, often calling them "commies." What views of their opponents do the students convey in these slogans? What sort of society do they advocate? What methods do they advocate for their cause?

With the French Sources 4 through 11, you must analyze pictorial attempts to mobilize opinion. The artists conveyed these messages graphically in pictures, with a minimum of words. Here you must ascertain the nature of the message and the goals of the students and workers.

The visual evidence is of several types. In 1968 posters appeared all over the university district of Paris in defiance of long-standing laws against posters on public buildings. Often they were fairly sophisticated in execution because many advanced art students put their skills in the service of the May revolt. The political cartoon also flourished in a number of new radical publications in Paris. The cartoons presented here originated in *L'enragé* (*The Madman*), a publication that consisted entirely of cartoons critical of established authority in France.

Cartoons and posters often magnify the physical characteristics of public figures, sometimes to ridicule but also to make perfectly clear the subject of the message. Thus you will find the prominent nose of President de Gaulle quite exaggerated, as well as certain poses. De Gaulle often embellished his speeches by raising both arms, the same gesture he used when leading the singing of the national anthem, *La Marseillaise*, a frequent occurrence after a public address. This pose is duplicated in

Chapter 13

The Perils of

Prosperity:

The Unrest of

Youth in

the 1960s

the cartoons and posters along with his uniform of a French general, complete with the cylindrical cap known as a *kepi*, making him instantly recognizable. Artists further identified de Gaulle by including in their pictures the Cross of Lorraine, the symbol of his World War II resistance movement, with its two transverse bars.

In analyzing the material, remember that political posters and cartoons, though based on real events, are not intended to report those occurrences accurately. They are meant instead to affect public opinion. By carefully examining the posters and cartoons, you can discover the artists' views of events and how they wished to sway public opinion. What action does each picture represent? What message is the artist trying to convey? What reaction does he or she wish to evoke in viewers? What do the pictures tell you about the participants, methods, and aspirations of the French movement?

Now let us examine the Czechoslovakian sources. The Czechoslovakian writings should be examined with the same methods you applied to the French. Source 12 is a tract that circulated illegally in Czechoslovakian literary circles as early as April 1967 and was republished in a Prague student publication in March 1968. Notice first the use of language. What effect do the authors seek in condemning their opponents as "knaves"? What view does the statement as a whole express toward established ideologies, both Soviet Marxist and U.S. capitalist? What methods for change are

advocated? Did young Czechoslovakians follow the course of action recommended in the tenth commandment? Why should the intellectuals, students, and professors be the leaders in change?

Source 13 is an extract from a statement that appeared in an influential publication, *Literární Listy* (*Literary Papers*), the journal of the Czechoslovakian Writers' Union. *Literární Listy* was the chief forum in 1968 in which intellectuals expressed their views on reform. It had a large circulation (300,000 copies in June 1968), and it published the manifesto for change, "Two Thousand Words." Source 13 appeared on March 5, 1968, as one of a number of replies to the question of the nation's political future posed by the editors: "Wherefrom, with Whom, and Whither?" The answer reprinted here was made by Ivan Sviták, a philosophy professor and reform leader. Notice his choice of language. Who, in his view, was the enemy of change? How does he characterize these people? What sort of social and political system did Czechoslovakian intellectuals seek?

Source 14 presents excerpts from the Action Program drafted by Alexander Dubček and his supporters that was adopted by the Central Committee of the Czechoslovakian Communist party on April 5, 1968. In his memoirs Dubček noted that this program, intended for submission to the next party congress for adoption as official policy, attempted to characterize a plan of sweeping reform as one entirely consistent with established party doctrine. Published in the official party newspaper *Rudé*

Právo, the program thus sought to allay the suspicions of old party functionaries and watchful Soviet authorities while rallying support among Dubček's countrymen for significant change. In what areas did this program initiate change? How did it propose to deal with economic problems, nationality issues, and the very nature of the Czechoslovakian political system? How did the plan succeed in placating the Soviets' resistance to change?

Sources 15 through 17 are cartoons drawn from *Literární Listy* and its successor, *Listy*. Use the same methods of analysis here as you employed with the French posters and cartoons. You again will note exaggeration of certain physical features to clarify the cartoon's message. Alexander Dubček had a large nose, as de Gaulle did, and it was exaggerated by Czechoslovak cartoonists, just as French artists exaggerated de Gaulle's nose. The Czechoslovakian cartoonists represented here also used symbols to illuminate their messages. The Phrygian cap worn by the woman in Source 15, for example, represents revolution and liberty.

The crushing of the Czechoslovakian experiment in democracy did not silence the voices of those seeking to rally citizens to resist authoritarian government. The means to express their messages, however, changed radically with the government's reimposition of censorship. Music was much harder to control than the press; it could be performed in isolated rural venues, and recordings could circulate widely. Indeed, a musical underground developed after 1968, and

Source 18 presents the words for a song of protest. The song, "The Twenty-Year-Old Today," was the composition of a rock band, The Plastic People of the Universe, whose name even carried a message. "Plastic" was a term dismissively used by young people of the 1960s to describe the materialism of modern consumer culture. The dissonant music of this group, which made great use of percussion instruments, gathered immediate attention because it was the very antithesis of the conventional, sentimental music approved by the government. But Plastic's name and sound were the least of the problems that the band posed for the regime. The group, like many rock bands today, deliberately used language chosen for its shock value, and the song in Source 18 provided its listeners in 1969 with a brief history lesson. The fall of Alexander Dubček and the restoration of rigid communist rule is the obvious cause of the "disgust" of the twenty-year-old. Czechoslovakians forty years of age, however, would also have remembered the communist coup of 1948 that ended their democracy. Those in their sixties would have recalled the events of 1968 and 1948 and the Nazi conquest of Czechoslovakia in 1939. In linking the events of 1968 with those of 1948 and 1939, what message did Plastic convey? Why do you think it drew the attention of the authorities, who first banned Plastic from official cultural events and then tried and imprisoned the group's original members?

An individual who facilitated performances by Plastic and who pro-

Chapter 13

The Perils of

Prosperity:

The Unrest of

Youth in

the 1960s

tested their conviction was the playwright and author Václav Havel. The communist government of Czechoslovakia was automatically suspicious of Havel's millionaire background, and his writing justified that suspicion because it criticized the communist regime. Censorship forced the clandestine circulation of much of his writing; it was part of what was called *samizdat* (from the Russian for "self-published") in much of communist-dominated Central and Eastern Europe. Such writing was often not even really "published" in our sense of that word; it circulated surreptitiously as handwritten manuscripts, carbon copies of typescripts, or mimeographed texts. Source 19 circulated widely as a

piece of *samizdat* writing, a copy of a protest letter that Havel courageously mailed in 1975 to Gustav Husák, Dubček's replacement as party secretary. What sort of regime had Husák imposed on the country? What pressures did his regime employ to ensure Czechoslovakians' acquiescence in the new order?

Using the analytical methods described here, you should be able to answer the central questions of this chapter: What aspects of the modern state and economy provoked the events of 1968? What vision of the future did leaders of the French and Czechoslovakian movements embrace? How did they propose to achieve it?

THE EVIDENCE

FRANCE

Sources 1 through 3 from Vladimir Fišera, editor, Writing on the Wall, May 1968: A Documentary Anthology *(London: Allison & Busby, 1978), pp. 133–134; p. 137; pp. 125–126. Reprinted by permission of W. H. Allen Publishers.*

1. The March 22 Movement, "Your Struggle Is Our Struggle," May 21, 1968

We are occupying the faculties, you are occupying the factories. Aren't we fighting for the same thing? Higher education only contains 10 percent workers' children. Are we fighting so that there will be more of them, for a democratic university reform? That would be a good thing, but it's not the most important. These workers' children would just become like other students. We are not aiming for a worker's son to be a manager. We want to wipe out segregation between workers and management.

There are students who are unable to find jobs on leaving university. Are we fighting so that they'll find jobs, for a decent graduate employment policy? It would be a good thing, but it is not vital. Psychology or sociology graduates will become the selectors, the planners and psychotechnicians who will try to organise your working conditions; mathematics graduates will become engineers, perfecting maximum-productivity machines to make your life even more unbearable. Why are we, students who are products of a middle-class life, criticising capitalist society? The son of a worker who becomes a student leaves his own class. For the son of a middle-class family, it could be his opportunity to see his class in its true light, to question the role he is destined for in society and the organisation of our society. We refuse to become scholars who are out of touch with real life. We refuse to be used for the benefit of the ruling class. We want to destroy the separation that exists between those who organise and think and those who execute their decisions. We want to form a classless society; your cause is the same as ours.

You are asking for a minimum wage of 1,000 francs in the Paris area, retirement at sixty, a 40-hour week for 48 hours' pay.

These are long-standing and just demands: nevertheless, they seem to be out of context with our aims. Yet you have gone on to occupy factories, take your managers as hostages, strike without warning. These forms of struggle have been made possible by perseverance and lengthy action in various enterprises, and because of the recent student battles.

These struggles are even more radical than our official aims, because they go further than simply seeking improvements for the worker within the capitalist system, [;] they imply the destruction of the system. They are political in the true sense of the word: you are fighting not to change the Prime Minister, but so that your boss no longer retains his power in business or society. The form that your struggle has taken offers us students the model for true socialist activity: the appropriation of the means of production and of the decision-making power by the workers.

Our struggles converge. We must destroy everything that seeks to alienate us (everyday habits, the press, etc.). We must combine our occupations in the faculties and factories.

Long live the unification of our struggles!

2. "Producers, Let Us Save Ourselves," May 22, 1968

To ten million strikers, to all workers:

No to parliamentary solutions, with de Gaulle going and the bosses staying.

No to summit negotiations which give only a new lease of life to a moribund capitalism.

No more referenda. No more spectacles.

Don't let anybody speak for us. Maintain the occupation of all workplaces.

[377]

Chapter 13

The Perils of

Prosperity:

The Unrest of

Youth in

the 1960s

To continue the struggle, let us put all the sectors of the economy which are hit by the strike at the service of the fighting workers.

Let us prepare today our power of tomorrow (direct food-supplies, the organisation of public services: transport, information, housing, etc.).

In the streets, in the local committees, wherever we are, workers, peasants, wage-earners, students, teachers, school students, let us organise and coordinate our struggles.

FOR THE ABOLITION OF THE EMPLOYERS, FOR WORKERS' POWER.

3. Sorbonne Occupation Committee, Slogans to Be Circulated by Any Means, May 16, 1968

(leaflets—announcements over microphones—comics—songs—painting on walls—texts daubed over the paintings in the Sorbonne—announcements in the cinema during the film, or stopping it in the middle—texts written on the posters in the underground—whenever you empty your glass in the bistro—before making love—after making love—in the lift)

Occupy the factories.

Power to the workers' councils.

Abolish class society.

Down with a society based on commodity production and the spectacle.

Abolish alienation.

An end to the university.

Mankind will not be happy until the last bureaucrat has been strung up by the guts of the last capitalist.

Death to the pigs.

Free the four people arrested for looting on 6 May.

THE ENEMY

Sources 4 through 8 from Bibliothèque Nationale, Les Affiches de Mai 68 ou l'imagination graphique *(Paris: Bibliothèque Nationale, 1982), p. 64; p. 15; p. 9; p. 63; p. 47.*

4. Poster, May 1968

6. Poster: "Light Salaries, Heavy Tanks," May 1968

SALAIRES LEGERS

CHARS LOURDS

5. Poster: "Let Us Smash the Old Gears!,"
May 1968

BRISONS
LES VIEUX ENGRENAGES

8. Poster: "Less than 21
Years of Age: Here Is Your
Ballot," May 1968

MOINS
DE
21ANS
voici votre
bulletin de
VOTE

REVOLUTIONARY METHODS

7. Poster: "Beauty Is in the Street!," May 1968

LA BEAUTÉ
EST DANS LA RUE

Chapter 13

The Perils of

Prosperity:

The Unrest of

Youth in

the 1960s

THE STUDENTS' VISION

Sources 9 and 10 from Bibliothèque Nationale, Les Affiches de Mai 68 ou l'imagination graphique, *p. 10; p. 24.*

9. Cartoon: "Each One of Us Is the State," May 1968

L'ETAT C'EST CHACUN DE NOUS

10. **Cartoon: "Popular Power," May 1968**

Chapter 13
The Perils of
Prosperity:
The Unrest of
Youth in
the 1960s

THE STUDENTS IN DEFEAT

Source 11 from Jean-Jacques Pauvert, editor, L'enragé: collection complète des 12 numéros introuvables, mai–novembre 1968 *(Paris: Jean-Jacques Pauvert, 1978).*

11. Cartoon, June 17, 1968

CZECHOSLOVAKIA

Sources 12 and 13 from Ivan Sviták, The Czechoslovak Experiment, 1968–1969 *(New York: Columbia University Press, 1971), pp. 17–18; p. 16. Reprinted by permission of the author.*

12. "Ten Commandments for a Young Czechoslovak Intellectual," March 1968

There are no more knaves than before; it is only that their field of activity is larger. . . . And so all of us are living in close collaboration with a few knaves.

LUDVÍK VACULÍK, in *Orientation, 1967*[4]

1. Do not collaborate with knaves. If you do, you inevitably become one of them. Engage yourself against the knaves.

2. Do not accept the responsibility forced upon you by the knaves for their own deeds. Do not believe such arguments as "we are all responsible," or the social problems touch "all of us," or "everyone has his share of guilt." Openly and clearly dissociate yourself from the deeds of the knaves and from arguments that you are responsible for them.

3. Do not believe any ideology that consists of systems of slogans and words which only speculate about your feelings. Judge people, political parties, and social systems concretely, according to the measure of freedom they give, and according to how tolerable the living conditions are. Judge them according to results, not words.

4. Do not solve only the narrow generational problems of youth; understand that the decisive problems are common to all human beings. You cannot solve them by postulating the demands of young men, but by vigorously defending the problems of all people. Do not complain about the privileges of one generation, but fight for human rights.

5. Do not consider the given social relations as constant. They are changing in your favor. Look forward. If you do not want to be wrong today, you must think from the point of view of the year 2000.

6. Do not think only as a Czech or a Slovak, but consider yourself a *European*. The world will sooner adapt to Europe (where Eastern Europe belongs) than to fourteen million Czechs and Slovaks. You live neither in America nor in the Soviet Union; you live in Europe.

---

4. **Ludvík Vaculík:** a novelist and one of the leaders of the Czechoslovakian reform movement; he also drafted the manifesto "Two Thousand Words."

Chapter 13

The Perils of

Prosperity:

The Unrest of

Youth in

the 1960s

7. Do not succumb to utopias or illusions; be dissatisfied and critical. Have the sceptical confidence of a negotiator, but have confidence in the purpose of your negotiations. The activity has its own value.

8. Do not be afraid of your task in history and be courageous in intervening in history. The social changes and transformations of man take place, no doubt, without regard to you, but to understand these changes and to influence them with the limited possibilities of an individual is far better than to accept the fatal inevitability of events.

9. Do not negotiate out of good motives alone; negotiate with sound arguments and with consideration of what you can achieve. A good deed can rise from a bad motive and vice versa. The motives are forgotten, but deeds remain.

10. Do not let yourself be *shot* in the fight between the interests of the power blocs. *Shoot* when in danger. Are you not in danger right now when you collaborate with the few knaves? Are you a knave?

13. Ivan Sviták, "Wherefrom, with Whom, and Whither?," March 5, 1968

From totalitarian dictatorship toward an open society, toward the liquidation of the power monopoly and toward the effective control of the power elite by a free press and by public opinion. From the bureaucratic management of society and culture by the "hard-line thugs" (C. Wright Mills)[5] toward the observance of fundamental human and civil rights, at least to the same extent as in the Czechoslovakia of bourgeois democracy. With the labor movement, without its *apparatchiks*;[6] with the middle classes, without their groups of willing collaborators; and with the intelligentsia in the lead. The intellectuals of this country must assert their claim to lead an open socialist society toward democracy and humanism.

5. **C. Wright Mills** (1916–1962): a Columbia University sociologist, the author of influential books including *White Collar* and *The Power Elite* and a severe critic of modern institutions.

6. *apparatchik*: a Russian word describing an individual who is part of the existing power structure.

Source 14 from Alexander Dubček, Hope Dies Last: The Autobiography of Alexander Dubček, *edited and translated by Jiri Hochman (New York: Kodansha International, 1993), pp. 297–299, 301–307, 313. Originally published in* Rudē Pravō, *April 10, 1968; translation revised from CTK, Prague, 1968. Reprinted by permission of Kodansha America, Inc. Excerpted from* Hope Dies Last *by Alexander Dubček published by Kodansha America, Inc. (1993).*

14. The Action Program of the Communist Party of Czechoslovakia, Adopted at the Plenary Session of the Central Committee of the Communist Party of Czechoslovakia, April 5, 1968

THE LEADING ROLE OF THE PARTY—A GUARANTEE OF SOCIALIST PROGRESS

At present it is most important that the Party practice a policy fully justifying its leading role in society. We believe that this is a condition for the socialist development of the country. . . .

In the past, the leading role of the Party was often conceived as a monopolistic concentration of power in the hands of Party bodies. This concept corresponded to the false thesis that the Party is the instrument of the dictatorship of the proletariat. This harmful conception weakened the initiative and responsibility of state, economic, and social institutions, damaged the Party's authority, and prevented it from carrying out its real functions. The Party's goal is not to become a universal "caretaker" of the society, to bind all organizations and every step taken in life by its directives. Its mission lies primarily in arousing socialist initiative, showing the ways and real possibilities of Communist perspectives, and in winning over all workers to them through systematic persuasion and the personal examples of Communists. This determines the conceptional character of Party activity. Party bodies do not deal with all problems; they should encourage activity and suggest solutions to the most important ones. At the same time the Party cannot turn into an organization which influences society only by its ideas and program. . . .

Within the framework of democratic rules of a socialist state, Communists must continually strive for the voluntary support of the majority of the people for the Party line. Party resolutions and directives must be modified if they fail to express the needs and possibilities of the whole society. The Party must try to ensure for its members—the most active workers in their spheres of work—suitable weight and influence in the whole society and posts in state, economic, and social bodies. This, however, must not lead to the practice of appointing Party members to posts, without regard to the principle that leading representatives of institutions of the whole society are chosen by the society itself and by

[387]

Chapter 13

The Perils of

Prosperity:

The Unrest of

Youth in

the 1960s

its individual components and that functionaries of these components are responsible to all citizens or to all members of social organizations. . . .

Only down-to-earth discussion and an exchange of views can lead to responsible decision-making by collective bodies. The confrontation of views is an essential manifestation of a responsible multilateral attempt to find the best solution, to advance the new against the obsolete. Each member of the Party and Party bodies has not only the right, but the duty to act according to his conscience, with initiative, criticism, and different views on the matter in question, to oppose any functionary. . . . The Party realizes that a deeper democracy will not hold in this society if democratic principles are not consistently applied in the internal life and work of the Party and among Communists. Decisions on all important questions and on filling cadre posts must be backed by democratic rules and secret ballot. . . .

NO RESPONSIBILITY WITH RIGHTS

. . . The whole *National Front,*[7] the political parties which form it, and the social organizations will take part in the creation of state policy. *The political parties* of the National Front are partners whose political work is based on the joint political program of the National Front and is naturally bound by the Constitution of the Czechoslovak Socialist Republic. It stems from the socialist character of social relations in our country. The Communist Party of Czechoslovakia considers the National Front to be a political platform which does not separate political parties into government and opposition factions. It does not create opposition to state policy—the policy of the whole National Front—or lead struggles for political power. Possible differences in the viewpoints of individual component parts of the National Front or divergency of views as to a state policy is to be settled on the basis of the common socialist conception of National Front policy by way of political agreement and unification of all component parts of the National Front. . . .

Voluntary social organizations of the working people cannot replace political parties, *but the contrary is also true. Political parties in our country cannot exclude common-interest organizations of workers and other working people from directly influencing state policy*, its creation and application. Socialist state power cannot be monopolized either by a single party, or by a coalition of parties. It must be open to all political organizations of the people. *The Communist Party of Czechoslovakia will use every means at its disposal to develop such forms of*

7. **National Front:** the coalition of political parties of the center and left that governed Czechoslovakia after World War II. These included the Communists, the National Socialists (no relation to the German party of that name), the Popular (Catholic) party, the Social Democrats, and the Liberal Democrats. With the Communists coup of 1948, that party gained complete political power but sought greater legitimacy by claiming to govern in the name of a national alliance of parties. In reality, from 1948 until 1968, Czechoslovakia was a one-party state.

political life that will ensure the expression of the direct voice and will of the working class and all working people in political decision-making in our country. . . .

The implementation of the *constitutional freedoms of assembly and association* must be ensured this year so that the possibility of setting up voluntary organizations, special-interests associations, societies, etc., is guaranteed by law and the present interests and needs of various strata and categories of our citizens are lended to without bureaucratic interference and without a monopoly by any individual organization. Any restrictions in this respect can be imposed only by law and only the law can stipulate what is antisocial, forbidden, or punishable. Freedoms guaranteed by law and in compliance with the constitution also apply fully to citizens of various creeds and religious denominations.

The effective influence of views and opinions of the working people on the policies and a firm opposition to all tendencies to suppress the criticism and initiative of the people cannot be guaranteed if we do not ensure constitution-based freedom of speech and political and personal rights to all citizens, systematically and consistently, by all legal means available. . . .

THE EQUALITY OF CZECHS AND
SLOVAKS IS THE BASIS FOR THE
STRENGTH OF THE REPUBLIC

Our republic, as a joint state of two equal nations—Czechs and Slovaks—must continually check to be sure that the constitutional arrangement of relations between our fraternal nations and the status of all other nationalities of Czechoslovakia develop as required to strengthen the unity of the state, foster the development of the nations and nationalities themselves, and correspond to the needs of socialism. It cannot be denied that even in socialist Czechoslovakia, in spite of outstanding progress in solving the problem of nationalities, *there are serious faults and fundamental deformations* in the constitutional arrangement of relations between the Czechs and Slovaks. . . .

In preparing the 14th Congress of the Party and the new constitution, it is necessary to submit a professionally and politically backed proposal for a constitutional arrangement of relations between our two nations that will fully express and guarantee their equality and right of self-determination. The same principles shall be applied to the pattern of the Party and social organizations. . . .

SOCIALISM CANNOT DO
WITHOUT ENTERPRISING

The democratization program in economy links economic reform more closely with the process facing us in the sphere of politics and the general management of society, and stimulates the determination and application of new elements to develop the economic reform even further. *The democratization program of the economy places special emphasis on ensuring the independence of enterprises and enterprise groupings and their relative independence from state bodies,*

Chapter 13

The Perils of

Prosperity:

The Unrest of

Youth in

the 1960s

the full implementation of the right of the consumer to determine his consumption and his style of life, the right of a free choice of working activity, the right and real possibility of various groups of the working people and different social groups to formulate and defend their economic interests in shaping the economic policy. . . .

THE PEOPLE'S VISION

Source 15 from Literární Listy, *in Sviták,* The Czechoslovak Experiment, 1968–1969, *p. 2.*

15. Cartoon: "If There Are No Complications the Child Should Be Born in the Ninth Month," 1968

THE ENEMY

Source 16 from Literární Listy, *in Robin Alison Remington, editor,* Winter in Prague:
Documents on Czechoslovak Communism in Crisis *(Cambridge, Mass.: MIT Press,
1969), p. 289.*

16. Cartoon, "Workers of All Countries Unite—Or I'll Shoot!," August 28, 1968

Chapter 13
The Perils of
Prosperity:
The Unrest of
Youth in
the 1960s

IN DEFEAT

Source 17 from Listy, *in Remington,* Winter in Prague, *p. 373.*

17. Cartoon: "It Is Only a Matter of a Few Tactical Steps Back," January 30, 1969

JDE JENOM O NĚKOLIK
TAKTICKÝCH ÚSTUPKŮ...

Vladimír Jiránek

Source 18 from Michael Long, Making History: Czech Voices of Dissent and the Revolution *of 1989, 2005, p. 10. Reprinted by permission.*

18. The Plastic People of the Universe, "The Twenty-Year-Old Today," 1969

Whoever is twenty today,
Feels like throwing up from disgust,
But those in their forties
Want to puke even more.
Only the sixty-year-old
Can nurse his sclerosis in bed.
But whoever is twenty today,
Only hurls with disgust.

19. Václav Havel, "Dear Dr. Husák," April 1975

Dear Dr. Husák,

In our offices and factories work goes on, discipline prevails. The efforts of our citizens are yielding visible results in a slowly rising standard of living: people build houses, buy cars, have children, amuse themselves, live their lives.

All this, of course, amounts to very little as a criterion for the success or failure of your policies. After every social upheaval, people invariably come back in the end to their daily labors, for the simple reason that they want to stay alive; they do so for their own sake, after all, not for the sake of this or that team of political leaders.

Not that going to work, doing the shopping, and living their own lives is all that people do. They do much more than that: they commit themselves to numerous output norms which they then fulfill and over-fulfill; they vote as one man and unanimously elect the candidates proposed to them; they are active in various political organizations; they attend meetings and demonstrations; they declare their support for everything they are supposed to. Nowhere can any sign of dissent be seen from anything that the government does.

These facts, of course, are not to be made light of. One must ask seriously, at this point, whether all this does not confirm your success in achieving the tasks your team set itself—those of winning the public's support and consolidating the situation in the country. . . .

I make so bold as to answer, No; to assert that, for all the outwardly persuasive facts, inwardly our society, far from being a consolidated one, is, on the contrary, plunging ever deeper into a crisis more dangerous, in some respects, than any we can recall in our recent history.

I shall try to justify this assertion.

The basic question one musk ask is this: Why are people in fact behaving in the way they do? Why do they do all these things that, taken together, form the impressive image of a totally united society giving total support to its government? For any unprejudiced observer, the answer is, I think, self-evident: They are driven to it by fear.

For fear of losing his job, the schoolteacher teaches things he does not believe; fearing for his future, the pupil repeats them after him; for fear of not being allowed to continue his studies, the young man joins the Youth League and participates in whatever of its activities are necessary; fear that, under the monstrous system of political credits, his son or daughter will not acquire the necessary total of points for enrollment at a school leads the father to take on all manner of responsibilities and "voluntarily" to do everything required. Fear of

Chapter 13

The Perils of
Prosperity:

The Unrest of

Youth in

the 1960s

the consequences of refusal leads people to take part in elections, to vote for the proposed candidates, and to pretend that they regard such ceremonies as genuine elections; out of fear for their livelihood, position, or prospects, they go to meetings, vote for every resolution they have to, or at least keep silent. . . .

The question arises, of course: What are people actually afraid of? Trials? Torture? Loss of property? Deportations? Executions? Certainly not. The most brutal forms of pressure exerted by the authorities upon the public are, fortunately, past history—at least in our circumstances. Today, oppression takes more subtle and selective forms. And even if political trials do not take place today—everyone knows how the authorities manage to manipulate them— they only represent an extreme threat, while the main thrust has moved into the sphere of existential pressure. Which, of course, leaves the core of the matter largely unchanged.

Notoriously, it is not the absolute value of a threat which counts, so much as its relative value. It is not so much what someone objectively loses as the subjective importance it has for him on the plane on which he lives, with its own scale of values. Thus, if a person today is afraid, say, of losing the chance of working in his own field, this may be a fear equally strong, and productive of the same reactions, as if—in another historical context—he had been threatened with the confiscation of his property. Indeed, the technique of existential pressure is, in a sense, more universal. For there is no one in our country who is not, in a broad sense, existentially vulnerable. Everyone has something to lose and so everyone has reason to be afraid. . . .

Somewhere at the top of the hierarchy of pressures by which man is maneuvered into becoming an obedient member of a consumer herd, there stands, as I have hinted, a concealed, omnipotent force: the state police. It is no coincidence, I suppose, that this body should so aptly illustrate the gulf that separates the ideological facade from everyday reality. Anyone who has had the bad luck to experience personally the "working style" of that institution must be highly amused at the official explanation of its purpose. Does anyone really believe that that slimy swarm of thousands of petty informers, professional narks, complex-ridden, sly, envious, malevolent petits bourgeois, and bureaucrats, that malodorous agglomeration of treachery, evasion, fraud, gossip, and intrigue "shows the imprint of the working man, guarding the people's government and its revolutionary achievements against its enemies' designs"? . . .

It would be hard to explain this whole grotesque contrast between theory and practice, except as a natural consequence of the real mission of the state police today, which is not to protect the free development of man from any assailants, but to protect the assailants from the threat which any real attempt at man's free development poses. . .

QUESTIONS TO CONSIDER

France and Czechoslovakia were two very different countries at opposite ends of Europe. Let us compare the events of 1968 as they unfolded in these two locations. Do they illustrate a common response to problems basic to modern life in the noncommunist and communist West?

Consider first the demands of French and Czechoslovakian protest leaders. Examine again the written and visual evidence, and consider the protesters' views on working conditions in France. What problems do they identify in Sources 1, 2, and 3? How are these problems defined graphically? Why do you think that the artist in Source 4 portrayed modern capitalism as a puppeteer? What is the significance of the puppeteer's appearance? Why did the artist show de Gaulle as part of the industrial gears of France in Source 5? Turn next to the Czechoslovakian statements on working conditions. Notice particularly Source 13, with its references to management by "hard-line thugs" and "apparatchiks." What great lie about communism (whose slogan is "Workers of the World Unite!") do the Czechoslovakians discern in Source 16? What common theme do you find in French and Czechoslovakian protesters' ideas on the conditions of labor in the modern economy?

Next consider the political vision of the 1968 activists. Take the French first. What sort of government did the formulators of Source 3 envision? How is that idea amplified in Sources 9 and 10? These cartoons spell their messages in words, but their art contains a message, too. Look closely at Source 9. How does the artist see the individual faring against big government, industrial giants, and powerful unions? What solution does the artist propose in the caption? Which groups did the creator of Source 10 hope would seize political power?

The Czechoslovakians also had a political vision. Review Sources 12, 13, and 14. What political outlook do these statements express? What groups did Czechoslovakian reformers expect to lead change? Combine this message with Source 15. How do the reformers regard their chances for success? How were the political visions of the French and Czechoslovakian reformers similar?

Both movements also expressed images of their opponents and the methods to be employed in their struggles. What sort of action does the artist of Source 7 recommend to the French? What secondary message do you think underlies the portrayal of the fighter as a woman? Source 8 shows a close-up view of a Parisian paving stone. What message do you find in its accompanying statement? In Sources 6 and 11, we find some statements of the reformers' view of the opposition and its power. Why do you think the artist pictured a silhouette of a tank in Source 6? The final French selection, Source 11, is a cartoon that appeared on the cover of *L'enragé* after the defeat of the students and workers. What significance do you find in the portrayal of de Gaulle? What has crippled him? What supports him? What view of

[395]

Chapter 13

The Perils of

Prosperity:

The Unrest of

Youth in

the 1960s

the government does the shape of his crutches convey?

The Czechoslovakian sources also characterize the reformers' opposition and their chances of success. In Source 15 what does the woman's obvious pregnancy represent? When does Dubček predict the birth? How long did the Czechoslovakian experiment in greater democracy actually last? What does Source 16 remind Czechoslovakians about the fate of their experiment?

The last cartoon, Source 17, reflects Czechoslovakia in defeat. Many alleged that making peace with the country's Russian conquerors would be simple: "It is only a matter of a few tactical steps back!" Where do the steps backward lead in this case?

What does this tell us about the fate of the reform movement? What was the response of the young to the failure of reform in Source 18? What common sentiment do you detect in the French and Czechoslovakian evidence regarding the reformers' chances for meaningful success in the face of the modern state? What sort of regime resulted from these "steps back," according to Source 19?

Answering these questions should prepare you to formulate your replies to the central questions of this chapter: What aspects of the modern state and economy provoked the events of 1968? What vision of the future did leaders of the French and Czechoslovakian movements embrace? How did they propose to achieve it?

EPILOGUE

As you continue your reading on the history of Western civilization through the events of the 1970s, 1980s, and 1990s, it will become clear that the student unrest in France and other parts of Western Europe as well as events in Czechoslovakia is of enduring importance.

Perhaps in partial response to this agitation, significant political changes occurred in much of the West in the 1970s and 1980s. In most Western democracies, eighteen-year-olds won the vote. In many countries, too, at least a partial reversal of political centralization began, perhaps in some measure stemming from youthful demands for more "power to the people." This impulse to diminish

state authority defied ideological labels. In France and Sweden it was begun by socialist governments, whereas in the United States it has been the work of conservative administrations. No country, however, has yet approached the French students' vision of autogestion.

In France, where student movements amassed the broadest nonstudent support, other changes occurred. His power tarnished by the events of 1968, de Gaulle resigned within a year of the student strikes over a minor issue of government reform. Universities and their curricula were radically restructured in an attempt to meet some student demands, and working conditions in the factories were improved. Even in France, however, fundamental educational and industrial policy remained firmly in the hands of government officials and corporate managers. Student political activism and bitter labor disputes, many originating in issues raised in 1968, persist.

Elsewhere, the student revolt garnered less support, produced fewer changes, and led some frustrated student radicals to turn their energies from protest to brutal political violence in the 1970s. In West Germany, some student radicals formed terrorist groups like the Baader-Meinhof gang, which lashed out violently at West German symbols of the conservative consumer society and American military installations. The Red Brigades terrorist groups in Italy had the same roots and objectives.

In the 1980s youthful discontent in Western Europe partially manifested itself in the Green movement. Especially strong in the West Germany, this movement represents the continued alienation of many from the West's industrial economy and modern society. The Green movement attacks the effects of modern industry on our environment and particularly the failure of traditional governing parties effectively to address environmental issues. The Green in West Germany also advocated an end to their country's participation in the North Atlantic Treaty Organization (NATO). While not always well organized, Greens entered the political life of a number of countries and by 1992 had elected members to parliaments in Germany and Switzerland as well as to the European Parliament. Indeed, from 1998 to 2006, the Greens became part of the governing coalition (with the Social Democratic party) in

Germany, and the party's leader became foreign minister. Such a governing role led the Greens to accept NATO membership for Germany.

Eastern Europe felt the effects of Soviet actions in Czechoslovakia in 1968 for two decades, as those seeking political, economic, and social change in that region consciously confined reform within the boundaries established by the Brezhnev Doctrine. Discontent with communist rule and Soviet domination, however, grew in the 1980s, led by the rise in Poland of an independent, noncommunist labor movement, Solidarity. By the late 1980s, events in the Soviet Union also actually fostered change in Eastern Europe. Soviet President Mikhail Gorbachev (1985–1991) proclaimed a policy of *glasnost* (openness) and *perestroika* (restructuring) and abandoned the Brezhnev Doctrine, allowing Eastern European nations to determine their own destinies. The result was a largely peaceful revolution in 1989, when one-party communist political systems collapsed in Poland, Hungary, East Germany, Romania, and Czechoslovakia. Indeed, by the end of 1991, the ultimate result of Gorbachev's new path was the dissolution of the Soviet Union and its one-party communist political system, replaced by the Commonwealth of Independent States. Events in Czechoslovakia provide an example of the rapidity of Eastern European change in 1989 and remind us of the enduring importance of the events of 1968 in promoting that change.

In Czechoslovakia the rigid, one-party communist rule reimposed by

Chapter 13

The Perils of

Prosperity:

The Unrest of

Youth in

the 1960s

Soviet arms in 1968 proved particularly resistant to change. The government dealt harshly with those favoring change: 500,000 dissidents lost their party memberships, hundreds of thousands of others linked with reform endured exclusion from professional employment for which they were qualified, and Dubček found himself demoted to work as a mechanic. Nevertheless, opposition continued. In January 1977, a number of dissidents established Charter 77 to pressure the government to respect human rights. Its leaders included the playwright Václav Havel and the philosopher Jan Patocka. Havel spent five years in prison for his reform efforts, and Patocka died after police questioning, but by the mid-1980s the success of Solidarity in Poland and the reforms of Gorbachev in the Soviet Union inspired new hope for change.

In 1988 widespread demonstrations against the communist regime began, despite the authorities' consistently forceful responses to this dissent. The year 1989 opened with a massive demonstration commemorating the twentieth anniversary of the death of the student Jan Palach protesting the loss of the Prague Spring reforms. Indeed, a demonstration by students was key in bringing down the communist government. On November 17, 1989, the authorities permitted a seemingly harmless student observance in Prague of the fiftieth anniversary of an act of student resistance to Czechoslovakia's occupation by Germany in World War II. The commemorative event quickly turned into a demonstration for greater democracy that drew 100,000 participants. Armed riot police brutally dispersed the unarmed crowd, seriously injuring 291 and arresting over 100 persons. But the brutality revolted the country, especially as founded rumors of a student death circulated, and opposition to the government dramatically rose. Students seized university buildings. Reformers, led by Havel, who had recently been released from prison, founded Civic Forum in the Czech lands and Public Against Violence in Slovakia to coordinate resistance. A general strike on November 27 brought the country to a virtual halt, and additional demonstrations for democracy were widespread in late November and in December. Faced with great opposition, Communist party leaders finally relinquished power in late December. The country's legislature selected a new presiding officer for its deliberations, Alexander Dubček, the reformer of 1968, and a new president for the country, the playwright Václav Havel. In what has been called the "Velvet Revolution" because so little bloodshed occurred, Czechoslovakia reestablished the democratic system it had in the coup of 1948. The newly democratic Czechoslovakia was not safe, however, from some of the problems that had undone its former communist regime. By 1992 long-standing nationalist tensions between the country's two chief language groups, the Czechs and the Slovaks, broke the country into two separate nation-states, the Czech Republic and Slovakia. Thus, many of the issues of 1968, here, as elsewhere, still affect the West.

CHAPTER FOURTEEN

THE EUROPEAN NATION-STATE AND

REGIONAL ETHNIC NATIONALISM

THE PROBLEM

The nation-state, a sovereign political unit (a state) extending over the area inhabited by an ethnic group with a common cultural and linguistic heritage (a nation), long has been the foundation of the European political system. Indeed, certain of the traditional major powers, like Britain and France, can trace their origins as nation-states back a millennium or more. But the evolution of modern European nation-states often reflected the imposition of the political and cultural hegemony of a dominant ethnic group over one or more minority ethnic communities. At times of great political stress, or in periods of sweeping political change, such countries sometimes have dissolved along regional ethnic lines. One such period, of course, was at the end of World War I. In 1917 and 1918, amidst military defeat, the multiethnic Russian, Austro-Hungarian, and Ottoman Empires dissolved into a number of smaller states whose boundaries approximated regions historically occupied by distinct ethnic groups. Another such period is the late twentieth and early twenty-first centuries.

During much of the twentieth century, a period marked by two world wars and the cold war, which jeopardized the survival of many nation-states as independent entities, most Europeans subordinated their ethnic differences to the more immediate need to preserve national independence. Beginning in the last years of the twentieth century, however, a number of developments weakened national unities that had always been more apparent than real. After the 1989 end of the cold war, with its pressure on each European nation to present a united front in support of the Soviet Union or the United States, many Europeans focused their attention on ethnic problems within their countries. At the same time, the growth of democratic political processes in former totalitarian states, like Portugal and Spain in the west and the erstwhile satellites of the Soviet Union in the east, allowed for the first time in decades political dissent that often reflected age-old ethnic conflicts. Finally, the supranational institutions of the European Union potentially diminished somewhat the importance of the traditional nation-state itself. It is not surprising, therefore, that the last two decades of the twentieth century and the first years of the twenty-first have been marked by ethnic conflict. In a number of European countries objection to the traditional, centralized nation-state arose most often from regional ethnic minorities that had retained their particular linguistic and cultural identities. These groups sought to control their own destinies by attaining greater political and cultural autonomy for their regions or by achieving independence from the nation-states of which they were a part.

Such ethnic issues mean that at the outset of the twenty-first century we must ask basic questions about the future of the European nation-state. What national and ethnic issues now challenge the traditional European nation-state? Why have such issues proven very divisive in Europe? What do you think will be the character of the European nation-state in the twenty-first century?

SOURCES AND METHOD

This final chapter, like all of the others in *Discovering the Western Past*, assembles a diverse body of evidence. It will require you to employ a number of the analytical techniques that you have mastered in earlier chapters, while also presenting some new ones. As usual, we provide background information on the individual sources essential for their analysis, and we will begin with sources from western Europe.

Source 1 presents a selection that reminds us of the importance of language in defining national identity, and it comes to us from Ireland. The Irish, a people with a distinct regional identity focused on their home island, a rich history, and a unique culture and language, had first been conquered by the English in the twelfth century. In the course of the nineteenth century, however, the English had integrated Ireland politically into the United Kingdom of Great Britain and Ireland, and the culture and Gaelic language of the Celtic natives of Ireland was disappearing within a nation-state defined by English language and culture. This is the problem addressed by Douglas Hyde (1860–1949), a language scholar who taught much of his life at University College Dublin. An Irish nationalist, Hyde founded the Gaelic League (*Conradh na Gaeilge* in Gaelic) in 1893 to try to save Gaelic from extinction and to preserve Irish identity. Irish nationalists quickly recognized the unifying power of their historic language in countering a centralized state imposing on its subjects the English language of its dominant ethnic group. In Source 1, Hyde outlines a path for future advocates of the rights of ethnic minorities by asserting the need to preserve unique languages and cultures. His message was key in the development of the modern Irish nationalism, which propelled his country to independence from Britain, and in recognition Hyde's countrymen selected him as the first president of the Republic of Ireland (*Eire* in Gaelic) in 1938. Why did Hyde see the preservation of Gaelic as so important? How did he treat the Celtic past? How could such cultural nationalism built around a unique language and culture translate into a drive for political independence from Britain?

Of course, the Irish subjects of Great Britain for whom Hyde spoke in the nineteenth century were just one of many European regional ethnic groups whose identities rested on language and historic regional homelands and who constituted reluctant citizens of nation-states dominated by other language groups. Source 2 presents Europe's major regional ethnic minorities near the end of the cold war. In order to interpret the information in this source, we must first understand its nature. The statistics in Source 2, formulated by language scholars, are estimates, because there often exists no precise census of a nation's citizens classified by their languages. Many nations, perhaps cognizant of the power of language to disrupt the unity of the modern, centralized nation-state, maintain that all of their citizens belong to the national community and therefore compile no official data on minorities. Second, we must understand that the data in Source 2 present only the largest ethnic minorities concentrated in their own distinct provincial or regional homelands. Numerous smaller regional ethnic groups and indigenous linguistic

minorities that are widely dispersed, including the Roma (frequently called "Gypsies") present in every European country, are not shown in this source. Thus, the actual language picture in most European countries is considerably more complex than Source 2 suggests, and a standard linguistic study identifies a total of twenty-nine European tongues spoken within France and thirty-three such languages spoken in Italy.[1] What do these data suggest to you about the extent of regional ethnic minorities in Europe in the late twentieth century? Which countries have the largest regional ethnic minorities? Remembering the importance that Hyde placed on language in shaping national identity, what conclusions might you draw about the ethnic unity of a number of European nation-states?

We can discern several responses by governments to the aspirations of their ethnic minorities. One possible response is typified by that of France, a country which Source 2 reveals to have substantial regional ethnic minorities. In recent years, many French government leaders and intellectuals have spoken of "the French exception," by which they mean every way in which their country and its people differ from other European countries and peoples. On matters of ethnicity, the French exception is that the nation's leaders largely remain steadfast in their belief that France ought to be a democratic, secular, centralized state in which all citizens,

1. Raymond G. Gordon, Jr., ed., *Ethnologue: Languages of the World*, 15th ed. (Dallas, Tex.: SIL International, 2005). Online version: http://www.etnologue.com.

[401]

even non-European immigrants, become culturally "French." Thus, the state has developed a system of public education intended to make all citizens French speakers and, despite recent concessions of some instruction in regional tongues, sees no need to assemble data on the languages of its citizens. This policy has met resistance among both European and non-European ethnic minorities. In the 1990s, the state's assertion of its secular, French character precluded Muslim girls from wearing the headscarves emblematic of their faith and culture in French public schools, generating considerable outcry at the time among Muslim citizens. And occasional acts of terrorism have resulted from the frustrations of indigenous minorities, like the Bretons and the Corsicans, who also object to the loss of their language and cultural identities within a state committed to the linguistic and cultural uniformity of its citizens. Indeed, French problems in Corsica are the origin of Source 3.

The traditional language of the Mediterranean island of Corsica is a non-French tongue, Corsu. That language, and the island's distinctive culture, long have been the foundation of separatist movements that have made Corsica an administrative problem for the French state. When France acquired the island in 1768 from Genoa, it immediately had to subdue a Corsican independence movement. In the late twentieth century Corsican separatism persisted in occasional terrorist acts against the government, and in 2000, Prime Minister Lionel Jospin, preparing to run for the French presidency in 2002,

proposed greater autonomy for Corsica in return for peace. His plan stalled in the national legislature, and another plan for less sweeping, administrative reorganization of Corsica designed to enhance Corsican identity within France failed to gain a majority vote in a 2003 referendum on the island. Corsica, therefore, remains an integral part of the French state.

Source 3 is a statement of opinion published in 2000 at the time of Jospin's proposal of Corsican autonomy. Such opinion pieces, when they are the work of highly regarded figures and appear in respected publications, are often quite influential. This is the case of Source 3. This editorial by Jacques Attali (1943–), a well-known economist and an adviser to the government of France from 1981 to 1991, appeared in the influential news magazine *L'Express*. What is Attali's view in regard to Corsica? Note how his reference to "the headscarf affair" portrays the threat of European minorities to the French nation-state as more serious than the growing presence of non-European minorities. Why does he take this position? What do you think that he meant by "the French exception"? How are his views almost the exact antithesis of those of Douglas Hyde?

Most western European nations have done more than France to accommodate the aspirations of regional ethnic minorities. Indeed, the Council of Europe, an international organization of forty-six European democracies, sponsored a "European Charter for Regional or Minority Languages" in 1992, which twenty-one nations, not including France, now have ratified.

Those countries minimally pledged to offer their indigenous-language minorities (the agreement specifically excludes immigrant groups) the right of public education and the conduct of public business in their languages in what amounts to state recognition of official status for minority tongues. Referring back to Source 2, how many western European nations are endeavoring, at least in principle, to meet their commitments by according official status to more than one tongue?

Constitutional documents, which state the principles on which a government is founded and the practices that it will follow, sometimes embody nation-states' efforts to meet the desires of their regional ethnic minorities. Source 4 offers excerpts from the Finnish constitution of March 1, 2000. That document, considered a model of peaceful accommodation of the desires of regional ethnic minorities, summarizes linguistic policies that had been in place for some time. Why would you describe the constitution as promoting a policy of true, regional bilingualism? How does the constitution go beyond bilingualism in accommodating the Swedish minority in one region? What other ethnic minorities' needs does the constitution address?

Other nations have implemented constitutional efforts to meet the desires of ethnic minorities that not only grant official status for minority tongues but also accord to their speakers a considerable amount of political autonomy. Typically the latter effort involves the creation of a federal system of government, one that transfers substantial power from the central government to the governments of regions or provinces that often have unique ethnic characters. This is the case in Belgium, a country whose 10 million citizens speak three major languages (refer again to Source 2) and have a long history of conflict between the French-speaking minority in the south and the majority in the north speaking a Dutch dialect (Flemish). Thus, the complex Constitution of 1993 provides for each language community's linguistic and cultural independence and a large measure of political autonomy. The United Kingdom has not gone as far as Belgium's federal system, but it did institute in 1999 a policy of "devolution" fundamentally changing the relationship of the country's two largest regional ethnic groups, the Scots and the Welsh, to a nation-state long defined on English terms. Scotland secured its own parliament, which administers funds from the British central government for matters of regional concern, including health, education, housing, transport, and economic development, while Wales got its own assembly with somewhat less authority and funding. Both secured enhanced recognition of their cultural identities with new rights to education and broadcasting in their individual Celtic tongues.

Spain, a country long divided by the efforts of the government in Madrid to forge a unitary state dominated by speakers of Spanish, also recently has tried to meet at least some of the wishes of its linguistic minorities. Thus, the Constitution of 1978 conceded to the main ethnic minority groups (see Source 2) limited political autonomy and official status for the language of each within their respective regions. At the same time, however, the constitution reserved control of national defense, justice, and foreign policy for the central government, and many Catalans and Basques find this unacceptable. The Catalans, whose cultural center is Barcelona, largely have confined their dissatisfaction to political maneuvering that has won the region greater autonomy and that recently also has included an effort to have their language ranked as one of the official languages of the European Union. Achievement of such status, of course, would recognize something more than simple regional autonomy for their land. But some violence has occurred among the Basques, a people who speak a language unrelated to any other European tongue and who largely still inhabit their formerly independent homeland in northern Spain and southwestern France.

Modern ethnic violence in the Basque region erupted in 1959 to protest efforts by the dictator Francisco Franco to govern Spain as a centralized state. The founders of the paramilitary nationalist group ETA (*Euskadi Ta Askatasune*, Basque for "Basque Homeland and Freedom") tried to advance its cause by assassinations and kidnappings that cost some 900 lives prior to a cease-fire in March 2006. Source 5 is a 1978 manifesto of Basque national aspirations, "The KAS (initials for the Basque name of the "Coalition of Socialist Patriots") Alternative," that greatly influenced the members of

ETA and other organizations. What were the political, linguistic, and military aspirations of the Basque nationalists? Why might you conclude that a document that calls for both amnesty for those who had broken the laws of the central government and expulsion from Basque lands of that government's police fundamentally contradicts the existence of a unified Spanish state? Why do you think compromise with such principles has been so difficult that the Basque problem endures to the present day? Why might such a manifesto have implications for France as well as Spain? How might the Catalans' aspirations within the European Union to realize greater recognition of their regional ethnic identity offer a model for a peaceful resolution of conflict in the Basque lands?

In eastern Europe the unrest of regional ethnic groups has had even more far-reaching effects. Post–World War II communist governments in Central and Eastern Europe long had concealed profound regional ethnic tensions, and the end of the cold war led to the outright dissolution of several multiethnic states in the region. Sometimes this was a peaceful process. Thus, Czechoslovakia, whose Slovak citizens long had felt dominated by the Czechs, peacefully separated into two nations, the Czech Republic and Slovakia, on January 1, 1993. But the region's greatest political change occurred with the dissolution of the Union of Soviet Socialist Republics (USSR), one of the leading powers in the cold war, on December 25, 1991.

The USSR stretched over six thousand miles, from Eastern Europe to the Pacific Ocean, and included within its boundaries 127 officially recognized linguistic groups. Like its predecessor, the imperial government of the tsar, the communist government of the USSR endeavored to hold these diverse national groups together in a highly centralized nation-state dominated by speakers of Russian, the country's largest single language group. Thus, the state mandated instruction in Russian in all schools and required the adoption of Russian Cyrillic characters in place of the Latin alphabet traditionally used by some of its eastern citizens. In contrast to the reality of this centralized, Russian-dominated state, however, Soviet authorities proclaimed a hollow policy of autonomy for non-Russian groups that fooled few of them and that prompted a number of them to proclaim independence as the power of the USSR's government ebbed in the last decade of the twentieth century. The map in Source 6 suggests the ethnic complexity of the former USSR and tells us much about its political structure in principle, if not in practice.

In principle the USSR was a federal state, and the borders of its component political units were intended to coincide with the regions inhabited by many of the country's linguistic groups. The largest groups resided in their own union republics that, again in principle, were politically autonomous units with the right of secession from the union. The largest of the fifteen union republics, the Russian Soviet Federated Socialist Republic (RSFSR), was created for the Russians, and the map also shows other political units in addition to the union republics. Autonomous republics, in principle, provided homelands to ethnic groups less numerous than those accorded union republics, although in practice a few autonomous republics had more population or territory than some union republics. Smaller ethnic groups resided in autonomous *oblasts* (provinces), and the smallest groups possessed their own *okrugs* (districts, the basic administrative units into which the entire union was divided). Observe the map closely, for these administrative divisions offer a simplified regional ethnic map of the USSR. What do you note about the ethnic composition of the fifteen republics? Why would it be difficult to divide the USSR along the lines of those republics?

Source 7 is a table presenting the ethnic populations of the fifteen republics that emerged from the USSR by 1991. How many of these are ethnically homogeneous in population? In how many of the republics do you find ethnic Russians? Why might you anticipate ethnic tensions within the European and Asian successor states of the former USSR?

Ethnic tensions particularly have troubled the largest of the successor states of the USSR, the Russian Federation, which, like the former USSR, in principle is a federal state of ethnic republics. Also like the former USSR, the Russian Federation perpetuates the domination of the state by the majority ethnic group, people who speak the Slavic Russian language and who are Orthodox Christian in their religious heritage. In one of the twenty-one republics of the Russian Federation,

Chechnya (numbered 20 in Source 6), ethnic tensions erupted at the moment of the Russian Federation's creation. Chechens, who speak a non-Slavic language and are largely Sunni Muslims in religion, had been reluctant subjects of a Russian-dominated state since their nineteenth-century conquest by the Russian Empire. Outright rebellion among the Chechens has tended to erupt whenever the Russian state has been preoccupied with external or internal crises. One such rebellion coincided with World War II, and in response the communist government of the USSR forcibly resettled more than 1 million Chechens and other peoples of their northern Caucasus region in Siberia and Central Asia at a cost of thousands of lives. Only in 1956 did the state allow the return of the Chechens to their homeland, and enduring anti-Russian sentiment there led militants to seize control of local government and declare Chechen independence in 1991.

The Russian Federation refused to recognize Chechen independence for two chief reasons. First, the government feared that Chechen secession would prompt other regional ethnic groups to leave the federation. Second, the proximity of Chechnya to the great oil and gas reserves of the Caspian Sea caused strategic concerns in the Russian government. The result was two bloody Chechen wars. In the first, Russian forces proved unable to control the country in the face of guerrilla warfare that the Chechens declared a *jihad* (Muslim holy war). This conflict, which cost the lives of perhaps 5,500 Russian soldiers and as many as 100,000

Chechens, forced the Russian Federation to agree to a cease-fire and troop withdrawal in December 1996 that represented de facto independence for Chechnya. The second Chechen war erupted in 1999, as Russian forces again attacked the breakaway republic in an attempt to bring it back into the Russian Federation. Chechens responded with guerrilla warfare, suicide bombings, and terrorist attacks within Russia itself, but federation forces extended sufficient control over the country to reestablish a Russian-dominated government in 2003 and to secure a cease-fire with some elements of the Chechen resistance in February 2005. Nevertheless, sporadic resistance continues.

Civilian loss of life in this second war was perhaps as great as in the first one, in part because of the brutality of Russian troops. Source 8, which conveys something of this ethnic warfare, is the work of a Russian investigative journalist, Anna Politkovskaya (1958–2006). Politkovskaya was a courageous and relentless critic of Russia's current authoritarian president, Vladimir Putin, who sought to silence critics of his regime by reasserting Soviet-era state ownership of most electronic media and by pressuring print journalists to silence their criticism. Politkovskaya was a particular critic of the Chechen war, which the Putin regime sought to portray as just another theater in the global war on terrorism. She traveled extensively in Chechnya, publishing eyewitness reports of the war that documented Russian atrocities that continued into 2006. Politkovskaya's reports, always controversial, sometimes elicited threats to her life, and as she was about to publish a story on continuing Russian torture in Chechnya, she was murdered on October 7, 2006. The nature of her contract-style shooting caused many to link her slaying to persons in the government. Here she reports an incident in the second Chechen war, carefully distinguishing between the Russian army's reluctant young draftees and the criminal elements of the irregular units, referred to in Source 8 as "contract soldiers," which Politkovskaya earlier had linked to the Russian Justice Ministry. What are the ethnic and religious conflicts revealed in the incident Politkovskaya reported? Why do you think incidents like this one will have an enduring impact in Chechnya? How does the author feel about the government's mode of fighting this war?

The tragic end of the Yugoslav republic also illustrates bloody ethnic violence in eastern Europe. Yugoslavia arose out of the ruins of the Austro-Hungarian monarchy after World War I in an area of great ethnic diversity. It was a state of many ethnic groups, but seven chief ethnic groups, speaking several languages and possessing diverse cultures and histories, dominated its history in the last years of the twentieth century. Four of these main groups—the Serbs, Croats, Montenegrins, and Bosniaks (Muslim inhabitants of the area of Bosnia-Herzegovina)—all speak essentially the same language with relatively minor pronunciation differences. But the four peoples are culturally and historically distinct.

Thus, Serbs and Montenegrins use the Cyrillic alphabet and largely are Orthodox in religion, while the Bosniaks and the largely Roman Catholic Croats use the Latin alphabet. In addition, Croatian, Montenegrin, and Serbian nationalists all retain memories of earlier political independence. The three other ethnic groups, the historically Muslim Albanians, the largely Catholic Slovenes, and the predominantly Orthodox Macedonians, all had quite distinct languages.

Prior to World War II, Yugoslavia had experienced extensive conflict between its ethnic groups as a result of attempts by Serbs to dominate the state. The World War II communist resistance leader Josip Broz Tito (1892–1980), however, repressed assertions of ethnic differences in his capacity first as prime minister and then as president of Yugoslavia, from 1945 until his death. Tito configured Yugoslavia as a federated state of six ethnic republics, Serbia (with two autonomous provinces, ethnically mixed Vojvodina and largely Albanian Kosovo), Croatia, Bosnia and Herzegovina, Macedonia, Slovenia, and Montenegro. Under his authoritarian rule, Yugoslavia experienced considerable economic prosperity while its communist government charted a cold war foreign policy quite independent of that of the USSR. At Tito's death, however, the federation came under growing ethnic stress. Part of the problem was economic in nature: the two northern republics, Croatia and especially Slovenia, had enjoyed a disproportionate part of the country's economic growth and shared little in common with the four poorer republics of Yugoslavia. But the largest part of the problem was ethnic conflict largely fueled by an ambitious Serb politician, Slobodan Milošević (1941–2006). Seeking to amass a political following in Serbia by inciting Serb nationalism, Milošević first gained control of the Serb Communist party in 1987 and then the presidency of Serbia in 1989. As communism collapsed, Milošević's attempt to forge a Serb-dominated nation-state provoked the dissolution of Yugoslavia. Slovenia, Croatia, and Macedonia declared their independence in 1991, followed by Bosnia and Herzegovina in 1992. The result was five wars between the country's ethnic groups in eight years.

In the first, the Serbian-dominated Yugoslav army launched a brief and unsuccessful attack on secessionist Slovenia in 1991. A second, far bloodier, war raged in 1991 and 1992, as Serbs within secessionist Croatia rose up in a revolt aided by the Yugoslav army. Bosnia and Herzegovina, the most ethnically diverse of the former Yugoslav republics, suffered even more grievously in the third and fourth wars. The third war was a brief conflict in 1993 between Bosnia and Herzegovina's Croat and Bosniak residents over a Croat attempt to carve a separate Croatian state out of the former republic. In a fourth conflict, the Serbs of Bosnia and Herzegovina, refusing to accept rule by the Bosniak-Croatian majority, rebelled and created a Republika Srpska ("Serb Republic"). Backed by Milošević and Yugoslav forces, the Serbs sought to solidify their control of Republika Srpska through a brutal policy of "ethnic cleansing" to expel or kill Muslims of the territory. Culminating in 1995 in a massacre of some 8,000 Bosniak males in Srebenica, the largest mass killing in Europe since World War II, this genocidal conflict shocked the world. The fifth war, equally shocking, erupted in 1999 in Kosovo, where the government of Milošević provoked rebellion by its policy of "cleansing" that region of its Albanian majority.

Together, these conflicts took the lives of perhaps 300,000 persons, and the international community eventually intervened. When the United Nations (UN) proved unable to re-establish peace, North Atlantic Treaty Organization (NATO) air forces heavily bombed Serbian forces. The result, in 1995, was a peace agreement for Bosnia and Herzegovina that provided for a large NATO peacekeeping force there. In Kosovo, NATO air warfare in 1999 against Serbia finally forced Milošević to remove Serbian forces, which were replaced by international peacekeepers. Domestic criticism of his policies finally drove Milošević from office in 2000, and in 2001, the Serbian government turned him over to an international tribunal for trial on charges of genocide and war crimes. He died before a verdict in his case.

Source 9 presents a map of Yugoslavia before these wars illustrating both the original boundaries of the republics and the regions inhabited by the various ethnic groups, including the Bosniaks, whom the map key identifies as "Muslims." Are the boundaries of the language zones coextensive with those of the republics? Why might you describe an ethnic map of the former Yugoslavia as a "patchwork" of intermingled ethnic groups? Why might these residential patterns explain much about the ethnic warfare in the former Yugoslavia in the 1990s?

Source 10 offers us a firsthand account of the genocide in Bosnia by Emir Suljagić, a Bosniak who was seventeen in 1992. Like many from his region, he eventually sought refuge in Srebrenica, where a UN force seemed to offer protection. There, his knowledge of English led to his employment as a translator for UN soldiers, and because he was an employee of the UN, he escaped the slaughter of Bosniak males when Srebrenica fell to the Serbs. He survived to study at the University of Sarajevo, work as a journalist, and testify about the events in Srebrenica at the trial of Milošević. In this selection, he describes the eruption of "ethnic cleansing" in April

and May 1992 as he and his father hid in the countryside and then made their way to Srebrenica. How would you describe the relations between Bosniaks and Serbs in the years prior to 1992? Why do you think that a state composed of different ethnic groups seemed to have worked before Milošević and his followers stirred up Serb nationalism? What was the cost of such ethnic intolerance for the family of this young man?

As you read the sources that follow, keep in mind the questions that we have posed about each of them. They should guide your analysis of this chapter's evidence and aid you in answering the central questions of this final chapter. What national and regional ethnic issues now challenge the traditional European state? Why have such issues proven very divisive in Europe? What do you think will be the character of the European nation-state in the twenty-first century?

THE EVIDENCE

Source 1 from Douglas Hyde, Revival of Irish Literature and Other Addresses *(London: Unwin, 1894), pp. 117–131.*

1. Douglas Hyde on the Revival of Gaelic, 1892

When we speak of "The Necessity for de-Anglicizing the Irish Nation," we mean it not as a protest against imitating what is best in the English people, for that would be absurd, but rather to show the folly of neglecting what is Irish, and hastening to adopt, pell-mell, and indiscriminately, everything that is English, simply because it is English. . . . If we take a bird's-eye view of our island today, and compare it with what it used to be, we must be struck by the extraordinary fact that the nation which was once, as everyone admits, one of the most classically learned and cultivated nations in Europe, is now one of the least so. . . .

I shall endeavor to show that this failure of the Irish people in recent times has been largely brought about by the race diverging during this century from the right path, and ceasing to be Irish without becoming English. I shall attempt to show that with the bulk of the people this change took place quite recently, much more recently than most people imagine, and is, in fact, still going on. I should also like to call attention to the illogical position of men who drop their own language to speak English, of men who translate their euphonious Irish names into English monosyllables, of men who read English books, and know nothing about Gaelic literature, nevertheless protesting as a matter of sentiment that they hate the country which at every hand's turn they rush to imitate.

I wish to show you that in Anglicizing ourselves wholesale we have thrown away with a light heart the best claim we have upon the world's recognition of us as a separate nationality. What did Mazzini say?[2] . . . That we ought to be content as an integral part of the United Kingdom because we have lost the notes of nationality, our language and customs. It has always been very curious to me how Irish sentiment sticks in this halfway house—how it continues apparently to hate the English, and at the same time continues to imitate them; how it continues to clamor for recognition as a distinct nationality and at the same time throws away with both hands what would make it so. . . .

What lies at the back of the sentiments of nationality with which the Irish millions seem so strongly leavened? . . . Of course it is a very composite feeling which prompts them; but I believe that what is largely behind it is the half unconscious feeling that the race which at one time held possession of more than half Europe, which established itself in Greece, and burned infant Rome, is now—almost extirpated and absorbed elsewhere—making its last stand for independence in this island of Ireland;[3] and do what they may the race of today cannot wholly divest itself from the mantle of its own past. Through early Irish literature, for instance, we can best form some conception of what that race really was, which, after overthrowing and trampling on the primitive peoples of half Europe, was itself forced in turn to yield its speech, manners, and independence to the victorious eagles of Rome. We alone of the nations of Western Europe escaped the claws of those birds of prey; we alone developed ourselves naturally upon our own lines outside of and free from all

2. **Mazzini:** Giuseppe Mazzini (1805–1872), an Italian nationalist and the founder of Young Italy, a nationalist group that aspired to free Italy of foreign rule and to unify its people under one government. He wrote extensively on problems of European nationalism.

3. Here Hyde portrays the accomplishments of the ancient Celts, a group of tribes occupying lands from the British Isles to Asia Minor. The ancient Celts were hardly a unified people, although Celtic warriors led by Bennus did sack Rome.

Roman influence; we alone were thus able to produce an early art and literature, *our* antiquities can best throw light upon the pre-Romanized inhabitants
of half Europe, and—we are our father's sons. . . .[4]

What the battleaxe of the Dane, the sword of the Norman, the wile of the
Saxon were unable to perform, we have accomplished ourselves.[5] We have at
last broken the continuity of Irish life, and just at the moment when the Celtic
race is presumably about to largely recover possession of its Celtic characteristics, cut off from the past, yet scarcely in touch with the present. It has lost
since the beginning of this century almost all that connected it with the era of
Cuchullain and of Ossian, that connected it with the christianizers of Europe,
that connected it with Brian Boru and the heroes of Clontarf, with the O'Neills
and O'Donnells, with Rory O'More, with the Wild Geese, and even to some
extent with the men of '98.[6] It has lost all that they had—language, traditions,
music, genius, and ideas. Just when we should be starting to build up anew
the Irish race and the Gaelic nation—as within our own recollection Greece
has been built up anew—we find ourselves despoiled of the bricks of nationality. The old bricks that lasted eighteen hundred years are destroyed; we
must now set to, to bake new ones, if we can, on other ground and of other
clay. . . . In a word, we must strive to cultivate everything that is most racial,
most smacking of the soil, most Gaelic, most Irish, because in spite of the little
admixture of Saxon blood in the northeast corner, this island is and will ever
remain Celtic at the core.[7]

---

4. Despite their conquest of Britain, the Romans never came to Ireland.

5. **Dane, Norman, Saxon:** Vikings from Denmark conquered parts of Ireland in the eighth
century. The Norman conquerors of Saxon England began Ireland's conquest in the late
twelfth century under King Henry II. Hyde probably uses "Saxon" here as a synonym for
the English.

6. In this sentence Hyde seeks to build national pride by invoking the names of Irish heroes.
Cuchullain was a legendary hero who reputedly defended his northern Irish province of Ulster.
Ossian was the legendary bard who sang the praises of his father, the heroic Fionn mac Cumhail.
Brian Boru (940?–1014) was the Irish king who broke the Vikings' hold on Ireland at **Clontarf.**
Shane O'Neill (1530?–1567), earl of Tyrone, fought the English. **Hugh Roe O'Donnell** (1571?–1602),
earl of Tyrconnel, led a failed rebellion against the English in 1601. Descendants of O'Neill and
O'Donnell were part of the **Wild Geese** who left Ireland in 1607 to continue the fight against England
in the forces of France and Spain. **Rory O'More** was one of the leaders of the Irish rebellion of
1641, and **the men of '98** were part of an abortive uprising led by Wolfe Tone (1763–1798).

7. Hyde refers here to Ulster. The British authorities displaced Irish residents here with English
and Scottish settlers after a failed Irish rebellion in the seventeenth century.

Source 2 from Barbara F. Grimes, editor, Ethnologue: Languages of the World, *twelth edition Copyright © 1992. Reprinted by permission of SIL International.*

2. Significant European Regional Ethnic Minorities, ca 1989

Nation State	Population	Speakers of Official and Regional Languages
1. Austria	7,595,000	German (official nationwide) 7,500,000 Croatian (official in Burgenland province) 28,054 Slovenian (official in Carinthia province) 45,000 Hungarian (Magyar) (official in Burgenland province) 19,117
2. Belgium	9,895,000	Dutch 5,640,150 French 4,000,000 German 150,000
3. Czechoslovakia	15,695,000	Czech (official) 10,004,800 Slovak (official) 4,865,450
4. Finland	4,977,000	Finnish (official) 4,900,000 Swedish (official) 340,000
5. France	56,184,000	French (official) 51,000,000 Alsatian 1,500,000 Breton 500,000 Corsican 200,000
6. Italy	57,657,000	Italian (official) and Italian dialects 55,00,000 German (official in Alto-Adige region) 225,000 French (official in Aosta Valley) 100,000 Slovenian (official in Trieste and Gorizia provinces) 100,000
7. Netherlands	14,864,000	Dutch (official) 13,400,000 Frisian (official in Friesland) 700,000
8. Spain	39,623,000	Spanish (official nationally) 28,173,600 Catalan (official regionally) 10,700,000 Galician (official regionally) 3,173,000 Basque (official regionally) 615,000
9. Switzerland	6,628,000	Swiss German (official) 4,225,000 French (official) 1,235,000 Italian (official) 195,000 Romansch (official) 65,000
10. USSR	285,743,000	127 languages[8]
11. United Kingdom	57,121,000	English (official) 55,000,000 Welsh 575,102 Scots 100,000 Gaelic (Irish) 120,000 Gaelic (Scottish) 88,892

8. See Sources 6 and 7.

Nation State	Population	Speakers of Official and Regional Languages
12. Yugoslavia	23,834,000	Serbo-Croatian (official) 17,000,000 Albanian (official) 1,600,000 Macedonian (official) 1,386,000 Slovenian (official) 2,000,000

Source 3 from Jacques Attali, "La fin d'une France," L'Express international, no. 2560 (July 27, 2000), p. 15. Translated by Julius R. Ruff. Reprinted by permission of L'Express International and the author.

3. Jacques Attali, "The End of One France," 2000

Globalization, new communication technologies, group and individual demands for autonomy, the construction of Europe:[9] all of these demand that we again think of the State. In doing so, we must raise a single question: What ought to remain of the nation? Everywhere, many aspects of state power are in the process of disappearing. Nationalized industries, the power of the civil service, . . . justice, and even someday the means of defense will be privatized, regionalized, Europeanized. All that will remain to the nation will be that which constitutes the heart of its identity, that is, the sense of belonging to one community, with a common destiny, speaking one language, concerned to share the best of what it has among all of its members and their descendants. . . .

What has happened with Corsica, therefore, attacks the very heart of the national identity by giving a fraction of the nation the right to differentiate itself from the rest by virtue of its language and social solidarity. While we could see in this a very easy solution for a unique problem on the nation's periphery, history teaches us that what happens on Corsica quickly will become the rule for other regions, which will not be satisfied until they have the same rights as their noisy countrymen.

The consequences of this universal demand for diversity will be disastrous. First, other peripheral regions will reject language uniformity and demand that we adopt Basque, Breton, Alsatian, or Creole as the language of instruction for their children. And since no parents, even those not native to a region, will have the courage to stand up against the local language by refusing to allow their children to be instructed in that dialect, all French people will soon have two mother tongues. Second, using the same principles, the central

9. **construction of Europe:** refers to the construction of the institutions of the European Union, which, by their supranational nature, diminished the powers and prerogatives of its member states.

[413]

regions of the country will refuse to assume the financial burdens of the periphery. Thus, for example, the Ile-de-France,[10] under the principles today applied to Corsica, will refuse to pay its share of the taxes to support Corsican officials. In the end, nothing will allow us to refuse the demands of migrants resisting integration into the settled population. Religious, ethnic, and linguistic groups scattered around the country will obtain the right to observe their own ways or even to congregate in a fixed territory. The headscarf affair thus will appear to be a trifle compared to the opportunities that concessions made to Corsican nationalists will open to religious groups hostile to the modern, secular state.

Thus, without having sought to do so, regionalization will reveal itself as the chief ally of the worst side of globalization, that which destroys state institutions while replacing them with nothing other than a territory open for criminalization. Those who have organized this sorry process in order to win the good favor of a terrorist faction before the presidential election may think that they have thus prevented terrorist actions. That is an illusion. If the Corsican reform takes effect, it will be the end of the French exception, an exception that for a thousand years has protected our land from the dictatorship of minorities, which is the worst enemy of democracy. In the end, it can only transform France at best into a big Belgium, or worse into a small Russia.

Source 4 from International Constitutional Law Documents, http://www.oefre.unibe.ch/law/icl/fi00000_.html.

4. Excerpts from the Finnish Constitution, 2000

SECTION 17 RIGHT TO ONE'S LANGUAGE AND CULTURE

(1) The national languages of Finland are Finnish and Swedish.

(2) The right of everyone to use his or her own language, either Finnish or Swedish, before courts of law and other authorities, and to receive official documents in that language, shall be guaranteed by an Act. The public authorities shall provide for the cultural and societal needs of the Finnish-speaking and Swedish-speaking populations of the country on an equal basis.

---

10. **Ile-de-France:** the region around Paris, French speaking in language and the historic center of France. Its medieval rulers eventually created the unified French state.

(3) The Sami,[11] as an indigenous people, as well as the Roma and other groups, have the right to maintain and develop their own language and culture. Provisions on the right of the Sami to use the Sami language before the authorities are laid down by an Act. The rights of persons using sign language and of persons in need of interpretation or translation aid owing to disability shall be guaranteed by an Act.

SECTION 51 LANGUAGES USED IN PARLIAMENTARY WORK

(1) The Finnish or Swedish languages are used in parliamentary work.

(2) The Government and the other authorities shall submit the documents necessary for a matter to be taken up for consideration in the Parliament both in Finnish and Swedish. Likewise, the parliamentary replies and communications, the reports and statements of the Committees, as well as the written proposals of the Speaker's Council, shall be written in Finnish and Swedish.

SECTION 79 PUBLICATION AND ENTRY INTO FORCE OF ACTS

(1) If an Act has been enacted in accordance with the procedure for constitutional enactment, this is indicated in the Act.

(2) An Act which has been confirmed or which enters into force without confirmation shall be signed by the President of the Republic and countersigned by the appropriate Minister. The Government shall thereafter without delay publish the Act in the Statute Book of Finland.

(3) The Act shall indicate the date when it enters into force. For a special reason, it may be stated in an Act that it is to enter into force by means of a Decree. If the Act has not been published by the date provided for its entry into force, it shall enter into force on the date of its publication.

Acts are enacted and published in Finnish and Swedish.

SECTION 120 SPECIAL STATUS OF THE ALAND ISLANDS[12]

The Aland Islands have self-government in accordance with what is specifically stipulated in the Act on the Autonomy of the Aland Islands.

---

11. **Sami:** a people, formerly called the "Lapps," who are native to the northern parts of Finland, Norway, Russia, and Sweden. Today numbering perhaps only 85,000 persons, they traditionally earn their living by hunting, fishing, and herding reindeer.
12. **Aland Islands:** a group of islands between Sweden and Finland whose population is about 95 percent Swedish speaking. By the Act of Autonomy, Swedish is the only official language there.

SECTION 121 MUNICIPAL AND OTHER REGIONAL SELF-GOVERNMENT

(1) Finland is divided into municipalities, whose administration shall be based on the self-government of their residents.

(2) Provisions on the general principles governing municipal administration and the duties of the municipalities are laid down by an Act.

(3) The municipalities have the right to levy municipal tax. Provisions on the general principles governing tax liability and the grounds for the tax as well as on the legal remedies available to the persons or entities liable to taxation are laid down by an Act.

(4) Provisions on self-government in administrative areas larger than a municipality are laid down by an Act. In their native region, the Sami have linguistic and cultural self-government, as provided by an Act.

SECTION 122 ADMINISTRATIVE DIVISIONS

(1) In the organisation of administration, the objective shall be suitable territorial divisions, so that the Finnish-speaking and Swedish-speaking populations have an opportunity to receive services in their own language on equal terms.

(2) The principles governing the municipal divisions are laid down by an Act.

Source 5 from Luis Núñez Astrain, The Basques: Their Struggle for Independence, *translated by Meic Stephens, p. 45. Reprinted by permission of Ashley Drake Publishing, Ltd.*

5. "The KAS Alternative," 1978

1. Amnesty: the release of all Basque political prisoners.

2. Democratic rights: the legalization of all political parties seeking Basque independence without any reduction in their status.

3. The expulsion from the Basque Country of the Civil Guard, the Armed Police and the General Police Corps.

4. The improvement of living and working conditions for the common people and the working class in particular.

5. A Statute of Autonomy which fulfils the following minimum conditions:

   * its simultaneous application to all four historic regions of the southern Basque Country[13]

13. The regions of the southern Basque country (*Euskal Herria* in Basque) are all within Spain. Their names, in Spanish, are Alava, Vizcaya, Gipuzkoa, and Navarra.

* recognition of the national sovereignty of the Basque Country and the right to self-determination, including the right to form an independent State

* recognition of the national links that exist between the north and south of the Basque Country[14]

* the Basque language to be official and to have priority

* the civil defence forces replacing the present oppressive forces to be created by the Basque Government and to be answerable to it alone

* the armed forces garrisoned in the southern Basque Country to be under the control of the Basque Government

* the Basque people to have sufficient powers to allow it always to have economic structures which it deems to be best suited, in social and political terms, to its progress and well-being.

14. The northern Basque country is in southwestern France; it includes the Basse-Navarre, Labourd, and Soule.

Source 6 from Robert J. Kaiser: The Geography of Nationalism in Russia and the USSR *(Princeton: Princeton University Press, 1994), p. 155.*

6. Federal Structure of the Union of Soviet Socialist Republics, 1989

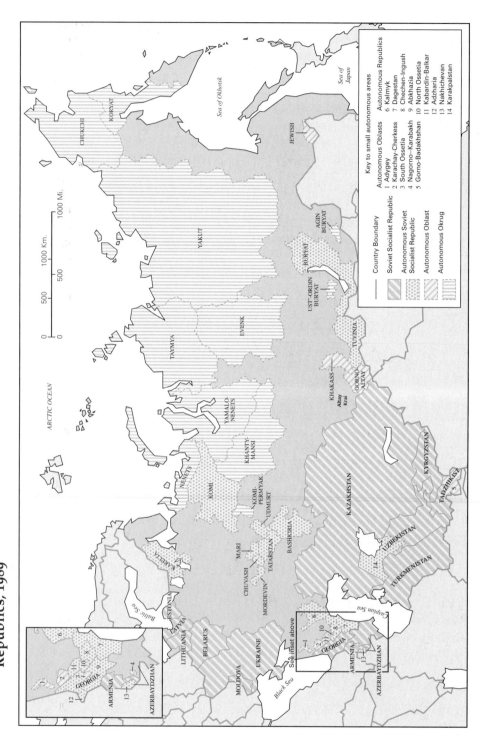

Source 7 from Archie Brown, Michael Kaser, and Gerald S. Smith (eds.), The Cambridge Encyclopedia of Russia and the Former Soviet Union, pp. 26–27. Copyright Cambridge University Press, 1994. Reprinted with the permission of Cambridge University Press.

7. Ethnic Composition of the Soviet Union's Successor States in the 1989 Census

Ethnic groups	Population (thousands)	Ethnic groups	Population (thousands)	Ethnic groups	Population (thousands)
Russian		Hungarians	163	**Belarus**	
Russians	119,866	Romanians	135	Belorussians	7,905
Tatars	5,522	Others	675	Russians	1,342
Ukrainians	4,363		51,452	Poles	418
Chuvash	1,774			Ukrainians	291
Bashkir	1,345	**Uzbekistan**		Jews	112
Beloruassians	1,206	Uzbeks	14,142	Others	84
Mordva	1,073	Russians	1,653		10,152
Chechen	899	Tajiks	934		
Germans	842	Kazakhs	808		
Udmurt	715				
Mari	644	**Tatars**	**468**	**Azerbaijan**	
Kazakhs	636	Karakalpaks	412	Azeris	5,805
Avars	544	Crimean Tatars	189	Russians	392
Jews	537	Koreans	183	Armenians	391
Armenians	532	Kyrgyz	175	Lezghins	171
Buryats	417	Others	846	Others	262
Ossctes	402		19,810		7,021
Kabarda	386				
Yakuts	380	**Kazakhstan**			
Others	4,939	Kasakhs	6,535		
	147,022	Russians	6,228	**Georgia**	
		Germans	958	Georgians	3,787
Ukraine		Ukrainians	896	Armenians	437
Ukrainians	37,419	Uzheks	332	Russians	341
Russians	11,356	Tatars	328	Azeris	308
Jews	486	Uygurs	185	Ossetes	164
Belorussians	440	Belorussians	183	Greeks	100
Moldovans	325	Koreans	103	Abkhaz	96
Bulgarians	234	Others	716	Others	168
Poles	219		16,464		5,401

Ethnic groups	Population (thousands)	Ethnic groups	Population (thousands)	Ethnic groups	Population (thousands)
Tajikistan		**Lithuania**		**Latvia**	
Tajiks	3,172	Lithuanians	2,924	Latvians	1,388
Uzheks	1,198	Russians	344	Russians	906
Russians	388	Poles	258	Belorussians	120
Tatars	72	Belorussians	63	Ukrainians	92
Others	263	Others	86	Others	161
	5,093		3,675		2,667
Moldova				**Estonia**	
Moldovans	2,795			Estonians	963
Ukrainians	600	**Turkmenistan**		Russians	475
Russians	562	Trukmen	2,523	Ukrainians	48
Gagauz	153	Russians	339	Belorussians	28
Bulgarians	88	Uzbeks	317	Finns	17
Others	137	Kazakhs	88	Others	34
	4,315	Others	256		1,565
			3,523		
Kyrgyzstan					
Kyrgyz	2,230				
Russians	917	**Armenia**			
Uzbeks	550	Armenians	3,084		
Ukrainians	108	Azeris	85		
Germans	101	Kurds	56		
Tatars	70	Russians	52		
Others	282	Others	28		
	4,258		3,305		

Source 8 from Anna Politkovskaya, A Dirty War: A Russian Reporter in Chechnya, *translated and edited by John Crowfoot, 2001, pp. 84–85. Reprinted by permission of Editions Robert Laffont Paris.*

8. Anna Politkovskaya, "Monsters and Human Beings," November 1999

We know of instances when air-force pilots jettisoned their bombs into the river on the outskirts of villages so as not to commit the sin of bombing their peaceful inhabitants.

We know cases of quite the opposite kind. The pilots deliberately fired on the Rostov-Baku Highway when refugees were fleeing along it from the war zone, and then flew past a second, third and even a fourth time when they saw that someone below was still moving. The war is rapidly acquiring two faces and each potential victim hopes and prays that they will be lucky and meet the "kind" face of this war.

Asya Astamirova, a young 28-year-old inhabitant of the Katyr-Yurt village in the Achkhoi-Martan district, has looked at both the one and the other. She survived physically because some soldiers saved her. But she is now dead to the world because other soldiers carried out a dreadful and cynical atrocity before her very eyes.

On 16 November Asya was bringing the body of her husband Aslan back to be buried in Katyr-Yurt. He had died in the Sunzhensk district hospital from the wounds he received when he came under fire. With her in the car were her children, six-year-old Aslanbek and two-year-old Salambek. In another car were Aslan's older sister Oeva, a mother of two, and their two uncles who were no longer young men. At the checkpoint between Achkhoi-Martan and Katyr-Yurt they were stopped and, without a word, the soldiers opened fire on both vehicles. When the first burst into flames Asya and the little boys leapt out. "For Allah's sake, save us!" they cried. The contract soldiers in their bandannas, who were not raw youths, continued shooting and told her: "There's no Allah, you Chechen bitch! You're dead."

They fired directly at her and the children. Aslanbek fell unconscious, Salambek screamed and Asya saw the car and her husband's body burn. Young conscripts observed the whole scene from a distance. When the contract soldiers had finished and went off to rest, the conscripts loaded the wounded Asya into an armoured vehicle and took her away. After several hours driving across the fields, avoiding the military posts, the soldiers unloaded the wounded family outside Sunzhensk hospital and without a word to anyone they left.

Asya is still in a state of shock. She gazes blankly round ward No 1 where she and the children were placed. Her mother Esita Islamova asks each new visitor: "How can I tell anyone after this that we belong together, that we're citizens of Russia? I can't!"

I try to stroke tiny Salambek's hair—his right leg is encased in plaster where fragments hit him—but the boy begins to scream and cry. He turns away and hides in the pillow.

"He's afraid," Esita explains. "You're a Slav, like the contract soldiers."

· "But what about the conscripts, they're also Slavs?"

"He's only a child. . . . It's what he remembers and that's what he's reacting to."

Our losses are immeasurable as we let the army get out of hand and degenerate into anarchy. By allowing such a war to be fought in our own country, without any rules, not against terrorists but against those who hate their own bandits[15] perhaps even more strongly than we do, we are the losers and the loss is irreversible.

INGUSHETIA[16]

15. **bandits:** a reference to the breakdown of law and order in Chechnya during the wars. Real crime thus flourished, but Russian officials often referred to Chechen guerrilla fighters as "bandits," too.

16. Although Politkovskaya filed her story from Ingushetia, a republic bordering Chechnya, the event at the checkpoint described here occurred just within the territory of Chechnya.

Source 9 from Panikos Panayi, An Ethnic History of Europe since 1945: Nations, States and Minorities *(New York: Longman, 2000), p. 43.*

9. National and Ethnic Minorities in the Former Yugoslavia

Serbs	
Croats	
Muslims	
Slovenes	
Monenegrins	
Macedonians	
Albanians	
Hungarians	
Bulgarians	
Romainans, Slovaks	

Source 10 from Emir Suljagić, Postcards from the Grave, *translated by Lejla Haveric, pp. 17–21, published by Sagi Books, in association with the Bosnian Institute. Copyright © 2005. Reprinted by permission.*

10. Emir Suljagić, "Ethnic Cleansing" in Bosnia, 1992

On the day of 12 May 1992 when Radio Bosnia-Herzegovina announced that Lieutenant General Ratko Mladić[17] had been nominated commander of JNA[18] troops in the country (or more precisely commander of the Second Military District of the JNA), Muslim villages around Bratunac started being set on fire. It was a coincidence—such a widespread persecution of the population must have been planned much earlier—but it was a coincidence that did not augur well. We had been hiding for two weeks already, since mid April, and were by now well into May without knowing what was to come. That day all our doubts were set at rest.

News from the cut off and occupied town were brought to us by Ibro S., a boy nicknamed *Žuto* [yellowy] because of his yellow-ginger hair and the countless freckles of the same colour on his face. He was fifteen or sixteen years old, but because of his size no one would have thought him older than twelve. . . .

Along with cigarettes he brought information, relating whereabouts he had seen each of our Serb neighbours, now wearing camouflage uniforms and carrying machine guns. He was the first to tell us, to our horror, that the Serbs were gathering men from nearby villages in the basement of the Vuk Karadžić primary school. Terrified, I heard how a certain Idriz had been killed, a man I knew only as the driver of my school bus. Serb soldiers had put him against a wall and repeatedly driven the bus into him until he died.

That day, when Ibro returned from town, he told us how he had been let through the barricade by Ranko Obrenović, a house-painter from a neighbouring village who had lost his left hand while playing with a bomb found a couple of years after the Second World War. I knew that story, I had heard it before from his son Aleksandar Obrenović, my best friend from school. I had been to his house countless times, I had shared a school desk with him for eight years. His father was now manning a barricade, one-armed, clumsy as he must have looked with a rifle. And my memories flooded back.

During my last year of primary school, as Slobodan Milošević's 'anti-bureaucratic revolution' was well underway, as the leaderships in Montenegro, Vojvodina and Kosovo were removed and tension grew in other parts of the former Yugoslavia, I witnessed the impact those events had on everyday life. A boy from my class—actually the child of a mixed marriage, which is

17. **Ratko Mladić:** the commander of the Bosnian Serb army during the war. Mladić (born in 1943) was present in that capacity at Srebenica during the massacres of July 1995. He was indicted in 1995 by the International Criminal Tribunal for the Former Yugoslavia on charges of genocide and crimes against humanity; he remains free and in hiding.
18. **JNA:** Yugoslav People's Army (*Jugoslavenka Narodna Armija*).

probably not irrelevant to this story—cursed my 'Turkish mother'[19] during a lesson. I realised then for the first time that, for reasons beyond my understanding, I was somehow different from some of my schoolmates.

Of course, I waited for him after class. I was deeply hurt and wanted to return the insult with interest. Aleksandar joined me as a partisan observer. We knocked him down and started kicking him. As he rolled about in pain, Aleksandar kept kicking him and saying through clenched teeth: 'Fuck your Chetnik mother.[20] He, a boy carrying the name of the heir to the Serbian throne assassinated in 1902, defended my 'Turkish honour' back then. A couple of years later his father stood armed at a barricade. . . .

Soon after Ibro told us about what he had seen and heard in town, thick pillars of light-coloured smoke started rising from villages on the hills around the town. We watched, for the first time we watched with our own eyes how other people's houses burn, just as we would later see our own houses burning. And we did not want to believe it. Or rather we did not dare to believe it, because it meant that a point of no return had been reached. On the right—the Serbian—bank of the Drina, a long column of big trucks covered in white tarpaulins grew steadily longer. We counted up to thirty of them and then gave up as the trucks headed towards Bratunac. While the villages burned, Serb soldiers chased the population out of the hills down to the main road where, in an incredibly synchronised operation, trucks waited for them in a line whose end was still in Serbia.

That night my father woke me up and whispered to me to get dressed quickly. Still half asleep, I obeyed and got dressed in the dark, hurrying to leave the house and join him outside where he was waiting impatiently. With him walking in front of me we set off, I did not know where to. After nearly an hour's trudge through the woods, we got to a clearing where a couple of hundred men had already gathered. It was way after midnight and the hubbub on the meadow rose as dawn broke. A fairly big group of people, some of them armed, separated and continued on further towards villages deep in the hills. The largest group stayed put on the meadow wondering what to do.

Father and I left at dawn. With us was Juso C., our cousin and neighbour, who had been to Podloznik several times. This was a village on the border between the two municipalities of Bratunac and Srebrenica that was difficult for Serb APCs[21] to reach. The expelled population from the Drina valley was already gathering there. . . .

19. **Turkish:** Bosniaks were natives of the region who converted to Islam during the years from the late fifteenth century to 1878, when Bosnia and Herzegovina were under the direct rule of the Muslim Turks.

20. **Chetnik:** a royalist irregular soldier in Yugoslavia during World War II. Chetniks fought both the occupying Germans and the communist partisans of Tito. With the collapse of communism in 1989, the term came to refer to all Serb extremists.

21. **APC:** armored personnel carrier.

Tired from the journey, I fell asleep curled up in the doorway, on the front step of a house belonging to one of the many of our cousins I was to meet. I woke up in a bed where my father had probably carried me. A complete stranger lay next to me, fully dressed like myself, a man I had never seen before. But my father was not in the room. I got up and started looking for him in the overcrowded house. He was outside with my mother and sister, who had arrived the pervious night in a group of several hundred women and children. Mother told us that all the other relatives, nearly the whole neighbourhood, had surrendered to the new Serb authorities who had guaranteed them safety and free passage to Tuzla. What is more Granny, father's mother, had been to look for us the day before in our hideout in the woods, in order to try and persuade us to surrender. Three months later we found out that all our relatives who had surrendered had been executed by firing squad. The elderly who obeyed the authorities' order to stay in the village and look after the cattle were collected into a house, killed and then burnt.

From there we went on to another village, Storesko. Mother knew of another distant relative there, with whom we could stay for a night. I do not know how long we stayed there. . . . In the meantime, Mother remembered we had yet another cousin in Skenderovići and father heard on the radio the news that Srebrenica was free. The next day we set off for the town, the first of many thousands who were to follow our example.

None of my companions on that journey is alive. Juso, with whom I left home, died in July 1995 near free territory, in a group that was trying to get through from Srebrenica to Tuzla on foot. Nihad, who brought me to Srebrenica, did not survive July 1995. My father returned home and died in his garden in December 1992.

QUESTIONS TO CONSIDER

This final chapter in *Discovering the Western Past* allows us to reflect on both the ramifications of modern nationalism and the condition of Europe at the start of a new century. Nationalism, a force that we have seen profoundly reshaping the eighteenth-, nineteenth-, and early-twentieth-century West, continues to be a potent force in the late-twentieth- and early-twenty-first-century world. Regional ethnic nationalism of this period especially raises questions at several levels for historians to answer.

At a most basic level, historians must examine the origins of ethnic challenges to the modern nation-state. What role did language and regional identity play in reinforcing ethnic identities different from those of the rulers of modern nation-states? How, for example, did Douglas Hyde not only call for Gaelic's revival but also give his audience a sense of pride in its past? What do you think the distinct regions or homelands of the Irish, Basques, Scots, Welsh, and other groups contributed to the development of ethnic identities at odds with the traditional nation-state? What sort of threat did such developing identities pose for Jacques Attali? Why did he see the nation-state inextricably bound up with language? How could the educational policies of a dominant ethnic group stymie the development of the ethnic identity projected by Hyde? Why do you think the ideas expressed by Attali were probably not just a "French exception"?

Second, historians must consider the goals of ethnic minority groups in contemporary Europe. Some, obviously, are satisfied with increased rights for the use of their traditional languages and perhaps even some limited political autonomy. Which ethnic groups fall into this category? What tactics have they used to pursue their goals within democratic societies? Where have the aspirations of ethnic minorities led to independence movements and violence?

What aspects of state policy probably helped to provoke that violence?

Finally, historians must consider the results of the ethnic problems that we have examined. Where has the centralized state resisted the demands for greater rights for regional ethnic minorities? What countries have remained unitary states while devolving some political authority and linguistic freedom to regional ethnic groups? Where have centralized states broken down, whether peacefully or violently, into weak federations or into new small nation-states?

Your answers to these questions should assist you in responding to the central questions of this chapter. What national and ethnic issues now challenge the traditional European nation-state? Why have such issues proven very divisive in Europe? What do you think will be the character of the European nation-state in the twenty-first century?

EPILOGUE

We reach this final section of *Discovering the Western Past* to find the traditional European nation-state quite likely on the threshold of far-reaching change in the twenty-first century. Three chief developments suggest that the nation-state, which we traditionally have studied as a single linguistic and cultural entity administered by a centralized governmental apparatus, will not long endure precisely as we have known it.

First, as we have seen in this chapter, the indigenous, regional ethnic groups within almost every country increasingly are contesting the traditional order of the nation-state. They demand instruction in their traditional languages and, more recently, media broadcasts in them as well. Indeed, the electronic media of the twenty-first century may well perpetuate and even expand the use of minority European tongues that linguists were writing off as dying languages fifty or one hundred years ago. We thus increasingly see a Europe of ethnically distinct regions challenging the tradition of a Europe of nation-states.

A second development also challenges the model of the ethnically unified European nation-state. Europe is receiving increasing numbers of non-European immigrants, many of whom are fundamentally different from the traditional citizens of their host countries. Racially, some are non-Caucasian, and religiously many do not subscribe to the Judeo-Christian religious tradition of Europeans. All come to Europe in the same quest that brought immigrants to the United States: the search for the opportunity for a better life. Integration of such groups into European society has not always been smooth. Almost every European country has produced right-wing political movements urging the limitation of such immigrants, or even their expulsion. And immigrant riots in democracies like France and Great Britain over recent decades suggest that immigrants have felt the sting of discrimination in employment, housing, and justice. Whatever solutions individual countries work out for the problems that produce such explosions, one thing is clear: European states in the future will be not only multilingual, but also multiracial and multicultural.

A third development further erodes the traditional nation-state as we enter the twenty-first century. The evolution of European international organizations like the European Union over the past fifty years has considerably changed the character of the nation-state. The European Union, for example, pursues a common economic policy with far-ranging impact. Thus, most European member states subscribe to a policy of free movement for the citizens of member states around the community, facilitated by international coordination of a plethora of regulations involving matters from education to professional licensing and social security benefits. The result is even greater ethnic diversity in every European Union country. But the community's economic policies do not only foster ethnic diversity. The economic institutions of the community also erode the traditional prerogatives of the governments of its members. Thus, many community members have adopted a common currency, the Euro, to encourage trade and international development among them. The common currency, however, has mandated a central European bank to impose uniform monetary policies on the Euro community. The bank and institutions like it are assuming powers traditionally held by the governments of nation-states, making them less relevant in the lives of their citizens than in the past.

Thus, the evidence that you have analyzed in this chapter is a key to understanding the future of Europe. National identity will continue to be an issue there, although the tragic experiences of Chechnya and the former Yugoslavia may yet yield to peaceful and democratic resolution of ethnic conflict. The one thing that is certain is that continuing change awaits the European continent.